D0821418

Freedom Rights

CIVIL RIGHTS AND THE STRUGGLE FOR BLACK EQUALITY
IN THE TWENTIETH CENTURY

SERIES EDITORS
Steven F. Lawson, Rutgers University
Cynthia Griggs Fleming, University of Tennessee

Freedom's Main Line: The Journey of Reconciliation and the Freedom Rides
Derek Charles Catsam

*Subversive Southerner: Anne Braden and the Struggle for Racial Justice
in the Cold War South*
Catherine Fosl

*Constructing Affirmative Action:
The Struggle for Equal Employment Opportunity*
David Hamilton Golland

Becoming King: Martin Luther King Jr. and the Making of a National Leader
Troy Jackson

Civil Rights in the Gateway to the South: Louisville, Kentucky, 1945–1980
Tracy E. K'Meyer

Democracy Rising: South Carolina and the Fight for Black Equality since 1865
Peter F. Lau

Civil Rights Crossroads: Nation, Community, and the Black Freedom Struggle
Steven F. Lawson

This Little Light of Mine: The Life of Fannie Lou Hamer
Kay Mills

After the Dream: Black and White Southerners since 1965
Timothy J. Minchin and John A. Salmond

For Jobs and Freedom: Race and Labor in America since 1865
Robert H. Zieger

Freedom Rights

New Perspectives on the Civil Rights Movement

Edited by
Danielle L. McGuire
and John Dittmer

THE UNIVERSITY PRESS OF KENTUCKY

Copyright © 2011 by The University Press of Kentucky

Scholarly publisher for the Commonwealth,
serving Bellarmine University, Berea College, Centre
College of Kentucky, Eastern Kentucky University,
The Filson Historical Society, Georgetown College,
Kentucky Historical Society, Kentucky State University,
Morehead State University, Murray State University,
Northern Kentucky University, Transylvania University,
University of Kentucky, University of Louisville,
and Western Kentucky University.
All rights reserved.

Editorial and Sales Offices: The University Press of Kentucky
663 South Limestone Street, Lexington, Kentucky 40508-4008
www.kentuckypress.com

15 14 13 12 11   5 4 3 2 1

Cataloging-in-Publication data is available from the Library of Congress.

ISBN: 978-0-8131-3448-2

This book is printed on acid-free paper meeting
the requirements of the American National Standard
for Permanence in Paper for Printed Library Materials.
♾

Manufactured in the United States of America.

Member of the Association of
American University Presses

Contents

Dedications   vii

Introduction   1
  Danielle L. McGuire

Long Origins of the Short Civil Rights Movement, 1954–1968   9
  Steven F. Lawson

Hollywood, the NAACP, and the Cultural Politics of the Early Civil
Rights Movement   39
  Justin T. Lorts

The Young Women's Christian Association's Multiracial Activism in the
Immediate Postwar Era   71
  Abigail Sara Lewis

James and Esther Cooper Jackson, Communism, and the 1950s Black
Freedom Movement   111
  Sara Rzeszutek Haviland

Till They Come Back Home: Transregional Families and the
Politicization of the Till Generation   137
  Krystal D. Frazier

The Johns Committee, Sex, and Civil Rights in Florida, 1963–1965   163
  Stacy Braukman

Joan Little and the Triumph of Testimony   191
  Danielle L. McGuire

Gender, Jazz, and Justice in Cold War Freedom Movements   223
  Jacqueline Castledine

EEOC Politics and Limits on Reagan's Civil Rights Legacy   247
  Emily Zuckerman

Race and Partisanship in Criminal Disfranchisement Laws   277
  Pippa Holloway

"The Community Don't Know What's Good for Them": Local Politics in the Alabama Black Belt during the Post–Civil Rights Era   305
    George Derek Musgrove and Hasan Kwame Jeffries

"I Want My Country Back, I Want My Dream Back": Barack Obama and the Appeal of Postracial Fictions   329
    Brian Ward

List of Contributors   365
Index   369

Dedications

Freedom Rights: New Perspectives on the Civil Rights Movement is dedicated to Steven F. Lawson, whose lifelong devotion to the scholarship and history of the modern civil rights movement inspired this anthology. Anyone interested in the history of race and American politics cannot get very far without encountering and engaging Lawson's groundbreaking body of work. When he published *Black Ballots* thirty-five years ago, civil rights historiography was in its infancy. Most of the books about the black freedom struggle had been written by journalists or activists, and the major historical works by scholars such as Clayborne Carson, William Chafe, David Garrow, and Charles Payne would not appear until years later. Lawson set the bar for the rest of us. *Black Ballots* combines social and political history to explain how and why African Americans and their allies persuaded a reluctant federal government to pass voting rights legislation in the 1950s and 1960s. His second book, *In Pursuit of Power,* focuses on how the black vote impacted local, state, and national politics at a time when the liberal agenda of the 1960s had fallen victim to a conservative backlash culminating in the election of Ronald Reagan in 1980.

In those two volumes Lawson dramatically demonstrates the relationship between grassroots activists and national political figures. While early civil rights historians wrote about great men and their organizations, and later scholars emphasized local movements, Lawson shows that the gains of the 1960s depended on concerted action at both the local and the national levels and that the landmark legislation was a result of sophisticated political lobbying as well as taking it to the streets. His 1991 *American Historical Review* essay titled "Freedom Then, Freedom Now" examines "the intersection of national and local undertakings," providing a conceptual framework for viewing the civil rights movement that has stood the test of time, influencing a new generation of scholars. To this day Lawson remains actively engaged in the debates over the direction of civil rights historiography, as his brilliant critique of the "long civil rights movement" that begins this book makes clear.

Lawson is a great teacher, both in the classroom and in print. He has reached out to undergraduates and to a larger audience of general readers in his *Running for Freedom: Civil Rights and Black Politics since 1941,* now in its third edition. Included there is a trenchant analysis of the rise and fall of Jesse Jackson and the political and racial factors that made the election of a black president possible. He and Charles Payne collaborated on *Debating the Civil Rights Movement,* which supplies basic facts about the movement and an analysis of the impact of local politics on public policy. It has become a standard text in college classrooms. Aware of the need to keep key documents relating to civil rights in the public domain, Lawson edited and wrote introductions for *To Secure These Rights,* the compilation by President Harry Truman's Committee on Civil Rights, and *One America in the 21st Century,* the report resulting from President Bill Clinton's initiative on race. With college students in mind, Lawson and his partner Nancy A. Hewitt are completing a U.S. history survey textbook, *Exploring American Histories.*

Time and space do not permit me to carry on at length about Lawson's extracurricular activities and the awards he has received. Suffice it to say that his participation in conferences and seminars, his service as a consultant on such important documentaries as *Eyes on the Prize,* and his expert testimony in voting rights cases have enhanced his reputation in the field while providing valuable resources to the larger nonacademic community.

Steven Lawson and I are extremely fortunate to have come of age at a time when this country was on the verge of a social revolution (the likes of which had not been seen since the abolitionist crusade of the mid-nineteenth century), when black people across the South risked their livelihoods and their lives in an ongoing struggle to take charge of their destiny. To have been able to record those monumental events is a great honor. And nobody has written about them with more analytical clarity than Steven Lawson.

—John Dittmer

Steven Lawson's teaching career began forty-two years ago at the Kingsborough Community College in Brooklyn, New York. Over the years, he has taught at City College of New York, the University of South Florida, the University of North Carolina–Greensboro, Duke University, the University of Cambridge, and Rutgers University, where he is currently Professor Emeritus. Lawson's deft storytelling and passionate engagement of the intersections of American politics, gender, and race have breathed life into textbooks and cast spells on hundreds if not thousands of undergraduates and graduate students. His demand for excellence combined with a generosity of spirit has inspired, guided, and motivated students to ask harder questions and come up with better answers. Most important, he encourages students to think for themselves and is always supportive, even when he disagrees. As a mentor, Lawson is both exacting and nurturing, demanding rewrites, setting deadlines, and challenging ideas one day while opening his home and providing a warm meal and some good-natured ribbing the next. Lawson's long-term commitment to his students is commendable—long after we defend our theses and dissertations and land jobs, he continues to advise, encourage, and edit. He has become a dear friend to me and to many of us—attending our weddings, kvelling over our books and our babies, and kvetching about the latest political news and baseball standings. More than anything, the example he sets as a scholar, teacher, and writer will energize future students of American history and will continue to inspire those of us who have had the honor to work with him.

—Danielle L. McGuire

Introduction

Danielle L. McGuire

In 1991 historian Steven F. Lawson traced the contours of civil rights historiography from the 1970s to the early 1990s in his seminal article "Freedom Then, Freedom Now: The Historiography of the Civil Rights Movement." While celebrating the contributions of early scholars, who focused primarily on national campaigns and charismatic leaders, Lawson called for a broader and more interactive model of the modern civil rights movement. He urged researchers to connect "the local with the national, the political with the social," and he asked scholars to "examine the external influences on national political struggles," to probe the "internal dynamics of movements" and investigate "relations between the sexes and races" of organizers. Lawson challenged historians to study the ideological roots of the freedom struggle, particularly the labor-liberal coalitions in the 1930s and 1940s; the role of women as participants, organizers, and leaders; and the international and economic concerns of all segments of the movement. In other words, Lawson called for scholarship that includes a more complete synthesis of the civil rights movement—work that is complex, nuanced, and exciting.

Two decades later it is impossible to read a book or an article about the civil rights movement without recognizing Lawson's influence, both as a scholar and as a teacher. However, much has changed, and it is time for a new assessment of the civil rights historiography and a new history of the civil rights movement. This volume of original essays reflects the current state of the field. It not only answers Lawson's call for a more dynamic history of black freedom movements but also lays a solid foundation for all future civil rights historiography. The essays in *Freedom Rights* point to a black freedom movement that is multiracial, cross-regional, and international, with local and national actors and organizations working in concert. The contributors investigate the role of domestic politics—from World War II and McCarthyism to the Reagan "revolution"—and its impact on individual activists as well as organizations such as the NAACP and the Justice Department. They also provide a gendered analysis of civil

1

rights activism and activists and investigate the role of family, sexuality, and sexualized violence in the long struggle for freedom.

The origins and end points of the modern civil rights movement are hotly contested. The latest debate centers on the idea of a "long civil rights movement," which began, as historian Jacquelyn Dowd Hall argues, in "the liberal and radical milieu of the late 1930s, was intimately tied to the rise and fall of the New Deal Order, accelerated during World War II, stretched far beyond the South, was continuously and ferociously contested and in the 1960s and 1970s inspired a 'movement of movements' that defies any narrative of collapse."[1] Steven Lawson was one of the first historians to challenge the chronology of the "master narrative" of the modern civil rights movement, which typically begins in 1954 with the Supreme Court's decision to end school segregation in *Brown v. Board of Education* and ends in 1968 with the assassination of Martin Luther King Jr. He argues against the notion of a long civil rights movement in his essay "Long Origins of the Short Civil Rights Movement, 1954–1968." Although Lawson acknowledges the contributions of historians who locate the movement's origins in earlier struggles for justice and equality, he argues that focusing too heavily on continuity "blurs the lines of historic changes within the black freedom struggle that give the period from 1954 to 1968 its distinct context and character." Lawson offers a hearty debate on the origins of the movement but also provides a clear and compelling narrative of how a distinct—and limited—campaign for civil rights became the most important mass social movement of the twentieth century.

The role of the NAACP in African Americans' long struggle for freedom is undeniable, and most scholars focus on the association's monumental legal and lobbying efforts in the areas of school desegregation, antilynching legislation, voting rights, and elimination of the poll tax. In "Hollywood, the NAACP, and the Cultural Politics of the Early Civil Rights Movement," Justin T. Lorts breaks new ground by analyzing the organization's cultural activism—especially efforts to eliminate negative comic stereotypes from television and film—as part of the emerging postwar struggle for racial justice. Drawing on articles, opinion pieces, private correspondence, and the NAACP's own papers, Lorts argues that beginning in 1942 the association waged a series of campaigns against Hollywood for perpetuating false images of African Americans that helped maintain white supremacy and black inequality. These campaigns highlighted the relationship between culture and politics and the importance of mass media in the emerging civil rights movement. Though never as successful as the NAACP's legal efforts to end school segregation, these Hollywood campaigns, which culminated in the 1951 boycott of the *Amos 'n' Andy* television show, helped eliminate some of the most harmful depictions of African Americans and played an important role in shaping the media landscape so that the civil rights movement could be successful.

Most scholars recognize the prominence of the NAACP in the civil rights movement, but few would consider the Young Women's Christian Association (the Y) a leading multiracial organization in the postwar era. Yet, as Abigail Sara Lewis persuasively argues in "The Young Women's Christian Association's Multiracial Activism in the Immediate Postwar Era," the Y reconstituted itself as a leader among similar organizations in the field of desegregation and race relations after World War II. As a national organization, the Y sought better interracial relations, but the horror of Japanese internment propelled it to desegregate and adopt a national policy on race in 1946. Known as the "Interracial Charter," this policy—and the organization's efforts to guarantee its fulfillment—made the Y a "pioneer in the interracial field." Its publications and studies on race relations were useful to other organizations seeking to desegregate and helped the Y become known throughout the country for its integration efforts. By the early 1950s, Lewis notes, the Y was cited as the only multiracial organization effectively fighting for civil rights and racial equality as a national issue, not just a sectional problem.

As the Y became a leader in the field of race relations and organizational diversity in the early 1950s, radical and leftist civil rights activists who had been organizing for racial equality and human dignity since the early 1940s found themselves the targets of vicious red-baiting and domestic anticommunism. Included among this group were James and Esther Cooper Jackson, a black Communist couple active in the Southern Negro Youth Congress, a Popular Front organization dedicated to racial justice through working-class unity. Focusing on their struggles, Sara Rzeszutek Haviland highlights how the domestic effects of Cold War politics "shaped the civil rights movement specifically by shaping the family lives of black activists." As Haviland demonstrates in her essay "James and Esther Cooper Jackson, Communism, and the 1950s Black Freedom Movement," the domestic Cold War undermined those militant black activists who had built interracial and cross-class coalitions with leftists, labor unions, and progressives during World War II. While anticommunism destroyed the possibility of a more radical movement for racial and economic equality, it also shaped a liberal civil rights agenda that gained popularity in the late 1950s. By focusing on the Jacksons' personal experiences in the early Cold War, Haviland sheds light not only on the shift from the Popular Front era to the modern civil rights movement but also on gender and family politics within the freedom struggle.

Family politics played a major role in both sparking and expanding the civil rights movement. As Krystal D. Frazier argues in "Till They Come Back Home: Transregional Families and the Politicization of the Till Generation," black family culture played a transformative role in nationalizing the freedom struggle, particularly in the aftermath of Emmett Till's murder. His death resonated with African Americans not just in the South but also across the country, and it helped politicize a new generation of young blacks—often called the "Till generation"—whose southern roots and northern upbringing created what Frazier calls a "cross-regional migrant culture." These migration-fostered political exchanges within families, Frazier argues, "shaped a generation that understood the complexities and possibilities of interracial life in the United States in ways not experienced by generations before them." Ultimately, this cross-regional diaspora would transform the nation and resonate around the world.

While the murder of Emmett Till nationalized issues of racial brutality, it also drew attention to the power of gender and sexuality in both maintaining and challenging white supremacy. By the mid-1960s segregationists and conservatives moved away from an overtly race-based articulation of white supremacy to an ostensibly color-blind defense of individual rights in order to discredit the civil rights movement as an immoral, if not outright prurient, campaign led by Communists and sexual deviants. In "The Johns Committee, Sex, and Civil Rights in Florida, 1963–1965," Stacy Braukman argues that "the seeds of this critique of liberalism had been sown in the immediate postwar years, but the commingling of conservative and segregationist attacks on the morals of blacks and whites on the Left forged a crucial bond with nonsouthern conservatives that would resonate for decades." Although the Florida Legislative Investigation Committee—commonly known as the Johns Committee for its founder, conservative state senator Charley Johns—could not use the fear of communism and homophobia to stem the tide of protests that engulfed Florida in the late 1960s, its sexual McCarthyism and racial fear-mongering became staples of New Right organizations outside the Sunshine State. Indeed, as Braukman perceptively argues, by the mid to late 1960s, "echoes of postwar anticommunism and massive resistance" could be heard throughout the country in conservative attacks against civil rights, Lyndon Johnson's

Great Society programs, antiwar activists, and "many other ominous signs of moral decline facilitated by federal encroachment."

Sex and civil rights were definitely connected, but not in the ways conservatives suggested. From the time of slavery through the better part of the twentieth century, African American women struggled to defend themselves and their bodily integrity from white men, who sexually assaulted them with alarming regularity. Indeed, black women's antirape activism was rooted in African Americans' long struggle for human dignity and constituted a crucial part of the modern civil rights movement. From the slave narratives of Harriet Jacobs to the fiery orations of Ida B. Wells and Fannie Lou Hamer's stark public testimony about a forced hysterectomy and brutal beating in 1963, many black women refused to remain silent about sexual violence. Instead, they organized public protests, testified about their assaults, and used their voices as weapons in the long struggle for freedom. In "Joan Little and the Triumph of Testimony," Danielle L. McGuire argues that the 1975 trial of Joan Little, a twenty-year-old black inmate from Washington, North Carolina, who killed her white jailer after he allegedly sexually assaulted her, tested the right of African American women to defend themselves from sexual assault. The Free Joan Little Campaign, as it became known, drew national and international attention to the long history of sexualized violence against black women and sparked spirited debates about a woman's right to self-defense. The broad coalition of supporters who rallied to Little's defense—from the National Organization for Women to the Black Panther Party—reflected the enormous social, political, and economic changes wrought by the civil rights movement, the women's movement, and the emergence of the New Left and Black Power.

Black women's desire for dignity, respect, and bodily integrity sparked larger campaigns for freedom throughout the entire African diaspora. In "Gender, Jazz, and Justice in Cold War Freedom Movements," Jacqueline Castledine examines artistic expression as a form of activism. Highlighting American performers Nina Simone and Abbey Lincoln and South Africans Dorothy Masuka and Miriam Makeba, she shows how these recording artists challenged the legitimacy of white supremacy in protest songs from 1950 to 1980. Often they did so at great personal cost. Masuka and Makeba, the former wife of Black Panther Party leader Stokely Carmichael, were exiled; Simone exiled herself in France. With their voices, Castledine argues, "this cohort skillfully maneuvered through male gendered spaces fighting white supremacy and, at times, assumptions about women and politics." Examining their activism underlines the significance of women's cultural expression in the struggle for freedom in both the United States and South Africa, as well as the international aspects of the freedom struggle.

As the mass civil rights movement eventually gave way to a broad conservative counterrevolution, Ronald Reagan promised to fundamentally change the civil rights policies that movement activists had fought for and helped develop over the previous two decades. The Reagan administration focused on color blindness and equal opportunity instead of equal results, promoted "reverse discrimination cases," and appointed staunch conservatives and critics of affirmative action to key positions in the Justice Department. However, as Emily Zuckerman argues in "EEOC Politics and Limits on Reagan's Civil Rights Legacy," instead of dismantling the civil rights machinery that had been in place since 1964, Clarence Thomas, head of the Equal Employment Opportunity Commission (EEOC), at first resisted Reagan's changes. Thomas's EEOC continued to fund and settle large cases, pressed other federal agencies to report their equal employment opportunity progress, and opposed the administration's position in a so-called reverse discrimination case. Thomas's role, along with the slow pace of bureaucratic change, resistance from some figures within the administration, the dedication of career EEOC staffers, and the unstoppable tide of change in the workplace (led by activists without regard to whether they could rely on the government as an ally), ensured that all was not lost during the Reagan years.

Although all was not lost, the disfranchisement of African Americans and other voters remains an ongoing civil rights issue. As Pippa Holloway points out in "Race and Partisanship in Criminal Disfranchisement Laws," the enforcement of these laws is far from a recent development. Throughout the early twentieth century the Democratic Party often manipulated laws that disfranchised felons by specifically targeting African American voters to protect its own political dominance. Holloway highlights early-twentieth-century instances of this practice by examining the partisan-oriented pardon process that restored voting rights for supporters and blocked the franchise for political opponents. She also examines African Americans' resistance to disfranchisement for (in many cases, wrongful) criminal convictions.

Passage of the Voting Rights Act in 1965 outlawed discrimination at the ballot box, but freedom, as Ella Baker put it, "is a constant struggle." In "'The Community Don't Know What's Good for Them': Local Politics in the Alabama Black Belt during the Post–Civil Rights Era," George Derek Musgrove and Hasan Kwame Jeffries reveal that black political organizations in Alabama overcame white fraud and voter suppression in the late 1970s and 1980s to secure control of county government. They used sophisticated get-out-the-vote techniques to achieve high voter turnout, which was a legacy of the "freedom politics" of the movement years. Once in power, however, black political organizations abandoned freedom politics and adopted styles of political mobilization and decision making that made them susceptible to charges of fraud. The white minority constantly leveled such charges at black politicians and enlisted friendly state and federal law enforcement agencies in an effort to undo black political victories through repeated investigations. Musgrove and Jeffries examine three voter fraud investigations (1984–1985, 1995–1997, and 2005–2008) to show the continuing efforts of the white minority to disfranchise African Americans, and they call for a return to the freedom politics that allowed blacks to secure majority control of the Black Belt in the 1980s.

Many viewed the election of Barack Obama, the first African American president, in 2008 as the end of the conservative ascendancy unleashed during the late 1960s. Some historians have argued that Obama's win represents the fulfillment of social and political developments first set in motion during the civil rights movement of the 1960s. Brian Ward's essay "'I Want My Country Back, I Want My Dream Back': Barack Obama and the Appeal of Postracial Fictions" explores the enormous popular investment in linking Obama and Martin Luther King Jr. and the belief that Obama's victory fulfilled King's dream that "race would no longer be an impediment to opportunity and achievement." Despite pronouncements that the election of its first African American president ushered the United States into a "postracial" era, Ward documents the ongoing significance of race and the continuing "blight" of racism in America. Still, he argues that the vogue for postracialism, which turned "Obama into a simulacrum, a romantic projection of a better, fairer, more just America" and harnessed citizens' desire for racial reconciliation and a redeemed America true to its core civic ideals, may actually be the "most radical aspect" of Obama's election.

The rich scholarship, new analysis, and compelling narrative style of the essays in *Freedom Rights* promise to reach a wide audience of students, scholars, and general readers interested in the civil rights movement, African American history, racial and gender politics, and ongoing struggles for dignity and justice. These essays represent the latest research and scholarly debates in the field of civil rights and will set the standard for future movement historiography. By engaging issues of gender, family, sexuality, and sexual violence in the civil rights movement; highlighting local, national, and international connections and cross-currents within the freedom struggle; attending to cultural as well as legal and political developments; and investigating the movement's roots and legacies, *Freedom Rights* does more than answer Lawson's call for a more dynamic, interactive history of the civil rights movement—it redefines it.

Note

1. Jacquelyn Dowd Hall, "The Long Civil Rights Movement and the Political Uses of the Past," *Journal of American History* 91 (March 2005): 1235.

Long Origins of the Short Civil Rights Movement, 1954–1968

Steven F. Lawson

> The charm of history and its enigmatic lesson consists in the fact that from age to age nothing changes and yet everything is completely different.
>
> —Aldous Huxley, *The Devils of Loudon*

Recently Michael Wright, a northerner who went to the South in the mid-1960s to organize for the Student Nonviolent Coordinating Committee (SNCC), drew on his practical experiences to consider the idea of beginnings. While working in Alabama and Georgia he learned that twenty years earlier, in the 1940s, there had been another group with an acronym pronounced "Snick"— the Southern Negro Youth Conference (SNYC). "Yes," he declared, "a 'snick' organization in the south doing exactly what we were doing 20 years later." Yet hardly anyone in SNCC knew anything about SNYC or about the campaigns in the South by the Congress of Industrial Organizations (CIO) during the Depression or about Marcus Garvey's United Negro Improvement Association in the 1920s or about the efforts of the Communist Party in the region throughout this period.[1] However, according to Wright, "this historical ignorance" did not matter one bit "as far as the movement of the 60s was concerned. The movement of the 60s might have been *sui generis* as far as most 60s activists were concerned." He was undoubtedly correct in his assessment, but his comments underscore a debate about the origins of the civil rights movement that has generated a good deal of heat over the past several years.

In general, the field of civil rights history has not produced the kind of controversy that has characterized other periods of U.S. history. Historians have not lined up on opposite sides in their interpretation of the civil rights movement in the way their colleagues have about the American Revolution, slavery, Reconstruction, populism, progressivism, the New Deal, and the Cold War. The history of civil rights has been written mainly by sympathizers who lived through the movement or by their students and intellectual descendants who favor the cause. True, historians have argued about whether to approach civil rights history from the top down or the bottom up and whether to focus on charismatic or community-centered leaders.[2] And in the politically conservative post-1960s era, New Right conservatives have portrayed the civil rights movement in a manner that emphasizes race-neutral principles and undermines affirmative action programs. Despite these skirmishes, those who write about civil rights share a consensus view of this struggle as the most influential mass social movement of the twentieth century. They applaud the courage of its participants and marvel at their accomplishment in toppling American apartheid.[3]

Yet Michael Wright's admission of historical amnesia concerning the previous battles against racism in the South speaks directly to a fundamental question about the civil rights movement over which historians increasingly disagree: when did it begin and when did it end, if at all? Historians are in the business of marking the past through periodization; we recognize continuity as a standard rule of operation, but we value the notion of change even more. If the past remained static, we probably would not need historians—sociologists, political scientists, or literary scholars could do the job. Of course, discerning between change and continuity is not an either-or exercise. Change and continuity are symbiotic. Change produces counterforces to restore continuity, and continuity breeds dissatisfactions to generate change. Too much emphasis on continuity blurs distinctions based on shifting context and demography; too much emphasis on change masks the origins of events and misses the cohesive forces tying disparate events together. Striking the right balance is the challenge to good history.

With respect to civil rights, good historians disagree over the issue of chronology. The so-called master narrative of the movement—the one popularized by the media, national celebrations, and high school textbooks—is well known. It starts in 1954 with the Supreme Court's ruling against school segregation in *Brown v. Board of Education* and ends in 1968 with the assassination of Dr. Martin Luther King Jr. and the replacement of civil rights with Black Power. In between, according to this chronicle, male leaders committed to nonviolence (mainly black ministers) awakened the moral conscience of the nation at places such as Montgomery, Birmingham, and Selma, Alabama; Albany, Georgia; and the Mississippi Delta, forcing the government to enact civil rights legislation that tore down legal segregation and extended the right to vote to the majority of black citizens.

Furthermore, the movement demonstrated the possibilities of interracial cooperation, although these were too quickly deflected by Black Nationalism.[4] This master narrative is seriously outdated, and no historian who has read the literature on civil rights since the mid-1970s accepts this version. We may lament the public's slowness in catching up to the scholarship, but we can rest assured that civil rights history no longer reads this way.

As early as the mid-1970s, some scholars, including myself, challenged the chronology of the civil rights movement by pushing it backward. Richard Dalfiume located the early period of the modern civil rights struggle in World War II, with its antifascist ideology and empowerment of black soldiers. Around the same time Harvard Sitkoff went back even further to President Franklin D. Roosevelt and the New Deal liberalism of the 1930s. In his monumental treatise on the *Brown* case, Richard Kluger adeptly traces its origins to the founding of the National Association for the Advancement of Colored People (NAACP) in 1909 and the local communities that spawned other cases after World War II.[5] The 1980s witnessed the beginning of pathbreaking community histories of Greensboro, North Carolina; Tuskegee, Alabama; and St. Augustine, Florida, which refocused movement scholarship from the national to the local level and discovered the movement's roots in different periods according to the specific locale.[6] From there, the writing of community studies exploded, expanding our understanding of the social networks that gave birth to and sustained protest throughout the South and on which the national civil rights movement was built. In these histories the vital role of women and ordinary men emerged to challenge the predominance of charismatic male leaders and even the few well-known female participants, such as Rosa Parks, in the struggle for equality.[7]

As far as the end of the movement, most scholars express dissatisfaction with the traditional terminus of either 1965 (Selma and the Voting Rights Act) or 1968 (King's death). Some have called for a recalibration of the movement's finish line, pushing it further ahead in time, and others have recognized that in some communities the movement did not take hold until after 1965.[8] This essay, however, focuses on beginnings rather than endings.

Redesigning the chronology of the civil right movement, especially its early years, has enlarged our understanding of it but has also led to a distortion of the movement's historicity. For example, some scholars have pushed the start of the movement back to the introduction of American slavery. Leon Litwack recently wrote that the "civil rights movement began with the presence of enslaved blacks in the New World, with the first slave mutiny on the ships bringing them here."[9] Others have chosen Reconstruction or the formation of the NAACP. In doing so, they equate all or nearly all of African American history with the civil rights movement. Without question, the quest for liberation from white supremacy has propelled African American history—from slavery, Jim Crow, and institutional racism. Whereas this overarching struggle for black freedom encompasses the civil rights period of the 1950s and 1960s, it is much broader and longer than what we traditionally refer to as the civil rights movement, and it has characteristics and contours separate from this shorter era. Charles Eagles has questioned this kind of all-encompassing version of civil rights history because scholars fail to see it as "a discrete episode . . . within the stream of time."[10] Indeed, the civil rights movement occurred at a particular time and place and must be viewed as historically distinct from other aspects of the black freedom struggle that preceded it and, for that matter, followed in its wake.

A far more sophisticated argument in favor of an extended chronology has emerged in the last generation of civil rights scholarship. Summarized and exquisitely articulated by Jacquelyn Dowd Hall, this body of work depicts a "long civil rights movement" that transcended the "classic" phase (1954–1968) of the freedom struggle. Though she does not use the phrase or refer to it, Hall has borrowed a concept, the *longue durée,* from the French *Annales* school.[11] Historians such as Robert Korstad, Glenda Gilmore, and Hall contend that this *longue durée* originated in the 1930s with a biracial alliance in the South among labor union radicals. Acknowledging the importance of racial objectives, they nevertheless highlight the class dimensions of the struggle to transform the South economically. Locals of the CIO, especially the textile and tobacco workers in North Carolina; the Southern Conference for Human Welfare (SCHW) and its successor, the Southern Conference Educational Fund; the National Committee to Abolish the Poll Tax; Highlander Folk School; and the Communist Party played major roles in the initiation of this movement. These mostly white organizations were joined by largely black groups such as the SNYC and the National Negro Congress. The climax of this organizing during the New Deal era came in 1948 with the independent presidential campaign of Henry Wallace, who ran on a platform that opposed economic inequality and racial segregation. Wallace's dismal last-place finish in a field of four also marked the nadir of the biracial struggle of the 1930s and 1940s, as the anticommunist Cold War counteroffensive halted immediate prospects for radical change in the United States.[12]

Unlike previous historians who viewed the New Deal or World War II as the prelude to the civil rights movement, Hall asserts that "civil rights unionism was not just a precursor of the modern civil rights movement. It was its decisive first phase." In other words, continuity and capaciousness characterize this version of history. Moreover, Hall seeks to transform and reinterpret southern history in several ways. First, she rejects the notion that the South was distinct from the rest of the country in its practice of white supremacy as a combination of racial and economic control over blacks—"the trope of the South as the nation's 'opposite other.'" As she puts it, she wants to uncover "the broader and ultimately more durable patterns of privilege and exploitation that were American, not southern in their origins and consequences." Second, and closely related in purpose, Hall and others have recaptured a legacy of twentieth-century southern radicalism that has been largely overlooked in a region so closely tied to political and economic conservatism. Without neglecting the centrality of African Americans, they illuminate the presence of southern white radicals and restore their place in history within a national narrative of struggle for political, economic, and racial equality and justice. As Hall acknowledges, scholarship on the long civil rights movement serves as a counterpoint to the New Right's efforts to reinterpret the classic civil rights movement exclusively as an attempt to obtain individual opportunity on a color-blind basis, mainly through the right to vote, without challenging the existing economic or political system.[13]

In offering this conception of the long civil rights movement, Hall and others have made a number of valuable contributions. Searching for continuity, they emphasize a pre–civil rights southern past that is customarily overlooked in accounts that view the South as either monolithic or bipolar—consisting of reactionary whites and submissive blacks. In addition, because their histories delve into local communities and organizations, they have uncovered an impressive array of women and men who remained invisible in the traditional narratives of the movement. Indeed, the new scholarship has identified African American women—in their roles as organizers and movers and shakers in their neighborhood churches and civic associations—as the backbone of the movement.[14] Finally, these historians have reminded us that civil rights history was not inevitable, that there were alternatives to the courses taken, and that the outcomes might have been different.

For all its virtues, the historical validity of the long civil rights movement has serious shortcomings. There is something we can correctly call the black freedom struggle, but it transcends the civil rights movement. As historians and teachers, we commonly divide history into various eras to underscore change over time and also to make the past more comprehensible to our students. The so-called classic civil rights movement was significantly different in objective, technique, and consciousness from preceding efforts to achieve freedom, whether abolitionism, Black Nationalism, or the interracial Popular Front of the New Deal era. As August Meier, the distinguished pioneer of civil rights scholarship, commented on the subject of change and continuity: "I confess that the older I grow, the more impressed I am with discontinuities in history and how social activism is based so largely in the social context and in the activists' perceptions of those changes."[15] The concept of the long civil rights movement, though useful in locating antecedents, blurs the lines of the historic changes within the black freedom struggle that gave the period from 1954 to 1968 its distinct context and character.

There was a genuine movement for social change in the South during the New Deal era, but it took on a different shape from the civil rights movement that followed in the next two decades. Civil rights unions and the Popular Front constituted vital parts of the omnipresent black freedom struggle. Its adherents performed the work of extending civil rights and laid the groundwork for what followed, but this remained distinct from the civil rights movement.[16] The Popular Front, with its black-red alliance, sought to transform the South and the nation economically, reduce poverty, limit the power of corporations, and boost the strength of labor unions. It also linked economic justice and the attack on Jim Crow at home with promoting peace and anti-imperialism abroad—a strong internationalist perspective that often lined up with Soviet foreign policy. The struggle for civil rights was only one thread of this broader egalitarian struggle and anti-imperialist movement. Thinking more universally compared with today's so-called identity politics, progressives believed that blacks would gain political power and advance economically by joining labor unions. Class mattered more than race, and critics targeted capitalism as the source of black oppression. Unlike liberals, those further on the Left doubted that African Americans would gain their freedom merely through the extension of legal and constitutional rights. Rather, only through a restructuring of corporate capitalism would genuine economic democracy emerge and white supremacy collapse. Although African American progressives actively participated in unions, groups such as the SCHW, and the Wallace campaign, the leadership and membership of these organizations in the South consisted mainly of whites. The Communist Party, an important player in this movement, also remained largely in white hands.

Although many scholars have welcomed the notion of the long civil rights movement, this reconceptualization has also drawn considerable criticism. From a methodological vantage point, critics Sundiata Keita Cha-Jua and Clarence Lang argue that the model's greatest flaw "is its ahistorical totalizing perspective" and "tendency to flatten chronological, conceptual, and geographic differences."[17] In a similar vein, Adam Fairclough writes: "The trouble with such broad definitions . . . is that in stressing history's 'seamless web' they turn history into a homogenized mush, without sharp breaks and transformations."[18] Historian Richard King observes that undue emphasis on continuity "obscures what was fresh, original, and dynamic about the civil rights movement of the 1950s and 1960s."[19] More than thirty years ago, August Meier and Elliott Rudwick asked whether a continuous legacy of nonviolent direct action, the central tool of the modern civil rights movement, existed among African Americans. After exhaustive research, they reached "the unexpected conclusion that its roots lay not in any past tradition of nonviolent direct action, but in the changing context of race relations which had emerged by the middle of the twentieth century."[20]

Ironically, even those whose work constitutes the basis for the concept of the long civil rights movement provide strong evidence that the Popular Front movements of the 1930s and 1940s did not continue into the 1950s and 1960s. Robert Korstad and Nelson Lichtenstein first called this rupture "the lost opportunity thesis."[21] According to their interpretation, the onset of McCarthyism, and particularly its longer duration in the South, wiped out the biracial, radical labor and political movement that had promised to transform the nation. As a result, when the second phase of the long civil rights movement emerged around 1954, it looked markedly different and carried little potential for sweeping change, especially in the economic realm. To avert the taint of communism, groups such as the NAACP supposedly removed the economic component from their agenda and concentrated on securing legal and political rights, focusing on the edifice of public segregation and not the foundation of white supremacy, or what Hall terms "racial capitalism."[22] Historian Robert Self, who is sympathetic to the role black radicals played in the long civil rights movement, nevertheless acknowledges that the Cold War had a "profound effect," opening "fissures within African American intellectual and political circles" and forcing "black radicals on the defensive."[23] Lending support to this idea of dislocation, Charles Houston, a pioneer of NAACP litigation against seg-regated public schools and a leading black progressive, lamented in 1950 about the future of the freedom struggle: "We may have to stop and start over again [or] leave it to those who come after us."[24] Thus, some of those who shaped the concept of the long civil rights movement acknowledge that the Cold War and the persecution of those on the Left erected an iron curtain between the two eras and produced a very different and discontinuous civil rights movement.[25]

The lost opportunity thesis also rests on too narrow an evidentiary base. Most union locals in the South did not follow the course of the food and tobacco workers in Winston-Salem, North Carolina, so ably chronicled by Korstad. National union leadership, especially that of the CIO, may have been sympathetic to transforming the South on a democratic and egalitarian basis, but this did not prove to be the case with the white rank and file. As it had during earlier efforts in the South to organize blacks and whites under the banner of economic and political reform, racism stood fiercely in the way. Whites sought to preserve their workplace privileges, such as seniority, to the disadvantage of African Americans, who were kept out of the better-paying positions. Many white workers, despite their economic grievances, shared with their employers and neighbors the cultural belief in and commitment to the preservation of white supremacy, making inter-racial organizing a daunting if not impossible task. More than a few union members in the South expressed this loyalty through membership in the Ku Klux Klan. The Cold War did not doom civil rights unionism so much as the continued forms of racism that survived the New Deal and World War II eras.[26]

Still, the work of Korstad and Lichtenstein is widely cited in the new scholarship on the long civil rights movement, which depends on a favorable interpretation of the Communist Party and its activities in support of black freedom. Without venturing into the political minefield of scholarship on the Communist Party, it is fair to say that from its defense of the Scottsboro Nine in the early 1930s to its support of organizing sharecroppers in Alabama and factory workers in North Carolina in the 1930s and 1940s, the party played an important role in the black freedom struggle.[27] Whatever the Moscow line, black and white party members at the local level discarded or reinterpreted it to fit their needs. Still, there is danger in romanticizing Communist Party efforts. As scholars such as Eric Arnesen contend, party members sometimes subverted civil rights issues when instructed to do so. Fairclough further discounts the party's influence, claiming that its efforts in support of antiracism in post–World War II Louisiana were "marginal."[28] Moreover, as Arnesen points out, Communists get too much credit for their impact on the black freedom struggle, and anticommunist unionists, such as A. Philip Randolph and his Brotherhood of Sleeping Car Porters, receive too little. The brotherhood, for example, was far more successful than the Communist Party in stimulating the upsurge of black unionism in the 1930s and 1940s.[29]

Though unintentionally, proponents of the long civil rights movement have constructed a declension narrative. They do not contrast the "good," cohesive interracial community, nonviolent years of the civil rights movement with the "bad," divisive, separatist, armed self-defense years of the later Black Power movement. Those arguing for the long civil rights movement generally use the neutral term *phase* to highlight specific periods under their larger conceptual umbrella. However, they implicitly privilege the civil rights unionism–Popular Front phase as holding the key to a more thoroughgoing economic, social, political, and international realignment of class and race in the United States and achievement of peace throughout the world. If only the Cold War had not subverted progressive efforts for change, the struggle for racial and economic equality would have gone much further. Radicalism would have trumped liberalism to overthrow racial capitalism. In singling out Cold War anticommunism for blame, this declension narrative reduces the impact of institutional racism in the South (and North)—American apartheid—which made the achievement of change highly unlikely. Indeed, the genius of the civil rights movement of the 1950s and 1960s was the way it adapted to the contemporary political environment to dismantle the most blatant forms of white supremacy.

The Cold War did make a huge difference in ending Popular Front activism and halting its particular version of economic and racial equality. However, the Cold War also had a significant effect in stimulating the classic civil rights movement. As did World War II, the Cold War forced the federal government to try to narrow the gap between its democratic promises of freedom and the reality of white supremacy in the South. Without calling it such, African Americans resurrected the "Double V" campaign—victory at home and victory abroad—they had adopted during World War II. In casting aside the radical economic ideology of the Popular Front, groups such as the NAACP succeeded in using America's anticommunist foreign policy and the corresponding need to win allies in emerging Third World nations to pry civil rights measures from the national government.[30] The growing political power of blacks who had migrated to the urban North during the war provided the political muscle needed to prompt President Harry Truman, the architect of America's Cold War policy, to take favorable action on the civil rights front.[31] Not surprisingly, the government's brief in *Brown v. Board of Education,* submitted by Truman's Justice Department, argued: "It is in the context of the present world struggle between freedom and tyranny that the problem of racial discrimination must be viewed."[32]

This Cold War context marks the period between 1954 and 1968—the classic civil rights movement—as distinct from its emancipationist predecessors. Faced with a new set of political, economic, and international considerations, civil rights activists adopted strategies and tactics suitable to these altered conditions. As sociologist Doug McAdam notes, "Established civil rights organizations clearly recognized the unique framing opportunity which the Cold War afforded them. They framed civil rights reform as a tool in America's struggle against Communism."[33] Groups such as the NAACP and the Leadership Conference on Civil Rights, founded in 1950 by A. Philip Randolph and Roy Wilkins (among others), evaluated their prospects amidst the collapse of New Deal political alliances, prepared to meet new postwar realities, and adopted liberal economic positions in support of civil rights. To this end, they did not so much abandon the redistributionist economic positions offered by progressives as they embraced the pro-growth principles of the new liberalism, which sought to manage corporate capitalism to benefit all Americans and not just the wealthy few.[34]

Thus the Cold War did not divorce the demands of liberal civil rights groups from economic reform. Without question, liberals pursued a far more restrained economic agenda, but they continued to link antiracism with economic reform. Their emphasis on expansion of the constitutional right to vote was not an exercise in abstract legalism; it offered a strategy to boost black voting power and thus enhance efforts to extend minimum wage, full employment, and social security legislation; provide public housing; and repeal the antiunion Taft-Hartley Act. It must be remembered that the 1963 March on Washington, which was organized by Randolph and his associate Bayard Rustin and included the NAACP and the United Auto Workers, was aimed at obtaining jobs and freedom—in that order. At the same time, Whitney M. Young, director of the National Urban League, promoted a post–World War II–style "Marshall Plan" aimed at impoverished African Americans.

The distinctive civil rights movement of the 1950s and 1960s may have narrowed the focus of the black struggle concerning issues of economic class, but it succeeded in refocusing the movement along racial lines. Indeed, the most significant difference between the classic civil rights movement and the efforts of civil rights unionism and the Popular Front was that the former was led by and based in African American communities. Whites certainly played important roles in the civil rights movement, most memorably illustrated in the 1963 March on Washington, but they tended to serve as allies and associates rather than key leaders of national and community organizations. The concept of the long civil rights movement has opened up the pages of history to progressive southern whites in the 1930s and 1940s. These activists were courageous, visionary, and essential, but they composed only a tiny fraction of the southern population. Their influence should be neither ignored nor exaggerated. As Glenn Feldman has observed, "It would still take grassroots black activists, 'outside agitators' from the North, and considerable federal involvement to effect meaningful reform in the area of southern race relations."[35]

From the very beginning, the beloved community Dr. King summoned included whites; however, the path to that brotherhood was blazed primarily by those who had the most to gain: African Americans in the South. The civil rights movement embodied the racial identity and aspirations of an oppressed minority, in contrast to the class-consciousness of the Popular Front. This shift developed in part out of pragmatic considerations. Seeking to avoid public identification with sympathetic whites likely to be branded as Communist, black civil rights reformers drew on their own racial organizations for leadership and sustenance. The modern civil rights movement depended on three of the most important indigenous organizations in the black South—churches, colleges, and NAACP branches (which had grown enormously during World War II).[36] Indeed, from these and other community-centered groups, women emerged as central actors in the struggle.

If there is a direct link from the civil rights movement to the pre-1954 era, it stems not from civil rights unionism but from African American protests during the World War II era. Some well-known (at least to movement scholars) examples include the following: Randolph's March on Washington movement, which in 1941 persuaded President Franklin D. Roosevelt to create a Fair Employment Practice Committee; the founding of the Congress of Racial Equality (CORE) in 1943, which spawned future civil rights leaders Bayard Rustin and James Farmer, as well as the Freedom Rides (Journey of Reconciliation) in the upper South in 1947; sit-in protests initiated by students at Howard University in Washington, D.C., and by the Tuskegee Airmen at military bases in both the South and the North; the well-publicized hearings against white supremacist Theodore Bilbo in Jackson, Mississippi, in 1947, which gathered the testimony of African Americans and prevented Bilbo from taking his seat in the Senate; and the campaign throughout the South to register voters in the wake of *Smith v. Allwright,* the 1944 Supreme Court decision that overturned the critical all-white Democratic Party primary.[37]

In addition, as Danielle McGuire has perceptively demonstrated, the war years produced black protest against the failure to convict white men of raping black women, most notably the 1944 Recy Taylor case in Alabama. Such efforts in defense of black womanhood helped mobilize civil rights community activism, especially in the 1940s and 1950s. In fact, McGuire establishes a powerful linkage between the Taylor case and the overwhelming presence of women in the Montgomery bus boycott a decade later.[38] Although historians have emphasized the role of World War II in raising the consciousness of oppression among black men, especially military veterans, women shared in this growing awareness as the wives and mothers of soldiers, as wartime factory workers, and as key members of religious and civic organizations. In summary, the origins of the classic civil rights movement can be traced more directly to black communities and the protest activities that emerged from them than to civil rights unionists and the Popular Front.

In addition to the Cold War, a number of other significant forces encouraged the development of the civil rights movement in the mid-1950s. The decline of the labor-intensive plantation system, which resulted from New Deal agricultural policies and increased mechanization, together with the wartime migration of African Americans from rural areas to southern and northern cities, opened up a crack in the white supremacist system of racial control. By creating new spaces for African Americans to occupy, these forces released blacks from intense white oversight and reinvigorated black urban communities in both the South and the North. Southern blacks, especially, took advantage of this fissure to wrest some power for themselves through indigenous protest and pressuring the federal government for reform. Also, the dissemination of new technologies, especially television, generally worked in favor of southern civil rights activists, allowing them to publicize their grievances and creating a political constituency in the North to back their demands.[39] Finally, during the 1950s and especially the 1960s, blacks' income rose significantly, giving

African Americans extra leverage to conduct boycotts and sit-ins more effectively and connecting them more powerfully to the burgeoning consumer culture. This growing integration into the commercial mainstream helped diminish white resistance to some measure of integration into the civic polity. Such economic power did not exist in the 1930s during the Depression era, and it made a critical difference.[40]

In attempting to depict the struggle for civil rights as a discrete movement, it is necessary to define the relevant terms. In its simplest form, a *social movement* consists of collective action by a group or groups with a common ideology consciously striving to alter existing political, economic, and social relationships. McAdam has provided a more multifaceted way of identifying social movements. He argues that movements are made up of "contenders" who operate at multiple levels—local, state, and national—and include a variety of actors representing conflicting positions, such as civil rights advocates and white supremacists. Thus, one of the characteristics of the modern civil rights movement was its complexity both internally and externally. It consisted of a variety of national, regional, and local groups that worked both cooperatively and in conflict with one another. A division of labor existed that provided opportunities for groups to focus on what they did best: the NAACP as litigator and lobbyist; the Urban League as agent to the business community; and SNCC, CORE, and the Southern Christian Leadership Conference (SCLC) as vanguards of direct action protest. On the positive side, these activities generated the creative tension that brought about innovative tactics and experimentation.[41] However, competition for funding and publicity among these perennially cash-starved groups hampered the unity of the movement. Internal squabbling diminished its ability to exert maximum and concerted pressure on the federal government to respond to its programs.[42]

A social movement is built on consciousness, ideology, and organizational and mobilizing structures. These ingredients give the particular movement its character and vary with the historical context. Participants in movements, according to McAdam, "need to feel both aggrieved about some aspect of their lives and optimistic that acting collectively, they can redress their problem."[43] They have to be aware of their oppression and have hope of overcoming it.

African Americans did not need much prodding to recognize their subjugation, and the ideological contingencies surrounding World War II and the Cold War offered them optimism for impending change. Historians have argued whether *Brown v. Board of Education* initiated the civil rights movement and about the impact it had, but unquestionably, this landmark decision accelerated the ideology of black freedom. *Smith v. Allwright* and *American Dilemma,* Gunnar Myrdal's pioneering study published in 1944, had provided the legal and intellectual stimulus for the civil rights movement.[44] However, not until *Brown* did the national government affirm the principle of racial equality as the law of the land. For the civil rights movement, this proclamation became the modern equivalent of the Declaration of Independence. As a monumental ideological victory, *Brown* inspired Jo Ann Gibson Robinson and the Women's Political Caucus in Montgomery to press their demands for the fair treatment of black bus riders, an effort that would lead to the historic bus boycott in December 1955.[45] Although the desegregation decision encountered massive resistance from southern governments, citizens' councils, and Ku Klux Klan terrorists, which managed to block full enforcement for more than a decade, this backlash convinced civil rights advocates that they would have to step up their efforts to destroy Jim Crow.[46]

Another significant event in dating the beginning of the civil rights movement was the brutal killing of Emmett Till. While visiting his uncle in Mississippi during the summer of 1955, the fourteen-year-old from Chicago upset local whites when he allegedly made a pass at a white female store clerk. In retaliation, the woman's husband and his brother removed Till from his residence, viciously beat him, and threw his dead body in the Tallahatchie River. The subsequent murder trial resulted in an acquittal. The assassination and the verdict had a stunning effect on the rising generation of African American youth who were roughly Till's age. By the end of the decade, this teenage cohort would reach college age and, with the memory of Till still fresh, would add new troops and inject vital energy into the civil rights movement.[47]

By the time of the *Brown* decision and Till's murder, African Americans possessed the institutional structures necessary to mobilize to close the gap between their expectations of change and the brutal reality of white supremacy. At the national level the NAACP led the way, followed by the SCLC, CORE, and SNCC. Indeed, after *Brown,* state-led efforts to destroy the NAACP, considered the most radical of black organizations by southern white authorities, spurred the creation of new protest organizations locally and throughout the South. Black churches, civic associations, and informal community networks added organizational muscle to the demands for racial equality during the 1950s and 1960s.[48] Without these structures (discussed in the numerous community histories written in recent decades), the yearning for civil rights would not have grown into a movement, and people would not have taken action against the power of state-supported white supremacy. The organizational vehicles that blacks fashioned and that originated in their communities propelled the civil rights movement and gave voice to their aspirations.

In attempting to demarcate the boundaries of the civil rights movement and distinguish it from other components of the long struggle for black freedom, we must ask what we mean by *civil rights*. As Cha-Jua and Lang argue, "in political discourse, 'civil rights' refer to privileges the state grants its citizens and protections against unjustifiable infringement by either the state or private citizens."[49] For African Americans, these rights derive from the Fourteenth and Fifteenth Amendments. In contrast, *civil liberties* stem from the Bill of Rights and apply more generally to freedom of speech, the press, association, religion, and privacy; the right to bear arms; and procedural protections related to the judicial and criminal justice systems. In the early twentieth century the terms *civil rights* and *civil liberties* were often used interchangeably. In fact, in 1940 the Justice Department established the Civil Liberties Unit, largely to deal with corporations' efforts to stifle union organizing, as well as to prosecute civil rights crimes. Most telling for our purposes, in 1941 the name of the Civil Liberties Unit was changed to the Civil Rights Section, and it began to focus less on union activities and more on justice for blacks.[50] In short, this change foreshadowed the breakup of the Popular Front, the demise of civil rights unionism, and the onset of the civil rights movement.

A further example of the disaggregation of *civil rights* from *civil liberties* in relation to the status of African Americans came in 1947. In response to an outburst of racial violence in the South, President Harry S. Truman appointed a Committee on Civil Rights. Although the committee report referred to both civil rights and civil liberties, the panel clearly identified civil rights as pertaining to racial minorities, in particular, to African Americans. The committee broke down civil rights into four parts: the right to safety and security of the person, the right to citizenship and its privileges, the right to equality of opportunity, and the right to freedom of conscience and expression. Only the last part covered traditional civil liberties—that is, the First Amendment's protection of free speech, association, and religion. The committee made a token effort to study civil liberties, but it clearly directed its attention to the civil rights concerns of African Americans and, to a much lesser extent, some other racial minorities. The presidential committee's far-reaching recommendations to eliminate racial segregation and disfranchisement also included a proposal to elevate the Civil Rights Section into a division of the Justice Department.[51]

Another way of determining the historical boundaries of the civil rights movement is to uncover how participants at the time viewed it and how the press reported it. As Hugh Murray has pointed out, "the people who were involved in the movement in the 1950s and 1960s called it the civil rights movement."[52] Toward this end, a search of the term *civil rights movement* in the Pro Quest database for key white and black newspapers from 1930 to 1969 was conducted. Among the listings for five African American newspapers—the *Atlanta Daily World, Chicago Defender, New York Amsterdam News, Pittsburgh Courier,* and *Baltimore African American*—there were no entries for the 1930s, 6 for the 1940s (nearly all from late in the decade), 33 for the 1950s, and 2,820 for the 1960s (most occurring after 1962). An examination of the *New York Times* yielded similar results: no articles with the term *civil rights movement* appeared in the 1930s or 1940s; there were 7 in the 1950s and 1,759 in the 1960s.[53] This statistical breakdown lends credence to the argument that the term *civil rights movement*—and with it the conception that the broader freedom struggle had taken a new form—gained widespread use in the 1950s and became prominent in the 1960s.

One other characteristic of the classic civil rights movement that deserves emphasis is the presence of Martin Luther King Jr. Over the past several decades scholars have done a good deal to decenter the movement from King. The reasons for doing so stem from the antielitist politics of civil rights scholars and from the criticism that focusing on one heroic man obscures the role of multitudes of women and ordinary men. Despite the validity of this observation, King's presence helps explain why the civil rights movement was distinctive and relatively short. Certainly, King did not create the movement; rather, the movement thrust him into a position he did not covet. He had long roots in the black community and was chosen to lead by blacks, not by whites. That said, King's charismatic leadership gave a unique character to the movement from 1954 to 1968. The Montgomery to Memphis arc of civil rights history has lasting public appeal, for good reason. King's philosophy and tactics of nonviolent direct action, the campaigns he launched, and his distinct and inspirational voice shaped the popular perception of the movement for both blacks and whites. Enemies of the movement had many targets, but none as convenient or larger than life as King. Within the movement, no matter the organization's competing style, activists had to reckon foremost with King. He served as the movement's mediator among groups and as the ambassador to white America.

If one looks to the 1940s for comparison, what is missing from incipient black protest, civil rights unionism, and the Popular Front is charismatic leadership at the national level. Perhaps Randolph or the Reverend Vernon Johns, King's predecessor at the Dexter Avenue Baptist Church in Montgomery, might have filled this void, but neither they nor anyone else did. Pushing King from the center of the movement does not alter the fact that most southern blacks viewed him as the person who could inspire them to action, articulate their goals, and convey their grievances to those occupying the highest seats of power.[54]

This essay has focused on the beginning rather than the end of the civil rights movement, but a few words are in order about the movement's conclusion. Scholars such as Jacquelyn Dowd Hall and Thomas Sugrue have placed Black Power within the chronology of the long civil rights movement, which carries the movement through the 1970s and into the 1980s. Although civil rights and Black Power shared some common roots, objectives, and personnel, and although they overlapped in time after 1965, their differences are more striking than their similarities. With the emergence of Black Power, the freedom struggle took on a nationalist rather than an integrationist cast, promoted self-defense over nonviolence, and connected the movement more closely to Third World liberation battles and radical economic ideologies. In this way Black Power more closely resembled the black Popular Front of the 1940s than the short civil rights movement. Peniel Joseph has offered the most comprehensive narrative and summary of the Black Power movement. Although sympathetic to the view of the long civil rights movement, Joseph depicts Black Power and the classic civil rights movements as separate. In "contrast to the struggle for civil rights," Joseph asserts, "the black power movement . . . privileged a view of black empowerment that was local, national, and international in scope, held political self-determination as sacrosanct, and called for a redefined black identity that connected black Americans to a national and global political project based on racial solidarity and a shared history of racial oppression."[55] Operating on separate tracks that occasionally intersected, the two movements together shaped the struggle for black equality in the ensuing decades. Whatever efforts were made to overcome institutional racism and white supremacy, they combined the extension of civil and economic rights with the building of racial identity.[56]

The struggle for black freedom did not end in 1968, and one can argue that it is still ongoing, despite Barack Obama's presidential victory. After 1968, civil rights groups such as the NAACP, Urban League, Leadership Conference on Civil Rights, and numerous organizations at the local level continued to lobby, organize, and agitate for racial equality and desegregation. Indeed, in many towns and hamlets in the rural South, where the classic civil rights movement operated, the struggle to obtain first-class citizenship and economic power did not emerge until the late 1960s and beyond. Community organizing, protests, political activity, and various efforts to improve the economic condition of blacks continued in southern communities. These activities notwithstanding, many things had changed that made the 1954–1968 era distinct: most of the legislative goals had been accomplished; two of the leading organizations, SNCC and CORE, had collapsed, and the SCLC survived in a weakened state; some of the original leaders had moved on or died; the movement's direction had shifted from civil rights to Black Power; the federal government, especially the presidency after the election of Richard M. Nixon, abandoned civil rights forces as the nation moved to the political Right; and, with the acquisition of voting rights, a good deal of the movement's energies shifted from mass protest to electing black candidates to political office. Clearly, important elements of the civil rights movement persisted and even expanded into new areas, but the short civil rights movement, defined by the robust interconnections among the federal government, community activists, national and local organizations, and charismatic and group-centered leaders, had ended.[57] This did not mean that the struggle for freedom rights ceased, but it would take different forms throughout the rest of the century and beyond.

Calling the civil rights movement short is not meant to be pejorative. After all, as distinguished labor historian E. P. Thompson notes, "most social movements have a life cycle of about six years," during which time they have a "window of opportunity" to exert their impact.[58] Social movements require a constant infusion of energy to maintain strength and morale. A struggle like the civil rights movement saps the strength of participants, especially those on the front lines. Not surprisingly, they do not last long. It is difficult to keep people in motion without exposing them to battle fatigue. Furthermore, the enormous triumphs over racial segregation and disfranchisement gave weary activists and the public alike reason to declare victory, despite the recognition that much remained to be accomplished. Nonetheless, the civil rights movement from 1954 to 1968 lasted twice as long as most.

It is not necessary to construct a long civil rights movement to challenge conservative, New Right interpretations of what happened from 1954 to 1968 as an attempt to produce a color-blind society that exalted individualism, opposed race-conscious remedies such as affirmative action, and pursued integration as an end in itself.[59] One should not retreat from viewing the short civil rights movement as an extension of black identity emerging from black churches, schools, colleges, civic associations, and even the segregated military. This does not leave white people or integration out of the pages of civil rights movement history. Whites, both northern and southern, played vital roles through fund-raising, lobbying, and, most importantly, courageously putting their lives on the line in a variety of ways. Yet blacks led and whites supported.

The short civil rights movement concerned the collective goal of freedom, and it went about achieving this goal in complex ways. A group effort, the movement cloaked itself in the garb of morality, but its participants understood and pursued the vestments of power. It made the ballot a number-one priority, not simply for its legal badge of citizenship but as an instrument to obtain better jobs, health care, education, housing, and justice. The Cold War, though furnishing an opportunity for the movement to develop, did not diminish economic equality as an objective; however, it reshaped this objective along liberal rather than radical lines. Furthermore, the movement of the 1950s and 1960s was not about integration for its own sake; it was about the destruction of white supremacy and the revitalization of African American society and culture. Toward this end, women played an extraordinary role as the backbone of the movement. Look at photographs and videotapes from this period, and you see women dominating the frames in mass meetings and on picket lines. Male leaders of all persuasions, from King to Stokely Carmichael, grabbed the headlines, but women did the necessary work to keep the movement going.

And as for King, although his words have been co-opted by conservatives, he epitomizes the transformative qualities of this movement and its radical as well as liberal dimensions. His views evolved over this period according to the circumstances he and the movement faced. His core values, however, did not change, although they were sorely tested. He did not abandon the possibility of a "beloved community" or the use of nonviolence to attain it. He viewed the beloved community as a society free from materialism, militarism, and imperialism. By the end of his life, he was calling for "a radical redistribution of economic and political power" and an overhaul of the "architecture of American society"—statements very different from those gloriously uttered in his 1963 "I Have a Dream" speech. The context had changed, and as a result, so had King.[60]

Those scholars who see the long civil rights movement as a way to recover a usable past and a progressive legacy do not have to scrap the traditional periodization but only the outmoded "master narrative." They need look no further than Henry Hampton's prize-winning documentary *Eyes on the Prize* to see how the classic civil rights period can satisfy their objectives.[61] In an unprecedented manner, this series weaves together the national and the local, ordinary men and women with more recognizable leaders, intragroup cooperation and competition, and mundane concerns with the aim of transforming America to make it "a more perfect union." It tears down the myth that the accomplishments of this civil rights movement were easy and that its participants were merely dreamers. It moves beyond King while understanding that the movement would have been very different without him. Hampton's *Eyes on the Prize* has taken the civil rights movement master narrative and reformulated it to include multiple perspectives of the people, both black and white, who made the movement and those who opposed it, those who had formal power and those who did not, all the while showing where this short civil rights movement succeeded and where it failed.

We are best served historically and politically by returning to a focus on the classic civil rights movement as the *bref durée*. The struggle for black freedom has been long and enduring, and the civil rights movement has been a critical part of it. "The short Civil Rights Movement," as Stephen Tuck writes, "was a distinctive, even exceptional moment."[62] Its brevity notwithstanding, this monumental struggle against white supremacy and for racial equality and justice transformed the United States in the mid-twentieth century. By refocusing their attention in this way, scholars will be writing about the long origins of the short civil rights movement rather than about the long civil rights movement. They will not have to diminish evidence of continuity in order to highlight the importance of change represented by the civil rights movement of 1954–1968. The women and men who produced this change made enormous sacrifices, encountered huge obstacles, and suffered severe physical and psychological damage. In no way, either implicitly or explicitly, should this civil rights movement be considered a decline in vision compared with that of its immediate predecessor. And, with respect to accomplishments, the short civil rights movement remains unparalleled.

Notes

I especially want to thank Danielle McGuire and John Dittmer for editing this splendid collection, which I will always consider the ultimate tribute to my work as a historian and teacher. Also, many thanks to my wonderful former students whose fine works are included in this volume. Finally, I extend my thanks to those who read and commented on my own essay: Jacqueline Castledine, William H. Chafe, Dorothy Sue Cobble, David Colburn, Emilye Crosby, John Dittmer, Charles Eagles, Nancy Hewitt, Pippa Holloway, Hasan Jeffries, William P. Jones, Abigail Lewis, William A. Link, Danielle McGuire, Susan Thorne, Stephen Tuck, and Brian Ward. You all make a grown man cry with joy.

1. Michael Wright to Carol Hanish, May 13, 2009, sncc-list@list.mail.virginia.edu, courtesy of John Dittmer. It must be noted, however, that SNCC elders such as James Forman, the executive director of the group, and Ella Baker, its adviser, knew of these movements and sought to apply their lessons through their leadership.

2. Steven F. Lawson, "Freedom Then, Freedom Now," in *Civil Rights Crossroads: Nation, Community, and the Black Freedom Struggle* (Lexington: University Press of Kentucky, 2003), 3–28.

3. Steven F. Lawson and Charles Payne, *Debating the Civil Rights Movement, 1945–1968,* 2nd ed. (Lanham, Md.: Rowman and Littlefield, 2006). For challenges to the mainstream presentation, see Stephan Thernstrom and Abigail Thernstrom, *America in Black and White, One Nation, Indivisible* (New York: Simon and Schuster, 1999), and Raymond Wolters, *Right Turn, William Bradford Reynolds, the Reagan Administration, and Civil Rights* (New Brunswick, N.J.: Transaction Publishers, 1996). I have avoided addressing two controversial issues in this essay: the northern black struggle for equality and the relationship between civil rights and Black Power. For the record, I view the civil rights movement as mainly a southern phenomenon and Black Power as both overlapping with and distinct from civil rights. For literature on the northern black freedom movement, see Thomas Sugrue, *Sweet Land of Liberty: The Forgotten Struggle for Civil Rights in the North* (New York: Random House, 2009); Jeanne Theoharis and Komozi Woodard, eds., *Freedom North: Black Freedom Struggles outside the South, 1940–1980* (New York: Palgrave Macmillan, 2003); Matthew Countryman, *Up South: Civil Rights and Black Power in Philadelphia* (Philadelphia: University of Pennsylvania Press, 2007); Martha Biondi, *To Stand and Fight: The Struggle for Civil Rights in Postwar New York City* (Cambridge, Mass.: Harvard University Press, 2006); Robert O. Self, *American Babylon: Race and the Struggle for Postwar Oakland* (Princeton, N.J.: Princeton University Press, 2005); and Beryl Satter, *Family Properties: Race, Real Estate, and the Exploitation of Black Urban America* (New York: Metropolitan Books, 2009). On Black Power, see also Tim Tyson, *Radio Free Dixie: Robert F. Williams and the Roots of Black Power*

(Chapel Hill: University of North Carolina Press, 2001); Peniel E. Joseph, *Waiting till the Midnight Hour: A Narrative History of Black Power in America* (New York: Holt, 2007), and *Black Power Movement: Rethinking the Civil Rights–Black Power Era* (London: Routledge, 2006); and Sundiata Keita Cha-Jua and Clarence Lang, "The 'Long Movement' as Vampire: Temporal and Spatial Fallacies in Recent Black Freedom Studies," *Journal of African American History* 92 (2007): 270, 274, 275, 277.

4. For a statement and critique of this view, see Renee C. Romano and Leigh Ranford, eds., *The Civil Rights Movement in American History* (Athens: University of Georgia Press, 2006), xiv–xv.

5. Steven F. Lawson, *Black Ballots: Voting Rights in the South, 1944–1969* (New York: Columbia University Press, 1976); Richard Dalfiume, "The Forgotten Years of the Negro Revolution," *Journal of American History* 55 (June 1968): 90–106; Harvard Sitkoff, *A New Deal for Blacks: The Depression Decade* (New York: Oxford University Press, 1978); Richard Kluger, *Simple Justice: The History of* Brown v. Board of Education *and Black America's Struggle for Justice* (New York: Vintage, 1976). Sitkoff has argued that World War II was not a watershed; see Harvard Sitkoff, "African American Militancy in the World War II South: Another Perspective," in *Remaking Dixie: The Impact of World War II on the American South,* ed. Neil R. McMillen (Jackson: University Press of Mississippi, 1997), 70–92.

6. William H. Chafe, *Civilities and Civil Rights* (New York: Oxford University Press, 1981); Robert Jeff Norrell, *Reaping the Whirlwind: The Civil Rights Movement in Tuskegee* (New York: Knopf, 1985); David R. Colburn, *Racial Change and Community Crisis: St. Augustine, Florida, 1877–1980* (New York: Columbia University Press, 1985).

7. The list is too long to include here, but it starts with John Dittmer, *Local People: The Struggle for Civil Rights in Mississippi* (Champaign-Urbana: University of Illinois Press, 1994), and Charles Payne, *I've Got the Light of Freedom: The Organizing Tradition and the Mississippi Freedom Struggle* (Berkeley: University of California Press, 1995).

8. Hasan Jeffries, *Bloody Lowndes: Civil Rights and Black Power in Alabama's Black Belt* (New York: New York University Press, 2009). With respect to politics, I pushed the story ahead into the mid-1980s and saw the election of post–Voting Rights Act black politicians as carrying on the civil rights agenda. See Steven J. Lawson, *In Pursuit of Power: Southern Blacks and Electoral Politics, 1965–1982* (New York: Columbia University Press, 1985).

9. Leon Litwack, "'Fight the Power!' The Legacy of the Civil Rights Movement," *Journal of American History* 75 (February 2009): 3; Kavern Verney, *Black Civil Rights in America* (London: Routledge, 2000).

10. Charles Eagles, "Toward New Histories of the Civil Rights Era," *Journal of Southern History* 66 (November 2000): 815–48. See also David L.

Chappell, "The Lost Decade of Civil Rights," *Historically Speaking* 10 (April 2004): 40.

11. For a classic work of this school, see Fernand Braudel, *The Mediterranean and the Mediterranean World in the Age of Philip the Second* (New York: Harper and Row, 1972). For an important discussion of continuity and change in women's history, see Judith M. Bennett, "Theoretical Issues: Confronting Continuity," *Journal of Women's History* 9 (autumn 1997): 73–94. Bennett distinguishes between continuity in women's status and change in women's experiences.

12. Jacquelyn Dowd Hall, "The Long Civil Rights Movement and the Political Uses of the Past," *Journal of American History* 91 (March 2005): 1233–63. In a recent presentation Hall acknowledged the validity of some criticisms concerning the long civil rights movement's blurring of chronological distinctions and its detracting from the "dynamic uprising of the late 1950s and early 1960s." She affirms that her "goal is not to downplay that moment in history, but to shed light on its larger aims and place it in a context that we can see only as we look back from our *own* moment in time." Jacquelyn Dowd Hall, "Introductory Remarks: The Long Civil Rights Movement: Histories, Politics, Memories," University of North Carolina–Chapel Hill, April 3, 2009. See also Robert Rogers Korstad, *Civil Rights Unionism: Tobacco Workers and the Struggle for Democracy in the Mid Twentieth Century South* (Chapel Hill: University of North Carolina Press, 2003); Glenda Elizabeth Gilmore, *Defying Dixie: The Radical Roots of Civil Rights, 1919–1950* (New York: Norton, 2009); Patricia Sullivan, *Days of Hope: Race and Democracy in the New Deal Era* (Chapel Hill: University of North Carolina Press, 1996); Michael Honey, *Southern Labor and Black Civil Rights: Organizing Memphis Workers* (Urbana: University of Illinois Press, 1993); Thomas A. Krueger, *And Promises to Keep: The Southern Conference for Human Welfare, 1938–1948* (Nashville: Vanderbilt University Press, 1967); Linda A. Reed, *Simple Decency and Common Sense: The Southern Conference Movement, 1938–1963* (Bloomington: University of Indiana Press, 1991); John M. Glen, *Highlander: No Ordinary School* (Knoxville: University of Tennessee Press, 1996); Robin D. G. Kelley, *Hammer and Hoe: Alabama Communists during the Great Depression* (Chapel Hill: University of North Carolina Press, 1990); Gerald Horne, *Communist Front? The Civil Rights Congress, 1946–1956* (Rutherford, N.J.: Fairleigh Dickinson University Press, 1988); and Sara E. Rzeszutek, "'Eagles in Buzzard Country': The Southern Negro Youth Congress in the Struggle for Social Justice, 1937–1949" (undergraduate honor's thesis, History Department, Mount Holyoke College, 2003). In contrast to those who subscribe to the long civil rights movement, John Egerton has written a massive history of southern dissenters before 1954 titled *Speak Now against the Day: The Generation before the Civil Rights Movement in the South* (Chapel Hill: University of North Carolina Press, 1995). See also Kevin Boyle, "Labour, the Left, and the Long Civil Rights Movement," *Social History* 30 (August 2005): 366–72.

13. Hall, "Long Civil Rights Movement," 1245, 1239, 1243.

14. Christina Greene, *Our Separate Ways: Women and the Black Freedom Movement in Durham, North Carolina* (Chapel Hill: University of North Carolina Press, 2005); Belinda Robnett, *How Long? How Long? African American Women in the Struggle for Civil Rights* (New York: Oxford University Press, 1997); Peter Ling and Sharon Monteith, eds., *Gender in the Civil Rights Movement* (New York: Garland, 1999); Lawson, *Civil Rights Crossroads.* One group of southern white and black women that does not receive enough attention is the YWCA. See Sara Evans, *Personal Politics: The Roots of Women's Liberation in the Civil Rights Movement and the New Left* (New York: Knopf, 1979); Abigail Sara Lewis, "'The Barrier Breaking Love of God': The Multiracial Activism of the Young Women's Christian Association, 1940s to 1970s" (doctoral diss., Rutgers University, 2008); and Lewis's essay in this volume.

15. August Meier, "Toward a Synthesis of Civil Rights History," in *New Directions in Civil Rights Studies*, ed. Armstead L. Robinson and Patricia Sullivan (Charlottesville: University of Virginia Press, 1991), 214.

16. I thank Jacqueline Castledine for this insight.

17. Cha-Jua and Lang, "The 'Long Movement' as Vampire," 269.

18. Adam Fairclough, "State of the Art: Historians and the Civil Rights Movement," *Journal of American Studies* 24 (1990): 388; Eric Arnesen, "Reconsidering the 'Long Civil Rights Movement,'" *Historically Speaking* 10 (April 2009): 32; Glenn Feldman, "Prologue," in *Before* Brown: *Civil Rights and White Backlash in the Modern South* (Tuscaloosa: University of Alabama Press, 2004), 2; Manfred Berg, *"The Ticket to Freedom": The NAACP and the Struggle for Black Political Integration* (Gainesville: University of Florida Press, 2005).

19. Richard H. King, *Civil Rights and the Idea of Freedom* (New York: Oxford University Press, 1992), 4.

20. August Meier and Elliott Rudwick, "The Origins of Nonviolent Direct Action in Afro-American Protest: A Note on Historical Discontinuities," in *Along the Color Line: Explorations in the Black Experience* (Urbana: University of Illinois Press, 1976), 307. More remarkably, they concluded, "even if Gandhi's revolution had not developed in India, even if CORE and Randolph's 1941 March on Washington Movement had never existed, even if a conscious philosophy of nonviolent direct action had not emerged among Afro-Americans, the sit-ins and other demonstrations of the 1960s would still have occurred" (389). Howard Zinn first underscored the idea of a national racism of which the South was a part in *The Southern Mystique* (New York: Simon and Schuster, 1972).

21. Robert Korstad and Nelson Lichtenstein, "Opportunities Found and Lost: Labor, Radicals, and the Early Civil Rights Movement," *Journal of American History* 75 (December 1988): 786–811.

22. Hall, "Long Civil Rights Movement," 1243, 1249. See also Risa Goluboff, *The Lost Promise of Civil Rights* (Cambridge, Mass.: Harvard University Press,

2007). Comparable analyses of race and American foreign policy can be found in Penny Von Eschen, *Race against Empire: Black Americans and Anti-Colonialism, 1937–1957* (Ithaca, N.Y.: Cornell University Press, 1997), and Brenda Gayle Plummer, *Rising Wind: Black Americans and U.S. Foreign Affairs, 1935–1960* (Chapel Hill: University of North Carolina Press, 1996). For views that show the benefits of the Cold War, see Mary Dudziak, *Cold War Civil Rights: Race and the Image of American Democracy* (Princeton, N.J.: Princeton University Press, 2002), and Thomas Borstelmann, *The Cold War and the Color Line: American Race Relations in the Global Arena* (Cambridge, Mass.: Harvard University Press, 2003).

23. Robert O. Self, "The Black Panther Party and the Long Civil Rights Era," in *In Search of the Black Panther Party: New Perspectives on a Revolutionary Movement,* ed. Jama Lazerow and Yohuru Williams (Durham, N.C.: Duke University Press, 2005), 24.

24. Quoted in Sullivan, *Days of Hope,* 273.

25. Robbie Lieberman and Clarence Lang, eds., *Anticommunism and the African American Freedom Movement: "Another Side of the Story"* (New York: Palgrave Macmillan, 2009), 1–15.

26. See Korstad, *Civil Rights Unionism.* As Peter Lau has recently shown, southern blacks who were beginning to organize politically in the late 1950s and early 1960s were little affected by the Cold War and were more concerned with the day-to-day realities of combating racism. Peter F. Lau, *Democracy Rising: South Carolina and the Fight for Black Equality since 1865* (Lexington: University Press of Kentucky, 2006). For additional criticism, see Adam Fairclough, "Louisiana: The Civil Rights Struggle, 1940–1954," in *Before* Brown: *Civil Rights and White Backlash in the Modern South,* ed. Glenn Feldman (Tuscaloosa: University of Alabama Press, 2004), 146; Fairclough, "State of the Art," 189; Feldman, "Prologue," 15; and Cha-Jua and Lang, "The 'Long Movement' as Vampire," 272.

27. Kelley, *Hammer and Hoe.*

28. Arnesen, "Reconsidering," 33; Fairclough, "Louisiana," 149.

29. Eric Arnesen, "No 'Graver Danger': Black Anticommunism, the Communist Party, and the Race Question," *Labor* 3 (winter 2006): 13–52, and "Reflections on Responses," 75–79.

30. As Charles Houston pointed out in 1950, "a national policy of the U.S. which permits disfranchisement of colored people in the South is just as much an international issue as the question of free elections in Poland." Quoted in Doug McAdam, *Political Process and the Development of Black Insurgency, 1930–1970,* 2nd ed. (Chicago: University of Chicago Press, 1999), xxii.

31. See Steven F. Lawson, *To Secure These Rights: The Report of President Harry S. Truman's Committee on Civil Rights* (Boston: Bedford-St. Martin's, 2003).

32. It went on to say, "Racial discrimination furnished grist for the Communist

propaganda mills, and it raises doubt even among friendly nations as to the intensity of our devotion to the democratic faith." McAdam, *Political Process,* xxiii.

33. Ibid., xxii.

34. Alonzo Hamby, *Beyond the New Deal: Harry S. Truman and American Liberalism* (New York: Columbia University Press, 1973); Steven M. Gillon, *Politics and Vision: The ADA and American Liberalism, 1947–1985* (New York: Oxford University Press, 1987).

35. Feldman, "Prologue," 10.

36. According to Meier and Rudwick, "Origins of Nonviolent Direct Action," 399, "Black direct action was essentially an indigenous creation of the Negro community." See also McAdam, *Political Process,* 230; Fairclough, "Louisiana," 150, 161. On the postwar NAACP, see Patricia Sullivan, *Lift Every Voice: The NAACP and the Making of the Civil Rights Movement* (New York: New Press, 2009), and Berg, *"Ticket to Freedom."*

37. White pacifists played a predominant role in the founding of CORE. See August Meier and Elliott Rudwick, *CORE: A Study in the Civil Rights Movement, 1942–1968* (New York: Oxford University Press, 1973); Steven F. Lawson, *Running for Freedom: Civil Rights and Black Politics in America since 1941,* 3rd ed. (Malden, Mass.: Wiley-Blackwell, 2009); Raymond Arsenault, *Freedom Riders: 1961 and the Struggle for Racial Justice* (New York: Oxford University Press, 2007); and Derek Cotsam, *Freedom's Main Line: The Journey of Reconciliation and the Freedom Rides* (Lexington: University Press of Kentucky, 2008).

38. Danielle L. McGuire, *At the Dark End of the Street: Sexualized Violence, Community Mobilization, and the African American Freedom Struggle* (New York: Knopf, 2010).

39. Also influential was the movement's favorable coverage by national journalists, some of whom came from the South. Gene Roberts and Hank Klibanoff, *Race Beat: The Press, the Civil Rights Struggle , and the Awakening of a Nation* (New York: Vintage, 2007).

40. Elizabeth Cohen, *A Consumer Republic: The Politics of Mass Consumption in Postwar America* (New York: Vintage, 2003). Of course, there were consumer boycotts in the 1930s led by Communists and black leaders such as Adam Clayton Powell Jr. They occurred mainly in a few northern cities and had limited impact. The South did not experience boycotts with respect to civil rights. See Mark Naison, *Communists in Harlem during the Depression* (Urbana: University of Illinois Press, 2004). See also Meier and Rudwick, *Along the Color Line.*

41. Nancy J. Weiss, "Creative Tensions in the Leadership of the Civil Rights Movement," and David J. Garrow, "Commentary," in *The Civil Rights Movement in America,* ed. Charles Eagles (Jackson: University Press of Mississippi, 1986), 39–55 and 55–64, respectively.

42. The classic civil rights movement departed from other challenges to white supremacy that did not reach the level of a mass social movement. Disfranchised

black women's attempts to influence black men in exercising their vote after the Civil War, lobbying and litigation efforts by the early NAACP, and individual resistance to segregated buses and other facilities were certainly part of the long struggle for black freedom, but they lacked the necessary ingredients of a social movement. In contrast, see Elsa Barkley Brown, "To Catch the Vision of Freedom: Reconstructing Black Women's Political History, 1865–1880," in *African American Women and the Vote, 1837–1965,* by Ann Dexter Gordon with Bettye Collier-Thomas (Amherst: University of Massachusetts Press, 1997), and Robin Kelley, *Race Rebels: Culture, Politics, and the Black Working Class* (New York: Free Press, 1994).

43. McAdam, *Political Process,* x; William H. Chafe, *Women and Equality: Changing Patterns in American Culture* (New York: Oxford University Press, 1977), 83, 99, 101; Peniel Joseph, "Waiting till the Midnight Hour: Reconceptualizing the Heroic Period of the Civil Rights Movement, 1954–1965," *Souls* (spring 2000): 14.

44. On Myrdal, see Walter A. Jackson, *Gunnar Myrdal and America's Conscience: Social Engineering and Racial Liberalism, 1938–1987* (Chapel Hill: University of North Carolina Press, 1990). Other influential books promoting racial equality included Ruth Benedict and Gene Weltfish Benedict, *The Races of Mankind* (New York: American Association of Scientific Workers, Public Affairs Committee, 1946), and Carey McWilliams, *Brothers under the Skin* (Boston: Little Brown, 1943).

45. David J. Garrow, ed., *The Montgomery Bus Boycott and the Women Who Started It: The Memoir of Jo Ann Gibson Robinson* (Knoxville: University of Tennessee Press, 1987).

46. Michael J. Klarman, "How *Brown* Changed Race Relations: The Backlash Thesis," *Journal of American History* 81 (June 1994): 81–118.

47. Anne Moody, *Coming of Age in Mississippi* (New York: Dial, 1968); Stephen Whitfield, *A Death in the Delta: The Story of Emmett Till* (Baltimore: Johns Hopkins University Press, 1991); Ruth Feldstein, *Motherhood in Black and White: Race and Sex in American Liberalism, 1930–1965* (Ithaca, N.Y.: Cornell University Press, 2000); Keith A. Beauchamp, *The Untold Story of Emmett Till* (documentary film, 2005).

48. McAdam, *Political Process,* ix.

49. Cha-Jua and Lang, "The 'Long Movement' as Vampire," 274.

50. Jerold S. Auerbach, *Labor and Liberty: The LaFollette Committee and the New Deal* (Indianapolis: Bobbs-Merrill, 1966); Kenneth O'Reilly, "The Roosevelt Administration and Black America: Federal Surveillance Policy and Civil Rights during the New Deal and World War II Years," *Phylon* 48 (1987): 17. Goluboff has shown in *Lost Promise* that the effort to link labor with black civil rights in the 1930s and 1940s had come to an end by 1954 and the *Brown* decision. Civil Rights Section lawyers' use of the Thirteenth Amendment to challenge "involun-

tary servitude" in the rural South had given way to an emphasis on the Fourteenth Amendment's equal protection clause. Workers' rights were subordinated to protection against racial discrimination.

51. Lawson, *To Secure These Rights,* 52–54. The committee's discussion of civil liberties did not include labor union organizing; rather, the panel explored the problem of government employees who held radical political beliefs. The previous year, amidst the onset of the Cold War, President Truman had created a Loyalty Board to examine Communist infiltration of the federal bureaucracy. Although the committee cautioned the Loyalty Board to act without violating the due process rights of those under investigation, it also called for "all groups, which attempt to influence public opinion," to register with state and federal governments and to disclose "pertinent facts," such as the names of their officers and contributors (ibid., 177–78). Such an approach would prove detrimental to the NAACP operating in the South during the 1950s, as state governments sought to harass the organization by exposing its membership lists.

52. Hugh Murray, "Change in the South," *Journal of Ethnic Studies* 16 (summer 1988): 126. Murray goes on to warn, "The people engaged in struggle christened it—with sacrifice and in blood. Historians in pipe-filled rooms ought not to try to rename it."

53. Thanks to Justin Lorts for his assistance. With respect to the black newspapers, the number for the 1960s may be inflated because it includes citations from multiple editions of the *Defender.* Neil McMillen has shown through the use of oral history that black World War II veterans in Mississippi did not see the 1941–1954 period as being connected to the civil rights movement. Neil R. McMillen, "Mississippi Veterans Remember the War," in McMillen, *Remaking Dixie,* 109.

54. Lawson and Payne, *Debating,* 42–46.

55. Peniel E. Joseph, "The Black Power Movement: A State of the Field," *Journal of American History* (December 2009), http://www.historycooperative .org/cgi-bin/justtop.cgi?act=justtop&url=http://www.historycooperative.org/ journals/jah/96.3/joseph.html, para. 6.

56. The term *freedom rights* comes from Hasan Kwame Jeffries and expands the black civil rights agenda, especially at the local level, beyond constitutional rights to include economic power and political self-determination. Jeffries, *Bloody Lowndes.*

57. Lawson, *In Pursuit of Power.*

58. Arnesen, "Reconsidering," 31, quoting from Korstad and Lichtenstein, "Opportunities Found and Lost," 811.

59. For agreement on this point, see Hall, "Long Civil Rights Movement," 1252.

60. Quoted in Litwack, "'Fight the Power,'" 19.

61. Part 1 of the series, consisting of six episodes, aired on PBS in 1987 and covered the period 1954–1965. Part 2, consisting of eight episodes, aired in 1990

and extended coverage to 1985. Episodes one through ten cover the relevant 1954–1968 period. I served as a scholar-adviser to this series.

62. Stephen Tuck, *We Ain't What We Ought to Be: The Black Freedom Struggle from Emancipation to Obama* (Cambridge, Mass.: Harvard University Press, 2010), 8.

Hollywood, the NAACP, and the Cultural Politics of the Early Civil Rights Movement

Justin T. Lorts

In February 1942 Walter White, the executive secretary of the National Association for the Advancement of Colored People (NAACP), traveled to California to meet with producers and directors and discuss the portrayal of African Americans in film. Since the mid-1930s articles in the black press, including the NAACP's *Crisis,* had articulated a sustained criticism of the stereotyped and comical images of African Americans that dominated the Hollywood film industry. These criticisms accused Hollywood films of functioning as a form of propaganda that perpetuated a false image of African Americans and prevented blacks from achieving social equality. Recognizing that the way blacks were perceived culturally affected how they were treated politically and socially, these writers urged black audiences and civil rights leaders to protest against Hollywood and force producers and directors to portray African American life honestly. By the end of the decade the NAACP, led by White and assistant secretary Roy Wilkins, would articulate these same criticisms.

White's trip to Hollywood would mark the first time he directly lobbied those with the power to change the situation. White had been invited to speak by Wendell Willkie, the 1940 Republican presidential nominee and current chairman of Twentieth Century–Fox, with whom White had developed a close friendship and working relationship. The two men hoped that by presenting the NAACP's case directly to Hollywood producers and directors, they could force concrete changes in filmic depictions of African Americans. The trip came on the heels of a highly successful period in which the NAACP participated in two key victories—Marian Anderson's 1939 concert at the Lincoln Memorial and the passage of Executive Order 8802 by President Franklin Roosevelt, which outlawed discrimination in the defense industries—and saw its membership grow dramatically (seventy-one new branches were created in 1941 alone). Given this in-creased clout and influence, White hoped to change Hollywood not by organized protest, as some in the black press had urged, but through in-vestigation, education, and lobbying—tactics the association had utilized with considerable success over the previous decade.

White's nine-day trip initially netted very little. It was only on the last day, when he met with producers Darryl Zanuck and Walter Wagner, that White was able to lobby anyone with the power to change the situa-tion. Seizing this opportunity, White pressed the two men to cast African American actors in more realistic roles. At the end of the meeting Zanuck and Wagner agreed to arrange a follow-up conference later that summer with all the major Hollywood producers. Full of optimism, White returned to Hollywood in July, where he was the guest of honor at a luncheon at the Café de Paris on the Twentieth Century–Fox lot. Speaking before a star-studded group of seventy producers and industry executives, White pressed for better roles while assuring his audience "that he did not expect Negroes to be treated always as heroes but simply as human beings, or as any other persons would be treated under the same circumstances."[1]

White would ultimately make several trips to California during the decade, first in an attempt to lobby producers and black actors, and later to establish a permanent NAACP Hollywood Bureau to put the association's stamp on the film industry. These efforts, known collectively as the "Hol-lywood campaigns," represent the NAACP's clearest attempt to connect black representation to the civil rights struggle and to use its considerable influence to force cultural change in American entertainment media.

Scholars who have examined the activities of the NAACP during the two decades leading up to the modern civil rights movement have tended to focus on the association's monumental legal and lobbying efforts in the area of school desegregation, antilynching legislation, voting rights, and elimination of the poll tax.[2] Such an emphasis is understandable, as these efforts provided the legal and political foundations for many of the grassroots civil rights struggles that would emerge in the 1950s and 1960s. Yet by focusing solely on the NAACP's legal and political work, much of the civil rights historiography has ignored the association's impact in the cultural arena.[3]

The NAACP's Hollywood campaigns provide critical insight into how civil rights leaders understood the relationship between culture and politics and the role of the mass media in the civil rights struggle. Although critics both within and outside the NAACP were quick to dismiss the Hollywood campaigns as a distraction from the organization's civil rights mission, it is clear from White's public and private correspondence from the World War II era that he viewed his efforts to eliminate negative stereotypes from the Hollywood screen as part and parcel of the larger struggle for racial justice. Other civil rights leaders and journalists echoed this sentiment, throwing their support behind White and the NAACP.

White's efforts in Hollywood are part of a longer history of cultural activism by black leaders, artists, and intellectuals who challenged popular depictions of blacks as comic Sambos in an effort to win social equality. In his important article "The Trope of a New Negro and the Reconstruction of the Image of the Black," Henry Louis Gates Jr. posits that the Sambo and the New Negro "bear an antithetical relation to each other." For Gates, countering the negative image of the Sambo and reconstructing the black image as a political and cultural "presence" was one of the primary functions of New Negro writing both during the Harlem Renaissance and in the three decades prior. Writers such as Booker T. Washington intentionally crafted their publications "to 'turn' the new century's image of the black away from the stereotypes scattered throughout plantation fictions, blackface minstrelsy, vaudeville, racist pseudo-science, and vulgar Social Darwinism." Far from a mere literary concern, the recrafting of the black image was done to change black political fortunes because reality imitates art, and as Gates puts it, to "manipulate the image of the black was, in a sense, to manipulate reality."[4]

Gates provides a useful way of understanding why a civil rights organization like the NAACP would make challenging comic stereotypes part of its agenda during the World War II era. From its inception, the NAACP has involved itself in cultural politics and has attempted to police cultural production. One of the association's first mass efforts was a protest over D. W. Griffith's *Birth of a Nation,* in which NAACP members and their allies working at the local level attempted to lobby local film censoring boards in a largely unsuccessful effort to eliminate some of the more offensive scenes from the movie. During the Harlem Renaissance the NAACP's leaders—including young assistant secretary Walter White—hoped to use arts and letters as a way to advance the association's political agenda. Yet the NAACP's leaders had a narrow view of what forms of culture were useful in the struggle, and they were openly hostile to forms of culture that they felt presented the race in an unflattering light. As David Levering Lewis notes, "much of the condemnation stemmed from racial sensitivity, from sheer mortification at seeing uneducated, crude, and sappy black men and women depicted without tinsel and soap."[5] After the Renaissance ended, attention would shift to Hollywood, where the dominant black stereotypes were the comics and servants imported from minstrelsy. The NAACP would again articulate the relationship between comic images and the social position of blacks. For the NAACP, black comic stereotypes in film (and later television) made it difficult for whites to take seriously African American claims for civil rights and social opportunity.

Indeed, the connection between media representations of African Americans and their success in winning social and political equality became evident during the civil rights movement that emerged in the postwar era. In recent years civil rights scholars have argued that the entertainment and news media had a critical and usually salutary role in the success of the movement. Cultural forms such as music, dance, and sport as well as media forms such as radio, television, and film served as both sites of conflict and weapons of protest.[6] As historian Brian Ward argues, "African American art and culture did not just reflect . . . putatively more important developments in the formal, organized, conventionally 'political' freedom struggle; they also played an active role in creating that Movement, defining its goals and methods, and expressing them to both the black community and a wider, whiter American public."[7]

The impact of media images on the success of the civil rights movement is particularly clear when it comes to television news. Scholar, activist, and movement veteran Julian Bond argues that national television networks "crucially shaped popular perceptions of the Movement throughout the nation." For movement activists fighting to reach a national audience, the media, and particularly television, "brought the legitimate but previously unheard demands of southern blacks into the homes of Americans far removed from the petty indignities and large cruelties of southern segregation. These racial structures were indefensible; once challenged and exposed, they finally crumbled."[8]

Although an analysis of the NAACP's Hollywood campaigns demonstrates the importance of media imagery to the civil rights struggle, it also reveals deep tensions between the NAACP and its traditional allies about acceptable tactics, exactly which roles were problematic, and whether a civil rights organization based in New York was properly positioned to bring about change in Hollywood. When Walter White proposed setting up an NAACP Hollywood Bureau in 1945 to analyze scripts for objectionable content and suggest changes that would allow the film to pass NAACP muster, liberal allies cried censorship, black actors and actresses accused him of threatening their livelihood, and critics in the black press charged him with meddling in affairs he did not understand in order to stroke his own ego. Indeed, there is much to be said for the argument that the Hollywood campaigns were a pet project of White's rather than a shared goal of the entire NAACP. Film historian Thomas Cripps is critical of White's stubborn inability to cooperate with or solicit support from black Hollywood in an attempt to impose his own vision on the entire industry. Roy Wilkins, Cripps notes, referred to the Hollywood campaigns as "Walter's thing," suggesting that the rest of the NAACP's leadership did not share the secretary's enthusiasm.[9]

These tensions limited the effectiveness of the Hollywood campaigns, preventing the NAACP from establishing a powerful presence in the film industry. Unlike the association's legal and political efforts at the time, the results of the NAACP's cultural activism were more mixed. There was no watershed moment, no pivotal victory, no lasting legislation, organization, or program. Yet it is because of this mixed success that the NAACP's Hollywood campaigns are important. In analyzing why the NAACP did not achieve its goal, much is revealed about the limitations of trying to connect cultural activism to a civil rights agenda. Unlike many of the other arenas in which the NAACP was involved, there was never a clear consensus on exactly what was wrong with Hollywood's portrayal of African Americans or what should be done to remedy these harms. Were all roles in which blacks played comics or servants harmful, or only certain ones? What constituted a realistic portrayal of African American life? What criteria would be used, and who would be responsible for making these decisions? That the NAACP and its allies could not reach a consensus on even these basic questions suggests that the Hollywood campaigns, though perhaps noble and consistent with the civil rights struggle, were inherently flawed from the outset.

"Rabid Anti-Negro Propaganda": Civil Rights, Stereotypes, and Hollywood Film

"The 1930s," according to film historian Donald Bogle, "was for individual black actors a Golden Age."[10] Despite only a handful of Hollywood films in which black characters played a central role (*Imitation of Life, Green Pastures, Gone with the Wind*), black actors and actresses found steady work at Hollywood studios and helped establish a thriving black entertainment community centered around Los Angeles's Central Avenue.[11] For most black comedians, Hollywood was the pinnacle of professional achievement, and many comics tried their hand at films during the decade. Pigmeat Markham took a break from the stage in 1937 to pursue a Hollywood career, and Eddie "Rochester" Anderson, despite a prominent role on radio's *Jack Benny Show* and frequent personal appearances on the Apollo stage, also tried to break into films. During the decade several talented performers—including Clarence Muse, Louise Beavers, Hattie McDaniel, Bill "Bojangles" Robinson, Mantan Moreland, and Willie Best—became bona fide stars in their own right, complete with lucrative studio contracts and prominent coverage in both the black and the mainstream entertainment press.

However, whether one was a celebrity or an anonymous extra, black actors during this period were confined almost exclusively to roles that portrayed them as maids, servants, or janitors. The archetypal role for black Hollywood had been established by Lincoln Perry, better known to audiences as Stepin Fetchit. Fetchit got his start on the vaudeville circuit, where he was a part of a comedy team with Ed Lee. He rose to stardom in 1929 with appearances in two all-black pictures, *Hearts in Dixie* and *Hallelujah!* Although both pictures received mixed but generally positive reviews, critics were nearly unanimous in their praise of Fetchit's performances. With his exaggerated dialect, shuffling gait, and controlled physical comedy, Fetchit was a perfect fit for the new medium of talking pictures, and from 1929 to 1935 he appeared in twenty-six films, often playing the same slow-witted comic servant. Though controversial in the black community and notoriously difficult to work with on the set, Fetchit was the top black actor in Hollywood during this period, and his Sambo characters provided the template for black roles in film. When Fetchit's prominence began to slip after his flamboyant and contentious behavior led to increased friction with Fox studios, those actors that took his place found themselves playing the same servant roles. Significantly, these servant roles—whether performed by women or men, in bit parts or marquee performances—were almost exclusively comic.[12]

Although there were isolated criticisms in radical black publications such as the *Harlem Liberator,* entertainment writers in black newspapers and periodicals were overwhelmingly sympathetic to black Hollywood stars, and direct criticism was rare.[13] Black actors and actresses received generally positive, if gossipy, coverage, and some of them, including Stepin Fetchit, had their own columns, effectively making them an arm of the black press.[14] Indeed, as film historian Anna Everett has shown, throughout the 1930s the black press functioned as a "shadow auxiliary of Hollywood's promotional machine," reproducing apologist stories that highlighted black celebrity and repeated praise culled from Hollywood press releases.[15] Even though they occasionally printed exposés on discrimination and the lack of opportunities in Hollywood, black periodicals rarely criticized the actors themselves. *Opportunity,* the magazine of the National Urban League, greeted Stepin Fetchit's achievement of Hollywood stardom with effusive praise. Commenting on Fetchit's performance in the early talking picture *Hearts in Dixie,* humorist Robert Benchley lavished praise on the droll comic and credited him with making talking pictures believable. "I see no reason for even hesitating in saying that he is the best actor that the talking movies have produced," Benchley gushed. "His voice, his manner, his timing, everything that he does, is as near to perfection as one could hope to get in an essentially phony medium such as this."[16] Other articles in the 1930s similarly avoided the problematic nature of the newly acquired visibility of Fetchit and other black comics in favor of rags-to-riches stories that highlighted black actors' financial success and offscreen involvement in the black community.[17]

Even contributors to *Crisis,* the official organ of the NAACP, occasionally succumbed to such boosterism. In an article titled "Out of the Kitchen," Chauncey Townsend praised Louise Beavers for her role as Aunt Delilah in *Imitation of Life*—one of many servant roles Beavers had played to perfection over the years. To Townsend, Beavers's transition from an actual maid in Hollywood to her "triumph" in *Imitation of Life* demonstrated that "a level head, a firm belief in one's own possibilities, and a willingness to accept small, inconsequential parts and enact them well are necessary to climb from the level of mediocrity to a place of more than ephemeral distinction in motion pictures." Downplaying the stereotyped roles on which her success was founded, the article presented Beavers as an active woman who was "intently race conscious and public spirited."[18]

As Townsend's article demonstrates, black opinion on comic stereotypes in Hollywood films—even within the pages of *Crisis*—was far from monolithic. Beginning in the mid-1930s, however, the NAACP began laying the intellectual foundation for its assault on comic stereotypes in popular media through official pronouncements and *Crisis* articles. As the decade wore on and Americans mobilized for war, black opinion gradually coalesced around the NAACP's belief that the stereotypical image of blacks in film was detrimental to the overall goals of the civil rights struggle.[19] This would dramatically alter the way African Americans and their institutions related to and engaged with the Hollywood film industry. As Cripps has noted, film executives were largely insulated from black Americans, relying heavily on the opinions of a handful of black stars, the Production Code Administration, and southern white advisers employed by the studios to provide guidance on southern culture and etiquette. These forces conspired to give a conservative voice to the filmmaking process, limiting the portrayals of African Americans to those that would not offend the racial sensibilities of southern audiences. "The effect of this institutional system," Cripps concludes, "was to impose on whites an imagery that was ever more irrelevant to the actual changing status of African Americans."[20]

One of the earliest and most influential articles on this topic appeared in *Crisis* in 1934. Written by Loren Miller, an activist, lawyer, and former city editor of the *California Eagle,* "Uncle Tom in Hollywood" argued that black audiences were effectively giving their stamp of approval to movies that depicted them in "servant parts in which they are either buffoons or ubiquitous Uncle Toms." For Miller, the danger in this "rabid anti-Negro propaganda" was twofold: black audiences "fortif[ied] their inferiority complex by seeing themselves always cast as the underdog to be laughed at or despised," and audiences in the United States and around the world came to think of blacks in these terms, "making the breakdown of racial chauvinism more difficult."[21]

To eliminate these dangers, Miller encouraged black audiences to protest against the Hollywood film industry directly. He charged black leaders and organs of opinion with "establish[ing] an adequate critique" to "inculcate" a protest spirit in black audiences. According to Miller, black audiences "must be taught to recognize and resent anti-Negro sentiment in such a manner that their feelings can reach the box office. They must let Hollywood know that they object vigorously to being shown as buffoons, clowns, or butts for jest." Miller concluded, "So long as we sit acquiescent and give either passive or active support to the Hollywood bilge of the present we are guilty of teaching ourselves, our own children, and millions of white, yellow and brown movie-goers the world over that the Negro is an inferior. It's time we took up arms on the Hollywood front."[22]

Over the next decade the arguments in Miller's article would gain widespread currency among black and liberal white journalists, critics, academics, and civil rights leaders, and they defined the NAACP's stance on Hollywood. Central to this stance was the contention that black images in film were limited and grossly stereotyped, marking "the Negro [as] a clown, a buffon [*sic*], a trespasser in the world of 'make-believe.'"[23] "Most thoughtful people realize that there is a definite liability to the Negro in the treatment he receives at the hands of the movies," Cecil Halliburton wrote in a 1935 article for *Opportunity.* "The portrayal of stereotyped conceptions of black people is an established part of the movie pattern," Halliburton argued, "and all movie fans recognize instantly certain of these characterizations—the lazy, happy-go-lucky rustic; the servant terrified by ghosts, burglars, corpses; the faithful old retainer of the romantic South; the condemned Negro who sings spirituals on Death Row in prison pictures."[24] Celebrities such as Stepin Fetchit, Mantan Moreland, and Hattie McDaniel may have humanized the comic servant through the sheer force of their own talent, but they also legitimized roles that "discredit[ed] them and the race."[25]

To many in the black press and the civil rights community, these stereotypes on the film screen functioned as a form of "anti-Negro" propaganda. Black leaders were well aware of the effects film could have on national perceptions of the race. The portrayal of blacks as sexually charged brutes in Griffith's blockbuster *Birth of a Nation* had served to justify Jim Crow and southern racial violence and contributed to vicious attacks on African Americans following World War I. The images presented in films of the 1930s were less blatant but equally problematic; their effects were more subtle yet even more insidious. For instance, in the 1934 film *Imitation of Life,* starring Louise Beavers and Fredi Washington, Beavers plays a comic maid who strikes it rich thanks to her pancake recipe, and Washington's character is so ashamed of her race that she passes for white. A *Crisis* reader commented that "the effect of such a picture is much more baneful than one which doesn't pretend to be [anything] other than anti-Negro. . . . The impression given . . . is that the attitudes and viewpoints of the characters are typical."[26] Pointing to a growing body of social science research that linked motion pictures to racial attitudes, particularly among children, black writers argued that Hollywood was a "powerful medium for attitude formation" that directly hindered civil rights gains.[27] In his *Pittsburgh Courier* column, Hollywood editor Earl Morris accused the motion picture industry of "keeping alive racial hatred in America" and "hinder[ing] the progress towards nationalism."[28] An editorial in the leftist periodical *Film Survey* was even more damning:

The rope that lynches Negroes in America is woven by many strands. One of the toughest of these is the American motion picture, which year after year continues to regard the Negro as a stereotype for submissiveness, irresponsibility, gaiety, and sex perversion. Hollywood did not initiate the stereotype, but over the years it has contributed mightily to reinforcing and embellishing it in the public mind. Thus, it has contributed to new feeling against the Negro people, as well as vindicating the old. . . . But the stereotype goes on in the everyday film. The lie is so constantly impressed that many of us have ceased to pay it conscious notice, but it reinforces already existing prejudices, seriously influences inter-racial relations.[29]

In framing black representation in Hollywood films in this manner, these publications effectively made the case for motion pictures being, along with lynching itself, a civil rights concern.

Roy Wilkins incorporated many of these arguments into a November 1937 article in *Film Survey* titled "The Treatment of the Negro in Film." Recently appointed the editor of *Crisis* and assistant secretary of the NAACP, Wilkins's words carried significant weight, and his *Film Survey* article represented the association's early official position on blacks in Hollywood. Beginning with the premise that "of all races that go to make up America, the Negro suffers most, perhaps, from the stereotyped characterizations on the screen," Wilkins lists the comical and servile types to which black performers were limited. "Of course, all Negroes are not happy-go-lucky, all of them cannot do a buck-and-wing, surprisingly few can tap dance," Wilkins continues. Yet Hollywood has "leaned over backwards in throwing Negro stereotypes on the screen" in an effort to present an image that "pleases the ego of most whites" and avoids alienating the market in the South. Because the movies "have distorted practically every phase of American life," Wilkins was not surprised that they "have contented themselves with borrowing wholesale the ante-bellum Negro and the fiercely insistent propaganda of the post-war South." "Needless to say," Wilkins concludes, "Negro film-goers are increasingly resentful of these characterizations and are not confining themselves to mere vocal objections. . . . With indignation and organized opposition spreading, it may be that Hollywood will curb the use of black stereotypes."[30]

With white actors in blackface avoiding any real criticism during this era, black actors were forced to bear a significant degree of responsibility for the prevalence of destructive comic stereotypes in Hollywood. Though the black press would routinely print examples of behind-the-scenes racism in Hollywood, the challenges black actors faced, and actors' involvement in the black community, it was difficult to gloss over black actors' complicity in perpetuating these images. Stardom was a double-edged sword, and along with their newfound celebrity and handsome paychecks, black actors received increased scrutiny and were charged with the responsibility to ensure accurate portrayals of the race. In declaring himself "Minister of Negro Propaganda," *Pittsburgh Courier* columnist Porter Roberts took aim at black actors who "stoop to ridicule" the race for "the underpay they receive as so-called 'stars,'" at black artists who make guest appearances on white radio programs and use dialect language that "insult[s] the colored radio audience," at black actors who "raise the color-line within the color-line," and at "Jack Leg" preachers who appear on the screen and make a "mockery of the way some ignorant colored people worship."[31] When asked by representatives of the Motion Picture Actors Guild why it constantly challenged black actors about their roles in motion pictures, the *Afro-American* replied, "Great responsibility rests on the shoulders of the colored performer to see to it that his race is portrayed to the world in the best possible light." The black actor is the "only ambassador who transcends the lines of race" and is therefore a role model to black audiences who are "hero starved" and "anxious for somebody to look up to and admire."[32]

As the *Afro-American*'s response suggests, black actors received the bulk of the criticism because the roles they played on the screen were often imagined by white audiences to be representative of black life as a whole. Black actors' participation in the reproduction of these images lent them a certain credibility that was lacking in white actors' performance in blackface. Audience members would not equate Al Jolson with blacks in general, but many argued that they would see Stepin Fetchit, Clarence Muse, and Louise Beavers as representative of the race. "Thousands of people who go to the movies *don't* know anything . . . about Negroes," noted Halliburton, "and there is where the damage is done: in setting up erroneous and inevitably to some degree, prejudicial attitudes towards the Negro."[33] The effect was even more dramatic when viewed in a global context. NAACP secretary Walter White noted in 1941 that "sixty million Americans go every week to the movies. Other millions see American films from Tasmania to Tibet. In picture after picture with but rare exceptions the Negro is portrayed as scared of ghosts, addicted to tap dancing, banjo plucking and the purloining of Massa's gin. . . . Almost no moviegoer today can learn through the film medium that there are Negro businessmen, housewives, educators, or just plain John Does. Thus a stereotype is not only being perpetuated but spread around the globe."[34] Writing less than a month before America's formal entry into World War II, White was aware of the increasingly international scope of Hollywood films and their importance in terms of disseminating impressions of African Americans worldwide.

To repair the image of the race, many in the black press and the black entertainment community pushed for an increase in independent black film production. By the mid-1930s there were calls for films to be produced by blacks, for blacks. A black film movement had been attempted before, most notably by Oscar Michaeux, and critics such as Loren Miller recognized the limitations of this approach artistically, technically, and financially. Even if black producers created artistically successful films that did not "simply ape the white movies," theater owners would still be under considerable pressure to take the pictures offered by the Hollywood studios. The best Miller could hope for was a "'little movie' movement comparable to the 'little theater'" that relied on low-budget films shown in small halls.[35] These films could function as a sort of counterpropaganda, showing images of African Americans that challenged mainstream Hollywood depictions. The *Chicago Defender* wrote admirably of Clarence Muse's attempts to produce a sweeping epic, *Son of Thunder,* which would show blacks in a heroic light. "Our movies . . . continue to libel the Negro," Muse noted. "They push him into a menial and subservient position. There is a crying need . . . for . . . Negro motion picture producing units."[36] Despite Muse's vision and the enthusiastic support of the *Defender, Son of Thunder* was never made.

Muse's failure is indicative of the challenges faced by black film production companies. As Hollywood expanded into a global entertainment power, and as motion pictures became more technologically complex, independently produced black films had a hard time competing in terms of star power, production value, and aesthetics. Proposals for independent black film companies continued to circulate, and black newspapers continued to urge the black community to support "every Negro picture on the market" and thus promote the infant industry and help open up jobs for blacks from "every walk of life."[37] Reviews of the black-produced films that did emerge during the late 1930s were generally positive, even though the sense was that their primary benefit was seeing one's fellow members of the race on-screen in something other than the typical servant role. But as Miller argued, black films were often awkward imitations of white Hollywood films that did little to challenge distorted depictions of African Americans on-screen. In a 1938 *Crisis* review of movies produced by the nascent black film industry, Miller called them "distinctly mediocre from an artistic standpoint," offering little but "old fashioned, pot boiler melodramas." Conscious that these films had been made "in response to widespread criticism of Hollywood's habit of casting the Negro actor as a clown, a fool or an underling," Miller was nonetheless critical of their assumption that "the problem is solved by merely casting the Negro actor as the hero of a hackneyed gangster, success or love story." "Gangster melodramas or goo-goo success stories, using Negro actors, distort reality just as surely as did *Imitation of Life*," Miller concluded.[38]

For Miller and other writers, the goal was not "heavy-footed problem or propaganda films" but rather pictures that "tell the truth." This emphasis on the truth would be a defining feature of the rhetoric on blacks in films during this period and beyond. To convince black audiences that truthful depictions were the ultimate goal—not a greater presence of black actors in films (even in servant roles) or the casting of black actors in "positive" roles—Miller believed that black film critics and producers needed to move beyond merely publicizing black films; they had to educate their audiences in how to evaluate films for their social content. In a similar vein, the *Pittsburgh Courier* advocated the creation of a producers' association, similar to that of the major studios, which could "acquaint Negroes with the value of supporting all-colored pictures."[39] Once it was properly educated, the black filmgoing public could then assume the responsibility for policing the image of the race in Hollywood. Pointing to the responsibility of the "colored" fan, the *Afro-American* argued that "when a colored performer turns in a creditable performance the colored public should give spontaneous and mass response because public approval or disapproval is the only barometer by which the producers gauge public opinion. Therefore, if colored people find themselves portrayed contrary to their wishes, they have themselves, not the actor, to blame."[40]

What Miller and other writers ultimately concluded was that some sort of organized protest or boycott of Hollywood was necessary. Using language that would become prevalent in the early years of the civil rights movement, writers and civil rights leaders pointed to the growing purchasing power of black consumers and argued that this power should be leveraged against the film industry. Writing in *Opportunity,* Miller noted that "the so-called Negro market is far from negligible"; with an annual purchasing power of $2 billion, it was a significant component of the American consumer market.[41] Morris emphasized the economic strength of African American film audiences in a series of articles aimed at reforming the film industry. "There isn't a single group or race in America that spends as much proportionally to see motion pictures as the Negro," Morris noted, citing the $50 million a year that black Americans contributed to Hollywood's bottom line. The "vast buying power" of the black market—consisting of a population that could "swallow" that of Canada and Australia—was critical to Hollywood's success, yet the major studios virtually ignored its concerns. "This great race of ours, which spends nearly $50,000,000 annually to support elaborate Hollywood studios, is kicked in the face" by those same studios. "YOUR DOLLARS helped to build Hollywood," Morris insisted, and they "certainly should entitle you to recognition by the major studios." Although Morris stopped short of recommending that blacks mount an industry-wide boycott, he urged his readers to send letters of protest (along with clippings of his articles) to Will Hayes and the heads of the major Hollywood studios, expressing their objections to the "subtle propaganda" and "demand[ing] something else than 'Uncle Tom' roles for your stars."[42]

America's entry into World War II not only infused a sense of militancy into African American communities but also led to a convergence of goals among the NAACP, Hollywood, and the U.S. government. Under the banner of the *Pittsburgh Courier*-led "Double V" campaign—victory abroad and victory at home—blacks saw significant gains in the desegregation of the labor industry, local activism, and influence and participation in national politics.[43] Furthermore, NAACP membership grew exponentially during this period, from 18,000 in the late 1930s to nearly 156,000 by the end of the war, making the association a more powerful voice in airing black concerns.[44] Black images on film became part of the larger goals of black World War II activism. Canada Lee, in criticizing the treatment of black actors on the legitimate stage and screen, made the connection between wartime activism and changes in black images. "The war is giving colored people the chance to fight for their rights when the peace comes and should pave the way to a truer conception of them in the theater," the black actor and activist asserted.[45]

"The NAACP Will Not Be Deterred": The Hollywood Campaigns, 1942–1950

It was against this backdrop that White made the first of many trips to Hollywood in 1942 in an effort to present the NAACP's case to those who had the power to change the situation. White had hoped a direct appeal to the conscience of the Hollywood elite would result in immediate action and improvement. Many of them were Jews, and their sensitivity to issues of racism and discrimination had been heightened by the Nazis' atrocities in Europe.[46] He also hoped that with wartime unity a high priority, the federal government, through the Office of War Information, would take a more active role in ensuring the positive portrayal of blacks.

However, the quality of the offerings in 1943 was disappointing. The bulk of black roles may have shifted from servants to entertainers, but the comic stereotypes remained. The *Baltimore Afro-American* accused the film industry of "sidestepping" its pledge for better roles by continuing to "exploit colored talent either in jim crow films or as menials or clowns in white films."[47] As the *Afro-American* suggests, Hollywood's attempt to respond to black concerns by producing all-black films led to results that were, to some, just as offensive. "I am disheartened and unhappy over 'Cabin in the Sky,'" White wrote regarding the remake of the successful Broadway production featuring a who's who of black comic talent (including Ethel Waters, Eddie "Rochester" Anderson, Buck and Bubbles, Moke and Poke, Mantan Moreland, Willie Best, Rex Ingram, and Lena Horne). That film, along with another 1943 revue, *Stormy Weather,* presented blacks in typically comedic roles. Perhaps most insulting was a black version of the Disney classic *Snow White and the Seven Dwarfs* entitled *Coal Black and de Sebben Dwarfs.* In just ten minutes, White complained, *Coal Black* featured "every established stereotype ever concocted to depict the Negro," and it threatened national unity by turning the seven dwarfs into miniature black soldiers.[48]

If Hollywood executives were evasive or defensive, black actors and actresses often proved downright hostile to the NAACP's efforts. These performers took a considerable interest in the welfare of the race, and they often maneuvered behind the scenes to improve black roles in film: deleting certain words from the script, insisting on not using dialect unless the role called for it, lobbying producers for better roles. They felt that the NAACP trivialized these efforts and unfairly blamed them for the position of blacks in American society. "When I played theaters the better part of our race looked down on us, but now that a few of us have, through hard work and sacrifice, made a little progress they expect us to suddenly become champions of all the ill of the race and refuse to play parts which our profession demands," Mantan Moreland noted. He then asked, "Who is going to feed us if we do this?" As Moreland states, by refusing to perform the only roles available to them, black actors not only risked their careers but also limited their opportunities to improve the situation from the inside. Many actors believed this was the most effective way to ensure better Hollywood roles, and they viewed the efforts of White—who did not live in Los Angeles and had no experience in the film industry—as the misguided actions of an outsider. Because it dealt directly with producers and left black actors and actresses out of the loop, "the whole approach of the NAACP to the Hollywood question was wrong and ill-advised," argued Clarence Muse. "Walter White, as a committee of one, in company with Mr. Willkie, interviewed producers and wined and dined in Hollywood fashion."[49]

Despite these criticisms, White forged ahead with his efforts, and in 1945 he proposed the establishment of an advisory board that would give the NAACP a more permanent presence in the film industry. No longer able to rely on the support and connections of Willkie, who had died the previous October, White laid out preliminary plans for what he called the Hollywood Bureau in a letter to a selected list of 500 friends of the association. The bureau would serve as a "source of information, criticism and suggestions not only on what should be deleted from films, but what could constructively be added to pictures in order to give a truer representation of the Negro." Despite earlier support from the film industry, momentum for the project had stalled. Although the studios had offered to finance the bureau, White and Willkie, fearing that "he who pays the piper calls the tune," held out for an independent bureau that would cost approximately $15,000 annually—money the NAACP did not have in its budget. White's letter concluded by asking the NAACP's leading members whether they thought "such a Bureau should be established," and if so, whether they would be "sufficiently interested to contribute" to its financing. "We would be most grateful if you would let us know . . . how you feel about this."[50]

Reaction to White's proposal revealed the challenges the NAACP's cultural undertaking faced. With pledges of support from such prominent donors as Frank Schiffman (owner of the Apollo Theater), attorney Charles Houston, historian Rayford Logan, Benjamin Mays (president of Morehouse University), musician Duke Ellington, and writer Sterling Brown, the NAACP selected a committee to help establish the Hollywood Bureau. The committee consisted of a wide array of industry insiders and prominent liberals, including Marshall Field, Edwin Embree, William Hastie, Arthur Springarn, Major Matty Fox (vice president of Universal), Langston Hughes, and Lena Horne. "Meritorious and laudable . . . are the aims of this new NAACP bureau," wrote the editors of the sympathetic *Chicago Defender.* "Perhaps Hattie McDaniel and Louise Beavers would no longer cavort in servants' uniforms and Clarence Muse himself might not be called upon to put on a grass skirt and prance about as a jungle savage, ostensibly portraying an African."[51]

Despite the prominence of the committee, a genuine sense of support from NAACP donors, and backing within the black press, the bureau encountered significant resistance on two main fronts.[52] Many Hollywood producers and executives saw the Hollywood Bureau as a censorship arm; already regulated by the government, they resisted further encroachment. "We are naturally opposed to any groups that serve, even indirectly, to push us around and the danger of becoming further beset becomes greater all the time," replied Howard Dietz, vice president of advertising at MGM and one of White's allies. Others voiced similar concerns, noting that "there is a big difference between general criticism after a film is portrayed and specific criticism and direction beforehand, which in a sense does constitute a threat."[53]

The Hollywood Bureau also faced continued resistance from many actors in the black entertainment community. In January 1946 White traveled to California to gather support for his idea. After achieving "modest success in building a sound basis for the Bureau," White presented his plan at a dinner party hosted by the Los Angeles branch, to which all the "Negro movie folks" were invited. According to White, black actors came out in force "with hatchets." Most of these actors—including Clarence Muse, Louise Beavers, Jesse Graves, and Ben Carter—gave White "the works" and voiced familiar concerns about the NAACP—that it blamed actors rather than Hollywood executives, refused to cooperate with black actors, and interfered in affairs it did not understand at the expense of their livelihood. Beavers noted that "in her 18 years of show life she had always attempted to devote her other efforts to the progress and advancement of the race." She had worked behind the scenes to clean up scripts, just as the NAACP was trying to do now with the bureau, and she was particularly annoyed that the NAACP would try to establish a bureau without even consulting her or other actors. Only Lena Horne and Carlton Moss, whom White referred to as "the new type out here," came to the organization's defense. Given previous run-ins, this opposition was not unexpected, and White hoped "some good will come from letting them fire [at] the target they most wanted to shoot at."[54]

Hattie McDaniel, perhaps the most prominent actress in Hollywood at the time, did not attend the meeting. Since her appearance in *Judge Priest* (she had also had a role in *Imitation of Life*, but her scenes were left on the cutting room floor),[55] McDaniel had scored a number of important roles—including that of "Mammy" in David O. Selznick's *Gone with the Wind* (1939). Her performance garnered enthusiastic praise in the white press and an Oscar for Best Supporting Actress, the first such award won by an African American. Although the black press took pride in McDaniel's accomplishment—even *Crisis* featured her prominently on the cover following her Oscar victory—it also voiced considerable concern over the Mammy role she consistently performed. As historian Deborah Gray White has shown, the Mammy image was a burden that fell squarely on the shoulders of black women. Like the comic Sambo, the Mammy spoke to white fantasies of black women as servile, loyal, and nonthreatening. In its filmic incarnations, the Mammy figure was a "big, fat and cantankerous" servant who served both as a confidant to her employer (master) and as comic relief in the film.[56] Other women would take on the Mammy role (most notably, Louise Beavers), but McDaniel's version, largely because of her success in *Gone with the Wind,* received the most attention.

Though White was at loggerheads with many in the black Hollywood community, his disagreement with McDaniel was particularly bitter, personal, and public. Like other black actors, McDaniel thought White was meddling in affairs he did not understand. In refusing the invitation to "break bread with Walter White," she accused him of prejudice toward darker-skinned blacks (he had allegedly said she was too dark to entertain the troops overseas), and he framed his opposition to her in terms of class snobbery. "What is the difference [in] playing a maid's part on the screen than playing it in the actual home," McDaniel wondered. "Does Walter White's maid . . . become an Uncle Tom just because she works in his home?" McDaniel also complained that during the secretary's first trip to California he had referred to her as "Hattie" and spoke to her "with the tone of voice and manner that a Southern Colonel would use to his favorite slave." In defending her roles and her position in Hollywood, McDaniel advanced claims similar to those of other black actors. "When I won the Academy Award, I did not take pride for myself," McDaniel asserted. "I thought it would open the avenue of progress and opportunity for [the] Negro boy and girl that would be wanting a chance in Hollywood." Contrasting her involvement with that of White—who, she claimed, kept doors closed in Hollywood—McDaniel noted her own contribution to the advancement of blacks in the film industry. "Although Walter White has tried to imply that I would accept any role just to be working this is not true. I am trying each day to lift the position of my people and to create a deeper respect from the other side for us."[57]

Privately, the NAACP leadership had little patience with McDaniel, and White in particular seems to have held the actress in contempt. In a confidential memo an NAACP staffer suggested to White that although the secretary may "have been a little wrong about her career," McDaniel was "MEAN and vicious and resentful" and "*should be shut up* if for the sake of her *own kind.*"[58] White displayed a similar attitude toward other actors who disagreed with his approach. He refused to meet individually with his opponents in Hollywood, dismissed even their most constructive criticisms, ignored advice to work toward building an effective working relationship with actors' groups such as the Fair Play Committee, and questioned the "mental processes" of those who doubted his effectiveness. After the dinner party, White wrote to Roy Wilkins that the actors "overplayed their hand and revealed to everybody that they were interested in jobs only for themselves and to Hell with everything else."[59]

Publicly, the NAACP effectively positioned its opponents as operating out of their own narrow self-interests at the expense of the entire race. For the association, there was more at stake than just jobs for a few individuals. By eliminating negative comic stereotypes from the screen, the NAACP hoped to materially and politically improve the lot of all black Americans. Black actors may know more about acting, Wilkins granted, "but is that any guarantee that they know about the effects of the Hollywood stereotype on the aspirations of 14 million black Americans?" The debate could thus be framed as a question of what was more important— "jobs for a handful of Negroes playing so-called 'Uncle Tom' roles or the welfare of Negroes as a whole?" For White, it was clear which side of the debate the NAACP should come down on: "The NAACP has not hesitated to 'interfere' with lynching, disfranchisement, unequal educational opportunities and job discrimination. All of these evils are aided in part by Hollywood stereotypes. The struggle, therefore, to improve the treatment of Negroes in the medium which reaches more human eyes and emotions than any yet devised by man is part and parcel of that struggle for improvement of the Negro lot. And the NAACP will not be deterred by the attacks of those who have a vested interest in the status quo."[60] White later argued that black actors were "more to be pitied than attacked." However, by framing the issue in this way—jobs for black actors versus the progress of the race (as determined by himself and the NAACP)—White exposed a critical fault line that would hamper the association's cultural efforts for the remainder of the decade.[61]

The inherent limitations of the NAACP's Hollywood strategy had become evident the previous autumn—coinciding almost exactly with White's proposal of the Hollywood Bureau—with the controversy over *St. Louis Woman*. Based on the novel *God Sends Sunday* by Arna Bontemps, *St. Louis Woman* was the creation of Bontemps and fellow Harlem Renaissance luminary Countee Cullen.[62] Bontemps and Cullen had been seeking financing to turn the novel into a musical and perhaps a film for nearly a decade before it was picked up by Arthur Freed, a producer at MGM. Freed's involvement signaled that the musical would make the transition to film as well, following the formula pioneered by *Hallelujah!* and *Cabin in the Sky*.

Almost as soon as the production was announced, a chorus of objections ensued. The strongest and most widely publicized came from the newly formed International Film and Radio Guild (IFRG) and its executive secretary, Leon Hardwick. After reviewing an early copy of the script, the IFRG condemned the production as "another of those subtle but vicious instruments through which the entire Negro race is stereotyped." Although Freed's intentions may have been "of the highest," the guild criticized the script for its "atrocious dialect" and "the usual killing, vice, trash and passion, with absolutely no counterbalance injected into the plot which would tend to show that not all Negroes are of the low type." Of particular concern was the prospect of Lena Horne, "one of the race's finest and most glamorous artists," being cast in the principal role of Della. A "good looking but loose woman of the sporting variety," Della was an "insult to Negro womanhood," the IFRG contended, and for Horne to be "forced" to play such a role "would cause her reputation as a progressive artist of [the] race to be besmirched irreparably."[63]

While the IFRG was preparing to publicly protest *St. Louis Woman*, the NAACP's leadership was working behind the scenes to halt production of the play. Like the IFRG, Walter White and the NAACP seemed to be concerned primarily with Horne's career and the symbolic importance of the race's leading actress appearing in a potentially disreputable role. Having brought Horne to the attention of MGM in the first place, the secretary had a special, somewhat paternal affection for the young star, who could be counted on for her unwavering support of the NAACP. Upon hearing the news of Horne's potential involvement, White immediately conferred with her and contacted Freed. Horne "has won a place in the hearts of millions of Americans, colored and white, as the first lady of the screen," White wrote to Freed. To allow her to play the role of Della would "tear down" her career and "destroy all the hopes her people had that so charming and beautiful and talented a performer would be given a dignified and rewarding opportunity in the entertainment world."[64] White also contacted MGM chairman Louis Mayer, with whom White enjoyed a productive relationship, to obtain Mayer's assurances that the studio would not punish the star for rejecting a role she did not want.[65]

By placing Horne at the center of the controversy, White and others revealed the importance of black womanhood in debates about African American images in film. The character of Della—a woman of "loose morals"—was a clear embodiment of what Deborah Gray White calls the Jezebel. "Governed almost entirely by her libido," Jezebel was the exact opposite of proper womanhood.[66] Like the Mammy, Jezebel is useful in understanding the limitations placed on black female performers in the American cultural imagination. Horne had already played the seductress "Sweet" Georgia Brown in the film *Cabin in the Sky;* assuming a similar role in the theatrical (and likely cinematic) production of *St. Louis Woman* risked identifying her with the stereotype. The possibility that Horne, who had become a prominent spokesperson for the race, might be associated with the Jezebel stereotype (in the same way that Beavers and McDaniel were associated with the Mammy) threatened to undermine white impressions of black women. Playing a "loose woman" risks "treading a path already overdrawn," observed *Amsterdam News* columnist Abe Hill. "Therefore [s]he is following a pattern which says in effect—'tis a pity, but Negro women are loose or prostitutes.'"[67]

The debate over *St. Louis Woman* was more about representations of black womanhood than about anything specifically related to the musical, as evidenced by the fact that when the controversy first surfaced, only a handful of people—apparently including Hardwick—had seen a copy of the script. Having been delayed by his father's illness, Cullen was still typing a draft in late August and was unable to provide a copy to those who requested to see it.[68] Initially, Walter White could only point to vague "reports" in voicing his concerns about the production. Once the controversy spilled over into the press, those associated with the musical, including producer Arthur Freed, confessed that they had not seen a script either. Freed assured White and others that he would not do anything to harm Horne's career, but he was unable to refute any of the charges being made. When asked to comment, Rex Ingram could only reply, "I have never yet been connected with any unsavory theatrical venture and you can bet if there is anything in 'St. Louis Woman' which does not meet with my approval it will not be there when the curtain goes up."[69] Even Lena Horne, who was repeatedly asked to publicly state her intentions regarding the show, was forced to respond that she had not seen the final script.[70]

In mid-September, after unsuccessful attempts to get a copy of the script, White arranged for Cullen to read the play for a group assembled at White's home in Harlem. White invited a "small and select group" of NAACP leaders and allies, including Thurgood Marshall, Roy Wilkins, Henry Moon, William Hastie, and Earl Brown. Cullen and Bontemps invited Mabel Roane, the secretary of the Negro Actors Guild; Thelma Boozer, entertainment critic for the *Pittsburgh Courier;* and black literary luminaries Aaron Douglass and Alain Locke.[71] Despite Cullen's full cooperation, the meeting failed to move White and Wilkins, who perceived the play (and the potential film) as being in the same tradition as *Cabin in the Sky.* Wilkins maintained that there was "nothing good" in the script and that it would be "very unfortunate" if it were made into a musical or, worse, a movie.[72] In a highly antagonistic letter to Cullen, White noted the irony of two black authors writing a musical "which portrays every cliché and every hoary myth about the Negro which our enemies have attempted to perpetuate." Seeing nothing redeeming in any of the characters, White was particularly appalled by the "disparagement of dark Negroes" and the indecent female characters. In listening to the play, White "wondered if all the work which the late Wendell Willkie and others have been doing in Hollywood . . . has not been almost wholly in vain." "I beg of you and Arna for your own sakes as well as that of the cause for which we are fighting," White concluded, "to turn your talents towards writing [that] will not do harm."[73]

Privately, the controversy continued to grow even more divisive, particularly among White, Cullen, and Bontemps, as honest disagreement morphed into petty squabbles involving the literary luminaries. White, in a particularly petulant move, chided Cullen and Bontemps for inviting their own guests to White's home for the script reading. Such an "extraordinary" move, besides being rude, failed to disguise the writers' attempt "to insure the presence of those who had quite obviously been won over to favoring the play before hearing it in our home." (White, of course, failed to acknowledge that most of his invited guests had already been won over to disfavoring the play prior to hearing it.)[74] Though sufficiently apologetic in correspondence with the secretary, privately, the two men seethed. Bontemps disparagingly referred to White and Wilkins as "dictator[s] of Negro participation in drama (and perhaps the other arts)" and as the "gentlemen who have undertaken to protect Broadway from Della Green."[75] He was particularly upset by the news that White's daughter had accepted a role in *Porgy*, which some saw as a political move on the producer's part designed to prevent further criticism of the play.[76] Apparently, "a poor yellow girl can't take an occasional present from a gentleman, but a Spelman girl can be a Nonnie," Bontemps complained to Langston Hughes in an effort to label White's actions both nepotistic and classist.[77] For Bontemps, White's actions were not only hypocritical and misguided; they were traitorous to the race. "Not only does Walter's opposition to *St. Louis Woman* seem strange in view of the Nonnie role for Jane, but the claque which you describe would seem to suggest that he and Roy seem to have wearied of the fight against Negro's enemies and turned their guns on their comrades."[78]

Petty snipping aside, this public and private infighting reveals the degree to which artists and civil rights leaders were divided not only on the NAACP's tactics but also on exactly what constituted harmful stereotypes. The disagreements among Cullen, Bontemps, and White were in many ways a continuation of the debates of the Harlem Renaissance era. By the end of World War II most black Americans agreed that films limited blacks to comic roles at the expense of more realistic portrayals. And even many black entertainers would agree, at least in principle, that these portrayals complicated the social and political advancement of African Americans. Yet there was little agreement on exactly what types of roles were problematic. Were all comic roles off-limits, or only those that relied on exaggerated dialect and physical movement? What constituted a realistic portrayal, especially in the context of a heavily censored film industry? And who was the appropriate arbiter of such questions? The NAACP and its allies in the black press provided little critical guidance on how to evaluate films and black performances based on their artistic and aesthetic qualities, resulting in confusing criticisms that tried to identify whether they were "better" or "realistic." Such critiques did little to fundamentally alter the place of blacks in American film. As Cripps argues, "until White and his allies produced a genre that challenged the popularity of Hollywood's South . . . success [would be] measured in praise for giving dignity to a stock servant or exploiting some fissure in racial etiquette."[79]

Furthermore, there was little agreement on what role the NAACP should play in policing Hollywood. In many ways, the reading White hosted in his home reflected his vision of the Hollywood Bureau—a coterie of elite blacks whose cultural tastes mirrored his own evaluating the scripts brought before it. But the reaction to the Hollywood Bureau demonstrates that although actors might have supported the broader goals of the association, they did not believe that White and other leaders were the best arbiters of these matters. The fact that White and company dismissed the *St. Louis Woman* script out of hand, without offering any suggestions for its improvement so that it could meet with NAACP approval, suggested that the bureau's criticism would be far from constructive. Comic images might have implications for civil rights, but it was unclear whether a civil rights organization was an appropriate choice to lead the fight against them.

Horne ultimately declined the role of Della in late September. Although there were immediate reports, fed by *New York Mirror* columnist Walter Winchell, that she would be disciplined by MGM for refusing the role, the decision received little fanfare in the black press. Production continued through the end of the year, with Ruby Hill taking over the role intended for Horne.[80] Cullen died in January 1946, just before *St. Louis Woman* entered into rehearsals. The show premiered in New Haven, Connecticut, to lukewarm reviews. Critics praised the music and the lyrics but were less kind to the cast (the one exception was Pearl Bailey, who would go on to achieve considerable fame in the 1950s as a nightclub performer and actress).[81] *St. Louis Woman* then moved to the Martin Beck Theater on Broadway, where it had a successful but brief run, despite being plagued by sniping on the cast and criticism from the press. Unsure of its financial prospects, and perhaps wary of generating more controversy, MGM decided against turning the musical into a motion picture.

Ongoing Efforts

The efforts of Walter White and the NAACP to change the Hollywood film industry, as well as other forms of mass culture, continued throughout the 1940s. Beginning in 1947 (and continuing into the 1950s), the NAACP passed resolutions at each of its annual conventions denouncing "derogatory terminology and racial, religious or national stereotypes" in "movies, radio stations, newspapers and other publications." Thanks to its efforts, as well as those of producers and black actors, actresses, and audiences, Hollywood did change the way it depicted African Americans in films. Walter White could look approvingly on a number of films released during that period, including *Home of the Brave, Intruder in the Dust, Lost Boundaries,* and *Pinky,* and black audiences could realistically hope that

American entertainment in the 1950s would be free from images of shuffling Sambos, lawless hustlers, and lazy, inept workers.[82]

In the early 1950s the NAACP would shift its attention away from Hollywood films and toward the increasingly popular medium of television. From 1951 to 1953 the association led a nationwide protest against the minstrel comedy *Amos 'n' Andy*, which had made the transition from radio to television. Using much of the same rhetoric it had employed during the Hollywood campaigns, the NAACP led a coalition of civil rights, labor, and liberal organizations to protest against the show and, in a new twist, to boycott the products of the show's sponsor. Despite the association's aggressive stance, the campaigns against *Amos 'n' Andy* faced the same tensions and setbacks as the Hollywood campaigns. Although the show was removed from prime time in 1953, it ran in syndication until the 1960s, and scholars remain divided on the effectiveness of the NAACP's involvement.[83]

With the NAACP's victory in *Brown v. Board of Education* and the beginnings of the modern civil rights movement, concerns about comic stereotypes in American media took a backseat to the grassroots protests that swept the South and catapulted the issue of black civil rights to the national forefront. The association's work in Hollywood continued, albeit in a subtler form, under the leadership of Roy Wilkins, who worked hard to rebuild the relationships White had damaged. In 1957 the NAACP formulated a new industry-based strategy that pushed for equal treatment and opportunities beyond stereotyped roles, but it placed the responsibility for achieving these goals on the actors, directors, and producers.[84] The association had effectively taken itself out of the Hollywood game, and although it would remain concerned with depictions of blacks in the mass media, it would never again attempt to be a leading force in the movie industry as it had during the Hollywood campaigns.

Notes

I began writing this essay in 2008 during my time at the National Endowment for the Humanities Summer Institute at Harvard University. I would like to thank the institute's directors, Waldo Martin, Patricia Sullivan, and Henry Louis Gates Jr., as well as my colleagues Jeff Johnson, Mike Ezra, Dexter Blackman, and Derek Musgrove. I would also like to thank Susanne Wofford, dean of New York University's Gallatin School of Individualized Study, for graciously granting me leave to participate in this institute. Many thanks to Lauren Kaminsky, Ann Fabian, Keith

Wailoo, and, of course, Steven Lawson, who provided valuable insight and support. Finally, I would like to thank my wife (and fellow historian) Abigail Sara Lewis, who has supported my work from the very beginning.

1. Quoted in Kenneth Robert Janken, *White: The Biography of Walter White, Mr. NAACP* (New York: New Press, 2003), 269. For information on the NAACP's victories and White's trip to Hollywood, see ibid., 246–73; Thomas Cripps, *Making Movies Black: The Hollywood Message Movie from World War II to the Civil Rights Era* (New York: Oxford University Press, 1993), 44–56.

2. Manfred Berg, *The Ticket to Freedom: The NAACP and the Struggle for Black Political Integration* (Gainesville: University Press of Florida, 2005); Kenneth W. Goings, *The NAACP Comes of Age: The Defeat of Judge John J. Parker* (Bloomington: Indiana University Press, 1990); Jack Greenberg, *Crusaders in the Court: How a Dedicated Band of Lawyers Fought for a Civil Rights Revolution* (New York: Basic Books, 1994); Janken, *Biography of Walter White;* Gilbert Jonas, *Freedom's Sword: The NAACP and the Struggle against Racism in America, 1909–1969* (New York: Routledge, 2005); Armstead L. Robinson and Patricia Sullivan, *New Directions in Civil Rights Studies* (Charlottesville: University Press of Virginia, 1991); Patricia Sullivan, *Days of Hope: Race and Democracy in the New Deal Era* (Chapel Hill: University of North Carolina Press, 1996); Patricia Sullivan, *Lift Every Voice: The NAACP and the Making of the Civil Rights Movement* (New York: New Press, 2009); Mark V. Tushnet, *The NAACP's Legal Strategy against Segregated Education, 1925–1950* (Chapel Hill: University of North Carolina Press, 2004); Robert L. Zangrando, *The NAACP Crusade against Lynching, 1909–1950* (Philadelphia: Temple University Press, 1980).

3. Notable exceptions include Cripps, *Making Movies Black,* and Leonard C. Archer, *Black Images in the America Theater: NAACP Protest Campaigns— Stage, Screen, Radio and Television* (Brooklyn, N.Y.: Pageant-Poseidon, 1973). Archer's perceptive study is limited by the fact that scholars did not have access to the NAACP papers at the time.

4. Henry Louis Gates Jr., "The Trope of a New Negro and the Reconstruction of the Image of the Black," *Representations* 24 (1988): 129–55.

5. David Levering Lewis, introduction to *The Harlem Renaissance Reader* (New York: Viking, 1994), xxxii.

6. See Robin D. G. Kelley, *Race Rebels: Culture, Politics and the Black Working Class* (New York: Free Press, 1994); Waldo E. Martin, *No Coward Soldiers: Black Cultural Politics in Postwar America* (Cambridge, Mass.: Harvard University Press, 2005); Ingrid Monson, "Monk Meets SNCC," *Black Music Research Journal* 19, no. 2 (autumn 1999): 187–200; Ingrid Monson, *Freedom Sounds: Civil Rights Call out to Jazz and Africa* (New York: Oxford University Press, 2007); Barbara Savage, *Broadcasting Freedom: Radio, War, and the Politics of Race, 1938–1948* (Chapel Hill: University of North Carolina Press, 1998); Suzanne Smith, *Dancing in the Streets* (Cambridge, Mass.: Harvard University

Press, 2000); William Van Deburg, *New Day in Babylon: The Black Power Movement and American Culture, 1965–1975* (Chicago: University of Chicago Press, 1992); Brian Ward, *Just My Soul Responding: Rhythm and Blues, Black Consciousness and Race Relations* (Berkeley and Los Angeles: University of California Press, 1998).

7. Brian Ward, introduction to *Media, Culture, and the Modern African American Freedom Struggle* (Gainesville: University Press of Florida, 2001), 2–3.

8. Julian Bond, "The Media and the Movement: Looking Back from the Southern Front," in Ward, *Media, Culture, and the Modern African American Freedom Struggle,* 16–17.

9. Thomas Cripps, "'Walter's Thing': The NAACP's Hollywood Bureau of 1946—A Cautionary Tale," *Journal of Popular Film and Television* 33, no. 2 (July 1, 2005): 116–25.

10. Donald Bogle, *Toms, Coons, Mulattoes, Mammies, and Bucks: An Interpretive History of Black in American Film,* exp. ed. (1973; reprint, New York: Continuum, 1992), 36.

11. For information on black Hollywood in the 1930s, see Donald Bogle, *Bright Boulevard, Bold Dreams* (New York: Ballantine Books, 2005), 102–83.

12. Bogle, *Toms, Coons, Mulattoes, Mammies, and Bucks,* 38–44; Mel Watkins, *Stepin Fetchit: The Life and Times of Lincoln Perry* (New York: Pantheon Books, 2005), 69–93.

13. For an example of radical black criticism, see Cyril Briggs, "Art Is a Weapon," and J. C. L., "The Role Assigned the Negro in American Films," *Harlem Liberator,* September 9, 1933; Anna Everett, *Returning the Gaze: A Genealogy of Black Film Criticism, 1909–1949* (Durham, N.C.: Duke University Press, 2001), 233–61.

14. Charlene Regester, "Stepin Fetchit: The Man, the Image, and the African American Press," *Film History* 6, no. 4 (winter 1994): 504–6, 518.

15. Everett, *Returning the Gaze,* 193–205.

16. Robert Benchley, "The First Real Talking Picture (*Hearts in Dixie*)," *Opportunity,* April 1929, 122–23. For similar praise of the highly controversial comic, see Ruby Berkley Goodwin, "When Stepin Fetchit Stepped into Fame," *Pittsburgh Courier,* July 6, 1929.

17. See, for example, Goodwin, "When Stepin Fetchit Stepped into Fame"; Ruby Berkley Goodwin, "A Lawyer Turns Vitaphone Artist," *Pittsburgh Courier,* July 20, 1929; William G. Nunn, "Stepin Fetchit, Modern Martyr of the Movie World, Breaks Silence," *Pittsburgh Courier,* February 20, 1932.

18. Chauncey Townsend, "Out of the Kitchen," *Crisis,* January 1935, 15, 29.

19. Until recently, viewing black images in Hollywood film through the lens of stereotype or caricature was the dominant approach of most scholarship on the subject. See Bogle, *Toms, Coons, Mulattoes, Mammies, and Bucks;* Thomas Cripps, *Slow Fade to Black: The Negro in American Film, 1900–1942* (New York:

Oxford University Press, 1993); Ed Guerrero, *Framing Blackness: The African American Image in Film* (Philadelphia: Temple University Press, 1993); Marshall Hyatt and Cheryl Sanders, "Film as a Medium to Study the Twentieth-Century Afro-American Experience," *Journal of Negro Education* 53, no. 2 (spring 1984): 161–72; Daniel Leab, *From Sambo to Superspade: The Black Experience in Motion Pictures* (New York: Houghton Mifflin, 1975); and Edward Mapp, *Blacks in American Films: Today and Yesterday* (Metuchen, N.J.: Scarecrow Press, 1972).

20. Cripps, *Making Movies Black,* 10.

21. Loren Miller, "Uncle Tom in Hollywood," *Crisis,* November 1934, 329, 336.

22. Ibid.

23. Earl J. Morris, "Should Negroes Ban White Motion Pictures?" *Pittsburgh Courier,* September 24, 1938.

24. Bogle, *Toms, Coons, Mulattoes, Mammies, and Bucks,* 35–38; Cecil B. Halliburton, "Hollywood Presents Us: The Movies and Racial Attitudes," *Opportunity,* October 1935, 296–97.

25. Morris, "Should Negroes Ban White Motion Pictures?" See also Joseph Joel Keith, "Propaganda and the Negro," *Opportunity,* June 1942, 168–69.

26. Pauline Flora Byrd, letter to the editor, *Crisis,* March 1935, 91–92.

27. Halliburton, "Hollywood Presents Us."

28. Earl J. Morris, "American Whites, Negroes Being Shoved into Background in Movies by Jewish Film Owners," *Pittsburgh Courier,* August 27, 1938; Earl J. Morris, "Demands Negro Be Recognized in Hollywood," *Pittsburgh Courier,* July 2, 1938.

29. "12 Million Forsaken," *Film Survey* 2, no. 3 (August 1939): 2–3.

30. Roy Wilkins, "The Treatment of the Negro in Film," *Film Survey* 1, no. 5 (November 1937): 1–2.

31. Porter Roberts, "Praise and Criticism," *Pittsburgh Courier,* July 24, 1937.

32. "Why Are Colored Movie Artists Challenged?" *Baltimore Afro-American,* January 9, 1943.

33. Halliburton, "Hollywood Presents Us."

34. Walter White, "The Negro and Hollywood: Racial Types in Films Must Please the South," *New York Herald Tribune,* November 19, 1941, Roy Wilkins Papers, box 27, "Movies and Television, 1942–1958," Manuscripts Division, Library of Congress, Washington, D.C.

35. Miller, "Uncle Tom in Hollywood," 336.

36. Bob Richards, "Writer Says Clarence Muse Creates Miracle in Hollywood," *Chicago Defender,* February 10, 1940.

37. Morris, "Should Negroes Ban White Motion Pictures?"

38. Loren Miller, "Hollywood's New Negro Films," *Crisis,* January 1938, 8–9.

39. Morris, "Should Negroes Ban White Motion Pictures?"

40. "Why Are Colored Movie Artists Challenged?"

41. Loren Miller, "The Negro Market," *Opportunity*, February 1938, 38.

42. Earl J. Morris, "'Hollywood Ignores Black America'—Morris," *Pittsburgh Courier*, May 28, 1938; Earl J. Morris, "Hollywood Overlooking Sepia Goldmine," *Pittsburgh Courier*, June 25, 1938; Morris, "Demands Negro Be Recognized in Hollywood"; Earl J. Morris, "Major Film Companies Must Recognize the Negro," *Pittsburgh Courier*, July 16, 1938; Morris, "American Whites, Negroes Being Shoved into Background"; Morris, "Should Negroes Ban White Motion Pictures?"

43. See Sullivan, *Days of Hope*, 133–68; Harvard Sitkoff, *A New Deal for Blacks: The Emergence of Civil Rights as a National Issue* (New York: Oxford University Press, 1978).

44. Sullivan, *Days of Hope*, 141.

45. "Canada Lee Talks Out Loud in Criticizing Legitimate Theater," *Baltimore Afro-American*, April 10, 1943.

46. Pointing out the parallels between the treatment of Jews in Nazi Germany and the treatment of blacks in America and by Hollywood was a consistent theme of the NAACP's argument. See Walter White, "Untitled Syndicated Column," November 7, 1946, Wilkins Papers, box 34, "White, Walter Syndicated Column, 1946." See also Michael Rogin, *Blackface, White Noise: Jewish Immigrants in the Hollywood Melting Pot* (Berkeley and Los Angeles: University of California Press, 1996).

47. "Hollywood Sidestepping Pledge of Better Casting for Colored," *Baltimore Afro-American*, March 6, 1943; "Hollywood's Answer to Our Appeal for Better Roles in Pictures for Colored Actors," *Baltimore Afro-American*, March 20, 1943.

48. W. White to Marc Connelly, November 21, 1942, NAACP II A 274, "Films—Cabin in the Sky, 1942–1943"; "Movie Cartoon Pokes Fun at Negro Soldiers," April 30, 1943, NAACP II A 274, "Films—General, 1943," NAACP Papers, Library of Congress, Washington, D.C.

49. "The Truth about Hollywood and the Race Issue from the Actor's Viewpoint," *Baltimore Afro-American*, January 9, 1943.

50. Walter White, draft of letter to a selected list of 500 friends of the association, August 1945, NAACP II A 277, "Films: Hollywood Bureau."

51. "Hollywood and Walter White," *Chicago Defender*, February 23, 1946.

52. "That Hollywood Bureau," *Los Angeles Sentinel*, January 31, 1946; T. Young [of the *Norfolk Journal and Guide*] to W. White, September 3, 1945, NAACP II A 277, "Films: Hollywood Bureau, 1945–49."

53. H. Dietz to W. White, September 5, 1945; Arthur Garfield Hays to W. White, November 5, 1945, NAACP II A 277, "Films: Hollywood Bureau, 1945–49."

54. W. White to Roy [Wilkins] and the Office, January 25, 194[6], ibid.; H. McDaniel to T. L. Griffin, January 20, 1946, NAACP II A 502, "Publicity Protests—Hattie McDaniels [*sic*], 1945–1949"; Walter White Tells Plans for Hol-

lywood Bureau," *Los Angeles Sentinel,* January 24, 1946, 16; copy of statement regarding NAACP's establishment of Hollywood Bureau, NAACP II A 277, "Films: Hollywood Bureau, 1945–49."

55. Jill Watts, *Hattie McDaniel: Black Ambition, White Hollywood* (New York: HarperCollins, 2005), 105.

56. Deborah Gray White, *Ar'n't I a Woman? Female Slaves in the Plantation South* (New York: W. W. Norton, 1985), 46–61.

57. H. McDaniel to T. L. Griffin, January 20, 1946; [unsigned] to W. White, February 12, 1946, NAACP II A 502, "Publicity Protests: Hattie McDaniels [*sic*] 1945–1949."

58. [Unsigned] to W. White, February 12, 1946, ibid.

59. W. White to R. Wilkins, January 25, 1945, NAACP II A 277, "Films: Hollywood Bureau, 1945–49."

60. Roy Wilkins, "The Watchtower," *Los Angeles Sentinel,* February 28, 1946; copy of statement regarding NAACP's establishment of Hollywood Bureau, NAACP II A 277, "Films: Hollywood Bureau, 1945–49." This statement was published in whole or in part by several black newspapers throughout the country.

61. Walter White, "People, Politics and Places," *Chicago Defender,* March 9, 1946.

62. *God Sends Sunday* was first published in 1931 and was produced as a play in 1933 by the Charles Giplin Players at Karamu Theater in Cleveland under the direction of Mrs. Rowena Jelliffe. See Thelma Boozer, "Script Proves Lena's 'St. Louis Woman' No Reflection on Race," *Pittsburgh Courier,* September 22, 1945.

63. "'St. Louis Woman' Script Condemned," *New York Amsterdam News,* September 8, 1945; L. Hardwick to R. Wilkins, August 29, 1945, NAACP II A 280, "Films, St. Louis Woman, 1945–1947."

64. W. White to A. Freed, draft of letter, n.d., NAACP II A 280, "Films, St. Louis Woman, 1945–1947."

65. L. Mayer to W. White, telegram, October 6, 1945; R. Wilkins to L. Hardwick, September 12, 1945, ibid.

66. White, *Ar'n't I a Woman,* 26.

67. Abe Hill, "Broadway Stews over Current Negro Roles," *New York Amsterdam News,* September 29, 1945.

68. C. Cullen to W. White, August 24, 1945, NAACP II A 280, "Films, St. Louis Woman, 1945–1947."

69. Herman Hill, "Controversy Rages over MGM's 'St. Louis Woman,'" *Pittsburgh Courier,* September 8, 1945.

70. Lawrence LaMar, "Hollywood Blasts IFRG Attack on Lena Horne's Play, 'St. Louis Woman,'" *Chicago Defender,* September 22, 1945. The claims by those associated with the musical that they had not seen a final script were not entirely a dodge. The script went through several revisions up through rehearsals, and most drafts, now housed at the Beinecke Library at Yale University, were practically illegible.

71. W. White to Jane Bolin, September 10, 1945, NAACP II A 280, "Films, St. Louis Woman, 1945–1947."

72. R. Wilkins to W. White, memorandum, September 17, 1945, ibid.

73. W. White to C. Cullen, September 19, 1945, ibid.

74. Ibid.

75. A. Bontemps to L. Hughes, n.d. [ca. November 1945], Langston Hughes Papers, series I, box 18, folder 396, "Arna Bontemps," Beinecke Rare Book and Manuscript Library, Yale University, New Haven, Conn.

76. Abe Hill, "Walter White Looms as New Theater Czar," *New York Amsterdam News,* September 22, 1945.

77. A. Bontemps to L. Hughes, September 14, 1945, Hughes Papers.

78. A. Bontemps to L. Hughes, September 18, 1945, ibid.

79. Cripps, *Making Movies Black,* 67.

80. "Lena Horne Refuses Lead Role in MGM's 'St. Louis Woman,'" *Chicago Defender,* September 29, 1945. See also "Mayer Differs with Winchell in 'Disciplining' Lena Horne," *Atlanta Daily World,* October 13, 1945.

81. "Complete Change Can Fit 'St. Louis Woman' for Broadway, Critic Says," *Chicago Defender,* March 2, 1946.

82. Walter White, "An Honest and Courageous Picture," May 12, 1949, and "Recent Movies on Racial Themes Indicate Maturity," November 10, 1949, Wilkins Papers, box 34, "White, Walter, Syndicated Column 1949."

83. For information on the *Amos 'n' Andy* campaigns, see Melvin Patrick Ely, *The Adventures of Amos 'n' Andy: A Social History of an American Phenomenon* (New York: Free Press, 1991). For their connection to the larger civil rights struggle, see Justin T. Lorts, "Black Laughter/Black Protest: Civil Rights, Respectability, and the Cultural Politics of African-American Comedy, 1934–1968" (PhD diss., Rutgers University, 2008), chap. 2.

84. See Cripps, "'Walter's Thing.'"

The Young Women's Christian Association's Multiracial Activism in the Immediate Postwar Era

Abigail Sara Lewis

Attempting to explain how race relations were going to differ in the postwar era, the newsletter of the National Board of the 3 million–member Young Women's Christian Association (the Y) quoted an African American soldier who was overseas at the time: "A different American is coming home."[1] Thousands of voting delegates who had just returned from the Y's 1946 national convention (held triennially) were already aware of this "different American." Leadership emphasized that bettering race relations was a top priority, and although most of the Y's local branches had always been racially segregated, the attendees responded by unanimously voting to desegregate the entire organization.[2] To keep up the momentum, members received a newsletter reviewing discussions that had taken place at the convention and outlining new organizational policies and plans. The newsletter made it clear that a heightened racial consciousness was central to the association's conception of this "different American" and that the wartime experiences of racial minorities contributed to the Y's newly democratized sensibility.

The Y's construction of a "different American" was based on three events: wartime changes in the labor market for racial minorities; the service of "colored Americans" in the armed forces, "where they have witnessed both the possibilities and the inconsistencies of the democracy they were fighting to defend"; and the relocation and resettlement of Japanese Americans. Recognizing that race relations had altered considerably during the war to meet "the demands of this crucial hour," the Y strove to create a more racially inclusive membership to help build a more tolerant American society.[3]

The "different American" was coming home to a racially changed landscape. Wartime domestic migration had upset existing racial "balances."[4]

Most of the 2.5 million African Americans who left the South during the war years sought opportunities for employment or more racially hospitable areas such as Chicago, Detroit, and Los Angeles.[5] Also significant was the forced resettlement of more than 100,000 Japanese from the West Coast either to internment camps or to "approved" relocation cities such as Chicago, Minneapolis, and Detroit. Although these demographic shifts tested the Y's policies, practices, and attitudes, the association's work on Japanese American resettlement served as the cornerstone of its efforts to better race relations internally and externally in the postwar era.[6] In many cases, Japanese Americans served as a buffer between blacks and whites as their resettlement throughout the country prompted dialogues on race in local Y branches. As local chapters opened their doors to Japanese members rather than establishing separate branches, as had been the prewar norm, it seemed logical to begin dismantling other similarly segregated branches. The Y planned to be a proactive surveyor in this racially changed national terrain.

Even before the war ended, the association believed that a harmonious postwar Christian social order was possible.[7] As the country's largest multiracial and interfaith women's organization, the Y represented women of all races, classes, religions, and regions.[8] It was clear to the organization that in order to sit at the table of power in this new postwar society, it needed to expand women's roles and leadership, regardless of race. A different American was indeed coming home. A different organization was coming home too.

The Effects of Wartime Migration

The multiracial community the Y planned to create was rooted in its wartime work with the Japanese American and African American communities. Although branches were racially segregated, the Y had become more progressive about race relations in the late 1930s. To a greater or lesser degree, all branches segregated blacks and whites. Some had limited social or organizational integration; others had virtually none. Asian Americans, though segregated, were more likely to share facilities with white members when their numbers were small. During war mobilization the Y kept a close eye on opportunities for women, encouraging many industries to look past racially and sexually discriminatory labor practices.[9] Once the war began, the Y's focus, both locally and nationally, quickly moved to aiding its German, Italian, and rather large Japanese American membership.[10] With the issuance of Executive Order 9066, which ordered the evacuation and imprisonment of enemy aliens, the Japanese in local branches looked to the national Y for guidance. The Los Angeles and San Francisco Ys, for example, wrote to the National Board, expressing their concerns about the mistreatment of Japanese Americans.[11] It established a policy of full support for the Japanese American community during internment, promising, *"Wherever you go the YWCA will be there."*[12] As a result, the Y established chapters in each of the relocation centers and encouraged staff from local branches near the centers to visit often. National Board staff also visited on a regular basis.[13]

In addition to its work on behalf of the Japanese community, the Y commissioned an interracial practices study to examine its own internal practices, aimed at black-white relations.[14] Throughout the war, local branches received surveys and questionnaires asking about the racial makeup of their members, the attitude of the local communities, and what interracial committees had been formed or work undertaken. The Y was not the only organization to do such a study, but it was one of the first. In his important treatise on race relations in America, *Brothers under the Skin,* Carey Mc-Williams examines how the war spurred many community organizations to undertake "self-surveys, 'social audits,' and investigations." Because a "community's pattern of race relations illuminates nearly every phase of its civic life," he argues, a "'social audit' on race relations, if properly conducted, cannot fail to point up general problems of housing, health, education, employment, and similar issues."[15] Because the Y's study started prior to the war and continued throughout it, the association could not only gauge its internal practices but also acquire a better grasp of the evolving racial situation brought about by the war and respond more effectively.

Nationally, race relations were irrevocably altered by the massive migrations during this period, triggering sweeping changes throughout the country. More than 12 million people joined the armed forces, going to new locations for training before being shipped overseas. Another 15 million migrated in search of better economic and social conditions.[16] These migrations changed the "racial balance" in certain regions and cities, leading to race riots in some places, especially in 1943, but also to interracial community organizing.[17] Cities such as Detroit, Los Angeles, Chicago, and Portland, Oregon, grew rapidly, causing shortages in housing, education, and other social services. The Y joined with five other organizations to form the American War-Community Services (AWCS) to help communities ease these strains.[18]

Although many migrations were voluntary, the U.S. government forcibly resettled Japanese Americans away from the West Coast. The evacuation and internment of Japanese Americans devastated communities and sent ripples throughout the nation. Removing the Japanese from the West Coast also keenly affected the Y branches in the area. One member stated, "We are facing the fact that we soon will lose a number of our most active and valuable club members. . . . They are girls, who like ourselves, are workers in offices, stores, and banks, civil service, teaching, nursing, household employment, and the service occupations. . . . They are girls who have worked with us in clubs, council, and conferences; on committees and Boards of Directors. They have helped to build our western coast both economically and culturally."[19]

These forced migrations sent Y branches into a tailspin as programming, outreach, and policies had to keep up with the fast-changing populations. Many chapters wrote of these concerns to the National Board. Even with the drastic changes taking place nationally, the Y's membership increased throughout the war, especially among Japanese women, who remained the third largest group within the association. Faced with an increasingly vocal and visible multiracial membership, the association began to devise a more nationally inclusive view of race, which would become its cornerstone in future race relations work.

The Y was a leader in helping Japanese American women relocate prior to and during internment. The National Board considered this an opportunity to strengthen its overall race relations work, which included the building of "constructive community attitudes regarding the Japanese and other minorities," emphasizing Japanese community leadership, and maintaining a connection between those still in the camps and those who had been resettled. The Y hoped that the "lessons learned in this project" could be used "as tools to help in problems relating to other minorities."[20]

National staff visited branches that were experiencing varying degrees of anti-Japanese tension and reported common issues facing the Japanese: "housing and employment problems . . . no show of welcome from whites, possible labor trouble(s) . . . , family relationship problems, great homesickness and feelings of insecurity and discouragement."[21] Staffers also worked with the Japanese community to help ease the transition. The association became a trusted resource for the Japanese community. Esther Briesemeister, a lead staffer in the Japanese Project, noted:

The Y.W.C.A. serves as a thread in the individual's life. A person may have had contact with the Y.W.C.A. before evacuation. She identifies with the organization in the relocation center and then looks to the Association in the local community as she resettles. We have had a high degree of carry-over from the relocation centers to community organizations and the people from the centers have looked to our organization for a great many different types of services. Many who have not actively identified with the Y.W.C.A. in centers know about our work and seek the organization when they resettle.[22]

Community branches used the issues surrounding resettlement to start discussions and activities to decrease racial tensions in their areas. In Chicago, branch leaders noted that "staff members have all been alert to ways in which prejudices can be detected and broken down, have seized opportunities to make communities interracial (and this includes Japanese Americans as well as Negroes), and have taken the initiative to create opportunities for girls of different races to know one another."[23] In all destination cities for relocated Japanese Americans, the Ys collaborated with local War Relocation Committees in housing and labor situations and sponsored interracial gatherings.[24] The Minneapolis branch worked hard to welcome the burgeoning Japanese American community, bringing Japanese American leaders from other branches into their fold. Like Chicago, the Minneapolis branch pushed for greater tolerance, noting, "it has been possible for the club members to become acquainted with young women of Japanese-American ancestry. This has contributed toward the understanding of people of other races."[25] The increase in interracial dialogue encouraged members to become more inclusive in other ways. One of the Business Clubs at the Minneapolis branch had black, Japanese, and Jewish members. The club also planned a joint program with a similar group at the Emanuel Cohen Center, which "proved to be an interesting experience."[26]

Some localities were less enthusiastic. Mayor Fiorello LaGuardia of New York City hoped to dissuade officials in Washington from allowing the "relocation of Japanese-American citizens in New York City 'or in any of the states on the eastern seaboard.'"[27] The Y joined with the NAACP and other civil rights organizations in protesting the mayor's views, and the groups' representatives secured a meeting with Police Commissioner Lewis J. Valentine to discuss the matter.[28] Even in inhospitable communities, local staffs were often supportive of resettlement and the association's race relations goals. Lucie G. Ford, the general secretary of the El Paso, Texas, branch was happy to help. In a letter to a colleague who had referred a Japanese woman to her, Ford said, "I am so glad and was proud to know that you *knew* I would welcome a Japanese girl. I am fighting the *cause* with several such girls. . . . Texas, you know is not always tolerant to groups other than the 100 per centers & *pure* white!!"[29]

Some racial attitudes were directly challenged by the larger implications of resettlement. The segregated, white branch of the Y in Washington, D.C., was willing to hire Japanese women in clerical and food service jobs and was interested in widening "the scope of the branch's Interracial Committee," but some members were concerned that if the bathrooms were desegregated to accommodate Japanese, black women might want the same access.[30]

Resettlement not only spurred discussions concerning communities' racial mores but also challenged the association's unspoken racial policies. Prior to the war, local branches did not have integrated staffs, except when a white led a nonwhite group. The National Board used its work for the Japanese to change the organization's hiring practices. It sent letters to many branch summer camp programs, "suggesting that they consider including a Japanese-American counselor on their camp staff."[31] Soon Japanese women joined the professional ranks in local branches, including Buffalo, Cleveland, Chicago, Peoria, Milwaukee, and Kansas City, Kansas.[32] Black women also benefited from this change, though not as widely until after the war.[33] "Often a sense of comradeship developed between [black and white women]," notes historian Susan Lynn, "who accepted each other as allies in the struggle against racial injustice, and close friendships developed, linking black and white women into networks that endured for a lifetime."[34] Many young Japanese, blacks, and whites remained with the organization for decades, and the impact of wartime multiracial staff settings stayed with these women when they later moved to other branches. In fact, when the Atlanta Y's executive director Virginia Carrier, who initiated its integration, retired in 1971, she said the "most interesting experience was working closely with Japanese evacuees" at the Seattle Y during World War II.[35] As the postwar years gave way to the civil rights era, it was clear that these wartime relationships had a direct impact on the actions taken by the Y during the various freedom struggles.

Resettlement affected the West Coast differently, since staff had to respond to the absence of the Japanese—a sizable constituency (5,000 Asian American members by 1948).[36] Many held that "while [the Japanese] are away they will be considered absentee members of the YWCA."[37] They hoped that preserving the idea of a Japanese presence would further interracial member relationships.[38] Maintaining positive interactions was important, since staff believed they needed to "prepare public opinion in the interval between the time Japanese go away and the time they return."[39]

Massive migrations of whites and blacks to the West deeply affected the coastal cities, which were already reeling from the Japanese evacuations. New populations transformed the neighborhoods where the Japanese had once lived, and staff had to balance their work with the exiled Japanese while tending to new groups. The increased migration of African Americans to the West Coast sometimes led to new, stronger partnerships for branches. For example, to be more helpful to migrants moving into the Bay Area of San Francisco, the Y financed a study by Professor Charles S. Johnson of Fisk University (he later established the Race Relations Institute at Fisk in 1944). Bay Area associations recruited "a number of the agencies, churches, social groups and interested lay people" to carry out "the plans laid out by Dr. Johnson and his staff." Members and staff alike planned "to put our shoulders to [the] wheel to see that through these findings the adjustment of the rural Negro to urban life can be made easier."[40] This type of action cemented the Y's relationships with black-led organizations. Already working closely with the National Urban League (NUL) under the AWCS, the Y anticipated continuing this collaboration through "definite joint activities on the West Coast" in the postwar era.[41]

Just as local branches were responding to the needs of these new populations, Japanese Americans were allowed to return to the West Coast. This concerned local staff, who worried about the reintegration of the Japanese into communities that had been dramatically resettled by African American migrants.[42] National Board staff viewed these areas as "special tension spots" and worked to minimize friction.[43] National staffers Dorothy Height, a leader in the African American community, and Japanese American Dorothy Takechi were dispatched to Los Angeles to hold a meeting with a "select group of Negro women" to talk about "interracial residents and the need of intra group understanding" between blacks and Japanese.[44] The National Board gave Takechi a scholarship and sent her to work with the Los Angeles association in its postwar resettlement work.[45] These tensions quickly dissipated, as evidenced by a 1946 *Ebony* magazine article titled "The Race War that Flopped," which reported a "heartfelt kinship" between the two groups.[46] But perhaps the strongest evidence that this tension disappeared is the lack of any further problems reported by the media.

Throughout the West Coast, branches reacted differently to the returning Japanese. Prejudices were still apparent in Portland, Oregon, where the board agreed to aid only "loyal" Japanese, making it clear that there were still questions about the loyalty of the Japanese community.[47] For them, the term *loyalty* was fraught with ideas about citizenship and patriotism. In Seattle, returning Japanese looked to the Y for employment, leading the branch to review not only its hiring policy but also the extent and direction of its interracial practices.[48] There and in other parts of the country, hiring Japanese women led to further racial integration of the Y staff. The general secretary of the Spokane branch saw a direct correlation between resettlement work and the decision to employ "a Japanese Secretary in our front office, a Negro Secretary in the office of our Health Education Department, and one Japanese and one Negro woman on our board of directors."[49]

Nationwide, the different stages of resettlement led branches to discuss multiracial integration efforts. By the end of the war, many looked to the National Board to define what *interracial* meant.[50] The question would challenge the organization throughout the postwar era. Did integration mean opening the mainstream (i.e., white) groups to minorities, while allowing minorities to form or continue to participate in racially exclusive groups? Or did it mean insisting on absolute integration across the board? Plans to desegregate and enforce integration varied from branch to branch. Some members supported the opening of the association's facilities to all races yet resisted the integration of activities and programs; some branches eliminated one-race clubs, but this caused a membership drop among all the races. In other branches, such as Portland, Oregon, the public embrace of racial integration led to an increase in members of color and a subsequent decrease in white members.[51] Meanwhile, in the South, there was generally no change in practice, although there was certainly more discussion of the matter.[52]

The way the Los Angeles Y handled these challenges is illustrative of how many branches coped with the impact of integration. By mid-1945 the Los Angeles association was preparing to implement more inclusive interracial practices throughout its branches. The Board of Directors enthusiastically endorsed the reopening of the Japanese branch and its residence hall (closed during the war), providing financial backing and lending staff to the effort. It decreed that both the branch and the residence hall would be interracial. The center was renamed the East Third Street Branch, and the residence was named the Magnolia Residence Hall.[53]

To the board's surprise, this decision reverberated negatively within the Japanese community. No former leaders had been consulted on this matter, and many balked at the decision to integrate. A group of Issei members, with the aid of a Japanese minister, threatened a lawsuit demanding that the building remain strictly Japanese.[54] The board relented, though it "stipulated" that if the buildings were to remain affiliated with the Y, administration had to be interracial. The Los Angeles association continued to campaign for branch integration, and eventually the Japanese leadership recommended the integration of the branch and the hall.[55]

The association seemed oblivious to the stressful effects of evacuation and internment on the Japanese, and its insensitivity went beyond the integration of the East Third Street Branch. In preparation for resettlement, the board created a Japanese Relocation Plan that included a Committee on Reorientation of Japanese Membership, intended to help educate the Japanese on the new interracial practices. Los Angeles association leaders requested that returning leaders of the branch meet with the Y's "Interracial Committee so that they may understand the new plan of operation."[56] White leaders believed that their actions were antiracist, but as historian Gary Okihiro has observed, the desire for inclusion "may be fundamentally racist if it means the forced absorption or assimilation of a group."[57] In this case, the Y was not trying to assimilate the Japanese community into the white mainstream, but it wanted to force its view of appropriate race relations on them. Postwar America was certainly not a bastion of multiracial inclusiveness; in fact, the Y was forcing its own ideal community on its members. The white staff's initial insensitivity to the reactions of former Japanese members made their antiracist work on behalf of the entire association not an "unmixed good."[58] Nevertheless, some Japanese supported the new interracial plans, including Dorothy Takechi, who served both the National Board and the Los Angeles association.[59] Esther Briesemeister privately wrote about the issues facing Takechi, including the desire of first-generation Japanese American members to have a "special place for them to meet." Already working to create such a place within the East Third Street center, Takechi did not want to disrupt the Y's integration goals. Briesemeister noted that Takechi "has had quite a struggle on the interracial aspects . . . as the Japanese are willing to live with anyone but the Negroes. However, there are some very fine Negro and Japanese women on the committee working on this and they are doing a good job of interpretation."[60] Briesemeister visited the branch in December 1945 to help Takechi and reported on its interracial progress to the National Board. In addition, the association was making a concerted effort to recruit more Latinas.[61]

The association's board did not force all the white branches to integrate on the same timetable. Briesemeister reported on the controversy surrounding Los Angeles's Clark Residence, which served only white women. Clark continued its policy of segregation, which Briesemeister called a constant "embarrassment to the total Association." She supported the recommendation that the Y "sever its connections" with Clark rather than enforce integration.[62] White staff seemed to feel more comfortable dictating the terms of integration within the nonwhite community than within their own. Still, this push for greater racial inclusiveness, coupled with the emphasis on better race relations by the National Board, encouraged leaders of the Los Angeles association to be more aware of their own racism. A 1948 program report noted that some of its branches relied on "token" racial participation, and "the inclusion . . . of one Japanese girl or woman, or one Negro does not warrant our saying we are interracial or intercultural." The report continued, "if we have examined these [prejudices], then we as board members, volunteers, and chairman must not stand by and see weaknesses and know they exist without realizing that we, too, are involved in them."[63] Members and staff alike were informed that by joining or working for the Y, they were implicitly agreeing to the larger philosophy and purpose of the national association, which included racial tolerance.

These issues were not unique to Los Angeles. During the immediate postwar era many branches confronted various forms of internal and external prejudice. Several southern branches, including Hot Springs, Arkansas, Atlanta, Georgia, and Tulsa, Oklahoma, applauded the National Board's move toward interracial sisterhood, but there was fear of community reprisals.[64] One southern branch director stated that even if she did not agree with integration, "the principle is superlatively Christian!"[65] Despite some reservations, most southern branches told the National Board that they were attempting to better race relations throughout the war. Exceptions included two Mississippi associations, which observed that, "unfortunately, interracial relations between Negroes and whites . . . worsened during the past three years in this community." Still, even these branches were "determined to restore and better these relations."[66] The mere fact that Deep South branches claimed to be attempting racial reconciliation could be considered a positive step toward changing attitudes in the region. In southern branches, postwar race relations continued to straddle the black-white binary, perhaps because so few women of other races or ethnicities were moving to the South. In the rest of the country, membership reflected the new multiracial population. For instance, in every region of the country except the South, there was an Asian American presence or an increase in the Asian American population between 1940 and 1950. The South was the only region that had double-digit percentages of African Americans in terms of population.[67]

As the National Board continued to push a multiracial agenda, it was clear to all concerned that there was uneven enforcement of racial policies and practices. The board declared that the "major emphases of the YWCA's of the United States—the Christian faith, democracy, and building a world community—with the deep implications these ideals have for the equality of peoples, give tremendous impetus toward a new era in race relationships."[68] The war had altered how local branches viewed race relations, and "working on the Japanese question has served as an impetus to associations to view more critically their work with Negroes and Mexicans." Members "discovered it was not possible to deal with one segment of the population without becoming aware of other groups with identical problems such as housing and jobs."[69] Local branches wanted to discuss how the association could best work on these new ideas at the Y's 1946 national convention.

The 1946 National Convention and Postwar America

The postwar period proved to be a chaotic time in race relations. Throughout the war, various individuals and groups had worked to create a national identity, regardless of race, in order to present a united front. But after the Allies declared peace, this identity was severely tested as disagreements surfaced over how fast the nation should be willing to grant civil and political rights to all citizens. Those first few months after the end of the war served as a time to reflect on the massive destruction that had taken place, but it was also a time of self-congratulation on the Allies' victory. Both these emotions fueled much of the social planning and action taking place, as many hoped to create a more inclusive nation and world. For the Y, this was a chance to establish "a more Christian social order which would be based on law that would promote the common welfare, secure justice and freedom for all peoples and banish war from the earth."[70]

The convention's agenda focused on taking stock of the lessons learned during the war, especially those concerning race. In preparation, the National Board sent local branches copies of *Interracial Practices in Community YWCAs,* published in 1944. That report, which "confirmed that community YWCAs remained largely segregated, and . . . recommended complete racial integration," was "slated for consideration by the 1946 national convention."[71] The National Board obviously wanted to create an official policy that could help branches "make clear that inclusiveness involves the joint sharing of common concerns rather than the independent activity of separate groups."[72]

Convention delegates were to vote on the Interracial Charter, which was based on the 1944 study written by Dr. Juliet Bell and Helen J. Wilkins, secretary of the Race Relations Committee.[73] The authors recommended that "community YWCAs in strictly segregated communities . . . plan interclub and intergroup activities to facilitate communication between segregated groups. In those communities where segregation was less extensive, the study urged community associations to launch integrated programs immediately. Associations with black branches were exhorted to reorganize these branches on an integrated basis. The study counseled community YWCAs to move as quickly as possible to open facilities, including residences, cafeterias, camps, and health education departments to all participants."[74] "It is a Negro-white study," Bell noted, "because Negroes are the largest minority in this country, 10 per cent of the total population, the largest minority in the YWCA."[75] Yet, she said, "it was hoped . . . that the findings of such a study might be used to interpret the relationship between white people and [other] racial minorities within the Association."[76]

Staff and members worked together to expand racial categories. In 1943 Annie Clo Watson, the head of what the Y called "nationality work," wrote a memo to the National Board that stated, "with [the] exception of general recognition of the Negro-white problem, there is not [a] well developed and active interest in national headquarters leadership in 'cultural minority' problems and program[s]." The work on behalf of the Japanese community had been stellar, but Watson was concerned that the lessons learned from this "special project" would not benefit other racial and ethnic groups; the association needed to be more responsive to the needs of the Chinese, Filipinos, and Mexicans, among others.[77] Shortly thereafter, the National Board became increasingly vocal about the importance of rights for all groups. Wilkins began to work more closely with Watson, incorporating her critique into their work and using it time and again to remind the association of the "growing realization of the similarity of problems of all of [the] people who face barriers of race or nationality."[78] In preparation for the convention, National Board leaders encouraged staff to review

Watson's memo and think about the importance of the Y as an intercultural and interracial organization.[79] Both Wilkins and Bell concurred that the scope of the Y's race work should be broadened, and they believed their study could "be applied to any other group relationships in the YWCA, Japanese-white nationality groups or minority religious groups."[80]

After publication of the study, Dorothy Height, a decades-long staffer at the Y and later president of the National Council of Negro Women, traveled around the country in her capacity as secretary of the Committee on Interracial Education to facilitate discussion and observe local branches' reaction to the study.[81] Her findings revealed varying views on segregation, immigration, and federal versus state power. During Height's visit to Memphis, the local board stated, "we accept the fact that the denial of the benefits of democracy is morally and religiously wrong. Therefore, we pledge ourselves to work without rest to secure the benefits of democracy to every American citizen."[82] Height's visits did not always go smoothly; her mere presence as a black woman evoked heated emotions at certain branches.[83] She also worked on multiracial issues with branches outside the South. For instance, Denver asked for assistance on "inter-minority relations," whereas Duluth, Minnesota, "needed more help on the question of Japanese Americans," and Delaware required input on the subject of "the American Indian."[84]

The war and resettlement work had changed the initial bifurcated understanding of race relations, broadening definitions of race and race work for the association. At the 1940 convention a proposed amendment to use the phrase "all racial minorities" instead of "Negro" failed.[85] Yet six years later, without any discussion, the Public Affairs Program began to use the term "minority groups" when referring to race work. This term was defined as including "Negro, Japanese American, Oriental, Mexican and Latin American, Foreign Born, [and] American Indian."[86] In addition, during the debate on implementing the recommendations of *Interracial Practices,* some spoke only of black-white relations, while others included Asian and Mexican Americans and equated them with African Americans in their speeches.[87] A representative from Salt Lake City asked, "If this report is on racial minorities, should not the Japanese be included?" In response, convention leadership made it clear that all racial groups would be included in the Y's future efforts involving race relations.[88]

Although the association was committed to a multiracial postwar society, the Y's focus on the desegregation and integration of black and white communities before, during, and after the war cannot be overstated.[89] The

Y saw itself not as "an organization of white women considering the situation of those of another race" but as a "Negro-white organization considering a problem that belongs to all of us."[90] At the 1946 convention the National Board made it clear that its work with the black community was a priority, since "the Negro represents the largest ethnic minority in the United States and the group for which racial tensions are most acute. Our program will, therefore, put special emphasis on this group."[91]

When not spearheading actions on its own, the Y often joined forces with other organizations, namely the NAACP and the NUL, to fight for the desegregation of the armed forces, agricultural reform, and the creation of a permanent federal Fair Employment Practices Committee (FEPC).[92] Representatives of both civil rights organizations had been regular attendees of past Y conventions and participated in 1946. Their support extended beyond simple attendance. Staff members worked with these groups in preparing participants for the racial climate of Atlantic City, New Jersey, where the gathering was held. The National Board created and distributed an informational card that listed New Jersey's race equality statutes, and it told attendees to carry this card with them to show to proprietors in case they were refused service at public establishments.[93] In addition, attendees had already received their March edition of the Y's monthly magazine *The Woman's Press,* which contained an article on the need for civil rights for all Americans written by Roy Wilkins, editor of the NAACP's *Crisis* magazine.[94] These groups were deeply interested in the outcome of the convention, hoping that if the largest women's organization in the nation took race relations seriously, then there was a real possibility for greater national action on this issue.[95]

Despite a steady dialogue on bettering race relations prior to and during the war, some Y members and staff were still hesitant to take the final step of desegregating the association. Participants at the convention understood that by choosing integration, they would be waging an uphill battle both internally and externally.[96] Some southern delegates argued that resistance to the charter would come not from members but from the men who sat on local community chest boards and controlled branch funding.[97] These same women acknowledged that "we women have moved further forward than men have in our thinking along these lines" and indicated that they would continue to support the charter.[98] Relieving some of the tension, it was agreed that where laws made it impossible to desegregate, intergroup activities would be planned.[99]

Mary Shotwell Ingraham, president of the National Board, understood that passage of the Interracial Charter was dependent on appealing to participants' religious beliefs, and she hoped these beliefs would trump ingrained social and regional mores. As a Christian organization, the Y often linked the observance of religious tenets to the taking of particular positions on a variety of issues, such as the struggle to improve women's access to education, the fight for economic justice, and the movement for the creation of "a more peaceful world order."[100] Ingraham expressed her opinion that true followers of Christianity naturally believed in racial tolerance and were willing to fight for it. A belief that personal faith was the foundation for one's commitment to progressive racial interaction dictated Y policy for the next two decades.[101]

Other convention leaders also connected Christianity to the fight for racial justice, including African American leader Benjamin Mays, the president of Morehouse College and vice president of the Federal Council of Churches of Christ in America. He told the women that "the future of democracy in the United States is with those who take the high road," and they had to imagine themselves as "crusaders for social justice" in the upcoming vote on the Interracial Charter.[102] Y leaders also hoped that this "crusade for social justice" would not be confined to the organization. Mrs. Legrand Tucker, chairwoman of the Commission to Study Interracial Practices, told delegates, "If you attack segregation at any point, the whole wall crumbles a little." She urged convention participants to "transfer our learnings from the Association to the world outside."[103] The charter was soon unanimously approved, although "a few southern white delegates left early to avoid the vote, and a few other [local] associations withdrew shortly afterward."[104]

Many progressive organizations, including the NAACP, the Congress of Industrial Organizations, and the National Association of Colored Women, applauded the Y for its Interracial Charter. Walter White, head of the NAACP, stated that the Y had "implemented more effectively than any other religious organization the tenets of true Christianity."[105] Some groups, while praising the Y, expressed concern about the heavy emphasis on black-white relations. A representative from the American Council of Race Relations sought and received confirmation that the Y was still committed to racial issues outside of black-white relations, especially within the Japanese community.[106]

The Y's passage of the Interracial Charter was the first of many race-related events in the postwar era. McWilliams characterized it as a period when "more has happened in the field of race relations in this country—

more interest has been aroused; more has been said and written; more proposed and accomplished—than in the entire span of years from the end of the Civil War to 1940. Of this there can be no doubt."[107] The immediate postwar era led many to believe that real progress was being made in race relations and that first-class citizenship would soon be a reality for all Americans. Some looked to the integration of baseball—when Jackie Robinson became a Brooklyn Dodger in April 1947—as a sign that the country was becoming more racially tolerant. The Cleveland Indians and St. Louis Browns followed suit that summer.[108] That same year, Pepsi Cola shook up the corporate world when it chose to promote positive racial images in its advertising and, within a few years, integrated its sales force.[109] Postwar America also saw the first real challenge to the infamous "one-drop" rule, which defined one racially as African American if there was one drop of "black" blood in one's veins.[110] In 1947 the Red Cross stopped segregating its blood supply, although it was another three years before it stopped designating the donor's race on blood bags.[111]

Even the federal government finally took steps to end Jim Crow. President Harry S. Truman created the President's Committee on Civil Rights, which issued its report *To Secure These Rights* in 1947.[112] The committee had been formed in large part to help quell the extensive and violent white backlash to struggles for civil rights and social equality.[113] This report, hailed as a blueprint for the modern civil rights movement, argued for the "establishment of a permanent civil rights division of the Justice Department, the creation of a Commission on Civil Rights, enactment of anti-lynching legislation, abolition of the poll tax, . . . desegregation of the Armed Forces . . . [and] enactment of a permanent FEPC."[114] Truman supported many of these suggestions and in 1948 signed Executive Order 9981, instituting the desegregation of the armed forces.[115] The Supreme Court also began to reverse itself, chipping away at legally sanctioned racial segregation in cases involving restrictive housing covenants, interstate transportation, and education.[116]

Although many of these advances dealt directly with the rights of African Americans, there was progress for other minorities as well. In 1948 the Supreme Court overturned California's Alien Land Law, which prohibited noncitizen Asians from owning property, ruling that the law violated the equal protection clause of the Fourteenth Amendment.[117] In a concurring opinion, Justice Frank Murphy wrote that the law's inherent racial discrimination was not only an "embarrassment" to the ideals of the U.S. Constitution but also an affront to "respect for, and observance of, human rights and fundamental freedoms for all."[118] Lower courts also invoked the Fourteenth Amendment in cases involving the unlawful segregation of Mexican Americans in public schools.[119] In 1948 Congress passed the Japanese American Claims Act, compensating some of the former internees for property losses.[120] Congress also passed the 1952 McCarren-Walter Immigration Act, which repealed any lingering Asian exclusion laws and allowed Japanese immigrants to become naturalized American citizens, the final immigrant group to gain such rights.[121]

The Y's Interracial Charter made the association a leader among social and civil rights organizations. In the fall of 1945 the American Civil Liberties Union (ACLU) conducted a survey of the racial practices of 141 "leading professional, scientific, and cultural organizations" in the nation. Twelve organizations reported having no black members, and only nine had more than 100. National organizations were divided into four categories: (1) those that were interracial nationally "but yield[ed] to local customs in excluding or segregating Negroes," (2) those that discriminated both nationally and locally, (3) those "that segregate[d] Negroes and refuse[d] them admission as members of the national organization," and (4) those that excluded blacks altogether. In the first category, the biggest included the Y, the Boy Scouts and Girl Scouts, the American Red Cross, and the Women's Christian Temperance Union. The American Bar Association and the American Veterinary Medical Association were in the second group, and the National Council of the YMCA and the Veterans of Foreign Wars were in the third. The General Federation of Women's Clubs and the Association of Professional Ball Players of America maintained a "white-only" policy.[122]

Within six weeks of publication of the ACLU survey, the Y and the Federal Council of Churches (FCC) moved to desegregate, integrate, and denounce Jim Crow.[123] The news of the Y's decision was broadcast nationally, and it was "believed [the charter] will set the tone for other organizations which presently follow a policy of racial segregation, if not down right racial exclusion."[124] By the end of the year the Congregationalists and the United Council of Church Women joined the discussion on racial equality.[125] Within a few years other denominations adopted the FCC's stance, including the Methodists.[126]

The Y and the FCC agreed that "unless Christian churches open their doors to all races they 'should cease to proclaim the doctrine of the fatherhood of God and the brotherhood of man.'"[127] As a hierarchical organization, the Y could have enforced its Interracial Charter throughout all its branches, but it did not. Although no branch was exempted from working toward this goal, there was a Christian understanding of those that had not fully worked out racial bias. There was faith that as long as there was persistent activity on this issue, "God will make known to our hearts the final answers to those questions on which we are now confused or uncertain or divided."[128] Acceptance of an inclusive fellowship (i.e., branch integration) was an individual religious experience, and it could not be forced, or else it would not be authentic. Nationwide, many branches grappled with ways to implement the charter immediately, while southern Ys debated the charter for the next twenty years without acting on it. For instance, staff at the Jackson, Mississippi, branch cited both the 1944 *Interracial Practices* study and the charter as the initial steps toward "achieving the goal" of trying "to learn each other."[129] For some in the black community, the fact that the Interracial Charter was making waves in Mississippi gave them hope that Jim Crow would soon be dead.[130] It was a slow death, however; the Jackson, Mississippi, branch would not fully desegregate until 1968.[131]

In addition to these hopeful signs, some black-led organizations took equally bold steps. In 1946 the oldest African American sorority, Alpha Kappa Alpha, opened its doors to all women, regardless of race.[132] A few years later the National Association of Colored Graduate Nurses, the largest group of African American nurses, disbanded; thanks to strides made toward integrating the nursing field, the association was no longer necessary.[133]

Many national social organizations supported and encouraged racial tolerance and equality, but they did not force their local groups to desegregate or integrate. A review of their race-related efforts reveals little mention of desegregation as a goal or acknowledgment of when it took place. Although the YMCA resolved to encourage local associations to eliminate racial discrimination and dissolved its national Colored Work Department, movement toward true desegregation was slow at best.[134] In some instances local and student YWCA and YMCA branches worked together on race issues, but seldom at the national level. In fact, throughout the postwar era the YMCA made repeated overtures to merge with the YWCA for financial, facility, and program reasons. But the Y was concerned that women's access to leadership and other empowerment measures, as well as its firm commitment to bettering race relations, would be lost through this union.[135] Other organizations, such as the Boy Scouts and Girl Scouts, led efforts to increase black membership and supported racial tolerance, but there was little effort to integrate its local troops.[136] Similarly, the American Association of University Women supported interracial efforts but had little power to enforce local compliance.[137] These weak efforts are important in understanding the struggle taking place during the postwar era as many groups attempted to create a racially tolerant environment.

The Y's leadership on race started immediately after the 1946 convention. In the forefront were the student Ys, which had a history of pushing the progressive agenda of the national organization.[138] In many cases student associations faced backlash on campuses and in the larger community as they pressed forward on integration. At the University of Oklahoma, student and administration leaders canceled a joint student Y–Girl Reserves event because of an invited black speaker.[139] Problems also arose at interracial student conferences. Since the 1920s, regional and national student Y conferences had been interracial in membership and leadership, except for those held in the South. Adoption of the Interracial Charter changed this. For example, in the summer of 1946 an interracial conference was held in Hendersonville, North Carolina, throwing the community into an uproar, and threats of violence ensued. In a letter to the editor one person wrote, "Such meetings are not welcome in this community. Ample facilities are available in other sections of the country, outside the south, for the accommodation of the interracial conferences."[140] National Board staffers were immediately dispatched to the town, and although they were assured that the students were safe, the Hendersonville sheriff "warned us emphatically that should we attempt to have another interracial conference, there 'would be a killing.'"[141]

Students were also involved in protesting the escalating violence against African American veterans and servicemen. After the 1946 lynching of veteran George Dorsey and his wife, his sister, and a friend in Monroe, Georgia, the cochairs of the student YW-YMCAs immediately wrote to Governor Ellis Arnall, urging that the "perpetrators of this crime be brought to justice."[142] The students alerted the National Board, prompting letters from the National Board president to both President Truman and Governor Arnall.[143] The governor quickly replied that he was doing everything within his power to investigate.[144] The Monroe lynching, as well as other cases of violence, led a variety of organizations to form the National Emergency Committee against Mob Violence.[145] The NAACP led the committee and asked the National Y to represent the different women's groups.[146]

Beyond cooperating with other civil rights organizations, the National Board and community branches continued to work toward the goals set out by the Interracial Charter. The Julius Rosenwald Fund sponsored the Y's "employ[ment of] a secretary for one year to work on a follow-up of the Interracial Study."[147] Some southern branches, including those in Miami, Austin, Oklahoma City, and Richmond, reported progress on integration efforts.[148] Out west, the Seattle branch protested both labor discrimination against Japanese Americans and blacks' lack of access to public establishments.[149] However, some other branches resisted this new emphasis on race relations. Shortly after the convention the Louisville, Kentucky, branch reported that it had ceased all integration efforts.[150] A few years later the Mobile, Alabama, Board of Directors sent a letter to all branches "expressing dissatisfaction with the Public Affairs Committee of the National YWCA, particularly those sections dealing with minority groups."[151] Still, a 1947 article in *Ebony* magazine, detailing the internal resistance to the 1946 charter, reported that the Y, "having come this far . . . [had] no intention of turning back."[152]

Even with local resistance to the charter, at the national level the Y stood apart from other organizations committed to civil rights. As one scholar noted, "In adopting a progressive policy the Y.W.C.A. was not unique—many philanthropic and religious bodies have also done so. What was unique was its determination to establish machinery within the organization to guarantee its fulfillment."[153] The Y continued to review its interracial practices after adoption of the charter, publishing numerous studies and reports on race relations that were deemed very "helpful" to other organizations.[154] Within a short time the Y had become "a pioneer in the inter-racial field and . . . [was] known throughout the country for its efforts toward full integration of minority groups in Association life."[155]

The Y also differentiated itself through its commitment to work with all racial and ethnic groups. Its multiracial foundation served as a springboard for its postwar activism. In her 1946 book *Step by Step with Interracial Groups*, Dorothy Height explained how the association had redefined the term *interracial work:*

> The word "interracial" has come to mean, for many, the relationship between Negro and white people. We must remember that our country has a number of racial minorities. Although many of the most difficult problems are in Negro-white relations because Negroes are the largest racial minority in the United States, *difficult problems face all minorities.* It has been agreed that progress in the solution of the problems in Negro-white relations is essential to a real assurance that we have genuine knowledge of how to

tackle, in any aspect, the problems of the minority. We shall be helped toward greater understanding and competence if we realize that solutions are related not to the kinds of *people* involved but to the kinds of *problems*.[156]

Other organizations and leaders also supported multiracial efforts in the fight for civil rights. Dr. Charles S. Johnson argued that the black community "should lend its conspicuous support to the campaigns against the manifestations and growth of anti-Semitism and against the undemocratic treatment of Japanese American citizens. This would not only win new friends and allies, but it would help preserve in our national tradition the American spirit of fair play."[157] The FCC encouraged congregations to be alert to how the "champions of white supremacy" were "organizing to deny freedom to Negroes and to persons of Japanese ancestry."[158] However, as historian Cheryl Greenberg points out, "most black and Jewish groups did little on behalf of interned Japanese Americans."[159] These groups "generally paid more attention to each other than to other minority communities," laying the groundwork for "sustained black-Jewish cooperation" in the civil rights movement.[160] Leadership fell to those organizations, like the Y, that believed in and practiced multiracial work before the postwar era.[161] By the early 1950s the Y was cited as the only multiracial organization effectively fighting for civil rights.[162]

The Y and the Changing Postwar Racial Scene

By the 1950s the association had made significant headway in terms of racial inclusiveness. At the start of the decade the Public Affairs Committee dissolved its Race Relations Subcommittee after seventeen years of existence because its work was now being "interwoven into the warp and woof of Association life."[163] Bettering race relations became the central goal of the organization.

The Y was distinctive, in that it fostered both an interracial and an ecumenical community. For many, it was the only place to have such an experience. Many members and staff participated in other social or religious organizations, but none of these groups offered the Y's diverse population. Women from the National Council for Negro Women (NCNW), the National Council of Jewish Women, and the Japanese American Citizens League joined the Y.[164] Many of these groups had similar agendas and often collaborated with the association, but women congregated at the

Y because the confluence of gender, race, and religion was seldom found elsewhere. Sociologist Belinda Robnett argues that black women "addressed issues of gender and race simultaneously. [However] when forced to choose, black women's identities . . . were strongly anchored to their Blackness."[165] This does not seem to hold true for many African American women who were highly active in the Y as members or staff. The Y shared more members with the NCNW than with any other organization, and although many Y members and staff were active in other single-sex organizations, the Y was the place to meet other women of all races who were committed to civil rights and racial tolerance. The Y's Christian purpose of building a fellowship of women and girls regardless of race united them in a way that superseded racial, ethnic, religious, and class boundaries. As the executive director of the Seattle Y explained, the Y's uniqueness was "due to a number of factors—partly because it is an organization by and for women, partly because it is an organization which both thinks and acts, partly because it crosses all lines and contains some of all kinds of people. . . . There is no dogma, but an odd sustaining unity among the groups making up the YWCA which holds it together."[166]

Thus, local Y branches became a place to forge multiracial and ecumenical ties. A member in Seattle who was the wife of a Buddhist minister knew the Y was the place to organize a club for Japanese war brides because these women "represented all faiths and did not want to affiliate with any church group."[167] It grew to include Australian and German war brides, furthering its amalgamation of different races and religions.[168] In 1954 black and white women in Aiken, South Carolina, looked to the Y for help in establishing an interracial branch, making it the first southern branch founded as such.[169] Some members who had limited contact with other races, "coming from . . . communities that have not yet freed their souls," were able to interact at regional conferences. One woman marveled at the chance to meet with women of different races, stating, "The YWCA is . . . the calm center of the whirlpool of our lives . . . a rock of Gibraltar, unmoved, amidst the tides of the ocean—an ocean of doubts, fears, hatreds, misunderstandings—that beset our world today. For God hath not given us the spirit of fear—but of power, through love."[170]

National leaders believed that the Interracial Charter and the campaign for racial inclusiveness had led to "a new day" at the community and student branches.[171] Although this inclusive fellowship initially emphasized black-white relations, the Y used the early postwar years to extend its fight against injustice to "religion [and] national origin."[172] The issue of multiracialism was never far from the Y's agenda, even after the 1954 *Brown v. Board of Education* decision challenged the country to reexamine its "democratic principles" with regard to the African American community.[173] One of the main reasons for the Y's interest in multiracialism was the presence of Japanese American staffer Dorothy Takechi. She started her career at the Y before the war in San Francisco, and the National Board was quick to note her leadership and intelligence. After getting her released from the internment camps, the Y furnished her with scholarships for college and graduate school. As noted earlier, immediately after the war she worked for the National Board, helping to alleviate racial tensions in Los Angeles. She then moved east and became the associate director of the Mount Vernon, New York, Y. In 1950 she was promoted to executive director, becoming the first nonwhite to hold that position in a main branch.[174] Soon she was back at the National Board working in the Leadership Services department and directing a major portion of the inclusiveness campaigns.[175] Leading up to the *Brown* decision, Takechi worked with the National Board's southern regional staff, putting together material on school desegregation for local and national staff members.[176] She served on various race-related committees, including ad hoc groups on *Brown* and desegregation.[177] Her memos during this time did not use the terms "Negro" or "white." Rather, Takechi used "race," "culture," and "all groups."[178] This was not accidental; Takechi sought to broaden racial categories since she did not fit into traditional biracial groupings. As the only Japanese woman at many Y conferences and meetings, her mere presence signaled to others that they too needed to think beyond the black-white paradigm.[179] Her presence also reinforced the Y's stature as a multiracial organization, as she was one of the Y's chief liaisons with other civil rights organizations with respect to programs, materials, and collaboration.[180]

The association's postwar challenge, like Takechi's, was to balance national multiracial activism and awareness with an increasingly biracial civil rights struggle. Urban migration slowed after the war, but the landscape was forever changed by the influx of nonwhites and the exodus of whites to the suburbs. In 1951 the Chicago branch broke its membership into "Foreign and Mixed Parentage; Foreign Born; and Negro"; it also counted "Roman Catholic, Hebrew, and Greek Orthodox" women among its majority Protestant membership.[181] Five years later the categories needed to be reformatted to reflect the increased membership of Japanese, Chinese, Mexican, and Puerto Rican women.[182] Similar changes occurred in other cities. Los Angeles, Seattle, and Minneapolis experienced increasing populations of Native Americans, and the Ys in those cities made concerted outreach efforts.[183] When a 1952 *YWCA Magazine* article reported steps the Seattle branch was taking toward racial inclusiveness, it stated, "by interracial, we mean Negro, Caucasian, *and Oriental.*"[184] Branches across the nation were experiencing similarly multiracial memberships.

Throughout the immediate postwar era, there was increased pressure by African American civil rights organizations and local groups to end racial segregation and discrimination, including the NAACP's legal campaigns for equal access to education and the 1953 Baton Rouge bus boycott.[185] Although the landmark *Brown* decision was the culmination of decades-long legal battles, the first direct action campaign to capture the nation's attention was the 1955–1956 Montgomery bus boycott.[186] This event refocused the nation's lens to view race relations as a regional, black-white issue.

Months prior to the Montgomery bus boycott, the Y held its Twentieth National Convention and recommitted to its local and national multiracial platform. Delegates were told to go back to their communities and ask, "Who are the people in my community and the areas round it, or on my campus? Are there Negroes among my fellow-townspeople? Are there Americans of Spanish-speaking background? Or Americans of Japanese or Chinese descent? Are there American Indians? If members of these groups or of other minorities which sometimes may be discriminated against live in our town, do they take part in the life of our YWCA? Do they feel welcome there?"[187] The convention also featured a debate regarding the ongoing segregation in the southern branches, but the National Board's focus was to strongly encourage members and staff to review broad community racial practices and to make connections among all the various racial groups' fight for equality and inclusion in every part of the nation.[188] The cover of the June 1955 *YWCA Magazine,* which recapped the convention, clearly showed white, black, and Asian delegates working together. At this point in the postwar era, the association still viewed the future of race relations in a multiracial sense.

After Montgomery, the black freedom struggle grabbed both the nation's and the association's attention. The *Brown* decision and the subsequent civil rights movement helped the Y further its agenda of racial inclusiveness, but it also forced the Y to refocus its attention from national goals to the South. The 1958 convention proved to be contentious, as the southern branches' reluctance to fully implement the 1946 Interracial Charter became the dominant issue. Debates between black and white southern members took center stage. No one disagreed with the goal of racial inclusiveness, but only how vigorously it should be implemented.[189] In the middle of the debate, one delegate from Los Angeles stated, "Mention has been made [of] integration only of Negroes, and we have in California, as you know, many, many representatives and many members of races other than Negro, and we would hope that in giving this consideration our good Spanish-American members, and particularly our Oriental members are also included."[190] This concern is indicative of where the Y's conversation on race was headed: it became increasingly focused on the South and on the civil rights movement. Clearly, a shift occurred after 1955, and for many, the attempts at multiracial coalition building in the late 1940s and early 1950s became an increasingly black-white struggle.

Notes

I would like to thank my dissertation committee members—Steven F. Lawson, Susan Schrepfer, Nancy Hewitt, Deborah Gray White, and Gary Okihiro—for their constructive critiques. None of my research would have been possible without the generous support provided by the Smith College Grierson Fellowship. Finally, I thank my husband, Justin Thomas Lorts, for believing in my project, and my father, Brian Arthur Lewis, for never tiring of editing and reading my work or listening to my stories of the Y.

1. Public Affairs Post Convention Newsletter, March 29, 1946, unprocessed box 3, 8, The YWCA of the USA Records, Sophia Smith Collection, Smith College, Northampton, Mass. (hereafter cited as YWCA of the USA Records).

2. Susan Lynn, *Progressive Women in Conservative Times: Racial Justice, Peace, and Feminism, 1945 to the 1960s* (New Brunswick, N.J.: Rutgers University Press, 1992), 49.

3. Public Affairs Post Convention Newsletter, March 29, 1946, 8.

4. Carey McWilliams, *Brothers under the Skin,* 8th ed. (1943; reprint, Boston: Little, Brown, 1964), 7.

5. For more on World War II migration, see Barbara A. Driscoll, *The Tracks North: The Railroad Bracero Program of World War II,* 1st ed. (Austin: University of Texas, 1999); Josh Sides, *L.A. City Limits: African American Los Angeles from the Great Depression to the Present* (Berkeley: University of California Press, 2003); Quintard Taylor, "A History of Blacks in the Pacific Northwest, 1788–1970" (PhD diss., University of Minnesota, 1978); Gerald D. Nash, *The American West Transformed: The Impact of the Second World War* (Bloomington: Indiana University Press, 1985); Lawrence Brooks De Graaf, Kevin Mulroy, and Quintard Taylor, *Seeking El Dorado: African Americans in California* (Seattle: University of Seattle Press, 2001).

6. "War Time Program: Division of Community YWCA's," July 13, 1942, microfilm reel 148, YWCA of the USA Records.

7. Elsie D. Harper, "Public Affairs, 1940–1945," November 8, 1945, unprocessed box 20, YWCA of the USA Records.

8. By the end of World War II, the Y had more than 3 million participants. Mrs. Arthur Forest Anderson to Senator Alexander Wiley, Chairman, Senate Judiciary Committee, February 5, 1948, unprocessed box 15, YWCA of the USA Records.

9. Letter from Sally Story to Eleanor Copenhaver Anderson, January 23, 1942, microfilm reel 149, YWCA of the USA Records; *Public Affairs News Bulletin,* January 10, 1941, processed papers, box 3, ibid.; memo from Rose Terlin to Elise Harper, March 3, 1942, unprocessed box 8, ibid.

10. Mary Ingraham to President Roosevelt, December 11, 1941, microfilm reel 99, YWCA of the USA Records; "Extracts from Letters Received by Los Angeles YWCA Recently," January 1942, microfilm reel 149, ibid. For more on the initial reprisals against the German, Italian, and Japanese communities, see Roger Daniels, *Concentration Camps USA: Japanese Americans and World War II,* Berkshire Studies in History (Hinsdale, Ill.: Dryden Press, 1971); Gary Y. Okihiro and Leslie A. Ito, *Storied Lives: Japanese American Students and World War II* (Seattle: University of Washington Press, 1999); Stephen C. Fox, "General John Dewitt and the Proposed Internment of German and Italian Aliens during World War II," *Pacific Historical Review* (1988); Stephen C. Fox, *The Unknown Internment: An Oral History of the Relocation of Italian Americans during World War II,* Twayne's Oral History Series No. 4 (Boston: Twayne Publishers, 1990); Timothy J. Holian, *The German-Americans and World War II: An Ethnic Experience* (New York: P. Lang, 1996); John Christgau, *"Enemies": World War II Alien Internment* (Ames: Iowa State University Press, 1985).

11. Letter from Grace Steinbeck to Helen Flack, February 27, 1942, microfilm reel 149, YWCA of the USA Records.

12. Memo from Helen Flack to presidents and general secretaries of associations in the Western Region, March 27, 1942, microfilm reel 148, YWCA of the USA Records.

13. For more on the Y's role in Japanese internment, see Abigail Sara Lewis, "'The Barrier Breaking Love of God': The Multiracial Activism of the Young Women's Christian Association, 1940s to 1970s" (PhD diss., Rutgers University, 2008).

14. Proceedings of the Sixteenth National Convention, unprocessed box 321, 217, YWCA of the USA Records.

15. McWilliams, *Brothers under the Skin,* 19.

16. Gerald D. Nash, *The Great Depression and World War II: Organizing America, 1933–1945,* St. Martin's Series in Twentieth Century United States History (New York: St. Martin's Press, 1979), 145.

17. For more on race and migration during the World War II era, see McWilliams, *Brothers under the Skin;* Kevin Allen Leonard, *The Battle for Los Angeles: Racial Ideology and World War II* (Albuquerque: University of New Mexico

Press, 2006); Sides, *L.A. City Limits;* Nash, *The Great Depression and World War II;* Taylor, "A History of Blacks in the Pacific Northwest"; Maggie Rivas-Rodriguez, *Mexican Americans & World War II,* 1st ed. (Austin: University of Texas Press, 2005).

18. Gretchen Knapp, "Experimental Social Policymaking during World War II: The United Service Organizations (USO) and American War-Community Services (AWCS)," *Journal of Policy History* 12, no. 3 (2000): 330.

19. *Public Affairs News Service,* Bulletin No. 6, May 12, 1942, microfilm reel 148, YWCA of the USA Records.

20. "War Time Program: Division of Community YWCA's," July 13, 1942.

21. Annie Clo Watson, "Informal Report on Japanese Situation. Confidential," April 26, 1942, microfilm reel 148, YWCA of the USA Records.

22. Esther Briesemeister, "Brief Outline of Y.W.C.A. Work in Cooperation with the War Relocation Authority" (marked "Confidential—Not to Be Circulated"), May 22, 1945, microfilm reel 149, YWCA of the USA Records.

23. "Memo Data and Trends," 1943 Interracial Practices Study, June 25, 1943, box 33, folder 17, 3, Chicago YWCA Papers, Special Collections, University of Illinois–Chicago Library (hereafter cited as Chicago YWCA Papers).

24. Some of these meetings did not go over well, as in the case of an August 1943 gathering where whites and Japanese refused to mingle. Charlotte Brooks, "In the Twilight Zone between Black and White: Japanese American Resettlement and Community in Chicago, 1942–1945," *Journal of American History* 86, no. 4 (2000): 1679.

25. "Annual Descriptive Report of the Year 1942," box 2, Minneapolis YWCA Papers, Social Welfare History Archives, University of Minnesota, Minneapolis (hereafter cited as Minneapolis YWCA Papers).

26. "Annual Descriptive Report for the Year 1942—Business and Professional," box 2, folder "Full Annual Report to National Board, 1942," Minneapolis YWCA Papers. The Cohen Center was a Jewish center.

27. Roy Wilkins, press release, April 27, 1944, NAACP Papers, II A 325, JA 12–15, Library of Congress, Washington, D.C. For more, see "Ickes Hits Mayor on Loyal Japanese," *New York Times,* April 28, 1944.

28. National Board Public Affairs Committee Meeting, 1944, unprocessed box 9, YWCA of the USA Records.

29. Lucie G. Ford to Mrs. Sickels, April 26, 1943, box 13, FF 204, International Institute of Minnesota Papers, Immigration History Research Center, Special Collections, University of Minnesota, Minneapolis.

30. Esther Briesemeister and Winona Chambers, War Relocation Authority Visit, October 3–5, 1943, microfilm reel 149, YWCA of the USA Records.

31. Betty Lyle, "Summary Report of the Japanese-American Project (August 1942–September 1943)," August 27, 1943, microfilm reel 148, YWCA of the USA Records.

32. Esther Briesemeister to Ann Elizabeth Neely, May 9, 1945, processed box 48, YWCA of the USA Records.

33. "Race Relations Subcommittee," May 9, 1945, unprocessed box 123, YWCA of the USA Records. For examples of black staff leadership, see "17th YWCA Convention Unmarred by 'Incidents,'" *Chicago Defender,* March 16, 1946. For an example of one local branch discussing the hiring of a black staff worker, see Program Planning Report (to San Francisco YWCA Board of Directors), by Llewellyn Toland McMahon, October 23, 1944, San Francisco YWCA Papers, San Francisco, Calif. (hereafter cited as San Francisco YWCA Papers).

34. Lynn, *Progressive Women in Conservative Times,* 53.

35. "Virginia Carrier Retires as YWCA Executive Director," *Atlanta Daily World,* August 1, 1971.

36. Mrs. Arthur Forest Anderson to Senator Alexander Wiley, Chairman, Senate Judiciary Committee, February 5, 1948, unprocessed box 15, YWCA of the USA Records.

37. "The Work of the YWCA, Fiscal Year 1941–1942," box 1, folder 18, Seattle YWCA Papers, University of Washington, Seattle (hereafter cited as Seattle YWCA Papers).

38. "Annual Report of Girl Reserves Department, Portland YWCA, for 1942," box 20, folder "YWCA Programs—Girl Reserves," Portland YWCA Papers, Lewis and Clark College, Portland, Ore. (hereafter cited as Portland YWCA Papers).

39. Elsie Harper and Helen Flack to Mabel Ellis, March 28, 1942, microfilm reel 148, YWCA of USA Records.

40. "Report of President Mrs. George V. Kulcher—Annual Meeting, 1944," San Francisco YWCA Papers.

41. "AWCS Minutes, January 25, 1944," processed box 47, YWCA of the USA Records. For more on African Americans in San Francisco during World War II, see Scott Tang, "Pushing at the Golden Gate: Race Relations and Racial Politics in San Francisco, 1940–1955" (PhD diss., University of California–Berkeley, 2002). For more on the YWCA and NUL in the AWCS, see Knapp, "Experimental Social Policymaking during World War II."

42. For more on the effects of resettlement in West Coast neighborhoods, see Taylor, "A History of Blacks in the Pacific Northwest," 224–25; Sides, *L.A. City Limits,* 36–56; McWilliams, *Brothers under the Skin,* 166; Scott Kurashige, "The Many Facets of Brown: Integration in a Multiracial Society," *Journal of American History* 91, no. 1 (2004); Thelma Thurston Gorham, "Negroes and Japanese Evacuees," *Crisis,* November 1945.

43. E. Monroe, "Statement Concerning the Need for a YWCA Worker on Interracial Matters with Special Emphasis on the Negro Situation," November 1945, processed box 41, YWCA of the USA Records.

44. Dorothy Takechi, "Meeting of the Metropolitan Los Angeles Group of the

National Negro Woman's Council," August 10, 1945, microfilm reel 149, YWCA of the USA Records.

45. Race Relations Subcommittee, May 9, 1945, unprocessed box 123, YWCA of the USA Records; Los Angeles Board of Directors Meeting, March 22, 1945, box 6, YWCA of Greater Los Angeles Papers, Urban Archives and Special Collections, California State University at Northridge (hereafter cited as Los Angeles YWCA Papers).

46. "The Race War that Flopped: Little Tokyo and Bronzeville Upset Predictions of Negro-Nisei Battle," *Ebony,* July 1946, 3. For more on this situation, see Kurashige, "The Many Facets of Brown"; Gorham, "Negroes and Japanese Evacuees."

47. Portland Board of Directors Meeting, December 12, 1944, box 13, Portland YWCA Papers. The adopted resolution stressed trust that the federal government would allow only loyal Japanese to move back to the West Coast. The resolution was published in the local papers. Portland Board of Directors Meeting, January 16, 1945, box 13, Portland YWCA Papers. Esther Briesemeister visited Portland and commented that although she discerned a prejudicial attitude toward Japanese and blacks, the board seemed committed to changing these attitudes. Esther Briesemeister, Portland Visitation Report, March 6–7, 1944, microfilm 207, YWCA of the USA Records.

48. Seattle Board of Directors Meetings, November 14 and December 12, 1944, box 17, folder 22, Seattle YWCA Papers.

49. "Excerpts from Letters to Mrs. Henry A. Ingraham: October 1, 1944 to March 1, 1945," Western Region, March 19, 1945, processed box 42A, YWCA of the USA Records.

50. Esther Briesemeister, Portland Visitation Report, February 21–23, 1945, microfilm reel 207, YWCA of the USA Records.

51. "Teenage Department Report, 1944–1946," box 20, folder "YWCA Programs—Girl Reserves," Portland YWCA Papers.

52. "Excerpts from Letters to Mrs. Henry A. Ingraham: October 1, 1944 to March 1, 1945," Southern Region, March 19, 1945, processed box 42A, YWCA of the USA Records.

53. See Los Angeles Board of Directors Minutes, September 28, 1944 (folder 1); February 22, April 12, and May 10, 1945 (folder 2); September 13 and October 25, 1945 (folder 3), box 6, Los Angeles YWCA Papers.

54. The group "produced a statement in the original deed which said the building was given for the use of the Japanese people." Laura Ault, Los Angeles Visitation Report, November 14, 1946, microfilm reel 163, YWCA of the USA Records.

55. Helen Flack, Los Angeles Visitation Reports, January 26 and October 10, 1947, microfilm reel 163, YWCA of the USA Records. A 1952 article marveled at the interracial living arrangements and gave the impression that everyone involved was supportive of the integration of Magnolia Hall from the start. "Magnolia Residence: YWCA's Interracial Home No Problem," *Los Angeles Times,* November 27, 1952.

56. Los Angeles Board of Directors Minutes, November 15, 1945, box 6, folder 3, Los Angeles YWCA Papers.

57. Okihiro and Ito, *Storied Lives,* xiii.

58. Ibid., 138.

59. See Los Angeles Board of Director Minutes, March 22, 1945 (folder 2), October 25, 1945 (folder 3), box 6, Los Angeles YWCA Papers.

60. Esther Briesemeister to "Nona," October 30, 1945, unprocessed box 48, YWCA of the USA Records.

61. Esther Briesemeister to Grace Stuff, February 2, 1945; Esther Briesemeister, Los Angeles Visitation Report, December 15, 1945, ibid.

62. Briesemeister, Los Angeles Visitation Report, December 15, 1945. The Clark Residence was not disaffiliated, although it remains unclear whether it desegregated, and if so, when.

63. Mrs. Edward B. Jamison, "Program Planning Progress Report," Metropolitan YWCA Board Meeting, June 17, 1948, box 9, folder 37, 2–4, Los Angeles YWCA Papers.

64. "Excerpts from Letters to Mrs. Henry A. Ingraham: October 1, 1944 to March 1, 1945," Southern Region, March 19, 1945, processed box 42A, YWCA of the USA Records.

65. "From Report of Findings from Nation-wide Discussion Issues of YWCA March–May 1945, Presented to N.B. 5/23/45," processed box 15, YWCA of the USA Records.

66. "Excerpts from Letters to Mrs. Henry A. Ingraham: October 1, 1944 to March 1, 1945," Southern Region.

67. The changes in census figures from 1940 and 1950 are as follows: Midwest, increase from 3.5 to 5 percent black, 0 to 0.2 percent Asian American; West, increase from 1.2 to 2.9 percent black, decrease from 1.5 to 1.2 percent Asian American; East, increase from 3.8 to 5.1 percent black, steady at 0.1 percent Asian American; South, decrease from 23.8 to 21.7 percent black, 0 percent Asian American in both years. Of course, these numbers would have fluctuated heavily during the war, especially in the South, which had two Japanese internment camps in Arkansas. Campbell Gibson and Kay Jung, "Historical Census Statistics on Population Totals by Race, 1790 to 1990, and by Hispanic Origin, 1970 to 1990, for the United States, Regions, Divisions, and States," Population Division, U. S. Census Bureau, http://www.census.gov/population/www/documentation/twps0056/twps0056.html.

68. "Traditional Position of the Young Women's Christian Association on Race," September 17, 1943, microfilm reel 93.2, YWCA of the USA Records.

69. Briesemeister, Los Angeles Visitation Report, December 15, 1945.

70. Elsie D. Harper, "Public Affairs 1940–1945," November 8, 1945, unprocessed box 20, YWCA of the USA Records.

71. Lynn, *Progressive Women in Conservative Times,* 46.

72. "Racial Equality in Y.W.C.A. Urged," *New York Times,* March 6, 1946.

73. Juliet Ober Bell and Helen J. Wilkins, *Interracial Practices in Community YWCAs* (New York: National Board, YWCA, 1944). Helen Wilkins was elected the first black National Board YWCA president in 1967; she was also the sister-in-law of Roy Wilkins, executive secretary of the NAACP, and the mother of Roger Wilkins, who served as the assistant attorney general of the United States from 1966 to 1969.

74. Lynn, *Progressive Women in Conservative Times,* 47.

75. Proceedings of the Seventeenth National Convention, processed box 2, 79, YWCA of the USA Records.

76. Ibid., 58.

77. Annie Clo Watson, "A Confidential Report . . . Organized Nationality Work in the YWCA," January 26, 1943, processed box 31, YWCA of the USA Records.

78. On Chinese and Filipino citizenship, see CP, "Miss Watson: This is an inter-office memo . . . ," April 12, 1943, box 32, YWCA of the USA Records. For work between Watson and Wilkins, see "Notes—Minutes—Committee of Nationality Communities—June 1, 1943," processed box 31, YWCA of the USA Records.

79. Margaret B. Gerard, "To: International Institutes and Foreign Community Departments," January 5, 1945, processed papers, box 36, YWCA of the USA Records.

80. Proceedings of the Seventeenth National Convention, 79.

81. Lynn, *Progressive Women in Conservative Times,* 48. For more on Height, see Dorothy I. Height, *Open Wide the Freedom Gates: A Memoir,* 1st ed. (New York: PublicAffairs, 2003).

82. "Race Relations Subcommittee," May 9, 1945, unprocessed box 123, YWCA of the USA Records.

83. Lynn, *Progressive Women in Conservative Times,* 48.

84. "Race Relations Subcommittee," May 9, 1945.

85. Public Affairs Program, 1940 National Convention, unprocessed box 15, YWCA of the USA Records.

86. Proceedings of the Seventeenth National Convention, xii–xiii.

87. Ibid., 72–74.

88. Ibid., 78.

89. For more on the Y's work with the black community prior to World War II, see Frances Sanders Taylor, "'On the Edge of Tomorrow': Southern Women, the Student YWCA, and Race, 1920–1944" (PhD diss., Stanford University, 1984); Nancy Marie Robertson, *Christian Sisterhood, Race Relations, and the YWCA, 1906–46* (Urbana: University of Illinois Press, 2007).

90. Myra Smith, "The Concern and Activities of the YWCA," October 6, 1944, processed box 41, YWCA of the USA Records.

91. Adopted Public Affairs Program, March 1946, unprocessed box 15, YWCA of the USA Records.

92. For more on the Y's efforts, see Jessie Vogt, "Report on the Council on National Defense Committee on Discrimination in Employment," July 23, 1941, processed papers, box 33, folder 8, YWCA of the USA Records; "Material Prepared for National Board Meeting Oct. 6, 1943—Compulsory Registration of Women," processed papers, box 8, YWCA of the USA Records; letter from Mabel T. Everett to Walter White, March 11, 1940, letters from Elizabeth B. Herring to Walter White, April 17, May 20, and June 26, 1941, and letter from Helen J. Wilkins to Roy Wilkins, September 18, 1940, NAACP Papers, NAACP II, 11 A 676 YWCA; and Knapp, "Experimental Social Policymaking during World War II." For more on World War II and blacks, see Robert Korstad and Nelson Lichtenstein, "Opportunities Found and Lost: Labor, Radicals, and the Early Civil Rights Movement," *Journal of American History* 75 (1988); Bruce Nelson, "Organized Labor and the Struggle for Black Equality in Mobile during World War II," *Journal of American History* 80 (1993); McWilliams, *Brothers under the Skin;* Leonard, *Battle for Los Angeles;* and Merl Elwyn Reed, *Seedtime for the Modern Civil Rights Movement: The President's Committee on Fair Employment Practice, 1941–1946* (Baton Rouge: Louisiana State University Press, 1991).

93. New Jersey Race Equality Statutes, 1946, unprocessed box 8, YWCA of the USA Records; Venice T. Spraggs, "YWCA Delegates Find Welcome at Atlantic City's Swank Hotels," *Chicago Defender,* March 16, 1946.

94. Roy Wilkins, "What Every American Wants," *Woman's Press,* March 1946.

95. Venice T. Spraggs, "Protestants, YWCA Drop Race Segregation Policy," *Chicago Defender,* March 16, 1946.

96. "Racial Equality in Y.W.C.A. Urged."

97. Ibid.; Irene Steyskal, "Racial Equality Policy Is Voted by Y.W.C.A.," *Chicago Daily Tribune,* March 6, 1946; Spraggs, "Protestants, YWCA Drop Race Segregation Policy," 1.

98. Steyskal, "Racial Equality Policy Is Voted by Y.W.C.A."

99. "Racial Equality in Y.W.C.A. Urged."

100. Lynn, *Progressive Women in Conservative Times,* 5.

101. Doug Rossinow, Sara Evans, and Susan Lynn have written on the use of Christianity in the Y as a way to foster racial tolerance. Doug Rossinow, *The Politics of Authenticity: Liberalism, Christianity, and the New Left in America* (New York: Columbia University Press, 1998); Sara M. Evans, *Personal Politics: The Roots of Women's Liberation in the Civil Rights Movement and the New Left,* 1st ed. (New York: Knopf, 1979); Lynn, *Progressive Women in Conservative Times.*

102. Lynn, *Progressive Women in Conservative Times,* 49.

103. Proceedings of the Seventeenth National Convention, 64.

104. Lynn, *Progressive Women in Conservative Times,* 49.

105. Spraggs, "Protestants, YWCA Drop Race Segregation Policy," 8.

106. Proceedings of the Seventeenth National Convention, 171.

107. McWilliams, *Brothers under the Skin,* 4.

108. For more on Jackie Robinson, the integration of baseball, and its impact on postwar race relations, see Jules Tygiel, *Extra Bases: Reflections on Jackie Robinson, Race, and Baseball History* (Lincoln: University of Nebraska Press, 2002); Neil J. Sullivan, "Baseball and Race: The Limits of Competition," *Journal of Negro History* 83, no. 3 (1998); Jules Tygiel, *Baseball's Great Experiment: Jackie Robinson and His Legacy,* expanded ed. (New York: Oxford University Press, 1997).

109. Douglas Martin, "Edward Boyd, 92, Marketer to Blacks, Dies," *New York Times,* May 6, 2007; Stephanie Capparell, *The Real Pepsi Challenge* (Detroit: Free Press, 2007).

110. For more on the issue of race and blood, see Spencie Love, *One Blood: The Death and Resurrection of Charles R. Drew* (Chapel Hill: University of North Carolina Press, 1996); Keith Wailoo, "Stigma, Race, and Disease in 20th Century America," *Lancet* 367, no. 9509 (2006); Keith Wailoo, *Dying in the City of Blues* (Chapel Hill: University of North Carolina Press, 2001).

111. "Red Cross Lauded for View on Blood," *New York Times,* June 11, 1947; "Red Cross to Omit Race Tag on Blood," *New York Times,* November 20, 1950. Although these events are significant, so was the backlash that occurred as demands for civil, political, economic, and social rights increased. For more on the backlash of the immediate postwar years, see Michael S. Sherry, *In the Shadow of War: The United States since the 1930s* (New Haven, Conn.: Yale University Press, 1995), 144–56.

112. Steven F. Lawson, ed., *To Secure These Rights: The Report of President Harry S. Truman's Committee on Civil Rights* (Boston: Bedford–St. Martin's, 2004).

113. For more on the early postwar backlash, see ibid.; Steven F. Lawson, *Black Ballots: Voting Rights in the South, 1944–1969* (Lanham, Md.: Lexington Books, 1999); Steven F. Lawson, *Running for Freedom: Civil Rights and Black Politics in America since 1941,* Critical Episodes in American Politics (New York: Mc-Graw-Hill, 1991); Kari A. Frederickson, *The Dixiecrat Revolt and the End of the Solid South, 1932–1968* (Chapel Hill: University of North Carolina Press, 2001); and Charles M. Payne, *I've Got the Light of Freedom: The Organizing Tradition and the Mississippi Freedom Struggle* (Berkeley: University of California Press, 1995).

114. William H. Chafe, *The Unfinished Journey: America since World War II* (New York: Oxford University Press, 1986), 90. For more on its significance to the civil rights movement, see Lawson, *To Secure These Rights.*

115. For more on the desegregation of the armed forces, see Bernard C. Nalty, *Strength for the Fight: A History of Black Americans in the Military* (Detroit: Free Press, 1986); Gail Lumet Buckley, *American Patriots: The Story of Blacks in the Military from the Revolution to Desert Storm,* 1st ed. (New York: Random House, 2001).

116. Whittington B. Johnson, "The Vinson Court and Racial Segregation, 1946–1953," *Journal of Negro History* 63, no. 3 (1978); August Meier and Elliott Rudwick, "The First Freedom Ride," *Phylon* 30, no. 3 (1969). There was also white backlash, including the formation of the Dixiecrat Party in 1948. See Frederickson, *Dixiecrat Revolt.*

117. For more on the law and similar actions against Asian immigrants, see Roger Daniels, *The Politics of Prejudice: The Anti-Japanese Movement in California and the Struggle for Japanese Exclusion* (Berkeley and Los Angeles: University of California Press, 1962).

118. "*Oyama v. State of California*," *American Journal of International Law* 42, no. 2 (1948): 476–77.

119. In the late 1940s both the Ninth District Court in California and the U.S. District Court, Western Texas District, ruled that "the placing of students of Mexican ancestry in different buildings was arbitrary, discriminatory, and illegal." For more on these cases, see Guadalupe San Miguel Jr., "The Struggle against Separate and Unequal Schools: Middle Class Mexican Americans and the Desegregation Campaign in Texas, 1929–1957," *History of Education Quarterly* 23, no. 3 (1983): 50; Frederick P. Aguirre, "*Mendez v. Westminster School District*: How It Affected *Brown v. Board of Education*," *Journal of Hispanic Higher Education* 4 (2005).

120. Cheryl Lynn Greenberg, "Black and Jewish Responses to Japanese Internment," *Journal of American Ethnic History* 14, no. 2 (1995): 19.

121. Prior to 1952 both Filipinos and Chinese were allowed to migrate to the United States, though in incredibly small numbers. For more on Asian immigration laws and the 1952 act, see Bill Ong Hing, *Defining America through Immigration Policy,* Mapping Racisms (Philadelphia: Temple University Press, 2004); Donna R. Gabaccia, *Immigration and American Diversity: A Social and Cultural History,* Problems in American History (Malden, Mass.: Blackwell Publishers, 2002); Bill Ong Hing, *Making and Remaking Asian America through Immigration Policy, 1850–1990,* Asian America (Stanford, Calif.: Stanford University Press, 1993).

122. "Survey Bares Professional Bias," *Chicago Defender,* January 12, 1946.

123. Spraggs, "Protestants, YWCA Drop Race Segregation Policy"; "Biggest Church Body in America Rips Jim Crow," *Chicago Defender,* March 16, 1946.

124. Spraggs, "Protestants, YWCA Drop Race Segregation Policy"; "Racial Equality in Y.W.C.A. Urged"; Steyskal, "Racial Equality Policy Is Voted by Y.W.C.A."

125. "Congregationalists Ask Racial Equality," *New York Times,* October 30, 1946; "Women Probe Race Issue," *Chicago Defender,* December 14, 1946. For more on the racial work on the United Council of Church Women, see Cherisse Renee Jones, "'How Shall I Sing the Lord's Song?' United Church Women Confront Racial Issues in South Carolina, 1940s–1960s," in *Throwing Off the Cloak*

of Privilege: White Southern Woman Activists in the Civil Rights Era, ed. Gail S. Murray (Gainsville: University of Florida Press, 2004).

126. "Five Denominations Oppose Segregation," *New York Times,* January 31, 1948; "Methodists Rap Past Bigotry, Urge Brotherhood, Give Negro Top Post," *Chicago Defender,* May 15, 1948.

127. "Open-Door Church Asked: Negro Leaders Challenge Whites on Segregation Issue," *New York Times,* December 16, 1944.

128. Grace Elliot, untitled speech, February 28, 1949, unprocessed box 228, 3, YWCA of the USA Records.

129. Venice T. Spraggs, "Miss. Bigots May Topple," *Chicago Defender,* March 23, 1946.

130. Ibid.

131. Eldri Dieson, "Report of Telephone Call, Mrs. Barbara Barnes, Executive Director, YWCA, Jackson, Mississippi," December 3, 1968, microfilm reel 295, YWCA of the USA Records.

132. "AKA Extends Membership to Women of All Races," *Chicago Defender,* October 12, 1946.

133. "Negro Nurses' Group Disbands Near Goal of 42-Year Effort to Attain Integration," *New York Times,* January 27, 1951. For more on black nurses, see Darlene Clark Hine, *Black Women in White: Racial Conflict and Cooperation in the Nursing Profession, 1890–1950* (Bloomington: Indiana University Press, 1989).

134. Even into the early 1950s, none of the YMCA's white southeastern or southwestern branches desegregated. See Nina Mjagkij, *Light in the Darkness: African Americans and the YMCA, 1852–1946* (Lexington: University Press of Kentucky, 1994), 127; Charles Howard Hopkins, *History of the Y.M.C.A. in North America* (New York: Association Press, 1951); "Race Bias Fight Voted by Y.M.C.A.," *New York Times,* May 18, 1946; "Top Y.M.C.A. Unit Asks Full Negro Equality," *New York Times,* May 21, 1950. Despite similar efforts in 1946, other scholars did not treat the YMCA as being on an equal footing with the YWCA in terms of its race efforts. See J. Oscar Lee, "The Status of Racial Integration in Religious Institutions," *Journal of Negro Education* 23, no. 3 (1954).

135. "Report of the General Secretary to the National Board," May 4, 1948, unprocessed box 226, 3, YWCA of the USA Records. For the YMCA's interest in race, see Orlin L. Donhow Jr., Associate Secretary YMCA, to Herbert P. Lansdale Jr., General Secretary of the National Council of YMCAs, May 22, 1961, processed box 25, YWCA of the USA Records. For more on the merger attempts, see Lynn, *Progressive Women in Conservative Times,* 115–16.

136. "Start Nation-Wide Drive for Negro Boy Scouts; Want 900,000," *Chicago Defender,* May 17, 1945; "Racial Harmony, World Food Aid Backed at Girl Scout Convention," *New York Times,* November 5, 1947; "Negro Girl Scouts Grow in Number," *Chicago Defender,* July 16, 1949.

137. The Washington, D.C., branch of the American Association of Univer-

sity Women (AAUW) refused to admit Mary Church Terrell, a black member of the national association. When the national AAUW told the branch to integrate or be dissolved, the D.C. branch sued and won. After losing its appeal, the national AAUW passed new bylaws at its 1949 convention requiring local branches to comply with integration efforts. Although the bylaws were passed overwhelmingly, the vote was not unanimous. For more, see "AAUW Gets Membership Ultimatum," *Washington Post,* April 7, 1948; "University Women Here Told to Admit Negro or Quit Group," *Washington Post,* April 11, 1948; "AAUW Branch Seeks Writ in Race Bias Row," *Washington Post,* April 17, 1948; "Court Upholds AAUW Branch on Racial Membership Issue," *Washington Post,* July 17, 1948; "Racial Test Barred by University Women," *New York Times,* June 23, 1949; "D.C. Court Upheld in AAUW Decision," *Washington Post,* June 14, 1949; "AAUW Takes Stand against Segregation," *Los Angeles Times,* June 23, 1949. For more on this incident, see Helen Laville, "'If the Time Is Not Ripe, Then It Is Your Job to Ripen the Time!' The Transformation of the YWCA in the USA from Segregated Association to Interracial Organization, 1930–1965," *Women's History Review* 15, no. 3 (2006).

138. Taylor, "'On the Edge of Tomorrow'"; Yolanda Barnett Wilkerson, *Interracial Programs of Student YWCA's: An Inquiry under Auspices of the National Student Young Women's Christian Association* (New York: Woman's Press, 1948).

139. Public Affairs Committee Meeting Minutes, April 17, 1946, unprocessed box 8, YWCA of the USA Records.

140. P. S. Finn Jr., letter to the editor, *Times News* (Hendersonville, N.C.), June 17, 1946, processed box 42B, folder "IN—the South, 1942–1947," YWCA of the USA Records.

141. Genevieve Lowry and Mary Sims to Helen Sheley, August 13, 1946, ibid. The Y was not the only organization facing this type of situation. In 1948, 100 Ku Klux Klansmen raided a Girls Scouts camp in Alabama because it was interracial. See "Klan Raids Girl Scouts Camp," *Chicago Defender,* June 19, 1948; "Scouts Ask U.S. Probe of Raid on Dixie Camp," *Chicago Defender,* June 26, 1948.

142. Dorothy Powell and Robert Schumpert to Governor Arnall, July 28, 1946, telegram attached to letter to Elsie Harper, July 28, 1946, unprocessed box 15, YWCA of the USA Records.

143. Mrs. Arthur Forest Anderson to President Truman and Governor Arnall, July 31, 1946, ibid.

144. Governor Ellis Arnall to Eleanor Anderson, August 2, 1946, ibid. For more on the 1946 Monroe lynching, see Laura Wexler, *Fire in a Canebrake: The Last Mass Lynching in America* (New York: Scribner, 2003).

145. Lawson, *To Secure These Rights,* 9.

146. Marjorie Mudge to Arthur Spigarn, August 14, 1946, unprocessed box 15, YWCA of the USA Records.

147. Rosenwald Fund, unprocessed box 34, folder "1946–1947," YWCA of the USA Records.

148. Myra Smith, "Dear Executive Director," April 4, 1946, processed papers, box 42A, YWCA of the USA Records.

149. Seattle Public Affairs Committee Meeting Minutes, May 21, 1946, box 23, folder "Public Affairs Committee—Meetings, 1946–1947," Seattle YWCA Papers.

150. Myra Smith, "Dear Executive Director," April 4, 1946.

151. Board of Directors Meeting, Portland YWCA, October 26, 1948, box 13, Portland YWCA Papers.

152. "YWCA Pioneers in Democracy," *Ebony,* August 1947, 39.

153. Horace R. Cayton, "A Study of Race Relations," *New York Times,* April 17, 1949.

154. Ibid. The Y's postwar publications include Wilkerson, *Interracial Programs of Student YWCA's;* Dorothy Sabiston and Margaret Hiller, *Toward Better Race Relations* (New York: Woman's Press, 1949); Dorothy I. Height, *Step by Step with Interracial Groups* (New York: Woman's Press, 1946).

155. Elizabeth Bradley, "Modern Women and Community Organization," *Journal of Educational Sociology* 23, no. 3 (1949): 164; Lee, "The Status of Racial Integration in Religious Institutions"; Lynn, *Progressive Women in Conservative Times,* 64–66.

156. Height, *Step by Step with Interracial Groups,* 1 (emphasis in original).

157. Charles S. Johnson, "The Next Decade in Race Relations," *Journal of Negro Education* 13, no. 3 (1944): 444. For more on Johnson's Race Relations Institute, see Katrina M. Sanders, *"Intelligent and Effective Direction": The Fisk University Race Relations Institute and the Struggle for Civil Rights, 1944–1969* (New York: Peter Lang, 2005).

158. "Federal Council Scores Racial Bias: Calls for Renunciation of Segregation in Proclaiming Race Relations Sunday," *New York Times,* February 6, 1947.

159. Greenberg, "Black and Jewish Responses to Japanese Internment"; Cheryl Lynn Greenberg, *Troubling the Waters: Black-Jewish Relations in the American Century* (Princeton, N.J.: Princeton University Press, 2006).

160. Greenberg, "Black and Jewish Responses to Japanese Internment," 8.

161. There were local multiracial coalitions led by black and Jewish groups and individuals, most notably in Los Angeles. As one scholar argued, it was "the uniqueness" of Los Angeles, as a truly multiracial and multiethnic city, that "demanded . . . an impetus for aligning the fight for black empowerment with that of other groups." Regina Freer, "L.A. Race Woman: Charlotta Bass and the Complexities of Black Political Development in Los Angeles," *American Quarterly* 56, no. 3 (2004): 624. One could argue that Los Angeles and the Y were similar, in that both represented multiracial populations before, during, and after the war. For more on multiracial efforts in Los Angeles, see George J. Sanchez, "'What's Good for Boyle Heights Is Good for the Jews': Creating Multiculturalism on the Eastside during the 1950s," *American Quarterly* 56, no. 3 (2004); De Graaf, Mul-

roy, and Taylor, *Seeking El Dorado;* David J. Leonard, "'The Little Fuehrer Invades Los Angeles': The Emergence of a Black-Jewish Coalition after World War II," *American Jewish History* 92, no. 1 (2005); Leonard, *Battle for Los Angeles.* For more on postwar coalitions in a broader context, see Ronald Takaki, *Double Victory: A Multicultural History of America in World War II,* 1st ed. (New York: Little, Brown, 2000).

162. H. H. Giles, "The Present Status and Programs of Private Intergroup Relations Agencies," *Journal of Negro Education* 20, no. 3 (1951): 412. In a survey on effective civil rights organizations, the top organizations listed (in order) were the NAACP, the NUL, the Y, the National Council of Jewish Women, the American Friends Service Committee (AFSC), and the Japanese American Citizens League, all of which were either race or religion based. Like the Y, the AFSC was a white-majority Christian organization, but it did not boast the same multiracial membership as the Y. Going into the early 1950s, the Y had more than 3 million participants, including over 600,000 members. Within the membership, 83,000 were black, 10,000 were white ethnic immigrants, 5,000 were Asian American, and 400 were Native American. Mrs. Arthur Forest Anderson to Senator Alexander Wiley, Chairman, Senate Judiciary Committee, February 5, 1948, unprocessed box 15, YWCA of the USA Records. For more on the AFSC, see Lynn, *Progressive Women in Conservative Times.*

163. "National Board Report: Progress toward Racial Inclusiveness: 1946–1958," March 1958, unprocessed box 171, 3, YWCA of the USA Records. New committees were formed throughout the decade, including the Committee on Racial Inclusiveness and the Interdepartmental Committee to Coordinate Work on Racial Integration.

164. It was also common for many to be members of nonracial and nonreligious organizations, such as the American Association of University Women and the League of Women Voters. But once again, these groups did not offer the same diversity as the Y.

165. Belinda Robnett, *How Long? How Long? African American Women in the Struggle for Civil Rights* (New York: Oxford University Press, 1997), 45.

166. Seattle Board of Directors Meeting, October 14, 1952, box 23, folder 1, Seattle YWCA Papers.

167. Seattle Program Planning Committee, "Basic Standards, Program and Services," May 28, 1951, ibid.

168. 1955 Info Sheet, box 23, folder 2, Seattle YWCA Papers.

169. Lois Gratz to Savilla Simons, December 9, 1954, unprocessed box 30, YWCA of the USA Records.

170. Mary Jane Willet, "Report of the Ad Hoc Work Group re: Implications of the Supreme Court Decision for Desegregation in the YWCA," October 8, 1954, unprocessed box 170, 5–6, YWCA of the USA Records.

171. Grace Loucks Elliot, "Ten-Year Report of the General Secretary to the

National Board," September 30, 1952, unprocessed box 226, Grace Elliot Papers folder, 5, YWCA of the USA Records.

172. Elliot, untitled speech, February 28, 1949, 9.

173. For more on the *Brown* decision, see Richard Kluger, *Simple Justice: The History of* Brown v. Board of Education *and Black America's Struggle for Equality* (New York: Vintage Books, 1977); Peter F. Lau, *From the Grassroots to the Supreme Court:* Brown v. Board of Education *and American Democracy,* Constitutional Conflicts (Durham, N.C.: Duke University Press, 2004).

174. Jessamine Fenner, "Fuller Inclusiveness for Professional Staff," *YWCA Magazine,* February 1956; 1949–1950 Narrative Report to National Board, box 10, folder 102, 10, Mount Vernon (N.Y.) YWCA Papers, Social Welfare Archives, University of Minnesota, Minneapolis. Dorothy Takechi served as the executive director of the Mount Vernon Y from 1950 to 1952. Prior to Takechi, the highest-ranking nonwhite branch staffer at a central Y was Marjorie Humber Jackson, an African American who served as the associate executive director at the Portland Y from 1946 to 1949. The first nonwhite woman elected president of the local board of a main branch was Helen J. Wilkins Claytor at the Grand Rapids, Michigan, branch in 1949. Claytor would later become the first black president of the National Board in 1967.

175. Dorothy Takechi, "Inclusiveness and the YWCA," 1954, processed box 15, YWCA of the USA Records.

176. Dorothy Takechi to Jean Willett, March 4, 1955, unprocessed box 30, YWCA of the USA Records.

177. "Ad Hoc Work Group re: Implications of the Supreme Court Decision for the YWCA, 1954," unprocessed box 30, YWCA of the USA Records; Amelia Wagner to Savilla Simons, January 3, 1955, ibid.

178. See Takechi, "Inclusiveness and the YWCA"; "Meeting on Desegregation, Atlanta University, Atlanta Georgia," December 15–18, 1954, unprocessed box 30, YWCA of the USA Records; Katherine Beppler, Personnel Services, to Dorothy Takechi, October 1, 1954, ibid.

179. Takechi was not the only Japanese American woman on the national staff at the time, but she was the most prominent and the highest ranking. By the time Takechi retired in 1978, her leadership and presence were no longer anomalies; it was common for women of all races to serve in leadership positions at both the local and national levels. For more on the active or absent presence of Japanese Americans and the subsequent impact on racial constructions in the Cold War, see Caroline Chung Simpson, *An Absent Presence: Japanese Americans in Postwar American Culture, 1945–1960* (Durham, N.C.: Duke University Press, 2001).

180. Dorothy Takechi to Roy Wilkins, June 25, 1954, NAACP Papers, II A 76 YWCA.

181. Report to National Board Committee on Basic Standards, September 1951, box 2, folder 6, Chicago YWCA Papers.

182. Executive Staff Meeting, January 4, 1956, box 17, folder 4, Chicago YWCA Papers.

183. Executive Director's Report, April 30, 1956, box 1, folder 22, Los Angeles YWCA Papers; PAC Meeting, January 27, 1958, box 23, folder "PAC—Meetings, 1958–1959," Seattle YWCA Papers; Ruth Marshall, Associate Executive Director, to Senator Edward Thys, April 14, 1947, box 9, "Indians—Misc. to 1955," Minneapolis YWCA Papers.

184. Myra A. Smith, "Progress toward Integration," *YWCA Magazine,* March 1952, 13.

185. For more on the NAACP legal campaigns, see Kluger, *Simple Justice;* Jack Greenberg, *Crusaders in the Courts: How a Dedicated Band of Lawyers Fought for the Civil Rights Revolution* (New York: Basic Books, 1994). For more on the Baton Rouge boycott, see Aldon D. Morris, *The Origins of the Civil Rights Movement: Black Communities Organizing for Change* (New York: Free Press, 1984), 17–25.

186. For more on the Montgomery bus boycott, see Adam Fairclough, *To Redeem the Soul of America: The Southern Christian Leadership Conference and Martin Luther King, Jr.* (Athens: University of Georgia Press, 1987); Jo Ann Gibson Robinson and David J. Garrow, *The Montgomery Bus Boycott and the Women Who Started It: The Memoir of Jo Ann Gibson Robinson* (Knoxville: University of Tennessee Press, 1987); Morris, *Origins of the Civil Rights Movement.*

187. Proceedings of the Twentieth National Convention, 1955, processed box 2, 50, YWCA of the USA Records.

188. Ibid., 237–39.

189. Proceedings of the Twenty-First National Convention, 1958, processed box 2, 145–98, YWCA of the USA Records.

190. Ibid., 151.

James and Esther Cooper Jackson, Communism, and the 1950s Black Freedom Movement

Sara Rzeszutek Haviland

On June 20, 1951, four-year-old Kathy Jackson's father, Communist leader James Jackson, disappeared, and her nightmares became reality. Her mother's hand would tighten around hers when they spotted FBI agents in fedoras and dark trench coats as they walked in their Brooklyn neighborhood. Her mother's normally pleasant Virginia accent turned harsh when she picked up the telephone and heard an unfamiliar voice. Grown men in suits watched Kathy play that summer, and when they approached her on the streets, she was so terrified that afterward she refused to leave her mother's side.[1] "They can't put little children in jail, can they?" she asked her mother.[2] Her big sister, eight-year-old Harriet, was tougher. She could draw strength from memories of her father that Kathy had not yet acquired. Harriet understood that her activist parents often faced such struggles, and she "contemptuously pointed [the FBI agents] out to her playmates."[3] Esther Cooper Jackson could not answer her younger daughter's questions about where her father had gone or when he would be back. Like other wives of disappeared Communist husbands, she simply did not know. She could only explain that he had vanished because he was trying to make a better future for his daughters and other children across the country, and the people in charge wanted to stop him.

Kathy quickly learned that the nation's highest law enforcement officers would not concern themselves with protecting her. Rather, they were out to frighten little children into betraying their families; they would haunt the children's imaginations and let them know that, whatever their fathers had done wrong, the children would pay the price. Esther Cooper Jackson believed the FBI agents were "particularly vindictive toward us because we're Negroes."[4] She and her family had left the Deep South in 1947, where their efforts to change the racial order had been met with both a white supremacist and an anticommunist backlash. On moving north and becoming active in Detroit, Cooper Jackson witnessed the way anticommunism shaped the experiences of its black residents, who sought to improve their political and economic conditions through union organization and economic activism. She and her family moved to New York City in 1950, and by the time her husband went underground a year later, Cooper Jackson fully understood the consequences of the early Cold War and McCarthyism on the black freedom movement and on her family's well-being.

Tangled notions of liberal democracy in the early 1950s resulted in the undemocratic treatment of the families of Communists and shaped the way activists approached the black freedom movement. In other words, the domestic effects of Cold War politics changed the black freedom struggle by shaping the family lives of black activists. For the Jackson family, the early Cold War represented an era of unparalleled fear and repression, but the injustice of the period motivated and empowered them to continue to work for change. In an era when images of the idealized nuclear family reinforced anticommunist liberalism, Cooper Jackson exposed the devastating effects that political repression had on her family. In addition, she argued that James Jackson's particular political predicament and the treatment of his family were symptomatic of a larger change in the struggle against racial injustice. While his wife fought for his freedom, James Jackson worked to reinvigorate Communist participation in civil rights as he moved about the country to avoid capture by the FBI. During his time away, Jackson wrote extensively on the black freedom struggle, and he believed that his absence would help create a better world for his daughters to inherit.

Cold War liberalism put a profound strain on the relationship between the 1950s civil rights movement and the Communist Party, USA (CPUSA), and James Jackson believed that rebuilding that relationship would go a long way toward fulfilling his overall purpose. Jackson's underground writing advised the party to become active in civil rights and criticized its outdated racial positions. As the party's southern regional director, Jackson maintained ties with activists working on civil rights. His connections and insights not only helped the party develop a realistic position on the situation in the 1950s South but also served to maintain a link between the CPUSA and black activists at a time when the relationship between the two was tenuous.

In 1951 James Jackson was indicted under the Smith Act for "conspiracy to teach or advocate the violent overthrow of the government." A peacetime sedition law, the Smith Act had originally been passed in

1940 as the Alien Registration Act. It allowed the government to pursue activists who discussed "overthrowing the government by 'force and violence'" and deport "aliens who had once belonged to an organization that advocated force and violence."[5] Instead of standing trial immediately in a potentially dangerous political climate, Jackson went underground until 1955, and his family became subjected to constant FBI harassment.

It is nearly impossible to trace James Jackson's time underground and verify his precise positions and activities. Jackson seldom spoke during his time away, even to his wife, or after he reemerged. As a black fugitive from 1951 to 1955, Jackson was in a more precarious position than that of his white counterparts. Finding suitable housing for Jackson and Henry Winston, another African American, proved challenging for the Communist Party (CP). As Gil Green notes, "If they lived in black ghetto communities, which were subject to far more rigorous police surveillance, accidental discovery was obviously a greater possibility. . . . Yet if Winston or Jackson were to live with white families, they would be trapped indoors."[6] Jackson spent some time in the Midwest, and he may have visited the South. Party member Charlene Mitchell once hosted Jackson in St. Louis, Missouri. He also spent some of his time on a farm in upstate New York, where locals knew him only as "Crazy Joe." During his time underground, Jackson continued to influence leftist thought on civil rights, writing articles under the pseudonym Charles P. Mann (i.e., "CP Man").[7]

Popular Front politics had vanished by the time James Jackson was indicted, and the interracial left-wing coalitions forged in the New Deal South were relics of a bygone era. In Birmingham, Alabama, a former center of the Popular Front civil rights movement, the City Commission outlawed not just the Communist Party but all "liberal and progressive organizations" on July 18, 1950. The ordinance was not unique to the Magic City; similar local laws gained popularity in Gary, Indiana; Peoria, Illinois; Chattanooga, Tennessee; Atlanta, Georgia; and other major and minor industrial hubs across the country.[8] At the federal level, loyalty oath programs led government employees to either hide their questionable political affiliations or face removal from their positions. Twelve top-tier CP leaders had already been indicted, tried, and convicted over the course of 1948 and 1949. Two years later the Supreme Court upheld their convictions in *U.S. v. Dennis,* a ruling that prompted Jackson and other indicted Communists to become fugitives.

In the South, conservative forces linked the CP's effort to court black activists with the fight against Jim Crow, effectively driving the Popular

Front's civil rights organizing and unionizing efforts out of business.[9] The connection between anticommunism and racism went beyond party-influenced groups, forcing moderate civil rights activists to downplay radical economic solutions. Although some radical groups remained active, including the Southern Conference Educational Fund, organizations across the Left were weakened.[10] Given the indictments of Communist leaders and the nationwide panic over any social critique that resembled socialism, even activists who had no direct ties with the CP faded into quiet conformity.

Although anticommunist hysteria led to the persecution of a range of individuals, the CP leadership bore more guilt in the public eye than did celebrities, activists, and ordinary citizens who were merely guilty by association.[11] After all, party leaders were charged with violating a specific law, the Smith Act, and as J. Edgar Hoover put it, they were responsible for trying "to poison our thinking about the issues of the day: social reforms, peace, politics, veterans', women's, and youth problems."[12] It was easy for anticommunists to generate fear and rally support around the Smith Act. On June 25, 1950, Soviet-equipped North Korea invaded U.S.-backed South Korea, making the peninsula the first hot spot of the Cold War. The U.S. military responded with a "police action" that lasted for more than three years.[13] In addition, the trial and 1953 execution of nuclear weapons spy Julius Rosenberg and his wife, Ethel, reminded Americans that they stood on the brink of disaster because of homegrown Communists.[14]

The first 12 CP leaders convicted under the Smith Act were awaiting sentencing when 126 additional individuals, including 21 "second-string" Communist leaders, were indicted in 1951.[15] The hostile political atmosphere intensified when the Supreme Court upheld those convictions in *U.S. v. Dennis*. This decision led the CP leadership to create the "second cadre," which would operate underground and included some of the leaders facing prosecution and prison. Of the initial twelve who were sentenced, only seven—Benjamin Davis Jr., Eugene Dennis, John Gates, Irving Potash, Jack Stachel, John Williamson, and Carl Winter—surrendered themselves immediately to serve their time. (William Z. Foster's case had been severed from theirs because of his failing health.) The remaining four—Gus Hall, Robert Thompson, Henry Winston, and Gil Green—went underground and were known by the CPUSA community as "unavailables." Among the second-stringers, Fred Fine, William Marron, Sidney Steinberg, and James Jackson "had not been at home when the FBI showed up."[16] They disappeared before standing trial.

The FBI launched a nationwide search for the missing men. News articles urged citizens "to join in the intense manhunt for the eight Communist leaders." Every American was "in a position to assist the FBI in locating and capturing the Red fugitives."[17] For the CP, creating the second cadre to operate underground was a viable alternative to having so many of its top leaders incarcerated. Putting some of the indicted and convicted Communists into the second cadre meant that if the remaining leadership faced indictment or incarceration in the hostile political environment, a covert group of experienced party functionaries could stay active.

Regardless of whether it was ultimately productive, given their situations, members of the second cadre and their families made reasoned political moves in the McCarthy era. James and Esther Jackson had envisioned a postwar world where the South would be united under a left-wing, interracial, labor-oriented NAACP. They imagined that "Double V" (victory at home and victory abroad) would be realized through socialist-influenced economic reform, political equality, and integration.[18] They knew the postwar era would not be without difficulties, but few anticipated the conservative backlash that drove so many of them underground. The second cadre and its support system of wives, children, and extended family kept alive some of the hope of the World War II years.

The CPUSA's response to the *Dennis* decision separated families by forcing members into hiding, and the FBI used the rhetoric of family as a weapon in its war on communism. In 1956 FBI director Hoover declared that in the fight against "crime and communism . . . there are no careers as important as those of homemaker and mother." Vice President Richard Nixon echoed that sentiment in 1959 during his "Kitchen Debate" with Soviet premier Nikita Khrushchev, stating that America's effort "to make easier the life of our housewives" was a common and democratic ideal around the globe.[19] Targeting suburban middle-class gender ideals became a simple way for politicians to gain support for their side in a complicated ideological struggle. To this audience, Jackson's alleged crime and subsequent disappearance constituted a heinous assault on U.S. democracy, and his family became a unique tool both in the FBI's pursuit of him and in his defense. Although his family had no contact with him for nearly five years, the FBI left no member of the extended Jackson and Cooper families alone.

For the families of the second cadre, McCarthyism introduced an era of fear that was unlike the anxiety about communism most Americans felt. The FBI waged a "war of nerves" against the families of Smith Act defendants.[20] Tactics included surveillance, harassment, threats, and interference in the ability to maintain incomes, homes, cars, and any semblance of normalcy. FBI harassment engendered opposition from activists on the Left, and these groups often comprised friends, family, and acquaintances of the unavailables. Esther Cooper Jackson and other activists recast questions of political affiliation and national loyalty as racial and gendered assaults that stood in contrast to the nuclear family–oriented language of liberal postwar democracy.

The FBI spent nearly $1 million a year to tail Smith Act families.[21] Agents forced their way into homes, intimidated neighbors, and used outright threats. For instance, FBI agents confronted Lillian Green, who was looking after her own children and her brother's children at a summer cottage, and made it clear that they meant business. Green implored them to leave, but they refused and said, "We don't use guns much . . . but sometimes a man we're hunting gets shot. Now you wouldn't want that to happen to your husband, would you?"[22] James Jackson's mother, Clara, also received a threatening call from the FBI. After she told them she did not know her son's whereabouts, the agents pressed harder. "Supposing your husband were to drop dead tonight, how would you get in touch with your son to let him know?" they asked.[23] Although they did not directly threaten to harm James Jackson Sr., the menacing call suggested to Clara Jackson that the FBI would go to great lengths to ferret out the fugitives.

In response to FBI harassment, the families of the unavailables formed the Families Committee of Smith Act Victims. The organization was composed primarily of women whose husbands faced prosecution, and they worked "to give financial, material, and emotional assistance to the children and spouses of the Smith Act victims and the prisoners themselves."[24] As sociologist Deborah Gerson argues, "the Families Committee resisted state repression with a strategy that made use of the valorization of family. The alliance between patriotism and familialism was challenged by women who pointed to the state as the destroyer of family freedom, security, and happiness."[25] Gerson suggests that the Families Committee provided Communist wives and mothers with an opportunity to become more politically empowered and take hold of their families' fates.[26] Esther Cooper Jackson worked with the Families Committee and made use of its support.

Race also gave meaning to Cooper Jackson's political activism on behalf of her family in the context of the liberal anticommunism of the 1950s. Historian Ruth Feldstein writes that in the 1950s it was "through [the] rendering of politics as personal and psychological that the 'good' and 'bad' mother—black and white—did political work in the reconfiguration of liberalism."[27] Cooper Jackson confronted cultural expectations that required a "good" black mother to be a loyal wife, a patriotic citizen, emotional, and active on behalf of her race.[28] These ideals created conflicts for Cooper Jackson. She could not simultaneously be construed as both patriotic and loyal to her husband, who had fled the justice system. She could not exemplify patriotism and remain active on behalf of her race through organizations that supported her loyalty to her fugitive husband. Her children needed a mother who was strong and composed, not emotional. Cooper Jackson navigated the cultural requirements for a black wife and mother as a victim of governmental harassment and as an activist who fought for a United States that embodied its own rhetoric of democracy.

As Cooper Jackson's situation illustrates, the FBI's assault on the Jackson family was not only contrary to the "valorization of family" but also a barrier to political unity within the movement. In the postwar years the NAACP responded to the need to distinguish itself from the Left. The NAACP was part of many progressive activists' résumés, including Cooper Jackson's, but to keep functioning as a liberal organization, the association followed suit, accepting the government's embodiment of Cold War liberalism. As the McCarthy era took hold, black activists who had worked toward civil rights in the Popular Front years needed to choose between groups that incorporated a Marxist influence and groups that worked within the existing political system, such as the NAACP. The path in between no longer existed.[29] When James Jackson went underground, his wife saw his absence and the assault on his communism as detrimental. Although the NAACP's postwar achievements were significant, Cooper Jackson believed that the greatest opportunity to defend her husband and the struggle for racial equality came from groups that fought the dominant political rejection of communism instead of embracing it.

Cooper Jackson pointed out the contradictions between the federal government's enforcement of civil rights and its pursuit of political fugitives as a way of highlighting the link between the persecution of families and the black freedom movement. The time and money the FBI devoted to harassing Smith Act families in the name of democracy was counterbalanced by the bureau's limited resources to enforce equal justice—a powerful symbol of that very democracy. The investigation of the murder of civil rights leader Harry T. Moore provides a case in point. Cooper Jackson demonstrated the contradiction between the FBI's inconsequential investigation of Moore's death and its constant harassment of her family. In so doing, she connected the welfare of her children with the advancement of the black freedom movement.

On Christmas evening in 1951, Florida NAACP leader Harry T. Moore and his family went to sleep in the small town of Mims. During the night an explosion rocked the household. A bomb had been placed underneath the house, and Moore died before Christmas was over. His wife, Harriette, died of her injuries a day after her husband's funeral. The FBI was a quiet presence in Mims after the murders. The bureau made little information public, and it eventually faced severe criticism for its inability to apprehend the killers. At the 1952 NAACP convention in Oklahoma City, delegates passed a resolution singling out the FBI for its failure in the Moore case. It asserted that the FBI was "almost invariably unable to cope with violent criminal action by bigoted, prejudiced Americans against Negro Americans." Over the next several years the FBI failed to solve the murders, even though at least twelve agents were officially assigned to the case. Yet one researcher who visited the area noted that "no FBI agents were to be found in the community."[30]

Although the case disappeared from public notice, Esther Cooper Jackson remained cognizant that the FBI never apprehended any suspects in the Moore bombing. After suddenly finding herself without her husband's financial or emotional support, and having no idea when he would return, Cooper Jackson was forced to cope with the immediate needs of her family alone. She secured a part-time job and set out to enroll four-year-old Kathy in nursery school. Kathy was admitted to Cleveland Day Nursery in Brooklyn, which provided subsidized child care for struggling families, but within two months Kathy was expelled because her mother allegedly had "undisclosed sources of income."[31] Cooper Jackson could not ascertain the source of this allegation, but she believed the FBI agents who had been hounding her family since June were to blame. She wrote, "unable to locate their father, the FBI has decided to take it out on the children and wife."[32] In a letter to the editor of the *Union,* Cooper Jackson connected her family's harassment to the Moore situation in Florida:

A month has passed and still no arrests in the Christmas night murder of Mr. and Mrs. Harry T. Moor [*sic*]! A month in which the authorities say an investigation is still taking place yet nothing of significance has been issued by the FBI or the Department of Justice. . . . Why are they so silent? Is it because they are busy elsewhere hounding the families of those very people whose life has been devoted to the things Harry Moor stood for—justice, equality and freedom? . . . This F.B.I. which utilizes great power and authority to hound young Negro children finds no funds or manpowers to unearth the killers of my people![33]

Kathy Jackson's expulsion from nursery school generated attention from the black press as well. Journalist James L. Hicks of the *Baltimore Afro-American* printed a front-page article on the issue, referring to the FBI's failure in the Moore case. He argued, "It looks like some of those eight FBI boys frittering away their time trailing innocent four-year-old children down the streets of Brooklyn could be more profitably employed tracking down bomb-throwing killers in the everglades of Florida."[34]

The suggestion that Cooper Jackson had unreported income was baseless, but Cleveland Day Nursery officials refused to allow her to appeal the expulsion. In response, she wrote to the editor of the *New York Daily Compass,* stating, "Since keeping [Kathy] in nursery school is the only way I have been able to seek and find employment, the effect of this expulsion order can only be interpreted as an attempt to starve the family and deny the children a chance at a normal life."[35] Cooper Jackson believed that Kathy's expulsion from nursery school was part of the FBI's efforts to disrupt the families of the fugitives, not an effort to "get its man."[36]

Until Cooper Jackson took her story to the public in January 1952, the New York Welfare Department flatly refused to help the family. But once Jackson's allies heard the appalling details of a child's persecution by the FBI, they sprang to action. The Families Committee of Smith Act Victims organized a response to Kathy's expulsion, highlighting the connection between political repression and racism.[37] The group sent a delegation of eighteen people to discuss the situation with John H. Lewis, community relations director of the New York Welfare Department, who informed the group that Kathy's case "would be decided without prejudice of color, race, or political belief."[38] But, as Families Committee leaders Peggy Dennis and Sophie Gerson noted, "The father of little Kathy Jackson is Dr. James Jackson, noted Negro Communist leader, who is being sought by the FBI. . . . Hoover's cloak-and-dagger men, in their fruitless efforts to locate the father, have held as virtual political hostages the two small daughters and the wife of Dr. Jackson. . . . Mrs. Esther Jackson, as a young Negro woman, had with difficulty found a suitable job and her continuance in that position is contingent upon her daughter's maintenance in a nursery school—a facility not easily available to a Negro child."[39] The Families

Committee argued that the Welfare Department's initial refusal to intervene "can leave no doubt that the issue of 'color, race or political belief' is very much in evidence in the shocking discrimination and victimization of the Jackson family."[40] After substantial protest from the community, educators, social workers, family, and friends, Cooper Jackson and the Families Committee convinced the Welfare Department on January 30 to stay the expulsion order indefinitely.[41]

The connection among race, Kathy's expulsion, the Moore murders, and the victimization of Smith Act families offers a window into an important moment in the history of the black freedom movement. The Popular Front's decline opened the door for moderate and liberal groups to make progress, yet black leaders in the Popular Front did not simply stop acting because they faced FBI harassment and public scorn. It is important to examine their continued activism in the early Cold War years because the experiences of individuals like Cooper Jackson offer insight into how the movement changed. Instead of fighting for earlier goals such as interracial working-class unity, black leftist activists in the 1950s needed to refocus their attention on more immediate issues of political liberty and freedom from harassment for the sake of their families. Cooper Jackson's activism became centered on protecting her family from political persecution and racial discrimination, and this shift reflects the changing nature of the black freedom movement during the Cold War.

In addition to working with the Families Committee, Cooper Jackson combined her dedication to her family with her devotion to the movement by supporting the National Committee to Defend Negro Leadership (NCDNL). When President Harry Truman's secretary of labor, Lewis Schwellenbach, proposed outlawing the Communist Party, individuals and groups with CPUSA ties formed the NCDNL in 1947. The group responded with a petition, urging the president to outlaw segregation and lynching instead. More than a dozen black newspapers ran the petition, which boasted the signature of Paul Robeson.[42] When those first twelve party leaders were indicted in 1948, the NCDNL emphasized the situations of fugitives Henry Winston and Benjamin Davis as important assaults on the black freedom movement. The organization characterized the Smith Act as "a menace confronting the Negro people."[43]

After her husband was indicted, Cooper Jackson argued that he had a democratic right to his Communist political affiliation and that his absence was a blow to the black freedom movement. Cooper Jackson wrote a pamphlet titled *This Is My Husband: Fighter for His People, Political*

Refugee, first published by the NCDNL in April 1953 and reissued in two additional printings later that year. The thirty-six-page pamphlet made a persuasive case for the intersection of the struggles of families victimized by the Smith Act and the struggles of the black freedom movement, all the while fusing Cooper Jackson's romantic love for her husband, her family's welfare, and their political goals.

This Is My Husband began with a statement on Cooper Jackson's emotional suffering, but she situated her pain in the context of the connections between politics and romance, setting the tone for the pamphlet. She wrote, "It is a hard thing to confine oneself merely to making words about one's beloved upon whose face one has not looked for what seems an eternity of time. I want so much to have now his warm comradeship; to hear again from his lips those winged words of exciting promise as he would give voice to his confident dreams of a free and bountiful new life for the world's humblest peoples."[44] She detailed the FBI's persecution of her family, again contrasting her situation to the bureau's desultory handling of the Moore case.

The pamphlet highlighted the impact of the Smith Act on black activists. Referring to the Supreme Court's upholding of the act in *U.S. v. Dennis,* Cooper Jackson quoted black lawyers Earl B. Dickerson and Richard E. Westbrooks as arguing, "The inevitable effect of the Supreme Court decision on the Smith Act is to undermine, if not destroy, effective protest with regard to government practices and policies inimical to the welfare of Negroes."[45] The lawyers suggested that the Smith Act intimidated black activists to the point of silence by prosecuting high-level black party leaders. The pamphlet suggested that governmental attacks on communism and Communist-influenced protest nourished the economic disenfranchisement of poor and working-class blacks, who had been empowered through the unionization efforts of the Popular Front years. The indictment of James Jackson, then, was an outright assault against attempts to build "a nation in which the workers will toil to enrich *themselves* and not a small set of exploiting industrialists, a nation in which poor farming folk will own the land they till."[46]

This Is My Husband offered readers a portrait of James Jackson as a real person, not a Communist subversive who was blindly taking orders from Moscow. It highlighted the growth of his political perspective within the context of his Richmond upbringing. James Jackson was raised by highly educated parents, and he was afforded opportunities that many of his friends were denied, but his exposure to extreme poverty within his community led him to apply Marxist theory to practical change.[47] Cooper Jackson mobilized her husband's upbringing in his defense, arguing that his observations of the "soul-killing drudgery" of his poor Richmond neighbors' "toil and sufferings, yet ever-hopeful spirit and striving for better things . . . inspired him to write, to speak, to join in and to lead struggles in their behalf."[48] Cooper Jackson invited readers to understand how a young boy's exposure to disparate opportunities for white and black, poor and privileged people in a neighborhood could lead to the development of a Marxist political perspective. James Jackson, she argued, was not an unfeeling Soviet dupe; rather, he was a compassionate man who sought to end the struggle and suffering of economically disadvantaged people, particularly those whose circumstances grew out of the South's racist culture.

Cooper Jackson never accepted the charge that her husband had committed a crime by acting on his political convictions and learning from the ideas of foreign leaders. She asked, "Should that search for answers to the most burning problems of every Negro and every worker stop at the continental borders of the United States? Concede this and our nation will soon become a benighted wasteland of 'super patriotic' bigots."[49] Cooper Jackson noted the exchange of revolutionary ideas between the United States and France and argued that the spirit of change abroad had inspired Thomas Jefferson to refine the democratic ideals in the early republic. Frederick Douglass had drawn strength, she argued, for the antislavery cause in the United States from Britain's abolitionist movement. *This Is My Husband* simultaneously articulated a firm political argument in her husband's defense and highlighted the couple's romantic and familial devotion, countering the common assumption that Communist families prioritized their political goals over their own unity.

While Esther Cooper Jackson was illustrating how her husband's disappearance and legal difficulties were direct assaults on her family and the black freedom movement, James Jackson continued to participate in civil rights discourse by encouraging Communists to change with the times. His "unavailability" afforded him certain freedoms. Party leaders who went to prison were unable to write as freely and extensively on political issues as those who went underground. As Peggy Dennis wrote of her husband's imprisonment, "a special ruling was made in Washington that . . . none of Eugene Dennis' [prison] letters could be published or quoted in public, and that he could not comment specifically on the Communist Party or 'communism.'" Had he done so, he would have faced solitary confinement and the revocation of his correspondence privileges.[50] Although Jackson was surely concerned with his family's well-being, he also believed that his decision to avoid prison would ultimately be beneficial to his children's futures, and he strove to make the most of his time out of the spotlight.

The party leaders who remained aboveground continued to rely on and express their appreciation for Jackson's sacrifice. In a statement they wrote, "We say to Comrade Jim Jackson, elected leader of the Party in the South and driven into hiding by the bankrupt US bourgeoisie—wherever you may be—you should know we are making good use of the legacy you have left us . . . and thus your leadership still guides us."[51] The CPUSA's statement suggests that the second cadre's influence was not diminished by its unavailability. Party leaders who were in hiding had left behind intellectual support for the aboveground operatives. The party also sought to support Esther Cooper Jackson and her two daughters and assured Jackson that "your family is now ours."[52]

Jackson continued to function underground as a prominent party expert on the issues black Americans were confronting. He covertly reported and analyzed the major developments in the freedom movement during the CP's period of tumult. Gil Green, who saw Jackson several times while the two were unavailable, recalled that Jackson continued to function as southern regional director from 1951 to 1955. He wrote that Jackson's "style of work was not all that different. Conditions in the South even prior to the witch hunt had never made possible the open functioning of the Party. . . . Even in the best of times, CP organizers worked in the South at their peril."[53]

While Jackson was in hiding, he worked on evaluating party policy on racial issues and highlighting black Americans' efforts in the South so that the CPUSA could uphold its reputation as a frontline fighter for racial equality. Jackson's key points in all his writings emphasized that although the civil rights movement was distinct from the CPUSA, it required the party's support. As a party centrist, he believed the CPUSA would benefit by adapting to changing U.S. political discourse and offering full support to civil rights organizations. His earlier work with the Southern Negro Youth Congress allowed him to see the emerging civil rights movement as a mass struggle the party could assist but should not co-opt. Jackson believed that racial oppression in the South required a people's movement that reflected the needs, desires, and ideas of black southerners, not party hard-liners.

Jackson focused on how black efforts to gain political rights and eliminate racial violence were relevant to the activism of other progressives, not how communism or other leftist movements were important in the lives of black southerners. This distinction offers insight into how Jackson employed communism in his own political life. For him, it was a relevant and vital means to achieving social and economic justice for all. But he saw clearly that black southerners were the primary agents of change in their own lives and were capable of making informed political decisions. By encouraging Communists and other progressives to lend their support to and act with black southerners, Jackson was attempting to move the discourse away from the notion that Communists were out to take advantage of African Americans. Instead, Jackson argued, "Communists . . . above all others must appreciate and energetically fight for . . . democratic reform . . . : first of all because it is right, and just, and would represent some measure of dignity to an outrageously oppressed people."[54] In other words, Communists should join with and follow other social movements, including the African American campaign for freedom.

Jackson's disappearance into the Communist underground represented one way Cold War tensions shaped the movement. Jackson's political affiliation drove his position on racial justice movements further from the mainstream. Meanwhile, movement tactics shifted in part as a response to the Cold War. In nearly every major civil rights crisis that emerged in the mid- and late 1950s, the image of U.S. democracy projected abroad was compromised. The United States could hardly promote American ideals abroad when it failed to implement them at home. As historian Mary Dudziak argues, "domestic racism and civil rights protest led to international criticism of the U.S. government. International criticism led the federal government to respond, through placating foreign critics by reframing the narrative of race in America, and through promoting some level of social change." Social change in the beginning of the Cold War was influenced by the "need for reform in order to make credible the government's argument about race and democracy."[55] Cold War civil rights reforms in the United States emerged from embarrassment and image-consciousness rather than from a purist vision of social justice. The United States could not continue to promote itself as a democratic nation if the Soviet Union could criticize and mock its racial caste system.

Black activists in the South saw an opportunity for mass action as McCarthyism began to fade and as the international political climate demanded that the United States embody the democracy it promoted. Over the course of the mid-1950s, blacks would see the beginnings of school integration in the South, along with the rise of major organizations and leaders who would fully reshape racial politics in the United States. In December 1955 Rosa Parks agreed to allow the Montgomery, Alabama, NAACP to use her arrest, after she refused to comply with segregation laws on a city bus, to kick-start a boycott and fight transportation segregation. The Montgomery Improvement Association and the Southern Christian Leadership Conference emerged from the Montgomery bus boycott and found in the Reverend Martin Luther King Jr. a charismatic leader.[56] Black activists proved through nonviolent tactics that "the philosophy of Thoreau and Gandhi can triumph."[57] In this context, Jackson's efforts to keep civil rights discourse at the forefront of the CP program reflected how Cold War politics shaped the Left's involvement in the freedom struggle.

Jackson's clearest expression of his opinion on the party's handling of civil rights came toward the end of his time underground, just as the civil rights movement was gaining momentum. In March 1955 Jackson and Henry Winston (writing as Charles P. Mann and Frederick C. Hastings, respectively) published an article in *Political Affairs* called "For a Mass Policy in Negro Freedom's Cause." In their essay Jackson and Winston criticized the party for being out of step with the growing civil rights movement and called on the CPUSA to revise its approach.

The CPUSA had not formally revisited its position on "the Negro question" since the 1928 "Black Belt thesis," which argued that black Americans living in the Deep South constituted their own nation. Modeled on the Soviet Union's system of republics, nation status afforded black southerners the right to self-determination.[58] The Black Belt thesis had been cited by many of the party's critics to suggest that Moscow was merely using American blacks to promote Soviet communism in the United States. Although official party policy prioritized class, arguing that it encompassed race, American Communists were unequivocal in their support of the notion of racial equality.[59] Jackson and Winston's effort to reform party policy on civil rights was an attempt to correct the misconception that the CP only wanted to use African Americans for its own ends, as well as an expression of unwavering solidarity with integration efforts in the Deep South. In "For a Mass Policy" they offered a proposal for bridging the divide between civil rights and the party. As black Communists with southern roots who were indicted, in hiding, and facing prison, the two were particularly interested in how the party positioned itself in relation to the civil rights movement.

Jackson and Winston contested Communist claims that the party's failure had led the "Negro masses to be taken over by the bourgeois reformist leaders."[60] Though their praise may have frustrated Roy Wilkins, the NAACP's anticommunist executive secretary, Jackson and Winston commended the NAACP's efforts toward school desegregation and applauded black Americans who mobilized the organization. "The N.A.A.C.P.," they argued, "is viewed by the Negro people as their own organized mass weapon which has won important battles for them in recent years." Nonetheless, the pair criticized the NAACP's leaders, calling them "reformist supporters of the white ruling class" who only followed the tide of protest, rather than initiating it, in order to "remain the leaders of the Negro people." If the NAACP had not followed the will of the people toward increased militancy, Jackson and Winston suggested, "the initiative and leadership exercised by the Communists and the Left would have resulted in the whole Negro liberation movement being organized and led by the working-class ideology and leadership of our Party."[61] Instead, they argued that the masses of poor, disenfranchised, and segregated blacks in the South were seeking practical leadership, and in spite of the NAACP's moderate reputation, the organization had become a vehicle for radical change.

"For a Mass Policy in Negro Freedom's Cause" was published shortly after the 1954 Supreme Court decision in *Brown v. Board of Education of Topeka, Kansas.* Jackson and Winston lamented the slow steps toward true desegregation in public schools and argued that Communists should be involved in implementing the ruling on the ground. The pair argued that blacks in the South needed the support of the CPUSA, but they did not need the party as a mobilizing force. They wrote, "The historic and heroic fight to implement the Supreme Court decision on outlawing school segregation and the fight to extend the right to vote and equal representation are such movements and struggles already involving millions."[62] The party did not need to ignite a struggle if one already existed, and such a suggestion distracted Communists from participating in a momentous movement. The primary goal, according to Jackson and Winston, should be to get involved with the organizations already working toward complete school desegregation, instead of pondering how to win the black masses over to a Communist-run organization working toward the same ends.

"For a Mass Policy in Negro Freedom's Cause" called on Communists to correct their flawed approach by reinvigorating Popular Front–style activism. Although they believed that the context of the 1950s differed from that of the 1930s, Jackson and Winston acknowledged that a similar approach could win the hearts and minds of the black southern masses and contribute to the mounting civil rights victories. "If our Party enters with both feet into the mass movement of the Negro people without losing its own identity and more advanced ideological and political program," they concluded, "then it can begin to regain rapidly its lost influence and leave its decisive mark on the future of the movement."[63]

The pair also implied that the party's isolation from the civil rights movement was in part a product of its perception that "bourgeois reformist" organizations such as the NAACP were the force to be conquered. Jackson and Winston believed that the true enemy of racial justice was obvious, but they made a point of reminding their readers that resistance to change in the South was powerful. Highlighting the surge of white citizens' councils, states' rights associations, the National Association for the Advancement of White People, the National Association to Defend the Majority of White People, and the Defenders of State Sovereignty and Liberty, Jackson and Winston argued that the "reign of terror against the Negro people" required immediate attention. They noted that even though the CPUSA characterized leaders of the NAACP as "reformists" who pandered to the white ruling class and to white supremacist organizations, there was no distinction between Communists and moderate black activists who advocated for desegregation.

Jackson and Winston pointed out that the citizens' councils in Mississippi "[applied] economic pressures to 'trouble-makers' [who advocated] compliance with the Supreme Court decision."[64] White supremacist organizations used foreclosure, credit denial, and other threatening and violent tactics to accomplish their goals, and any black Mississippians who had made it out of poverty put themselves in danger if they were not quiet about their politics. Jackson and Winston applauded NAACP efforts to provide financial support to business owners, home owners, farmers, and workers who risked their livelihoods to defend civil rights. They argued that the "unity displayed in Mississippi by all classes of Negro life cannot but inspire the entire democratic camp."[65] Jackson and Winston also noted that the NAACP and black leaders in Mississippi were "developing a new form of struggle, 'the economic boycott' as their answer to the economic terror of the white bankers, merchants, and plantation owners."[66]

The situation in Mississippi deteriorated in 1955 in response to *Brown*. According to NAACP leader Amzie Moore, white supremacists killed seven blacks that year. Among them was the Reverend George Lee, an organizer of the Belzoni, Mississippi, NAACP who was murdered after the group filed suit against a local sheriff who refused to accept poll taxes from potential African American voters.[67] In August, Mississippi's pattern of racial violence gained national attention with the murder of a fourteen-year-old Chicago boy, Emmett Louis Till. Till, who was visiting his uncle in Money, Mississippi, was unfamiliar with the particularities of Jim Crow. Although he was aware of racial separation, he was not versed in the gendered rules of segregation. Till was kidnapped, shot, and weighted down in the Tallahatchie River after a white woman in a convenience store reported that he had spoken to her inappropriately. His death, his open-casket funeral, and the trial of his killers catalyzed the civil rights movement across the South.[68] Although Jackson and Winston reemerged and began to confront their own legal problems just as the Montgomery bus boycott began, their praise for Mississippi leaders discussing boycott plans indicated that the Mississippi CP branch would have expressed support. Jackson and Winston closed the portion of their article on school desegregation by urging the party to "end our isolation and weaknesses which flow from the past underestimation of this question."[69]

Ending Communist isolation from the growing civil rights movement was the dominant theme in Jackson and Winston's article. They expressed general agreement with the party's goals but offered extensive criticism of how the CPUSA chose to become involved. The pair vehemently disagreed with a fellow comrade who "mechanically shouts 'working-class hegemony' and politically places his main emphasis not on the struggle to unite the Negro people as a people but on sharpening up the differences within its ranks."[70] Instead of further fragmenting the American Left, Jackson and Winston asserted, Communists needed to quietly bring their radical ideas to the front lines of the mounting struggles across the South. Unity among the masses would prevail over a splintered movement with similar goals but different means.

Jackson and Winston's article did more than articulate a clear stance on the CPUSA's involvement in the black freedom struggle. For these two men and for the rest of the second cadre, publishing articles under pseudonyms in *Political Affairs* allowed Communist discourse to continue in a period of censorship, repression, and fear. Though vociferous debate occurred regularly in the pages of *Political Affairs,* Jackson and Winston, writing as Mann and Hastings, had greater liberty to critique their comrades and the CP than if they had written under their own names. Particularly in the arena of civil rights, Jackson's underground writings allowed him to continue his involvement in party affairs and to voice his own views. Jackson's writings as Charles P. Mann served a dual function for the party as well. His pieces allowed the outward appearance of solidarity within party ranks, for the unavailables seemed to be completely behind the party line. But because Jackson's anonymity allowed him to express his opinions openly, those articles in *Political Affairs* contradicted the common assumption that the Communists were of one mind, following a single policy that came from Moscow. For the party leadership, criticism coming from underground operatives replaced the debate that might have occurred in actual meetings and helped the CPUSA retain some normalcy while it suffered the effects of McCarthyism.

Early in 1955 eight of the Communists who had gone to prison were released, and after nearly five years in hiding the underground fugitives were growing restless. They pressed the party leadership to call for their emergence.[71] James Jackson turned himself in at the Federal Courthouse Building in New York City on December 2, 1955. On learning of his surrender, U.S. Attorney Paul W. Williams told the *New York Times* that Jackson was "one of the most dangerous Communist conspirators in the United States."[72] The *Times* article also noted that Jackson was "the Party's top organizer in the South" and that his surrender was a critical step in ensuring the security of the United States.[73] The attention to Jackson's supposed threat to the United States and his role in the South illustrated the extent to which the Communist Party's potential position in the emerging civil rights movement was truly a national issue. Whereas black religious leaders, local business owners, domestics, and moderates in the South could ask for their rights and ruffle the feathers of only those whites who were most resistant to change, the idea of a Communist asking the South to sacrifice its traditions made the whole nation nervous.

Jackson was tried and found guilty. At the sentencing stage, Jackson made another attempt to prove himself a compassionate, thoughtful activist whose politics would benefit the masses. He grounded his statement to the court in his upbringing and the development of his political consciousness alongside the injustices of the Jim Crow South, drawing on the burgeoning civil rights movement rather than focusing solely on Communist dogma. "The freedom of choice in associates," Jackson argued, "the freedom of choice of membership in an association, are freedoms particularly dear to the Negro people. Involved is the essence of the right to pursue and secure relationships with other Americans in order to further our advance toward genuine equality and to realize our stature as free American citizens."[74]

Although most black Americans, Jackson asserted, "hold no brief for the Communist Party's program of socialism," the history of slavery, segregation, lynching, and disenfranchisement would lead them to believe in

Jackson's "right to pursue the struggle for their rights through this political party." According to Jackson, black Americans would "want the doors of political alternative left open to facilitate a greater responsiveness to their needs and demands on the part of the Democratic or Republican Party of their current choice."[75] Jackson also characterized his own communism as "a social science . . . and not . . . holy scripture."[76] He appealed to potential judicial appreciation for the emerging civil rights struggle in the nation, hoping that he could help the court make sense of communism's appeal. Also, his aging mother made an emotional plea for clemency on her son's behalf, stating, "He has done nothing in his life but work for his country and his people."[77]

While the appeals process was beginning for Jackson and his codefendants in 1957, the Supreme Court determined in *Yates v. United States* that, under the Smith Act, "advocacy, to be criminal, must be of some future *action,* rather than of the desirability of believing something," severely limiting the scope of the *Dennis* opinion.[78] The *Yates* decision affected nearly ninety Communists who either had been convicted or were awaiting prosecution.[79] Jackson's conviction was among those that were reversed.

When the ordeal of Jackson's trial, sentencing, and appeal was over, he focused on two priorities: reconnecting with his family and reconstructing the Communist Party as a useful organization in the progressive struggles across the nation. While he was away, Esther Cooper Jackson had regularly reminded her daughters that their father was trying to make the United States a better place for them to live as Americans, as black children, and as representatives to the world. As parents, the Jacksons believed that creating a better world for future generations meant being politically engaged on behalf of their family and on behalf of oppressed groups around the world. The context of the early Cold War made it impossible for politics and family life to be separated in the daily struggles of black activists, and the Jacksons fused leftist politics and family devotion in a way that reflected, answered, and influenced the changing nature of the black freedom movement.

Notes

I would like to thank Steven Lawson, Deborah Gray White, Mia Bay, and Robert Korstad for their comments, suggestions, and input on this essay. I deeply appreciate the support and feedback of my colleagues and friends, particularly John Adams, Rebecca Tuuri, and Katie Lee. Krista Haviland offered endless patience and support. I also extend gratitude to Danielle McGuire and John Dittmer for compiling this collection of essays.

1. Alfred Kahn, *The Game of Death: Effects of the Cold War on Our Children* (New York: Cameron and Kahn, 1953), 159.

2. Alfred Kahn, *The Vengeance on the Young: The Story of the Smith Act Children* (New York: Hour Publishers, June 1952), 9.

3. Ibid.

4. Ibid., 10.

5. Ellen Schrecker, *Many Are the Crimes: McCarthyism in America* (Boston: Little, Brown, 1998), 98.

6. Gil Green, *Cold War Fugitive: A Personal Story of the McCarthy Years* (New York: International Publishers, 1984), 105.

7. Esther Cooper Jackson interview with Sara Rzeszutek; James and Esther Cooper Jackson interview with Mary Helen Washington, in James and Esther Cooper Jackson Papers, Tamiment Library, New York University, New York; Green, *Cold War Fugitive.*

8. "Birmingham's Fascist Ordinance, Outlawing the Communist Party," Jackson Papers.

9. Works that address the changing black freedom movement from the Popular Front to the civil rights years include Robin D. G. Kelley, *Hammer and Hoe: Alabama Communists in the Great Depression* (Chapel Hill: University of North Carolina Press, 1990), 224–31; Patricia Sullivan, *Days of Hope: Race and Democracy in the New Deal Era* (Chapel Hill: University of North Carolina Press, 1996); Michael K. Honey, *Southern Labor and Black Civil Rights* (Urbana: University of Illinois Press, 1993); Robert Korstad and Nelson Lichtenstein, "Opportunities Found and Lost: Labor, Radicals, and the Early Civil Rights Movement," *Journal of American History* 75 (December 1988): 786–811; Catherine Fosl, *Subversive Southerner: Anne Braden and the Struggle for Racial Justice in the Cold War South* (New York: Palgrave Macmillan, 2002); Mary Dudziak, *Cold War Civil Rights: Race and the Image of American Democracy* (Princeton, N.J.: Princeton University Press, 2000); Penny Von Eschen, *Race against Empire: Black Americans and Anticolonialism, 1937–1957* (Ithaca, N.Y.: Cornell University Press, 1997); Nikhil Pal Singh, *Black Is a Country: Race and the Unfinished Struggle for Democracy* (Cambridge, Mass.: Harvard University Press, 2004); Brenda Gayle Plummer, *Rising Wind: Black Americans and U.S. Foreign Affairs, 1935–1960* (Chapel Hill: University of North Carolina Press, 1996); Carol Anderson, *Eyes Off the Prize: The United Nations and the African American Struggle for Human Rights, 1944–1955* (Cambridge: Cambridge University Press, 2003); Thomas Borstelmann, *The Cold War and the Color Line: American Race Relations in the Global Age* (Cambridge, Mass.: Harvard University Press, 2001).

10. Linda Reed, *Simple Decency and Common Sense: The Southern Conference Movement, 1938–1963* (Bloomington: Indiana University Press, 1994).

11. Hollywood writers and actors, newspaper editors, union organizers, gays and lesbians, and individuals who had been involved in civil rights and Popular

Front activism were questioned and persecuted for their political ideals. J. Edgar Hoover and the FBI also targeted people who had once been members of the Communist Party but had since withdrawn. See Mona Smith, *Becoming Something: The Story of Canada Lee, the Untold Tragedy of the Great Black Actor, Activist, and Athlete* (New York: Faber and Faber, 2004); Gerald Horne, *The Final Victim of the Hollywood Blacklist: John Howard Lawson, Dean of the Hollywood Ten* (Berkeley: University of California Press, 2006); David Robinson, *Chaplin: His Life and Art* (New York: McGraw-Hill, 1985); Martin Duberman, *Paul Robeson: A Biography* (New York: New Press, 1988); David Levering Lewis, *W. E. B. Du Bois: The Fight for Equality in the American Century, 1919–1963* (New York: Henry Holt, 2000); John D'Emilio, *Sexual Politics, Sexual Communities: The Making of a Homosexual Minority in the United States, 1940–1970* (Chicago: University of Chicago Press, 1983); Sally Belfrage, *Un-American Activities: A Memoir of the Fifties* (New York: HarperCollins, 1994).

12. J. Edgar Hoover, *Masters of Deceit: The Story of Communism in America and How to Fight It* (New York: Henry Holt, 1958), 82.

13. Thomas Patterson, *On Every Front: The Making of the Cold War* (New York: Norton, 1979).

14. For a discussion of the Rosenberg case, see Sam Roberts, *The Brother: The Untold Story of the Rosenberg Case* (New York: Random House, 2003).

15. Green, *Cold War Fugitive;* Deborah A. Gerson, "Is Family Devotion Now Subversive? Familialism against McCarthyism," in *Not June Cleaver: Women and Gender in Postwar America,* ed. Joanne Meyerowitz (Philadelphia: Temple University Press, 1994), 154.

16. Green, *Cold War Fugitive,* 68–69.

17. Ibid.

18. Sara E. Rzeszutek, "Love and Activism: James and Esther Jackson and the Black Freedom Movement in the United States, 1914–1968" (PhD diss., Rutgers University, 2009), 108.

19. Elaine Tyler May, *Homeward Bound: American Families in the Cold War Era* (New York: Basic Books, 1988).

20. Green, *Cold War Fugitive,* 71.

21. Kahn, *Game of Death,* 154.

22. Ibid., 156.

23. Kahn, "Vengeance on the Young," 11.

24. Gerson, "Is Family Devotion Now Subversive?" 151.

25. Ibid., 153–54. For additional material on families and Communist activists, see James R. Barrett, *William Z. Foster and the Tragedy of American Radicalism* (Chicago: University of Illinois Press, 1999); Peggy Dennis, *The Autobiography of an American Communist: A Personal View of Political Life, 1925–1975* (Westport, Conn.: Lawrence Hill/Creative Arts, 1977).

26. For a detailed discussion of women's activism in the CPUSA, see Kate

Weigand, *Red Feminism: American Communism and the Making of Women's Liberation* (Baltimore: Johns Hopkins University Press, 2001).

27. Ruth Feldstein, *Motherhood in Black and White: Race and Sex in American Liberalism, 1930–1965* (Ithaca, N.Y.: Cornell University Press, 2000), 85.

28. Ibid., 92–94. Feldstein discusses the way Mamie Till Bradley, mother of fourteen-year-old Mississippi murder victim Emmett Till, represented the ideal of "good" black motherhood. Bradley, a World War II widow, feared "that [Emmett Till's] murder would be used by the Communists for anti-American propaganda." Bradley's patriotism made her loss more profound; her husband had died serving "the American proposition that all men are equal," and her son's murder was a reflection of the war's failure to realize democracy for African Americans. Bradley's embodiment of "good" black motherhood in the wake of her son's murder energized the civil rights struggle and garnered sympathy among liberal whites and northerners. See also May, *Homeward Bound;* K. A. Cuordileone, *Manhood and American Political Culture in the Cold War* (New York: Routledge, 2005).

29. Manfred Berg, "Black Civil Rights and Liberal Anticommunism: The NAACP in the Early Cold War," *Journal of American History* 94 (June 2007): 75–96; Anderson, *Eyes Off the Prize;* Plummer, *Rising Wind.*

30. Kahn, *Game of Death,* 158n. For information on the Moore case, see Ben Green, *Before His Time: The Untold Story of Harry T. Moore, America's First Civil Rights Martyr* (New York: Free Press, 1999); Steven F. Lawson, *Civil Rights Crossroads: Nation, Community, and the Black Freedom Struggle* (Lexington: University Press of Kentucky, 2003).

31. Peggy Dennis and Sophie Gerson, "To the Editor of the Readers' Column," Jackson Papers.

32. Kahn, *Game of Death,* 157.

33. Esther Cooper Jackson to editor, *Union,* n.d., Jackson Papers.

34. Kahn, *Game of Death,* 158.

35. Ibid., 157.

36. Green, *Cold War Fugitive,* 175.

37. See Gerson, "Is Family Devotion Now Subversive?"

38. Dennis and Gerson, "To the Editor of the Readers' Column."

39. Ibid.

40. Ibid.

41. Kahn, *Game of Death,* 160.

42. Earl Ofari Hutchinson, *Blacks and Reds: Race and Class in Conflict, 1919–1990* (East Lansing: Michigan State University Press, 1995), 196–97.

43. Ibid., 200.

44. Esther Cooper Jackson, *This Is My Husband: Fighter for His People, Political Refugee* (New York: National Committee to Defend Negro Leadership, 1953), 5.

45. Ibid., 7.

46. Ibid.

47. Ibid., 7–17.

48. Ibid., 6.

49. Ibid., 34.

50. Eugene Dennis, *Letters from Prison* (New York: International Publishers, 1956), 5.

51. CPUSA Report, Jackson Papers.

52. Ibid.

53. Green, *Cold War Fugitive,* 118.

54. Charles P. Mann, "Universal Suffrage . . . The Gauge of the Maturity of the Working Class," unpublished manuscript, August 1952, Edward Strong Papers, Moorland-Spingarn Research Center, Howard University, Washington, D.C.

55. Dudziak, *Cold War Civil Rights,* 13–14.

56. Taylor Branch, *Parting the Waters: America in the King Years, 1954–1963* (New York: Simon and Schuster Paperbacks, 1988); Douglas Brinkley, *Rosa Parks* (New York: Penguin Group, 2000).

57. Maurice Isserman, *If I Had a Hammer . . . : The Death of the Old Left and the Birth of the New Left* (New York: Basic Books, 1987), 109.

58. Mark Naison, *Communists in Harlem during the Depression* (New York: Grove Press, 1984); Kelley, *Hammer and Hoe.*

59. Branch, *Parting the Waters;* Albert Fried, *Communism in America: A History in Documents* (New York: Columbia University Press, 1997); Gerald Horne, *Black Liberation/Red Scare: Ben Davis and the Communist Party* (Newark: University of Delaware Press, 1994); Isserman, *If I Had a Hammer.*

60. Charles P. Mann and Frederick C. Hastings, "For a Mass Policy in Negro Freedom's Cause," *Political Affairs* 8, Jackson Papers.

61. Ibid., 11.

62. Ibid., 29.

63. Ibid.

64. Ibid., 17–18.

65. Ibid., 18.

66. Ibid.

67. Charles Payne, *I've Got the Light of Freedom: The Organizing Tradition and the Mississippi Freedom Struggle* (Berkeley: University of California Press, 1995), 36–37.

68. Ibid., 39–40. Till's murderers were acquitted, and shortly thereafter they confessed to the murder in a magazine interview.

69. Mann and Hastings, "For a Mass Policy," 19.

70. Ibid., 21

71. Green, *Cold War Fugitive,* 150–51.

72. "Red Aide Missing since '51 Gives Up," *New York Times,* December 3, 1955.

73. Ibid.

74. James E. Jackson Jr., statement before sentencing, Jackson Papers.

75. Ibid.

76. Ibid.

77. "Mrs. Jackson's Plea," Jackson Papers.

78. David Caute, *The Great Fear: The Anticommunist Purge under Truman and Eisenhower* (New York: Simon and Schuster, 1978), 208 (emphasis in original).

79. Ibid.

Till They Come Back Home

*Transregional Families and the Politicization
of the Till Generation*

Krystal D. Frazier

Whenever he visited Chicago, Uncle Moses Wright vividly described the "good country life" in Mississippi, with its wide open spaces, riverside fishing, and long summer nights. Intrigued by the possibilities of adventure and the promise of fun with some of his favorite cousins, fourteen-year-old Emmett Louis Till pleaded to go south during the summer of 1955. His mother, Mamie Till Bradley, doubted that her Chicago-born son could understand "the things that ran deep in the awareness of people who lived in the South," and she was reluctant to let him go.[1] Emmett contended that if his mother could take in "two of Papa Mose's girls and raise them for years," then he ought to be allowed to travel south for a simple summer visit. Bradley eventually relented, and she prepared Emmett by giving him "the talk about strange things in a strange, new place" that "every black parent had with every child sent down South back then."[2] Their entire migrant community echoed her warnings, charging the lovable Emmett, who "thought he could talk his way out of anything," to deport himself carefully in Mississippi and avoid transgressing southern etiquette.[3]

That summer, while Emmett was visiting his family in Money, Mississippi, two white men brutally murdered him. J. W. Milam and Roy Bryant pledged to "scare the Chicago out of him" after they heard he had flirted with a white woman, Bryant's wife, Carolyn. Bryant and Milam stormed the Wright home, demanded "the one who did the talking," and drove Till to an isolated shed, where they beat him ruthlessly and gouged out his eye. They then shot him, tied a seventy-five-pound mill fan to his neck, and tossed his swelling body into the Tallahatchie River. Upon retrieval of the corpse, Mamie Till Bradley insisted on an open-casket funeral for her son. For four days that September, cameras captured the 100,000 mourners who filled Chicago's Roberts Temple Church of God in Christ. Images

137

of Emmett's mutilated body in *Jet* magazine, along with reports in black journals and major newspapers across the country, outraged thousands of Americans. The travesty of justice in the subsequent acquittal of Till's murderers by an all-white, all-male jury was made even more unpalatable by the extravagant and unrepentant confession the killers provided to *Look* magazine after their trial. "I'm tired of 'em sending your kind down here to stir up trouble," Milam reportedly said to Till, and "I'm going to make an example of you."[4] Milam's frustrations with northerners infiltrating Mississippi reflected long-standing traditions of cross-regional exchange that affected how black children interpreted Jim Crow.

In the aftermath of Till's death, Sheriff Clarence Strider, who oversaw the local investigation of the murder, also argued that northern aggression was the issue: "We never have any trouble," Strider said, "until some of our Southern niggers go up North and the NAACP talks to 'em and they come back home."[5] Of course, Till's murder was not the fault of the National Association for the Advancement of Colored People. Travelers were more likely to visit relatives than to meet with civil rights organizations outside the South, and black southerners had enough local motivation to resist Jim Crow. Nevertheless, Strider's comment contained some insight. The interactions between black southerners and their relatives in other regions had important implications for southern politics and the nation at large.[6]

This phenomenon was apparent in the widespread impact of Till's murder on young people across the country.[7] Sociologist Joyce Ladner, a veteran of the Student Nonviolent Coordinating Committee (SNCC), coined the term the *Till generation,* counting herself among the many youngsters who were stirred to activism after exposure to the Till case.[8] The Till generation included many children whose political sensibilities regarding regional differences were first heightened through experiences in and conversations with family members from different parts of the country. Understanding the cross-regional family culture of this cohort allows us to better contextualize the origins of the postwar black freedom struggle and provides a deeper revelation of Till's significance.

In part, the murder of Emmett Till helped politicize young African Americans across the country because his short life reflected the experiences of a generation of black Americans with southern roots, migrant upbringings, and varied regional encounters within politicized transregional families. This essay examines the experiences of children affected by migration and argues that their heightened political sensibilities shaped their understanding of the complexities and possibilities of interracial life in the United States in ways not experienced by generations before them. The culture of transregional African American families helped nationalize the civil rights movement and should be recognized as one of its origins.

Black Families and Postwar Migration

In 1924 Mamie Carthan, the future mother of Emmett Till, boarded a Chicago-bound train with her mother Alma, en route to meet her father. Two months after his arrival, Wiley Nash Carthan had found work at the Corn Products Refining Company and a place for his family to live in the sleepy town of Argo, Illinois (which the community of transplants termed "Little Mississippi").[9] The Carthans became pillars in the Argo community and in Roberts Temple Church of God in Christ, of which Alma was a founding member. She frequently extended herself on behalf of migrants, giving them, as her daughter later put it, "every reason to look forward, never back."[10] Yet many migrant families, including the Carthans, often looked back. Their folkways, political opinions, and economic aspirations were shaped by their experiences in the South. Migration, as historian James Gregory writes, "is often best understood as a circulation rather than as a one-way relocation because, in many instances, migrants at some point circle back toward home."[11]

The Carthans were part of the "Southern Diaspora," or out-migration of millions of black and white southerners in the first three-quarters of the twentieth century. Whites outnumbered blacks during each decade of the migration; however, African Americans often created a more significant impact by leaving the South at much higher rates than whites and by settling in regions with few nonwhite residents.[12] As blacks populated northern areas, the country had to address racial tensions that had previously been sectionalized to the South.

Black southerners who decided to migrate to the North departed in a series of waves. Around the First World War, contemporary observers termed the flight of 1.2 million African Americans from rural southern communities to industrial areas in the North and Midwest the "Great Migration." Several factors led to this exodus from the South: racial tyranny, disfranchisement, wartime industry, immigrant restrictions, agricultural futility, poverty, sexual exploitation and emotional and physical abuse, lack of education, and scarce employment opportunities. Indeed, for most migrants, leaving their friends, families, and homes was a social, political, and economic necessity.[13]

During the World War II era, migrants again fled the South, seeking redress from a variety of injustices. Southern communities were newly infused with the resentment of black World War II veterans, who had fought a war for democracy abroad but were unable to realize it on American soil. Many of them also practiced self-defense, and some left the South to avoid retaliation. John Wiley of Greenville, Mississippi, who had fought in World War II, almost pulled out his switchblade when a white man demanded his seat at the rear of a bus. Wiley was enraged that the man continued to harass him, refusing to sit in the all-white section, until the bus driver finally convinced the white patron to take a seat in the front. Soon after, Wiley and his family moved to Chicago.[14]

Other veterans channeled their frustrations into early civil rights activities across isolated southern communities. Amzie Moore, an African American veteran who returned to the Mississippi Delta after the war, became prominent in the Regional Council of Negro Leadership and the Mississippi NAACP. This activism set the stage for SNCC's work in Mississippi, including the 1964 summer project. Black veterans and local activists fought for justice in the Jim Crow South even though the possible repercussions of demanding political participation included bloodshed. Their efforts to exercise self-determination and secure economic autonomy led to race riots, lynch mobs, sexual exploitation, and other forms of racial terrorism throughout the country.[15]

Migrants often found that the abuses and limitations of the rural South had urban counterparts that were treacherous in their own right. In urban areas, race riots replaced lynch mobs, and overcrowded shantytowns and tenements stood in for dilapidated farm shacks. Moreover, the burdensome demands of factory work, public sanitation jobs, and domestic employment often proved comparable to the hard and dirty labor of the fields. Nevertheless, migrants appreciated the regular hourly pay, the freedom to leave a job without indebtedness, and the relaxed social code they experienced outside the South. Furthermore, migrants established networks that helped them negotiate life in these new locales and reflected the southern communities to which they remained connected.

These migrants and their southern counterparts developed and maintained the familial culture that shaped many members of the Till generation. Before they had ever heard of Till, young people affected by migration interacted with their families and friends in and from different regions and were tied to these networks by patterns of interdependence. Moreover, the substantial communities and new alliances black migrants formed outside the South provided the political leverage that later helped black northerners support the southern front of the civil rights movement and created a cultural system that moved information back and forth between the regions.[16]

Economic Interdependence: The Centrality of Children

Many migrants remained connected to southern family members through relationships of economic interdependence.[17] Migration patterns varied among male and female migrants, who rarely traveled in nuclear family groups. Most single male migrants worked their way north through what Darlene Clark Hine calls "secondary migration"—that is, "leaving farms for Southern cities, doing odd jobs, and sometimes staying in one location for a few years before proceeding to the next stop." Single black women, however, most often "traveled the entire distance in one trip" and "usually had a specific relative—or fictive kin—waiting for them at their destination" who could assist them with finding employment, establishing homes, and caring for children.[18] Emmett Till's grandmother, Alma Carthan, fulfilled this role in Argo for southern migrants, "taking in relatives and friends of relatives and some people even our *relatives* didn't know," Mamie Till-Mobley remembered.[19] Married couples often relocated through chain migration, whereby one spouse found work and then sent for the rest of the family. Charlie Russell, father of legendary Boston Celtics star Bill Russell, traveled to Detroit, found a job, and then relocated to Oakland, California, before calling his family to join him.[20] No matter how their parents reached their destinations, migrant children were often tied to the South by the same family networks that sustained the migration.

One of the most significant arenas for exploring migrant interdependence and cultural connection is that of child care and child rearing. Migrants who arrived in northern locales with few relatives to welcome them often left their children in the care of southern relatives during periods of transition or for the duration of their childhoods. Upon his wife's death, Charlie Russell refused to move his family back to their Louisiana home, "where he had kinfolk to pitch in and help." Nevertheless, as his son Bill explained, "By tradition, Mister Charlie could leave us in Louisiana with absolute assurance that we would be 'raised' even if no one ever heard from him again" because "the extended family would always be there like a safety net beneath all the children stranded by the hardships of the great black migration out of the South."[21]

Examples abound in support of Russell's thesis. Wilma Eason, a widow with five children, leaned on her siblings as she prepared to migrate from North Carolina to New York with her new husband, who had six children of his own. Wilma's sisters took in three of her children and assumed Wilma's role in caring for their aging parents after she migrated.[22] Even if they did not solicit permanent child rearing, many other migrant parents enlisted temporary or periodic assistance from relatives in the South. After the death of her husband in rural Hemingway, South Carolina, Julia Presley left her two small daughters in the care of her mother and began working in New York. She sent enough money home to build a new house and extend the family farm. By the time her daughter Sylvia migrated to New York and married, Julia was back at home and in a position to offer the same type of support she had received as a migrant parent. Three of her grandchildren completed grade school in South Carolina under Julia's care while her daughter and son-in-law built "Sylvia's" soul food brand in Harlem. With their children temporarily in the care of family members, migrants such as Wilma and Sylvia were better able to maximize industrial opportunities, which often benefited wide extended networks.[23]

Moreover, the children themselves often helped maintain family economies. Some children of migrants benefited their southern families by caring for ailing elders or smaller children while residing in the South. William Ray's mother joined her brother in New York and left her sons in the care of their grandmother until William wrote and asked his mother to rescue him from being overworked in Hoke County, North Carolina. Young sharecroppers like Ray sometimes compensated for the lost labor of adults who migrated off family farms, to which the family wage was essential. "While my uncle run up and down the road," he maintained, "I was farming. Doing what he was supposed to be doing." As adults, Ray and his wife Geneva worked and saved money in New York City, while Geneva's mother kept their two daughters in her South Carolina home for about three years.[24]

Migrant parents also sent their children home for extended holidays and summer visits, during which time southern children and their guests explored and compared folkways and experiences. As Mamie Till-Mobley notes, the 1950s saw a "great black migration to the North, but in the summer, there were quite a few black kids from cities of the North who went south to visit relatives. For our kids, it was as close to summer camp as they were going to get."[25] Adventures in the South included discovering variations in landscape, folkways, and family life, which often included many relatives living within a short radius. Southern Christian Leadership Conference executive Ralph David Abernathy recalled cousins visiting his childhood home in Alabama. "In such a world," he notes, "every child knows he is watched with love and concern by literally dozens of people in addition to his parents. I was well aware of the inescapable presence of my kin wherever I went, and I knew that if I misbehaved they would either step in to correct me or else tell my parents about the incident. But, if I was hurt or in danger, they were just as quick to come to my rescue or defense."[26] As Abernathy implies, embracing children in wide family networks helped shield them from Jim Crow and from racism in general.[27]

Sending children to other regions or back to the country in the summertime also kept them off the city streets and out of trouble. The parents of acclaimed author Claude Brown debated whether to send him south to abate truancy, but the matter was settled by a New York City court, which sentenced him to a one-year stint with his grandparents in South Carolina. Likewise, nearly every year, Askia Muhammad left the mean streets of South Central Los Angeles for Indianola, Mississippi, where he spent the summer in the care of his grandmother and uncle, out of the reach of California's dangerous gangs. This strategy applied to southern children as well. Doug Davidson's family left Mississippi "under a sort of emergency" in 1954, escaping possible retaliation after his "older brother and some of his friends had beaten up some white boys."[28] While attending Howard University, Courtland Cox, who represented SNCC on the 1963 March on Washington steering committee, recalled meeting southerners whose parents had sent them north to escape the racial terror of the South. Notably, after a harrowing year trying to desegregate Little Rock's Central High School, Minnijean Brown Trickey completed school in New York under the care of psychologists Kenneth and Mamie Clark, who opened their family home to her. In New York, Trickey was exposed to experiences that would forever alter her perceptions of the South and the United States at large.[29]

Changing Scenes and New Interpretations: Cultivating the Political Sensibilities of Black Children

Before they ever left home, children in transregional families developed interests in traveling as well as insights into how race functioned in other places, based on observing and listening to family members. Although she did not travel to the South as a child, northern-born Prathia Hall, a leader in the Albany, Georgia, movement, contended that she knew southerners because she "knew their relatives when they came north" and settled in transplant communities, like the one in her father's Philadelphia church.[30] SNCC activist Courtland Cox grew up in a Trinidadian American family but learned how to critique institutional racism on New York City streets from second-generation African American migrants. These youngsters had no direct reference to the South, but their worldviews were no doubt shaped by the voiced memories of their parents or by what other adults implied about the South, "the part that was more understood than talked about."[31] As they prepared their children for visits to southern relatives, migrant parents provided crash courses that emphasized deference and the dangers of traversing white southern mores. Such lessons were ingrained in children and were regularly reinforced with state-sanctioned markers and other modes of social hierarchy that were neither as abundant nor as apparent in the North.[32]

Young southerners most often learned about life in other regions through the stories of visiting migrants, who inspired images of the big-city life and tolerable racial codes. Future SNCC chairman and U.S. congressman John Lewis was "obsessed" with the North while growing up in Troy, Alabama. His uncles, who visited once a year from Buffalo, New York, intrigued him with accounts of desegregated schools and lunch counters.[33] Likewise, as Bill Russell pondered his family's impending move to Oakland, California, from Monroe, Louisiana, he wondered whether the Russells would "become like those families who return every summer to visit from the North, driving long cars, wearing shiny clothes and making people uncomfortable."[34] Russell and his brother were amazed at the prospect of life outside the South and envisioned "New York, Chicago and Los Angeles" as "huge fairylands."[35]

Similarly, in his memoir *Once upon a Time When We Were Colored*, Clifton Taulbert notes that his northern relatives "would always keep my head filled with dreams of life in a land where color bars were non-existent and colored people could eat in the same places with whites."[36] Anticipating the arrival of a cousin who had not been home in twenty years, Taulbert hoped to be the first to show him around town, "to be near this visitor from the alien and magical North."[37] One summer, as his well-to-do Aunt Georgia departed, she invited him to come live in Chicago, where her sons played and dined with their white neighbors. Although Taulbert was too young to leave, "from then on," he notes, "I began to look beyond the South, and to prepare myself for life in St. Louis, Chicago, or Detroit."[38]

Although Taulbert envisioned the North as a wonderful, mystical, and promising place, he also recognized that the pull north had the potential to separate loved ones and cause them to never return home again.[39]

Although they may not have longed to live there, some northern children were nearly as anxious to investigate the South as Taulbert was to see the North. Carolyn Dillon pleaded to be allowed to go south, like others in her Gary, Indiana, community. But Carolyn got only as far as the South Side of Chicago, where she spent childhood summers with a migrant aunt, who worried that the stubborn Carolyn might be harmed if a white person disrespected her in the South and she failed to respond as expected.[40] Moreover, although Carolyn's other aunt, Mollie Lipscomb, supported the idea of Carolyn visiting the South, she refused to allow her own daughter, Barbara, to travel to Gary, fearing that she might get "fancy Northern ideas in her head that would get her killed once she arrived back in Natalbany, Louisiana."[41] Despite the possibilities of danger, children like Carolyn and Barbara simply wanted to visit their relatives and explore whatever adventures lay across the Mason-Dixon Line.

Conversely, observations from adult migrants and visiting relatives taught some northern children that the South was no place they wanted to visit. Although his parents taught him how to distinguish southern "crackers" from local Harlem "Jews" by variations in their behavior toward African Americans, Claude Brown thought his parents' "minds were still down there in the South Carolina cotton fields." Moreover, he called his visiting relatives "crazy-acting, funny-dressing, no-talking people" whose odd behavior was likely attributable to "eating corn bread and biscuits all the time," and he had no interest in visiting their homes.[42] Likewise, Timothy L. Jenkins, part of the legal genius within SNCC, had no desire to travel south, where one was constantly "in life and death peril."[43] Although he never visited the South as a child, he learned about it from his Virginia-born father and the varied clientele that frequented their Philadelphia barbershop, where African American experiences were often discussed within international contexts.[44]

Listening to the conversations of northerners, transplants, distinguished members of the black elite, organic intellectuals, ministers, laymen, and everyday "blue-collar people," Jenkins discovered that lynching, rape, arson, and general discrimination were widespread across the South. He was so aware of the regular atrocities that Emmett Till's death was "not an isolated event," Jenkins remembered, but "one of a series that came to my attention as a youngster."[45] For Karen Edmonds Spellman, who distributed media reports from SNCC's Atlanta office and later in Lowndes County, the same was true, but with a very important distinction. "Fear never stopped us from protesting and demonstrating and doing what we knew had to be done," Spellman remembered. But, growing up in the all-black town of Langston, Oklahoma, she had an intimate understanding of terror, which, she recalled, "was all around you, all of the time in the South."[46] Many young northerners, like Jenkins, would not come face-to-face with such abiding fear until they entered the movement in the 1960s.

Nevertheless, Jenkins and other young men growing up in this context would have been at least somewhat aware that affiliating with white women could be dangerous for black males, even in the North. In light of what she perceived as her son's propensity toward "high-yaller" women, Claude Brown's mother, a South Carolina migrant, declared, "I sho am glad they ain't got no little white girls in these schools in Harlem, 'cause my poor child woulda done been lynched, right up here in New York."[47] This, along with the images of Emmett Till's funeral procession and anecdotal evidence about the hundreds of northern mothers and fathers who forced their male children to examine Till's corpse, confirms that migrant communities enforced protective measures against black male–white female fraternization. By contrast, regular assaults, acts of terror, and periodic trials consistently reminded young black southerners of what Richard Wright terms "the white death, the threat which hung over every male black in the South."[48] In fact, the *Jackson Daily News* attested to Till's probable ignorance of southern protocol, reporting that he must have been "feeble-minded" to whistle in a white woman's presence, since no mentally healthy black male teenager would have done so in the South.[49]

While southern black parents trained their children to try to abate racial violence, they simultaneously insulated the children from the immediate insults of Jim Crow in a variety of empowering ways that were not always available in desegregated northern spaces. African American southerners congregated at black-owned businesses and attended black churches and all-black schools, where black students were certain that their "teachers believed in them."[50] Moreover, in all-black communities containing a healthy supply of black professionals, landowners, and entrepreneurs, parents' admonishments that "there's nobody any better than you" were regularly confirmed.[51] Whereas northern black children were more likely to have opportunities to interact with amicable whites, southern children had greater exposure to injustices and inequities they could readily attribute to whites. As a result, southern parents often took more pains to minimize their children's contact with white people.[52] Ralph David Abernathy and his playmates considered his father's warning to avoid playing with whites as "merely hypothetical," since they "didn't sit around and brood about whether or not to play with whites" in their cohort; they had "never met any and had no desire to."[53] For Karen Edmonds Spellman and her sisters, the idea that they "were supposed to be considered as unequal or inferior . . . didn't even enter our minds."[54] In other scenarios, black southern children had more opportunity for direct contact with overt racism than did their northern counterparts. And such encounters were regularly shaped by the perplexing responses of adults. The interactions between Bill Russell's parents and white people "often added up to a mystery." In a single instance, "white strangers could be rude to my parents," Russell recalled, "and then pat me on the head without a second thought."[55] Children carried such interpretations into new familial contexts.

Youngsters gained their earliest impressions of regional inequities as they compared what they learned from adults and experienced at home with what they learned from family members in and from different regions. Through these intrafamilial exchanges, black children developed and quenched their curiosities, many of a political nature, and these often grew into political activism. Some of the most obvious differences were observed in public social spaces, such as the city scene that met John Lewis in the summer of 1951 in Buffalo, New York. His uncle Otis, a schoolteacher and principal, planned the trip expressly to indulge John's interest in the North. Most black children growing up in the South were taught to speak to whites only when spoken to, to never look them in the eye, and to move out of the paths of approaching whites in urban spaces. In light of this training, John's visit was like "stepping into a movie, into a strange, otherworldly place . . . the sidewalks crowded with people, black and white, mixing together as if it was the most natural thing in the world"—a sight unlike any he had witnessed in Alabama. At the end of his trip, Lewis was ready to go home because he missed his family. "But, home would never feel the same as it did before that trip," he said, "and neither would I." This exchange awakened something new in Lewis.[56]

This type of experience was not limited to southern children. Through familial exchanges, northern-born children often strengthened their identification with southern relatives and began to personally abhor Jim Crow. Carolyn Dillon learned a lot about her own environment in Gary, Indiana, when her cousin Barbara was finally allowed to visit from Louisiana. Barbara was "very impressed with how I lived," Carolyn recalled, and "I . . .

lived in a federal housing project!" Although much of Carolyn's world was segregated, Barbara was moved because Carolyn's large all-black school had "well-educated black teachers . . . real books, and school supplies." Carolyn thus gained a greater appreciation for her immediate resources and a personal reference for the experience of children in the South. While Barbara returned to Louisiana pondering the open seating on Gary's buses and in its movie theaters, thanks to Barbara, Carolyn watched the unfolding desegregation trials with a new sensitivity. She cried as she witnessed "the moms of *Fun with Dick and Jane* . . . throw tomatoes at a nice little colored girl who was trying to go to school," and she began to rethink the doctrine that whites would accept a better-educated black populace. Forced "to do a lot of growing up overnight," Dillon accused her migrant aunt of lying to her about "what we needed to do to be accepted." Her teary-eyed aunt replied, "'I believed it was true, too.'"[57]

As they interacted with their peers in different regions, black children like Carolyn and Barbara began to ask questions about their identity in relation to the experiences of their families and of black people in general. By the time her family migrated from Greensboro, North Carolina, to Connecticut, Karen Edmonds Spellman and her sisters were veteran protesters who quickly recognized the subtler displays of racism. "All of those symbols we had of racism and segregation in the South didn't exist in the North," Spellman explained, so the girls had to adjust to "a different set of conditions."[58] Unlike the members of the Edmonds family, who were "race people," questions of race and place abounded for less vigilant children exposed to similarly new contexts: "Why are some people treated one way and others another? How will I and the people I love be treated, and will that treatment be fair?"[59] Instead of a closer identification with relatives from different places, cross-regional exchanges sometimes resulted in children distancing themselves from their relatives in other regions. Claude Brown's one-year stint in his grandparents' home confirmed his perception of the South developed while entertaining southern relatives in Harlem: "Down South sure was a crazy place," and Claude never wanted to return. Yet he acknowledged that he learned many things in the South, including "how to say 'yas'm' and 'yas suh,'" a habit he denounced once he was on the train back to New York.[60] For a while, Brown had joined the southern children, for whom "playing by the rules became a self-conscious performance in which they 'got one over on' or otherwise manipulated whites."[61] During subsequent trips to the South, children like Claude would have a reference for the type of behavior demanded in the South, even as they realized how much they preferred home.

Likewise, southern children's exchanges with northern relatives sometimes encouraged them to see their experiences with a new perspective. Boston's segregated Roxbury neighborhood, where Spellman visited relatives in "small apartments on crowded streets," was disappointing. It could not compare to the "endless space to explore in rural and small-town southern communities, regardless of the other opportunities it might provide.[62] Ibrahim Mu'min grew up in an urban public housing community in Columbus, Georgia, where he first participated in desegregation protests at the age of nine. Mu'min became aware of the wide access to public accommodations and other clear advantages to life in the North when his migrant cousins visited. But they attended schools where they were unwelcome, whereas Ibrahim enjoyed a "nurturing and supportive" network in his all-black school. Moreover, Mu'min could not reconcile the large number of northern relatives who seemed to "always work for somebody else" with his family's entrepreneurial spirit, which also infused the general culture of black Columbus.[63] The same was true for future SNCC freedom singer Charles Neblett growing up in Robinson County, Tennessee. Although many of his relatives were doing quite well in migrant locales, during his visit to Chicago—the "real North"—Neblett was "surprised how bad some people were living," because they always seemed to return to Tennessee in fancy cars. His Tennessee community was filled with black-owned institutions that kept his family uninterested in migrating. Perhaps the greatest pull was the financial independence they enjoyed as landowners. "I just figured I was better off" than a lot of migrants, Neblett remembered.[64]

Likewise, in Langston, Oklahoma, Karen Edmonds Spellman was insulated in an all-black community with many black professionals, but she was also exposed to municipal inequities. Since the local school ended at the eighth grade, the Edmonds family migrated to Greensboro, North Carolina, where Karen's father joined the faculty of Bennett College, and the entire family participated in justice struggles. Dr. Edmonds also became head of the Greensboro NAACP, and under his leadership in the 1950s the city's civil rights movement flourished with boycotts, sit-ins, and protest marches. The Edmondses' activities drew the attention of white terrorist groups that targeted them with bomb threats and cross burnings, which were compounded by "endless investigations" by the FBI. They were eventually forced out of Greensboro in 1958 and found refuge in New Haven, Connecticut, where Karen completed high school.

The Edmonds family brought their strong tradition of activism to the North and soon began building awareness about conditions in the segregated South among blacks and whites in New Haven. The work was not easy. Spellman met a lot of northerners who thought they had "arrived" and did not understand their role in helping to end racial discrimination in the South. The Edmonds family, consisting of "seasoned, veteran protesters," was considered an oddity as they picketed the local nonsegregated Woolworth's—part of the national chain that included segregated southern facilities.[65]

Having grown up in the South and feeling accountable for the lives of people there, Spellman, Neblett, and Mu'min were among the many young southerners whose exchanges with migrants and northern communities encouraged them to remain committed to fighting injustices in the South and on the national scene. The death of Emmet Till helped many other disconnected grandchildren of the Southern Diaspora to reevaluate both their relationship to the Jim Crow South and the national significance of the struggle against it.

Till's Legacy: Uniting a Generation for Justice

Emmett Till became an instant martyr whose significance was linked to the aftermath of the landmark 1954 *Brown v. Board of Education* decision, which banned segregation in public schools. Riding the tailwinds of images of victorious third-grader Linda Brown atop the stairs of the Supreme Court were images of Till's mutilated corpse. This juxtaposition raised the consciousness of millions of Americans, including those who were not descendants of African American migrants.[66] In Chicago, Till's murder represented an attack on the best of what migration had to offer black families—a chance for their children to be healthy, happy, educated, and protected. In such black metropolises, "building communities in the big cities of America during an era when those cities monopolized important forms of power gave black migrants unique opportunities for influence."[67] As such, Chicagoans and blacks in other northern cities with substantial migrant populations pressured Mississippi officials to prosecute Till's assassins.[68] Chicago also housed some of the nation's most powerful black media outlets, including the *Chicago Defender, Ebony* and *Jet* magazines, and the Associated Negro Press. Other well-known figures, such as entertainers Louis Armstrong and Jelly Roll Morton and politician Oscar de Priest, all of whom represented African American success, resided in Chicago as well. In this context, Till's death was not just the horrific murder of a child but also a symbolic affront to African American progress.

Till's dead body provided a powerful source of the symbolic capital necessary for political transformation in any major movement and represented a new generation of freedom fighters to whom youngsters across the country could relate. Moreover, his family gave his death national significance by both commemorating his life and boldly condemning his killers.[69] Mamie Till Bradley bravely relived the unfathomable experience of identifying her son's mutilated corpse as she testified in front of a courtroom of unsympathetic spectators. The image of Till's uncle, Moses Wright, standing before the Leflore County court on September 21, 1955, and boldly pointing out the men who had abducted Till emboldened black people across the country, who recognized that what had happened to Till could happen to a member of their families. "The most frightening thing about the Till incident," sociologist Doug Davidson recalled, "was that it could have been me." Davidson's cousins visited him every summer in Mississippi until he moved north, and he returned to Mississippi to visit his grandmother each summer thereafter.[70] Meanwhile, Wright represented the weary elders who had preserved the dignity of African American families throughout the early twentieth century and fought American racism as best they could. Although it endangered his life, Wright's testimony helped pass the torch to the next generation. Both the publicity surrounding Till's death and the acquittal of his murderers inspired a new generation to join the fight for African American liberation.[71]

Indeed, many young black southerners were riveted by Till's death and the subsequent murder trial, helping to spawn a new generation of activists and reflecting the impact of transregional culture on African American families. Karen Edmonds Spellman recalled that Till's murder was just one of many atrocities. "I grew up in the South," she explained, "so it wasn't as if I was a northerner hearing about a young person killed in the South." Black southerners were constantly surrounded by terror, and according to Spellman, it was not surprising when young people "went missing." Till's death, she said, was "the first time people in the North knew about some of the violence that was going on," but it was not news to black people in the South, who faced it daily. Still, for future SNCC program director Cleveland Sellers, who hailed from the mostly black up-country town of Denmark, South Carolina, Till's death held a certain distinction. "The greatest realization of racial injustice" he recalled, and "the atrocity that affected me the most was Emmett Till's lynching."[72] "Emmett Till was only three years older than me," Sellers remembered, "and I identified with him. I tried to put myself in his place and imagine what he was thinking when those white men took him from his home that night. . . . There was something about the cold-blooded callousness of Emmett Till's lynching that touched everyone in the community. We had all heard the atrocity accounts before, but there was something special about this one."[73] Sellers was not alone. Hundreds of others had been lynched before Till. Yet the bravery of his mother, the relative security of her Chicago home, the growing national sensitivity to the rights of American children of all races, and the tenacity of the black press ensured that his death received unprecedented exposure. Black teenagers read the newspaper coverage of Till's death and imagined the final moments of one of their peers—so young, so terribly abused, and so unprotected. The image of his unrecognizable face provided vivid evidence that life was dangerous, if not deadly, for black people in America, and no matter how removed or insulated a young black person might feel, he or she was vulnerable to white supremacist violence.

Till's death forced black children in cross-regional families to recognize their shared vulnerability, and it influenced their decisions to become active in civil rights protests. The death of Emmett Till compelled Mississippian Anne Moody to examine her surroundings. Before Till was murdered, Moody had been too engrossed in helping her family and completing school to keep abreast of local happenings. After Till's death, Moody's employer, whom she described as "the meanest white woman in town," insisted that Till was one of those disrespectful northern Negroes who "think they can get away with anything" and that he had died "because he got out of his place with a white woman." Till's murder made Anne and other African American youngsters wonder exactly which actions merited death. "Probably just being a Negro . . . was enough," she feared. As Anne began asking questions and investigating the Till case, she became annoyed with the secretiveness surrounding the discontent in her community, evident in adults' refusal to answer her questions. At only fifteen, Anne began to hate people: Till's killers, white supremacists in general, and "Negroes . . . for not standing up and doing something about the murders." Moody transformed her resentment for what she interpreted as her community's complacency into activism. She later joined the Congress of Racial Equality and participated in sit-in protests, the 1963 March on Washington, and the 1964 Mississippi Freedom Summer.[74] The events surrounding the death of the young man some called the "Chicago boy" resonated across the South.

While growing up in Hattiesburg, Mississippi, Joyce Ladner "had always looked at northerners as less vulnerable, being able to go back home." But if Till, "an outside child," could be killed, her male relatives were also at risk for death, and she might be raped or otherwise horribly violated. "Optimistic that justice would prevail," Ladner somehow channeled her fear into activism in the NAACP and later SNCC. She also cited Till's murder as "one of the greatest influences that ultimately led" to her "becoming a scholar, a sociologist."[75]

John Lewis "felt like a fool" in the wake of Till's death, which crushed his hopes for justice spurred by the *Brown* decision.[76] "I was fifteen, black, at the edge of my own manhood, just like him," Lewis said. "He could have been me. *That* could have been me, beaten, tortured, dead at the bottom of a river."[77] Lewis decided that he had to change the context in which his family lived. "I loved my parents," he wrote, but "I couldn't accept the way things were." Experiencing the Till case within the context of transregional families helped give Lewis and his cohort new "expectations for how they should be treated."[78] Like Anne Moody and Joyce Ladner, Lewis chose to channel his anger and passion into working for change.

Historian James Horton had a similarly transformative response. Raised in the North, twelve-year-old Horton was visiting family in the South when Till was killed. Like countless other northern parents, Horton's mother shaped the occasion of the murder into a teachable moment and spent "most of the morning counseling me on 'being careful,' a nonspecific term which at the time I took to mean watching out for traffic on unfamiliar country roads," Horton said.[79] The knowledge of Till's death and Horton's later visits to the South "confirm[ed] my notion that the South and its white people were different and dangerous." His "need to understand" white southerners' behaviors led to his graduate studies in southern history and his decision to become a professional historian.[80] Likewise, Tim Jenkins employed the lessons he learned growing up in Philadelphia in his work for SNCC. As a liaison between southern leaders and northern movement activists, Jenkins helped equip black student leaders in the South with the type of international and theoretical critiques to which he had been introduced in Philadelphia and in the classrooms of Howard University. Transregional familial contexts prepared young people like Horton and Jenkins to invest in freedom struggles in ways that provided significant resources to the movement.

Their familial experiences distinguished the Till generation from their foreparents and helped equip them for the work of advancing the black freedom struggle in the postwar era. Moreover, Emmett Till's death highlighted a sense of continuity of identity within families that extended across various regions. Till's death brought the reality of lynching to the North and to a major migrant destination in a fashion that bore witness to the impact of such migration on African American familial life. As Karla F. C. Holloway eloquently argues, "Children's deaths made apparent both the persistence of memory and the necessity of memorial."[81] The national coverage of Till's murder made an especially strong impression on both southern and nonsouthern residents who empathized with the Till family. Many black youngsters could relate to the Till case because they too participated in cross-regional summer exchanges and could easily imagine themselves or their young relatives meeting a similar fate. With Till's death, northern children who were not allowed to go south for fear that they would get into trouble gained a better understanding of the dangers their caretakers were trying to protect them from, and young southerners were vividly forced to recognize their own vulnerability. Yet Till's murder also inspired activism, moving young people to express and channel the very anger and defiance that many of their elders had taught them to suppress.

Perhaps his mother best expressed the significance of Emmett's death to his peers. "To little black children who gazed upon the images of my son in the pages of *Jet* magazine," Mamie Till-Mobley said, "Emmett was the face of a harsh reality that left no place to hide. . . . To all black people," she continued, "he was a reminder of the common problem we faced in this country, whether we lived in the North or the South. He was a unifying symbol. And his name would be spoken at so many rallies and fund-raisers and even in congressional hearings."[82] Indeed, Till helped unite black families and justice activists across the regions because although he was northern born, he had a southern heritage—a product of migration and interdependent black families.

In light of the politicizing influence that transregional family culture had on African American youth in the postwar era, scholars of the civil rights movement must acknowledge the importance of African American family systems in the movement's origins. Although they lived in different regions, African Americans who remained in the South and those who migrated out were not a separate people. They were members of the same extended family groups that were intricately linked through economic, cultural, and political ties. Youngsters' various experiences while visiting family members in different parts of the country were accompanied by new understandings of blackness that inspired them to action in ways that would force the United States to begin closing the gap between its ideals and its practices. If not for the migration, the extension of familial systems, and the interfamilial exchange of political ideas and experiences, neither Emmett Till nor his legacy could have existed. Moreover, because Till's death was widely publicized, African American members of the Southern Diaspora were unable to disconnect themselves from their southern relatives' struggle for freedom. If child murder was a problem in the Mississippi Delta, it was also a problem in Chicago's black metropolis. If Jim Crow was the resident demon of the South, it also haunted those who left the region and made their homes in other locales. African American families could no longer play the roles that had nurtured Emmett Till in his cross-regional, northern migrant community without addressing the injustice in the South and, by extension, the entire nation. As they demanded justice, African Americans would continue to employ their flexible familial systems in the liberation struggles that accelerated after Till's death, enlivening the political consciousness of thousands of African American families.

Notes

My own transregional network of generous natural and adoptive kin sustained me through the writing of this essay. I am eternally grateful for the love and support of my parents, Otis and Wilma Frazier. Special thanks to Kimberly, Keston, Kendall, and Krystien Frazier; Jermaine, Kelly, and Jayson Deese; Kenya Anderson; Natasha Boyce; A. Sophia V. G. Heywood; Taneesha Johnson; Antonia Winstead; Sjocquelyn Winstead; and the Wrights, Richards, Akamigbos, Alonzos, Baileys, Bellamys, Brownes, Delk-Millers, Eustache-Joneses, Jameses, Joneses, Pauls, and Watermanns for their encouragement and hospitality while I completed the research and writing. Mia Bay, Steven Lawson, Deborah Gray White, Ann Fabian, Kimberley Phillips, Larry Hudson, Amrill Alonzo, Othell Miller, Gloria Delk, Tori Arthur, Jessica Wolfendale, and the editors of this volume provided myriad helpful critiques for which I am grateful. And finally, thank you to Dr. Bernice Johnson Reagon for her early consultation on this project and to the other gracious women and men of the Till generation who shared powerful recollections that gave me the confidence to construct this narrative.

1. Mamie Till-Mobley and Christopher Benson, *Death of Innocence: The Story of the Hate Crime that Changed America* (New York: Random House, 2003), 98. When Emmett Till was killed, his mother's name was Mamie Till Bradley; by the time she wrote her memoir, her surname was Till-Mobley. References to her in this essay reflect that transition.

2. Ibid., 101–2.

3. Ibid., 75.

4. Ibid., 139.

5. "People & Events: Clarence Strider (1904–1970)," in "American Experience: The Murder of Emmett Till," http://www.pbs.org/wgbh/amex/till/peopleevents/p_strider.html (accessed September 3, 2006).

6. Scholars of the civil rights movement have recently argued that normalizing the South in the history of civil rights struggles obscures the reality of racial segregation in the North as well as the impact of organized protests outside the South. For discussions that decentralize the South and challenge traditional periodizations of the movement, see Jeanne Theoharis and Komozi Woodard, eds., *Freedom North: Black Freedom Struggles Outside the South, 1940–1980* (New York: Palgrave Macmillan, 2003); Peniel E. Joseph, ed., *The Black Power Movement: Rethinking the Civil Rights–Black Power Era* (New York: Routledge, 2006); and Jacquelyn Dowd Hall, "The Long Civil Rights Movement and the Political Uses of the Past," *Journal of American History* 91, no. 4 (March 2005): 1233–63.

7. Clenora Hudson-Weems first argued for the restoration of Till's catalytic impact in the historical record based on her 1988 dissertation research. For her discussion of Till's neglect in the historical record and the role of union organizers in publicizing the case prior to the NAACP's involvement, see Clenora Hudson-Weems, *Emmett Till: The Sacrificial Lamb of the Civil Rights Movement* (Bloomington, Ind.: AuthorHouse, Parity, 2006), 46–57. After Hudson-Weems published her claims, scholars began paying more attention to the relationship between Till's death and early movement episodes such as the backlash against the *Brown* ruling, the Montgomery bus boycott, and the development of the student sit-in movement. Historian Rebecca de Schweinitz, *If We Could Change the World: Young People and America's Long Struggle for Racial Equality* (Chapel Hill: University of North Carolina Press, 2009), 217, powerfully argues that the lore surrounding Till's abduction presented defiant resistance as an alternative to accommodating Jim Crow and inspired militancy among his cohort. Jennifer Ritterhouse, *Growing Up Jim Crow: How Black and White Children Learned Race* (Chapel Hill: University of North Carolina Press, 2006), 17, reminds us that although Jim Crow's children were often more defiant than their parents, "the penalties for failing to perform according to the rules remained ever in force, demanding that black children suppress (although not entirely 'forget') their individual and contrary impulses."

8. See Ladner's comments in Charles Payne, *I've Got the Light of Freedom: SNCC and the Organizing Tradition in Mississippi* (Berkeley and Los Angeles: University of California Press, 1995), 54. For the purpose of limiting the sample, I classify the Till generation as those born within five years of 1940, so they would have been preteens to teenagers when Till was murdered and old enough to participate in civil rights activities by 1960 and have a distinct memory of his death.

Till They Come Back Home 157

Although Till's death affected youngsters with diverse backgrounds, this essay is limited to an examination of the ways in which transregional African American family culture shaped activists; therefore, it does not assess cross-regional exchanges within nonblack families.

9. Till-Mobley and Benson, *Death of Innocence,* 18–19.

10. Ibid., 18.

11. James N. Gregory, *The Southern Diaspora: How the Great Migrations of Black and White Southerners Transformed America* (Chapel Hill: University of North Carolina Press, 2005), xii.

12. Ibid., 16–17.

13. Darlene Clark Hine was among the first to add sexual exploitation and reproductivity concerns to this traditional list of "push-pull" factors that led to black southerners' decisions to migrate. See Darlene Clark Hine, "Black Migration to the Urban Midwest," in *Hine Sight: Black Women and the Re-Construction of American History,* with a foreword by John Hope Franklin (Bloomington and Indianapolis: Indiana University Press, 1994), 91. See Gregory, *Southern Diaspora,* 326, for more on the disproportionate impact of black migrants. The number of black residents nearly quadrupled in some northern locales after the second wave of migration around World War II. Several historical monographs explore the demographics of migration from specific states and regions. See Joe William Trotter, *Black Milwaukee: The Making of an Industrial Proletariat, 1915–1945* (Urbana and Chicago: University of Illinois Press, 1985), 41; Allen Ballard, *One More Day's Journey: The Story of a Family and a People* (New York: McGraw-Hill, 1984), 184; Denoral Davis, "Toward a Socio-Historical and Demographic Portrait of Twentieth-Century African Americans," in *Black Exodus: The Great Migration from the American South,* ed. Alferdteen Harrison (Jackson: University Press of Mississippi, 1991), 10; and Stewart E. Tolnay and E. M. Beck, "Rethinking the Role of Racial Violence in the Great Migration," ibid., 22. Isabel Wilkerson, *The Warmth of Other Suns: The Epic Story of America's Great Migration* (New York: Random House, 2010), provides detailed accounts of three migration stories— one from each decade between 1930 and 1960—that help debunk the culture of poverty theses that some scholars have traditionally applied to migrants.

14. George King, director and producer, *Goin' to Chicago,* presented by George King & Associates, Center for the Study of Southern Culture and Afro-American Studies Program, University of Mississippi (San Francisco: California Newsreel, 1994).

15. See Kimberley L. Phillips, *Alabama North: African-American Migrants, Community, and Working-Class Activism in Cleveland, 1915–45* (Urbana and Chicago: University of Illinois Press, 1999), 44–45; Ballard, *One More Day's Journey,* 13, 154–61.

16. Gregory, *Southern Diaspora,* 124. Chad Berry, *Southern Migrants, Northern Exiles* (Urbana and Chicago: University of Illinois Press, 2000), 138, argues

that many black migrant families in the North maintained a type of political accountability to the South, training children about the dangerous racial climate of the United States and wielding their newly acquired political mobility in favor of national reform.

17. I am still refining my ideas about what constitutes a cross-regional family. For purposes of this essay, I consider a cross-regional family to be one whose members moved out of the South but remained connected to other southern family members through visiting or other cultural practices. For example, although he dislikes the South, I consider author Claude Brown's family to be cross-regional because it maintained contact with southern relatives and folkways. I also consider Congressman John Lewis's family to be cross-regional because it was a southern family whose political ideas were shaped by members who resided in the North and brought northern cultural attributes with them when they returned. This discussion is part of an ongoing effort to explore African American identity and the question of when a migrant from the South becomes a northerner, despite maintaining lifestyle characteristics common to southerners.

18. Hine, "Black Migration to the Urban Midwest," 91.

19. Till-Mobley and Benson, *Death of Innocence,* 18.

20. Bill Russell and Taylor Branch, *Second Wind: The Memoirs of an Opinionated Man* (New York: Ballantine Books, 1979), 28.

21. Ibid., 34.

22. Carolyn Bonaparte, interview by Ray Allen of City Lore, July 26, 1993, transcript, African-American Migrants and Southern Folkways in New York City Oral History Project (AAMSFNYC), Schomburg Center for Research in Black Culture, New York, N.Y., 1–2.

23. Sylvia P. Woods, interview by Ray Allen, October 1, 1992, transcript, AAMSFNYC, 1–9.

24. William Thomas Ray, interview by Ray Allen, June 10, 1993, transcript, AAMSFNYC, 8.

25. Till-Mobley and Benson, *Death of Innocence,* 100.

26. Ralph David Abernathy, *And the Walls Came Tumbling Down: An Autobiography* (New York: Harper and Row, 1989), 15.

27. As Earl Lewis argues, black communities often focus on "congregation," turning inward to help strengthen their own institutions, as opposed to focusing on exclusion from the larger society. See Earl Lewis, *In Their Own Interests: Race, Class, and Power in Twentieth-Century Norfolk, Virginia* (Berkeley: University of California Press, 1991), 91–92, 104, 107. Gretchen Lemke-Santangelo argues that black children were especially important and valuable cultural assets who were trained to contribute to the families and communities of which they were a part. See Gretchen Lemke-Santangelo, *Abiding Courage: African American Migrant Women and the East Bay Community* (Chapel Hill: University of North Carolina Press, 1996), 147–49. Several migration monographs and other texts

mention this pattern of sending children south for summer visits. See Phillips, *Alabama North,* 141; Sam Gadsen, *An Oral History of Edisto Island: Sam Gadsen Tells the Story,* trans. Nick Lindsay (Goshen, Ind.: Goshen College, Pinchpenny Press, 1975), 6–7; and Clifton Taulbert, *The Last Train North* (New York: Penguin Books, 1995), 8–11.

28. Hudson-Weems, *Emmett Till,* 204.

29. Chester Butler, interview by Ray Allen, February 10, 1992, transcript, AAMSFNYC, 23; Claude Brown, *Manchild in the Promise Land* (New York: Touchstone, 1999), 21; Askia Muhammad, speech at tribute to Lawrence Guyot, 2009 (DVD in possession of Guyot); Courtland Cox, interview by the author, July 14, 2010, Washington, D.C.; Spirit Trickey, "Guiding My Mother's Place in History," *Crisis,* July–August 2005, 52.

30. Prathia Hall, interview by Sheila B. Michaels, February 23, 1999, Congress of Racial Equality/Student Nonviolent Coordinating Committee Veterans Oral History Project, Columbia University Oral History Archives, New York, N.Y., tape 1 of 2.

31. Till-Mobley and Benson, *Death of Innocence,* 18–19. Wilkerson, *Warmth of Other Suns,* 45, argues that many black migrants never shared their stories about the South with their children.

32. Ritterhouse, *Growing Up Jim Crow,* 110.

33. John Lewis with Michael D'Orso, *Walking in the Wind: A Memoir of the Movement* (New York: Simon and Schuster, 1998), 49.

34. Russell and Branch, *Second Wind,* 28.

35. Ibid.

36. Clifton Taulbert, *Once upon a Time When We Were Colored* (Tulsa, Okla.: Council Oak Books, 1989), 139–40.

37. Ibid., 139.

38. Taulbert, *Last Train North,* 10.

39. Taulbert, *When We Were Colored,* 140; Taulbert, *Last Train North,* 118–19.

40. Carolyn C. Dillon, comments on "Do You Remember," in "American Experience: The Murder of Emmett Till," http://www.pbs.org/wgbh/amex/till/sfeature/sf_remember.html (accessed September 3, 2006). Dillon's comments no longer appear on the website, where only comments from famous individuals remain. Dillon confirmed her comments in a telephone interview by the author. See also Ritterhouse, *Growing Up Jim Crow,* 104. Ritterhouse argues that, like their middle-class counterparts, lower-class parents trained their children in hard work, thrift, respect for community, and personal integrity but were more likely to emphasize deference.

41. Dillon, comments on "Do You Remember."

42. Brown, *Manchild in the Promise Land,* 37, 41–43, 275.

43. Timothy L. Jenkins, interview by the author, July 7, 2010, Washington, D.C. Jenkins was an executive member of SNCC, the National Student Associa-

tion (NSA), and Students for a Democratic Society. He continued working for the NSA and SNCC while in law school. He also contributed to the development of Title V of the Civil Rights Act, which included voter education initiatives. See Wesley C. Hogan, "Bridges North," in *Many Minds, One Heart: SNCC's Dream for a New America* (Chapel Hill: University of North Carolina Press, 2007), for a more in-depth discussion of the role of Jenkins, Casey Hayden, and others in taking the SNCC model outside the South, as well as strengthening the committee's leadership through exposure to resources from northern entities.

44. Jenkins interview. This exposure gave Jenkins his earliest "insights into the meaning of race in both America and the world."

45. Ibid.

46. Karen Edmonds Spellman, interview by the author, June 25, 2010, Washington, D.C.

47. Brown, *Manchild in the Promise Land,* 40.

48. Richard Wright, *Black Boy (American Hunger): A Record of Childhood and Youth* (New York: Harper Perennial, 1993), 202–3.

49. "Designed to Inflame," *Jackson Daily News,* September 2, 1955, 8. Karla F. C. Holloway, *Passed On: African American Mourning Stories* (Durham, N.C.: Duke University Press, 2002), 129–31, contrasts the thousands of mourners who viewed Till's casket in an era of persistent racial terrorism with the much fewer mourners and the higher incidence of violent death among black children by intraracial homicide that plagued African American families by the 1990s.

50. Charles Neblett, interview by the author, April 17, 2010, Raleigh, N.C.; Spellman interview; Ibrahim Mu'min, interview by the author, August 9, 2010, Washington, D.C.

51. Neblett interview.

52. Till-Mobley and Benson, *Death of Innocence,* 100.

53. Abernathy, *And the Walls Came Tumbling Down,* 29.

54. Spellman interview. Ritterhouse, *Growing Up Jim Crow,* 85, 110, argues that middle- and upper-class black southern children, like Spellman, were raised with a sense of respectability that emphasized worth, promise, personal dignity, and one's responsibility to racial advancement.

55. Russell and Branch, *Second Wind,* 28.

56. Lewis with D'Orso, *Walking in the Wind,* 49–51.

57. Dillon, comments on "Do You Remember."

58. Spellman interview.

59. Ritterhouse, *Growing Up Jim Crow,* 4.

60. Brown, *Manchild in the Promise Land,* 47, 50.

61. Ritterhouse, *Growing Up Jim Crow,* 17.

62. Spellman interview.

63. Mu'min interview.

64. Neblett interview.

65. Spellman interview.

66. Linda Brown was the daughter of the Reverend Oliver L. Brown, the principal plaintiff in the 1954 *Brown v. the Board of Education* case that denounced segregation as illegal and permitted young Linda to attend a white elementary school four blocks from her home. She had previously been forced to travel four miles to school. Mrs. Nettie Hunt posed for a photo with her daughter Nickie on the Supreme Court steps while holding a newspaper with the headline "High Court Bans Segregation in Public Schools." The image was widely circulated across the country.

67. Gregory, *Southern Diaspora,* 326.

68. Ibid.

69. After Till's death, his mother campaigned across the country with the NAACP and helped raise thousands of dollars for the organization's justice work.

70. Quoted in Hudson-Weems, *Emmett Till,* 204.

71. Katherine Verdery, *The Political Lives of Dead Bodies: Reburial and Post-socialist Change* (New York: Columbia University Press, 1999), 33, argues that dead bodies are "excellent means for accruing something essential to political transformation: symbolic capital. . . . Dead bodies . . . can be a site of political profit."

72. Cleveland Sellers, *The River of No Return: The Autobiography of a Militant and the Life and Death of SNCC* (New York: William Morrow, 1973), 14.

73. Ibid., 15.

74. Anne Moody, *Coming of Age in Mississippi* (New York: Dell, 1976), 104–11.

75. Quoted in Hudson-Weems, *Emmett Till,* 212.

76. Lewis with D'Orso, *Walking in the Wind,* 47.

77. Ibid.

78. de Schweinitz, *If We Could Change the World,* 51–90, 217. De Schweinitz provides a brilliant analysis of the Till case and the American ideals of childhood in 1955, noting how both the defense and the prosecution used images of childhood to support their clients and that the defendants, Milam and Bryant, asserted their appreciation of childhood by bringing their wives and children to the courtroom.

79. James Horton, comments on "Do You Remember," in "American Experience: The Murder of Emmett Till," http://www.pbs.org/wgbh/amex/till/sfeature/sf_remember.html (accessed September 3, 2006).

80. Ibid.

81. Holloway, *Passed On,* 139.

82. Till-Mobley and Benson, *Death of Innocence,* 199–200.

The Johns Committee, Sex, and Civil Rights in Florida, 1963–1965

Stacy Braukman

> We're not having any sex orgies or anything like that. This is a march for freedom.
>
> —Lester Maddox

In the summer of 1956, as part of a regional wave of resistance against the U.S. Supreme Court's *Brown v. Board of Education* decision, the Florida legislature created an investigating committee whose primary aim was to tarnish the reputation and hamper the efforts of the National Association for the Advancement of Colored People (NAACP). Across the South, in Alabama, Louisiana, Mississippi, South Carolina, and Virginia, legislators sought to expose what they believed to be the criminal activities and subversive ties of the NAACP and other groups advocating racial equality.[1] Unlike the other states, however, the Florida Legislative Investigation Committee (FLIC; commonly known as the Johns Committee after its founder, conservative state senator Charley Johns) expanded its antisubversive mission over nine years to include homosexual teachers, indecent literature and pornography, liberal professors, and student activists.

By 1965 the civil rights movement had penetrated American politics and culture, awakening the nation's conscience in a way that even jarring individual episodes in the 1950s—from Emmett Till's lynching to the venomous white mobs in Little Rock—had not. The stark contrast between the dignified resolve of nonviolent demonstrators and the rage of die-hard segregationists came into sharper relief during the era of the Freedom Rides, Birmingham, the March on Washington, and Bloody Sunday and the subsequent march from Selma to Montgomery. Many Americans came to sympathize with the abstract principles of black voting rights and equal access to lunch counters, but not (as was becoming increasingly clear) with the reality of African Americans moving into white middle- and working-class neighborhoods. At the very moment when the greatest constitutional victories in a century were being won, however, the movement itself was already changing. Growing student activism across a widening spectrum, from the increasing radicalism of the Student Nonviolent Coordinating Committee (SNCC) to the emergence of the New Left, seemed to portend the fulfillment of postwar conservatives' and segregationists' greatest fears.

In Florida the FLIC acted as both a sounding board and a mouthpiece for massive resistance and southern conservatism during these years. The committee monitored students who were active in civil rights and peace groups, defended an unpopular report on homosexuality, and published a leering account of Martin Luther King and the St. Augustine campaign of the Southern Christian Leadership Conference (SCLC). By 1964, with the passage of the Civil Rights Act and the conservative triumph within the Republican Party, massive resistance transformed from an overtly race-based articulation of white supremacy and fear of black contamination to an ostensibly color-blind defense of individual rights, particularly the freedom of association. The Johns Committee joined politicians, legislative committees, and the FBI to discredit the civil rights movement as tainted by communism, with a pronounced emphasis on sexual immorality. The seeds of this critique of liberalism had been sown in the immediate postwar years, but the commingling of conservative and segregationist attacks on the morals of blacks and whites on the Left forged a crucial bond with nonsouthern conservatives that would resonate for decades.

Charley Johns and FLIC counsel Mark Hawes addressed the legislature on April 18, 1963, to summarize the committee's activities over the previous two years. Hawes started by explaining that the committee had originally gone to the University of South Florida (USF) in Tampa to gather "information in the field of subversion and homosexual conduct." But members began "receiving complaints . . . in regard to the anti-Christian teachings and materials on that campus, and the alleged materials containing the vulgar and profane language out there." Hawes quoted FBI director J. Edgar Hoover's warning from *A Study on Communism* about the Communist Party's establishment of "a speaker's bureau for the purpose of making themselves available to go around and become members of the faculty of the universities of this country and to make one-shot and two and three-shot speeches." Hawes then outlined student and parent complaints about USF professors: their insulting and belittling of Christian beliefs and those who hold them; the teaching of "ethical relativity—the notion that there is no absolute standard of morality or immorality"; the use of "coarse and vulgar, profane and vile" language in reading assignments and classroom discussions; and homosexuality and inappropriate behavior with students. Worst of all, said Hawes, administrators and faculty were closing ranks and crowing about the sanctity of academic freedom, which, as construed by USF administrators, meant nothing more than "the right to bring communist sympathizers and communists themselves to teach and indoctrinate, [and] the right to take this ordinary, everyday filth which I call intellectual garbage off the newsstands and put it in the classrooms as required texts, and it includes the right for these people to do these things without any restraint or policy at all on behalf of the people or the elected officials."[2]

Similar controversies had plagued colleges and universities for decades, especially during the red scares following World War II. Across the country, schools compelled teachers and professors to take loyalty oaths because conservative anticommunists feared corrosive liberal influences in classrooms and campus organizations. Hoover never seemed to tire of warning about the Communist menace in schools and colleges. But many universities policed themselves, and they had policies dating back to the 1930s that denied employment to members of the Communist Party and barred them from speaking appearances.[3] Just to be sure, during the late 1940s and 1950s virtually every state passed or attempted to pass laws banning the hiring of Communists and requiring loyalty oaths. Because politicians believed Communist teachers' primary allegiance was to the Soviet Union rather than to intellectual integrity or autonomy, such teachers were viewed as unfit. Secrecy surrounding party membership was another strike against members. When the House Un-American Activities Committee (HUAC) made its first inquiry into subversive professors in 1953, it ushered in a new era of scrutiny and created a consensus in the academy "that it had to respond to the congressional hearings." As historian Ellen Schrecker put it, "once HUAC, SISS [Senate Internal Security Subcommittee], or Senator McCarthy questioned a teacher and raised the issue of Communism, the academic community rushed to investigate."[4]

In the post-*Brown* South, where schools and universities functioned as a different battleground—for the pro-segregation forces defending against Negroes, outsiders, and the federal government—university self-policing, political investigations, and other intrusions had become commonplace. Untenured professors at some Alabama colleges were dismissed for publicly supporting integration. A minister's speaking invitation to Ole Miss was rescinded when his NAACP membership was revealed.[5] And in the summer of 1963 the North Carolina legislature passed "An Act to Regulate Visiting Speakers at State Supported Colleges and Universities," which prohibited appearances by anyone who had been a member of the Communist Party, had advocated the overthrow of the state or federal constitution, or had pleaded the Fifth Amendment in any legislative hearing on subversion or communism. Although it applied to all state-funded universities, the law was directed at the University of North Carolina at Chapel Hill, which had a long tradition of liberalism and had recently made headlines as a source of student protests and civil rights demonstrations.[6]

In the early 1960s a young Jesse Helms railed against University of North Carolina rabble-rousers in his nightly editorials for Raleigh television station WRAL. Armistead Maupin (who later gained fame as a gay novelist), the conservative editor of the school's *Daily Tar Heel*, did the same. The object of their scorn was a group called the Student Peace Union, a local chapter of a national organization devoted to nuclear disarmament and civil rights founded in 1959. In March 1963 the group devoted itself to civil rights in the Raleigh–Durham–Chapel Hill area, and students began a series of highly publicized demonstrations at segregated restaurants, hotels, and theaters. North Carolina legislators were furious. As one historian argues, they responded to this flouting of southern custom by concocting the speakers' ban to "exercise direct political control over the university, some of whose students and faculty had been openly opposing the status quo."[7] The link between racial subversion and communism had been hammered into the southern white consciousness, and now with Helms editorializing about it night after night on television, the legislature played up universities as breeding grounds for liberal-inspired interracialism and moral corruption.

Demonstrations were gaining momentum in other southern cities as well, including St. Augustine, Florida, in 1963. There the local NAACP Youth Council, headed by a young dentist named Robert Hayling, led the picketing, marches, and sit-ins against segregated restaurants and city facilities. Hayling was relatively new to the area, having moved to St. Augustine three years earlier from Nashville, and he was more impatient with the city's entrenched white leadership and its refusal to desegregate than were his native colleagues. His militancy may have enhanced his appeal to the Youth Council, comprising high school students and a handful of college undergraduates. In early 1963 Hayling and other NAACP members wrote to Vice President Lyndon Johnson, urging him to cancel his upcoming visit to St. Augustine. Soon after they contacted President John F. Kennedy to demand that he quash a federal grant to help pay for the city's 1965 quadricentennial because of discrimination in its schools, stores, and recreational facilities. Both requests were ignored, but the gathering storm attracted the attention of the FBI, which dispatched agents to St. Augustine to monitor the growing racial unrest.[8]

The all-white city council proved equally uncooperative, refusing NAACP demands to desegregate public facilities, hire more African Americans in city government jobs, and establish a biracial committee. Meanwhile, fed up with the numerous death threats he had been receiving, Hayling further alienated St. Augustine whites when he angrily told reporters that he would not think twice about using violence, if necessary, for his own self-defense. Referring to the recent shooting in Jackson, Mississippi, he stated flatly, "We are not going to die like Medgar Evers."[9] Ten days later sit-ins began. Mayor Joseph Shelley publicly condemned the protests as Communist inspired. Unknown assailants fired shots at Hayling's house, and white employers began firing or threatening to fire black workers who participated in any demonstrations. Undaunted, the Youth Council, the NAACP, and local black citizens continued to picket and sit-in. From late summer into the fall the demonstrations grew in size, and the recriminations increased accordingly. The police displayed unnerving ease in their manhandling of black protesters, and various Ku Klux Klan groups and the John Birch Society, which had an active chapter in the city, got involved. By late October the Klan rallies and cross burnings gave way to gun violence on both sides. By the end of 1963 it was obvious that compromise would be impossible.[10]

Prior to 1963 the Johns Committee likely would have sent its chief investigator, R. J. Strickland, to investigate racial agitators such as Robert Hayling. But that summer the committee was in the middle of a shake-up, necessitated in part by the negative publicity surrounding the inquiry at the University of South Florida and by judicial rebukes suffered earlier in the year. On June 24 Strickland submitted his resignation.[11] That month, FLIC attorney Mark Hawes also resigned quietly. Neither was replaced until November. In addition, John Evans, former aide to Governor Farris Bryant, assumed the newly created position of staff director. Evans had also headed the Center for Cold War Education, a think tank devoted to teaching the evils of communism and the benefits of American democracy in Florida's schools.

While the committee was being overhauled and its members were sitting idly on the sidelines, a growing number of students were joining liberal groups, taking up leftist causes, and participating in public protests on behalf of racial equality. At Florida State University dozens of white students formed chapters of the Young People's Socialist League and Students Act for Peace (SAP). They also joined in the picketing and sit-ins aimed at integrating the capital city's movie theaters, restaurants, swimming pools, and recreational facilities. The Congress of Racial Equality (CORE), a nonviolent civil rights organization founded in the early 1940s, organized the demonstrations. Police arrested and jailed hundreds of students from the state's historically black school, Florida A&M University, along with a small contingent from Florida State and the University of Florida that participated in the protests.[12]

The upsurge in interracial civil rights activism during 1963 reflected both local circumstances and a national shift in priorities. In communities across the South, sit-ins and demonstrations had been taking place for nearly three years, resulting in little actual integration. Black patience wore thin, especially as white resistance stiffened. President Kennedy had finally been convinced to push aggressively for civil rights legislation that would address, among other things, public accommodations. He had watched in horror, along with the rest of the country, as Martin Luther King and the SCLC led a youth march on May 2 and Bull Connor's police force used violence against Birmingham's black elementary and high school students. White officers allowed their dogs to attack the black children; they sprayed the demonstrators with powerful fire hoses, hurling them against buildings, trees, and sidewalks; and they arrested and jailed the protesters for demanding equal access to city facilities. Images from the melee, broadcast to national and international audiences, thrust Kennedy yet again into the awkward position of opposing Marxism in Third World independence movements while trying to deflect criticism of the blight of segregation on his own nation's democracy. A week later, after the bombing of King's brother's house and the black-owned Gaston Motel in Birmingham, local blacks responded by attacking white police and firemen. The following month Alabama governor George Wallace made his infamous and symbolic stand in the schoolhouse door to prevent two black students from entering the University of Alabama. Wallace's actions made for great political theater, but they infuriated Kennedy and persuaded the president to endorse a comprehensive civil rights bill.[13] In many Florida cities and towns, including Tallahassee, St. Petersburg, Tampa, Gainesville, Daytona Beach, and Jacksonville, the NAACP, newly unburdened from the Johns Committee's harassment and energized by college and high school students, launched a new series of demonstrations against segregated movie theaters, restaurants, beaches, and other public spaces.[14]

Early in 1964 the white South was on the brink of losing its grip on legalized segregation. Although some segregationists may have hoped that southerner Lyndon Johnson would stand with them, even Richard B. Russell, longtime Georgia senator and Johnson's mentor, knew that the Texan's sympathies and political sensibilities meant that Kennedy's civil rights bill would pass. More ominously for segregationists, blacks were shifting their attention to voter registration and legal challenges to disfranchisement across the region, even as they stepped up sit-ins, picketing, and lawsuits against the public schools. The Johns Committee had been reorganized, discontinuing its investigations of homosexual teachers and subversives within the NAACP. The responsibilities of staff director John Evans tended almost entirely toward public relations, and chairman Richard O. Mitchell became the committee's public face, replacing Johns and Strickland. In 1964 the FLIC promised to investigate internal security, and in light of the proliferation of student activist groups and escalating tensions in St. Augustine, it believed this message would resonate with Floridians.

The FLIC could not legally interfere with the NAACP's announced voter registration drive that began in January, seeking to add 50,000 new names to the nearly 220,000 registered black voters in the state. The committee had begun recruiting informants at the University of Florida and Florida State University to infiltrate the Young People's Socialist League, the Liberal Forum, and SAP, but it would take time to gather enough "detailed information on some of the key links in these organizations" to propose any legislative action. Evans also coordinated FLIC meetings with members of various antisubversive groups that spring, including the HUAC, the Alabama Legislative Commission to Keep the Peace, and California's Senate Investigating Committee on Education.[15]

Given the FLIC's new focus, it is surprising that in March 1964 it issued what many viewed as a bizarre report on the threat of homosexuality, but releasing the report may have been one of the committee's few options. Plans for a report on the dangers of homosexuality had been in the works since a series of statewide educational conferences on pornography and homosexuality in 1961–1962. At one Florida Children's Commission

(FCC) advisory committee meeting in January 1962, a participant had recommended educating the public by disseminating an informational pamphlet on the problem.[16] Two months later the FCC announced in a press release that it had received suggestions from an undisclosed "committee on community education" that "all known information on the subject be compiled."[17] In June 1962 the Research Committee in Sexual Deviance, a subcommittee of Governor Bryant's Advisory Committee on Homosexuality, concluded that a "public education effort employing the so-called 'shock technique' may be needed immediately [if] the public is to be stimulated to want to do something about" homosexuality and pornography.[18]

Soon after being hired as the FLIC staff director, Evans began defending past campaigns and emphasizing the focus on creating new legislation. He also promised at the beginning of his tenure that the Johns Committee would produce "a definitive report, factual in nature and complete in its descriptions, of the relationship of homosexuality to sound citizenship in our state." And he reassured Floridians that "investigative leads in the Committee's files and which came to its attention were promptly and properly followed up by appropriate agencies." In public appearances, press releases, and personal correspondence, Evans tried to convince audiences that this new and improved committee was no longer focused on rounding up gays and lesbians but was still dedicated to investigating "organizations and individuals which can be broadly termed 'subversive.'"[19]

In January 1964 the committee completed its report on homosexuality, and members met at the end of the month to discuss how best to present their findings. State senator Robert Williams from Graceville, a small town near the Alabama line, proposed that distribution of the forty-four-page booklet be limited to "members of the Legislature, law enforcement officials, educators, members of the press, and to such groups as parent-teacher associations, city police departments, and others properly concerned." Johns seconded the motion.[20]

Homosexuality and Citizenship in Florida was supposed to be the Johns Committee's crowning glory, the culmination of years of exhaustive interrogations and surveillance. But the FLIC drastically overestimated the public's tolerance for being scared straight. Upon opening the swirling lavender cover, the reader was greeted by a black-and-white photograph of two men, naked to the waist, embracing and kissing on the mouth. On the next page the preface explained the importance of the report to "every parent and every individual concerned with the moral climate of the state," who "should be aware of the rise in homosexual activity noted here." The

beginning of the main text was positioned next to a full-page photograph—
"taken from a homosexual's collection"—of a teenage boy clad only in a
G-string and bound with ropes to a latticework door. As the caption explained, "the use of bindings is frequent in artwork of this nature" and is
"an apparently strong stimulant to the deviate."[21] Two other pictures were
included in the report. One, on the page opposite the "Glossary of Homosexual Terms and Deviate Acts," showed a man in a public restroom receiving oral sex from another man in the adjoining stall. The doors to both
stalls had been removed, to no effect. His hips pressed against the parti-
tion, his face turned toward the camera but obscured by a black rectangle
to conceal his identity, the man wore a plaid shirt with the short sleeves
rolled up. The man performing oral sex was seated on the toilet. The last
image, placed next to the "Bibliography on Sexual Deviations," showed
a series of images of a preadolescent boy in various poses and stages of
undress that resembled the popular muscle magazines of the day.[22]

These illustrations demonstrated what committee members had been
telling Floridians for years: homosexuals coveted children, they took and
traded dirty pictures, and they had anonymous sex in public places. This
exposé of homosexuality was bolstered not only by the report's frequent
references to "experts" and "authorities" or the hefty bibliography but also
by the most inflammatory photographic evidence, intended to instill fear.
Indeed, without these pictures, it is difficult to imagine the report causing as much of a stir. To be sure, it discussed sex frankly and contained a
glossary of gay terminology that certainly would have thrown 1964 audiences for a loop. Who knew (or needed to know) that *pygmalionism* (the
"sexual desire for a statue or statues") was a problem at all, much less one
related to homosexuality, or that a *dinge queen* was a Negro homosexual,
sea food referred to homosexuals in the navy, and *chicken* was slang for an
extremely young homosexual?

A blurb printed on the back of the pamphlet offered individual copies
for sale at twenty-five cents apiece. But there was considerable confusion
about who constituted the "properly concerned" or "properly qualified"
persons who were invited to order their own copies of the booklet. The un-
certainty was only heightened by a piece in the *New Republic* that claimed,
"Two thousand books were printed at a cost of $720. The first thousand
were sent off to legislators, newspapers, and other 'key' people, but anyone who sends the committee 25 cents can get one."[23] Despite committee members' claims that their intention had been to distribute the report
only to those with a vested interest in youth and education, the ambiguous

statement on the back of the pamphlet, coupled with national publicity about the shocking report, led untold numbers of people from around the country to mail in their quarters and their requests. The Dade County state attorney threatened legal action to prevent the sale of the report and called it obscene.[24]

In the opening pages committee members established their credentials by emphasizing their impartiality and reliance on "officials of Florida's mental health program, law enforcement agencies and courts" and their "extensive study of the many and divergent publications, both scientific and popular, in the field" to formulate "recommendations for effective recognition by the state of its present and potential bearing on the quality of citizenship in Florida." The report maintained that homosexuals constitute "a well organized society," including everything from separate customs to special meeting places and even "national organizations through which articulate homosexuals seek recognition of their condition as a proper part of our culture and morals."[25] The report represented homosexuals as a secretive, organized underground community whose political agenda was to make their abnormality normal in the eyes of American culture.

The idea that so-called perverts sought acceptance of their way of life as "normal" was central to postwar opposition to pornography and obscenity. The Cincinnati-based Citizens for Decent Literature (CDL) focused on the issue in its 1964 film *Perversion for Profit,* which was similar in tone and content to *Homosexuality and Citizenship in Florida.* Charles Keating Jr. founded CDL in the mid-1950s with the goal of restricting or eliminating altogether obscene paperback books, magazines, and tabloids. The organization grew rapidly in the early 1960s, claiming 300 chapters across the country by 1965. Local chapters sent members out into the community—to "PTAs, fraternal orders, women's clubs"—to enlighten them about the harm caused by this material. "After we had described the problem," explained one CDL member, "we'd pass around to the audience a typical group of pornographic publications. Invariably, everybody would be shocked."[26] Shock was the catalyst for action, as newly informed citizens wrote angry letters, joined the organization, or took other steps to try to clean up their communities' newsstands. In *Perversion for Profit,* narrator George Putnam, a popular news anchor in Los Angeles and later a conservative talk radio host, warned that obscene reading material enticed youth to "enter the world of homosexuals, lesbians, sadists, masochists and other sex deviates." Putnam held a placard with a picture of an octopus, tentacles outstretched, reaching into every corner of a map of the United States. As the camera zoomed in on the sinister image, the narrator intoned: "Here is the most vicious, the most insidious feature of these publications: they constantly portray abnormal sexual behavior as being normal; they glorify unnatural sex acts; they tell youngsters that it's smart, it's thrilling, it provides kicks to be a homosexual, a sadist, and every other kind of deviate." And, like Communists, such publications were insidious and sneaky, tricking young people into perversion gradually, while making this deviance appear perfectly normal, harmless, and downright fun. Girlie magazines that emphasized women's buttocks "appeal to the sodomist." Too many images of breasts turned healthy male appreciation into "a fetish." A normal heterosexual man who enjoys men's muscle magazines, Putnam announced, would eventually become perverted.[27]

The danger of allowing gays to serve as teachers, according to *Homosexuality and Citizenship in Florida,* was their corrupting influence on children. The theme of homosexual desire for youth ran through the entire report. In some places the author was careful to distinguish between the child molester—who "attacks, but seldom kills or physically cripples his victim"—and the homosexual, who "prefers to reach out for the child at the time of normal sexual awakening and to conduct a psychological preliminary to the physical contact. The homosexual's goal and part of his satisfaction is to 'bring over' the young person, to hook him for homosexuality." In perhaps the most concise summary of the post–World War II interpretation of homosexuality, the report called it "unique among the sexual assaults" because "the person affected by the practicing homosexual is first a victim, then an accomplice, and finally by himself a perpetrator of homosexual acts."[28]

The outcry was immediate. Some, like a writer in the *New Republic,* dismissed the booklet out of hand as silly and alarmist and questioned the logic behind hunting Communists and homosexuals together: "Possibly the two deviations have become confused in the committee's collective mind."[29] Racial moderate Bill Baggs, editor of the *Miami News* and close friend to *Atlanta Constitution* editor Ralph McGill and *Arkansas Gazette* editor Harry Ashmore, mocked the Johns Committee's gross miscalculation. Baggs wrote to Ashmore, "the author of the tract did such a splendid job in No. 1, Vol. 1, Florida Homo, that we shall never see No. 2." "This is but another testimonial," he said, "to the fact that Florida is not afraid to think new thoughts and explore new ranges. In short, we are at least not stuffy."[30]

Other critics included self-identified homosexuals. Hal Call, a leader in the San Francisco–based homophile group the Mattachine Society, noted the report's many flaws—starting with its failure to achieve its primary goal, which was to document the extent of homosexual infiltration of state agencies. Call pointed out that the committee quoted no authorities, despite the substantial bibliography, and offered no proof that homosexuals recruited the young, spread venereal disease, or were "a factor in other forms of sexual deviations, in major crime occurrences, and in security matters." He concluded by observing that "only about one-third of the material in the section on Florida laws has anything whatsoever to do with homosexuality," and "the remaining two-thirds was included in order to associate homosexuality with everything else that is considered abnormal or arouses emotional responses."[31] One man from Fort Lauderdale composed a scathing letter to committee chairman Richard Mitchell, telling him, "Your present ill-fame only serves to prove that you and your crowd have the dirtiest minds in the whole state."[32] Another scolded the Johns Committee for casting aspersions against all homosexuals: "Let me assure you there are thousands upon thousands of us right here in Florida who live sane and sensible lives. None of my friends would hardly know what one of your 'glory holes' is much less would we indulge in such degradation."[33]

Most people who commented publicly condemned the report for the lurid photographs and bizarre glossary, but not the message. As a *Tallahassee Democrat* editorial put it, although the report was "obscene" and "shocking," and "the subject it treats is offensive . . . it is a real subject that we have discussed too long behind the backs of our hands without recognizing the scope and implications of the pernicious problem it presents. This booklet contains information . . . that has only recently begun to dawn on the opened minds of some editors and reporters who like to think they are world-wise." On the issue of the photographs, the editors remarked that they "have seen some of the pictures the committee has had before it during its investigation, and we'd say the ones it published were among the least objectionable." Finally, the editorial warned readers not to dismiss the pamphlet or the committee out of hand or at the expense of gleaning a valuable lesson from the report, because there "might be something in it that will help you understand a public problem, or head off a family tragedy."[34]

Some Floridians, everyday citizens who may or may not have actually seen the report, agreed that despite its flaws, the message was important and should be heard amid the cries of obscenity. A father from Hollywood, Florida, whose son was entering college wrote, "The information as imparted in the booklet will be invaluable, in my guidance and counseling of my son, in his new environment, in this crucial period of his life." A Key West resident praised the committee for "enlightening both the public and officials on this subject which has been too hush-hush for many years, and which is now internationally recognized and dealt with in a much more sane fashion than in days past." A woman from Miami exclaimed, "It is about time some of our Legislators were shocked about the growing HOMOSEXUALS in our community. I admire you very much for publishing this booklet and I do hope it will shock our State Legislate [*sic*] into making some new and stiff laws to control these SEX DEVIATES." A mother of five and grandmother of ten wrote to Evans, urging him to "do something about it before many of our young people are ruined and little children are killed as a result of these perverts being loose in our society."[35]

Evans defended the report in a speech before the Florida Federation of Women's Clubs, gave numerous interviews, and responded to scores of letters from both opponents and supporters. He assured a Miami judge, in a rote recitation of the party line, that *Homosexuality and Citizenship in Florida* was "a definitive report, factual in nature and complete in its descriptions, of the relationship of homosexuality to sound citizenship in our state." He explained that the committee had formulated a strict policy about limiting distribution of the report to specific groups—an explanation that did not account for the statement on the back cover that individual copies were available for twenty-five cents each. Evans claimed, "The booklet has received wide use among the organizations for which it was intended, and if the reports that come back to us are any indication, it has made a significant contribution to better understanding and handling of the problem of homosexuality around the state."[36]

Two weeks before the report was released, the Southern Christian Leadership Conference held its annual meeting in Orlando. Black leaders from St. Augustine traveled there to ask King's advisers for his help in resuscitating their city's flagging integration movement. After C. T. Vivian visited the city and saw firsthand the influence of the Klan, the John Birch Society, and other segregationists within city government and law enforcement and felt the palpable racial disquiet in the muggy St. Augustine air, he recommended that the SCLC launch a campaign there.

The SCLC's first venture into St. Augustine lasted two weeks, but not long after the activists departed, the local movement floundered. The SCLC then announced that it would return to see the campaign through to the end this time, and on May 26 the second round of demonstrations began. This time it turned violent. Whites threw bricks, rocks, and whatever else was handy at the blacks who marched through downtown St. Augustine nightly. On a few occasions they beat up cameramen and demonstrators and shot at and set fire to King's rental beachfront cottage—whose address the *St. Augustine Record* had published. Unshakable city leaders, represented by Mayor Shelley, would not consider the activists' demands that the city add a handful of black police officers, firefighters, and clerical workers. An even greater sticking point was Shelley's refusal to appoint a biracial committee. The mayor had the support of most St. Augustine whites, whose numbers were increased by Klan groups from around the state as well as from neighboring Georgia and Alabama.[37]

Governor Farris Bryant was unable to stop the nighttime marches, which had become a magnet for violence during the summer of 1964, as had the wade-ins at local beaches. When a handful of African Americans went in the swimming pool at Monson's Motor Lodge, the proprietor immediately ran to a storage closet, pulled out a container of what he claimed was acid, and began pouring. The crowd dispersed, but not before one man was physically assaulted in the pool by a police officer. On July 2, when President Johnson signed the civil rights bill into law, King and the SCLC called off the demonstrations. But white resistance and resentment did not end with their departure, and many white businesses quickly returned to an aggressive de facto segregation.[38]

Racial tensions in the city were made worse by the ongoing public presence of Klan groups and right-wing extremists such as J. B. Stoner, Connie Lynch, and Holstead "Hoss" Manucy, who regularly led counter-demonstrations and rallies and seized every opportunity to condemn Communists and "nigger lovers." Manucy, who was from a small town north of St. Augustine, was the head of the Ancient City Gun Club, a white supremacist group that overlapped in membership with the Klan and collaborated in harassing civil rights demonstrators. In August 1964 *Time* magazine reported that he and his men had been enjoined from picketing in front of more than a dozen motels and restaurants with signs reading "Niggers Eat Here. Would You?" White proprietors reported that they had been cowed into resegregating their establishments. St. Augustine's black citizens, emboldened by the Civil Rights Act, did not hesitate to take them to court.[39] Stoner and Lynch were itinerant segregationist activists who had devoted the past several years to visiting civil rights hot spots and organizing white resistance in local communities. Stoner had served as chairman of the anti-Semitic, segregationist, anticommunist, and nativist National States' Rights Party since the group's founding in 1958. The Reverend Charles Conley "Connie" Lynch was a self-styled fundamentalist preacher whose career consisted of denouncing racial mixing and godless communism. In St. Augustine the three men received almost daily press coverage of their attacks against the civil rights "invasion," and their inflammatory words helped set the tone for the battle over integration.

FBI agents from nearby Jacksonville were there to keep tabs on both sides. Since the March on Washington the previous August, the bureau had stepped up its campaign to discredit the movement in general, and King in particular, as Communist tainted. Historian Kenneth O'Reilly argues that the massive demonstration in the nation's capital marked a critical turning point in the FBI's treatment of King and civil rights activists. He cites Hoover's "belief that blacks had gone too far with their protests and now posed an imminent threat to the established order" and the FBI director's inability to contain the civil rights movement through "a relatively passive surveillance policy on the intelligence front."[40] O'Reilly goes on to document the FBI's full-scale assault on King's private life and associations, reflecting both the pragmatism of a social conservative and a highly personal racist, sexualized animosity. But the connections drawn between perversion and subversion were not simply the product of one man's imagination. By 1963 they had been etched into the political landscape. O'Reilly claims that the "ease with which the FBI slid from the communist issue to the morality issue indicates that the director and his aides were looking for something—anything—that might work to discredit King." But it indicates much more—namely, that the Cold War had shaped people's way of thinking about political enemies, depicting them as morally degenerate and sexually perverse. Given this shift, coupled with enduring notions of black sexual licentiousness, the FBI's search was neither desperate nor grasping.[41] Hoover's targeting of King's extramarital affairs was more than a convenient ploy or a cheap attempt at character defamation. It was an expression of an anticommunist ethos that equated or linked sexual immorality with radicalism and un-Americanism.

The FBI followed King to St. Augustine in the summer of 1964, and in mid-August it sent copies of an intelligence analysis of "Communist plans" for the upcoming march in the city to more than forty government offices. Agents identified eight close associates of King and the SCLC as having Communist links. In the fall of 1963 Hoover had ordered a wiretap on King's home and office in Atlanta and had compiled voluminous reports on the civil rights leader's extramarital affairs and contacts with accused subversives such as Stanley Levinson, Jack O'Dell, and Bayard Rustin (who was further demonized for being a homosexual). Hoover, who in one infamous memo called King a "tomcat," increasingly criticized the civil rights movement for attracting "Communists and moral degenerates."[42] Mayor Shelley, citing Hoover in a speech to a local civic club, reported on "how deeply the civil rights movement has become involved with communism. A lot of people think what has happened in St. Augustine in the past year is a simple matter of segregation and integration," but "that's just a coverup, just a pattern of what is happening all over the United States. It is part of an American revolution."[43]

Rather than actually inserting themselves into St. Augustine's racial turmoil, members of the Johns Committee continued to observe Florida's white university students, who were joining various liberal causes in growing numbers. In Gainesville the Student Group for Equal Rights (SGER) took part in sit-ins and picketing at drugstores, restaurants, and movie theaters beginning in the summer of 1963. One SGER member, an anthropology graduate student, also attended regional SNCC meetings and became a founding member of the Southern Student Organizing Committee, an offshoot of SNCC created in 1964 to mobilize white support for the civil rights movement.[44] The committee's files on the SGER consisted mostly of the group's literature and newspaper clippings. Meanwhile, in Tallahassee, Board of Control member Charles Forman accused Florida State University president Gordon Blackwell of coddling the Young People's Socialist League, a subversive group that showed a "communist pattern." Because Blackwell had refused to ban the group (although he did try to "restrict" its activities), Forman claimed the president was fostering an "ultra-liberal" attitude on campus. At the end of July Blackwell resigned to become the president of Furman University.[45] The issue became a running theme in the governor's race, as Jacksonville's segregationist mayor Haydon Burns blustered on the campaign trail about the number of "pinks and commies" in the state's universities.[46] He went on to win the election.

The FLIC also spent the summer of 1964 monitoring a group of peace activists who, under the auspices of the Committee for Nonviolent Action (CNVA), were traveling from Canada to Cuba in support of nuclear disarmament. The CNVA had been founded in 1958, emerging from a loosely organized series of protests against nuclear testing in the Nevada desert. Early sponsors included the War Resisters League and the Women's International League for Peace and Freedom, and members included such well-known pacifists as A. J. Muste, Bayard Rustin, Barbara Deming, and Albert Bigelow. During the late 1950s and early 1960s CNVA activists picketed the White House, sailed into restricted waters in the Pacific where the United States conducted nuclear tests, and protested the construction of Polaris nuclear submarines. It was one of several organizations that contributed to a reinvigorated peace movement in the mid- to late 1950s, spurred by growing fears of nuclear testing, the danger of nuclear fallout, and Soviet expansion and influenced by Gandhi's nonviolent revolution in India as well as the American civil rights movement's use of Gandhian tactics at home. The most visible of these was the Committee for a Sane Nuclear Policy (SANE), founded in 1957. SANE's membership grew in state and local chapters concentrated largely in cities in the Northeast, Midwest, and West. By the early 1960s the group was splintering along tactical lines—pacifists versus direct action radicals—but it organized many high-profile marches and rallies against nuclear testing and arms proliferation.[47]

In 1960 the CNVA had launched a 6,000-mile, eleven-month "Walk for Peace" from San Francisco to Moscow. The group's second walk for peace began in the spring of 1963, originating in Quebec City and concluding prematurely in Miami (U.S. government travel restrictions made it impossible for them to reach their original destination, Guantánamo Bay, Cuba). In September 1963, as the marchers prepared to venture below the Mason-Dixon Line, the CNVA Walk Team issued guidelines for public behavior that stressed propriety—most importantly, prohibiting drug use, advising limited and discreet alcohol consumption, and urging that "displays of affection" be kept within "the bounds of good taste."[48] The admonition proved irrelevant. In Georgia the group met with cattle prods, harassment, and imprisonment in Macon, Griffin, and Albany in late 1963 and early 1964. The peace walkers were in Macon when Kennedy was assassinated; they suspended all protests and traveled to Atlanta, with the intention of resuming the walk after the funeral. But the Atlanta police "ordered them to leave the city" and threatened to arrest them if they stayed or "in the event of any demonstration."[49]

White southern conservatives saw the CNVA as a bunch of integrationist beatniks, and they were infuriated as they monitored the group's march though their region. As A. J. Muste put it, "the fact that white girls and Negro men walked side by side tended, for many Southerners, to blot out everything else." He also noted that in Georgia, "the fact that 'peace' people, 'peaceniks' were beaten and reacted nonviolently" established "a link of common action and suffering that has made the 'cause' of peace and the 'cause' of civil rights one in a way that could hardly have been accomplished otherwise."[50]

Florida was no exception, especially since the group was supposed to depart from Miami to reach Castro's Cuba. In 1964 the trek became an obsession for the Johns Committee, whose members watched as the civil rights movement exploded and St. Augustine became a flash point during the summer. The first sign of trouble came with the news that ten Florida State University students, members of SAP, had traveled to Albany, Georgia, to pressure officials there to release the jailed CNVA walkers. The Florida State delegation then drove the freed walkers to Koinonia Farm, the interracial Christian community in nearby Americus. Steve Baum, head of the Florida State University chapter of SAP, told the student newspaper that the marchers had decided to alter their Florida route and go through Tallahassee and Gainesville, the state's most important college towns and the sites of frequent demonstrations.[51]

The Johns Committee tabulated the racial and gender breakdown of the CNVA marchers and followed their southward progress daily. In one report the committee noted that there were thirteen white males, five white females, three "colored" males, and three who were unidentified. From diverse backgrounds—San Francisco, Portland, Boulder, Chicago, Atlanta, and Washington, D.C.—the marchers had attended or were attending some of the nation's best universities: MIT, Stanford, Rutgers, Wisconsin, Oberlin, and Morehouse. Most of them had also been active in the civil rights movement.[52] Although the CNVA had its share of detractors, Florida law enforcement officials made no attempt to arrest or otherwise harass the walkers. The FLIC reported in April, however, that two of the Negro marchers visited the apartment of two white women when the group reached Jacksonville. The foursome then went to Jacksonville Beach, "where they camped on a blanket and proceeded to engage in some heavy petting." When a crowd started to gather, police escorted the four off the beach. A few miles down the road, "several car loads of whites swooped down on the car carrying the Peace Marchers, stoned out its windows, shot out its tires and caused it to crash."[53] While in Jacksonville, the CNVA held demonstrations at three different naval bases. Some of the marchers stayed with members of the Florida Council on Human Relations, but the local branch of the NAACP made it clear that it would have nothing to do with the group because of its support for Cuba.[54]

After making protest stops at the Cape Kennedy Space Center and Patrick Air Force Base just south of Cocoa Beach, the peace walkers arrived in Miami at the end of May. There, angry Cuban exiles shattered the relative calm that had surrounded the march thus far in Florida. The first assault occurred as the group walked through Miami Beach and people in passing cars splattered them with red paint, spit on them, and called them "dirty Communists." The walk concluded with an antiwar demonstration at Bayfront Park, where Cubans again hurled insults at the protesters and ripped picket signs and pamphlets from their hands as the march coordinator called for peace between the U.S. and Cuban governments. The riot police stepped in just as the two opposing sides began to try to outsing each other, the exiles belting out the Cuban national anthem and the peace walkers breaking into choruses of "We Shall Overcome."[55] The CNVA marchers elicited a similar outcry from Cubans and local police when they reached Key West in late June. This time they were arrested and spent two days in the city jail.

By this point, staff director John Evans and one of the committee's investigators had resigned from the FLIC, claiming a difference of opinion about tactics and targets. Neither man felt entirely comfortable investigating the governor and his special police force in St. Augustine. They were also concerned that some of the committee members—namely, Charley Johns and Pinellas County representative Bill Young—were meeting in secret and initiating their own investigations.[56] At the end of September, however, with less than six months remaining before the next legislative session, Johns and the vice chairman also resigned, frustrated by the committee's plummeting reputation, the absence of a functioning staff, and the lack of a clear-cut target. Those left standing—George Stallings, Young, chairman Richard Mitchell (who had been sidelined by poor health for much of the past year), Bill Owens, and Leo Jones—refused to see the committee disbanded. "I disagree that there isn't much that could be accomplished," said Stallings. Johns, however, told reporters he probably ought to "close the office, lock up the records and save the taxpayers of Florida the remainder of the $155,000 appropriation."[57] That did not happen, and the remaining members spent the next several months putting together the promised report on St. Augustine.

The FLIC released its final report, *Racial and Civil Disorders in St. Augustine,* in February 1965. Just as *Homosexuality and Citizenship in Florida* had reinforced Cold War ideas about sexual deviance, this report revealed segregationists' obsessions with communism, sex, and outside agitators. The Johns Committee had stepped out on a limb with its report that told the public more than it cared to know about perversion. Now the committee retreated to more familiar representations that would be less shocking: black men as oversexed and a local movement exhorted to violence and disorder by troublemaking Communist outsiders.

Published almost six months after the events it described, *Racial and Civil Disorders in St. Augustine* constituted little more than a synopsis of the way race relations—allegedly amicable "for two centuries"—had rapidly deteriorated when newcomer Robert Hayling began advocating armed self-defense and King and the SCLC entered the city early in the summer of 1964. In retelling the story of the lunch counter sit-ins, the report focused on the "juveniles" and "teenagers" who carried them out. "When picketing and other forms of harassment continued," it stated, "those under seventeen were escorted home and their parents summoned to juvenile court." This subtle message about the criminality of blacks steadfastly refused to acknowledge nonviolent sit-ins as a legitimate form of protest and labeled them criminal harassment. The next paragraph, detailing episodes of interracial violence, did not mention shootings, physical assaults, bombings, or arson by whites. Instead, it highlighted "threatening or obscene telephone calls to white women" and the case of a white woman being "robbed and raped at knifepoint by an unidentified Negro." The report addressed the Klan's presence in the city with the disclaimer that "very few of them could be identified as citizens of St. Augustine."[58]

The next section dealt at some length with the SCLC's Florida Spring Project, which drew college students from New England to St. Augustine to participate in civil disobedience. When the mother of the Massachusetts governor arrived to join the sit-ins, she and the city of St. Augustine garnered the national publicity the movement sought. In the Johns Committee report, this was framed as an explicitly subversive strategy: "The tactic of inducing socially prominent and elderly ladies to act as 'cats paws' in order to win sympathy and wide publicity has long been a Communist and radical technique." Throughout the twenty-four pages of the report's main body, the authors regularly inserted a sentence, always italicized for emphasis, stating that "*most St. Augustine Negroes are not taking part in the movement*" or that participants had to be "*brought in from other states.*" In tallying arrest figures, the report emphasized that many "*were juveniles as young as fourteen years who gave their home addresses as being a thousand or more*" miles from the city. The report's authors punctuated this section with one of many sardonic references to King's "Non-violent Army."[59]

Racial and Civil Disorders in St. Augustine also included a timeline of "racial incidents," a slanted biography of Martin Luther King, a set of twenty-five appendices ranging from local newspaper articles about blacks arming themselves to letters from the NAACP and SCLC to President Johnson and the U.S. Commission on Civil Rights, Farris Bryant's executive orders, and outrageously biased police reports on blacks' demonstrations. The facts about King dwelled, in shopworn form, on his ties to the Highlander Folk School and the Southern Conference Education Fund (SCEF), and the report contained lengthy quotes from the Louisiana Joint Legislative Committee, which claimed in 1964, "The infiltration of the Communist Party into the so-called 'Civil Rights' movement through the SCEF is shocking and highly dangerous to this state, and the nation." The report also revealed that one of King's closest associates, Bayard Rustin, had been a member of the Young Communist League and, even worse, was a homosexual. Then followed the litany of subversives with whom King had long surrounded himself, which segregationists had been trotting out for years: Jack O'Dell, Aubrey Williams, James Dombrowski, and Carl and Anne Braden, "all identified as Communists before the Senate Internal Security Subcommittee."[60] Taken together, these exhibits were intended to impart to the reader two familiar narratives: one about outsiders stirring up racial discord, chaos, and disorder to weaken American democracy, and the other about integrationists as perverted race mixers.

Soon after the release of *Racial and Civil Disorders in St. Augustine,* the nation watched as thousands of blacks and whites joined together in a dramatic march from Selma to Montgomery, Alabama, to demand equal voting rights. On March 25, 1965, the triumphant procession made its way past Dexter Avenue Baptist Church to the steps of the capitol for an afternoon of freedom songs and political exhortations, including King's speech that famously asked, "How long?" and answered, "Not long." When the march ended, the ad hoc transportation committee, which had spent the previous five days shuttling volunteers and marchers along Highway 80 between Selma and Montgomery, still had work left to do. Dozens of participants needed rides to the airport or back home. In one of the transport cars, a 1963 Oldsmobile with a Michigan license plate, sat Viola Liuzzo, a thirty-nine-year-old white woman who had come to Alabama after watching the harrowing television coverage of Bloody Sunday from the comfort of her middle-class Detroit living room. In the passenger seat was Leroy Moton, an African American from Selma, who was twenty years her junior. That night, a car carrying four Klansmen, one an FBI informant, pulled up next to the Oldsmobile and opened fire. Liuzzo was fatally shot in the head.

The killing elicited yet another round of nationwide shock and grief and lent new urgency to the voting rights bill, but it also provoked a brutal character assassination from the Ku Klux Klan and the FBI, which leaked misinformation to the public about Liuzzo, claiming that she had been sitting "very very close" to Moton in the car, giving "all the appearances of a necking party," and had "puncture marks in her arms indicating recent use of a hypodermic needle."[61] The rumors confirmed many white southerners' assumptions about what kind of woman would forsake her husband and children to carouse with Negroes in an unseemly display disguised as a voting rights march. In historian Dan Carter's words, these "pamphlets, press releases, and speeches by conservative Alabamians, including George Wallace, reveal an obsession with 'orgies' and 'fornication' and 'debauchery.'" They also "foreshadowed the beginnings of the sexual culture wars that would resonate through American society in the 1960s and 1970s."[62] The Johns Committee, like other conservative and segregationist groups in the mid-1960s, served the same purpose, cementing the imagined links between sexual and political deviance within right-wing discourse.

Many smear campaigns emanated from Selma. In 1966 Selma sheriff Jim Clark published a memoir, *The Jim Clark Story,* artlessly subtitled *I Saw Selma Raped.* Robert M. Mikell, an Auburn graduate and a writer from Montgomery, penned a book at Clark's request called *Selma,* which he claimed to be a "comprehensive testimonial" about what really happened—as opposed to the "distorted facts and slanted reports" on television. Instead, it was an excuse to publish all the rumors and accusations that had circulated among angry Alabama whites during the most recent invasion of integrationists: public drunkenness and urination, men and women masquerading as priests and nuns, straggly beatniks and grubby Communists, and rampant and promiscuous sex. According to the witnesses whose affidavits Mikell read (most of whom turned out to work in law enforcement or state government), the Selma marchers, both black and white, simply could not stop having sex—sex in the streets, sex on front lawns, sex behind buildings, sex inside the SNCC office, and, most damning of all, sex on a church floor.[63]

The most provocative exposé appeared in *The True Selma Story: Sex and Civil Rights,* a tabloid-style magazine published in Birmingham in 1965. Its similarities to the Johns Committee's reports are worth noting in the context of the burgeoning conservative narrative of sexual, racial, and political subversion. The cover was an unremarkable cartoon illustration of the famous photograph of civil rights marchers bearing American flags, but in this representation they were marching under a Kremlin-red sky. The inside front cover featured a full-page photograph of white and black marchers standing near the state capitol in a large puddle with streams running down the street. The caption indicated that, moments before the photo was snapped, SNCC's James Forman had yelled to the group: "Stand up and relieve yourself!" On the next page, along with the table of contents, was a biographical sketch of the author, Albert "Buck" Parsons. An image of Parsons, with a cigarette in his mouth, a tough-guy scowl on his face, and a military-style buzz cut, accompanied it. He was a stringer for *Life* magazine, managing editor of an unnamed weekly Birmingham newspaper, and a pilot who had volunteered for the Bay of Pigs mission. Alabama congressman William L. Dickinson had enlisted Parsons to investigate the Selma-to-Montgomery march, and *The True Selma Story* was the result of his efforts.

The first section, the requisite retelling of Martin Luther King's personal peccadilloes and dubious associates, was titled "Black Knight of the Civil Rights Movement." The next section served as the centerpiece of the report, addressing sex and civil rights. It contained "sworn" statements about a "skinny white girl" having sex with a black man and then turning over to have sex with another black man lying next to the couple, a drunken black woman singing freedom songs and then violently attacking the police, and a white man who dressed up as a priest and had sex with young black girls. In one affidavit a witness claimed to have seen James Forman and a "red-haired white girl" engaging in an "abnormal sex act which consisted of each of the two manipulating the other's private parts with their mouths simultaneously"—an act commonly associated with male homosexuality and legally defined as sodomy. An Alabama state trooper swore that "one of the white beatniks, with a goatee, told one of my troopers" he was being paid and given free meals and "all the Negro p— he wanted."[64] A section devoted to "Bayard and Ralph: Just a Couple of the Boys" described Bayard Rustin as a "homosexual who solicits on city streets, whose life's work is the subversion of the moral fiber of the youth of America," and it called Ralph Abernathy a hypocrite who had seduced a fifteen-year-old girl in his congregation and performed "abnormal intercourse" with her.[65] This was the narrative that conservative white Alabamans, like conservative white Floridians, told themselves in an attempt to make sense of a world where their values were being threatened. It was a narrative rooted in a specific time and place, shaped by the conservative anticommunist conception of political subversion and sexual perversion, and used to defend segregation against liberal federal encroachment.

In the spring of 1965, with the eyes of the nation on Selma, Florida legislators decided against any effort to renew the FLIC for another two years. The committee had little to show for the 1963–1965 period, other than a controversial report on homosexuality and a little-noticed report on the integration crisis in St. Augustine. And it had done nothing to stem the tide of student activism at Florida's universities or demonstrations against segregated restaurants, theaters, and beaches in communities throughout the state. The FLIC's attempt to shock Floridians with *Homosexuality and Citizenship in Florida* had backfired, and it had raised the ire of liberals and moderates by interfering in the curriculum, pedagogy, and policies of the University of South Florida. Even conservative Democratic governor Haydon Burns said of the Johns Committee in early 1965, two months before the legislative session began, "I think it serves no purpose whatsoever."[66]

Many in Florida and elsewhere would have disagreed. The committee had served a purpose not just for the previous two years but for its entire duration. By the mid-1960s there was a groundswell of opposition against what some saw as a dangerous liberalizing trend in American politics and culture. From the John Birch Society to Citizens for Decent Literature, from Young Americans for Freedom to supporters of George Wallace and Lester Maddox, the echoes of postwar anticommunism and massive resistance could be heard in conservative attacks against the Civil Rights Act, welfare, the constitutional banning of prayer in school, the free speech movement in Berkeley, the loosening gender and sexual mores across a broad swath of American life, and many other ominous signs of moral decline facilitated by the federal government.[67] For them, the Johns Committee's purview or tactics might have come into question, but the larger weight of its mission had not. Even state agencies such as the Board of Control and the Board of Education appropriated some of the FLIC's ideology and duties, taking responsibility for keeping homosexuals and controversial books and speakers out of Florida's classrooms. School integration lagged for years. Attacking political, sexual, and racial subversion, increasingly under the umbrella of liberalism, became a staple of the New

Right. Conservatives in Florida who had found a champion in the committee so closely associated with Charley Johns did not disappear along with it in 1965.

Notes

I am indebted to Jacquelyn Dowd Hall, George Lewis, and Steven Niven for their careful reading of and insightful comments on earlier versions of this essay. And I am grateful to Amy Hurd for her love and encouragement.

Epigraph: *New York Times,* April 26, 1965, from an address during a protest march against President Lyndon Johnson's Great Society, sponsored by Americans for States' Rights, Private Property Rights and Private Enterprise, Atlanta, Georgia.

1. See Jeff Woods, *Black Struggle, Red Scare: Segregation and Anti-Communism in the South, 1948–1968* (Baton Rouge: Louisiana State University Press, 2004).

2. Report of the Florida Legislative Investigation Committee (FLIC) to the Florida Legislature, April 18, 1963, 3, 12, 21, Papers of John Egerton, box 1, Special Collections, University of South Florida Library, Tampa.

3. Ellen W. Schrecker, *No Ivory Tower: McCarthyism and the Universities* (New York: Oxford University Press, 1986), chap. 2.

4. Ibid., 105–6, 218.

5. C. Vann Woodward, "The Unreported Crisis in the Southern Colleges," *Harper's,* October 1962, 82–89; Stanley H. Smith, "Academic Freedom in Higher Education in the Deep South," *Journal of Educational Sociology* 32, no. 6 (February 1959): 297–308.

6. William J. Billingsley, *Communists on Campus: Race, Politics, and the Public University in Sixties North Carolina* (Athens: University of Georgia Press, 1999), 3–4.

7. Ibid., 62.

8. David R. Colburn, *Racial Change and Community Crisis: St. Augustine, Florida, 1877–1980* (Gainesville: University Press of Florida, 1991), 29–34; Taylor Branch, *Pillar of Fire: America in the King Years, 1963–65* (New York: Simon and Schuster, 1998), 35–40.

9. Branch, *Pillar of Fire,* 111.

10. Colburn, *Racial Change and Community Crisis,* 36–60.

11. Letter from R. J. Strickland, June 24, 1963, Records of the Florida Legislative Investigation Committee, box 2, State Archives of Florida, Tallahassee (hereafter cited as FLIC Records).

12. Glenda Alice Rabby, *The Pain and the Promise: The Struggle for Civil Rights in Tallahassee, Florida* (Athens: University of Georgia Press, 1999), 145–59.

13. Robert Dallek, *An Unfinished Life: John F. Kennedy, 1917–1963* (Boston: Little, Brown, 2003), chap. 17; Taylor Branch, *Parting the Waters: America in the King Years* (New York: Simon and Schuster, 1989), chap. 20.

14. *St. Petersburg Times,* June 4 and 19, 1963.

15. *Miami Herald,* January 12, 1964; FLIC staff report #8, February 7, 1964, FLIC Records, box 1; *Florida Flambeau,* February 12, 1964; John Evans to Francis J. McNamara, January 22, 1964, FLIC Records, box 1; FLIC staff reports #12, March 6, 1964, and #15, April 3, 1964, FLIC Records, box 1.

16. Florida Children's Commission advisory meeting report, January 22, 1962, 11, FLIC Records, box 1.

17. *Florida Times-Union,* March 6, 1962.

18. Memo from Wayne Yeager to Florida Children's Commission's Advisory Committee on Homosexuality, June 4, 1962, 3, Farris Bryant Administrative Correspondence, box 57, State Archives of Florida.

19. John E. Evans to Robert L. Shevin, July 13, 1964, 2, FLIC Records, box 2.

20. FLIC minutes, January 29, 1964, 7, Farris Bryant Administrative Correspondence, box 82.

21. FLIC, *Homosexuality and Citizenship in Florida* (Tallahassee, 1964).

22. Ibid.

23. Robert H. Williams, "Sex, Tallahassee," *New Republic,* May 23, 1964, 5.

24. *Tallahassee Democrat,* March 20, 1964.

25. FLIC, *Homosexuality and Citizenship in Florida.*

26. Norman Mark, "Censorship: Fanatics and Fallacies: The Anonymous Smut Hunters," *Nation,* July 5, 1965, 5.

27. Citizens for Decent Literature, *Perversion for Profit* (1964).

28. FLIC, *Homosexuality and Citizenship in Florida.*

29. Williams, "Sex, Tallahassee," 5.

30. Bill Baggs to Harry Ashmore, June 8, 1964, William C. Baggs Papers, box 1, Archives and Special Collections, Otto G. Richter Library, University of Miami.

31. Hal Call, "1964 Open Letter to the Florida Legislature's 'Johns Committee,'" in *Speaking for Our Lives: Historic Speeches and Rhetoric for Gay and Lesbian Rights, 1892–2000,* ed. Robert B. Ridinger (Binghamton, N.Y.: Harrington Park Press, 2004), 86–87.

32. "A Voter and a Good Citizen" to Richard Mitchell, n.d., FLIC Records, box 2.

33. "Another Mister X" to FLIC, June 28, 1964, FLIC Records, box 2.

34. *Tallahassee Democrat,* March 20, 1964.

35. Andrew E. Kroha to FLIC, March 18, 1964; Harold S. Dalton to FLIC, March 18, 1964; Mrs. A. B. Sawyer to FLIC, March 18, 1964; anonymous to John Evans, May 13, 1964, FLIC Records, box 2.

36. Evans to Shevin, July 13, 1964, 2.

37. Colburn, *Racial Change and Community Crisis,* chap. 4.

38. Ibid.

39. Michael Newton, *The Invisible Empire: The Ku Klux Klan in Florida* (Gainesville: University Press of Florida, 2001), 163; *Time,* August 14, 1964.

40. Kenneth O'Reilly, *"Racial Matters": The FBI's Secret File on Black America, 1960–1972* (New York: Free Press, 1989), 131–32.

41. Ibid., 141.

42. Ibid., chap. 4.

43. *St. Augustine Record,* July 31, 1964.

44. Gregg L. Michel, *Struggle for a Better South: The Southern Student Organizing Committee, 1964–1969* (New York: Palgrave Macmillan, 2004), chap. 1; Calendar of Events Connected with the Establishment of the Student Group for Equal Rights, n.d., University of Florida Student Organizational Files, box 1, University of Florida Archives, Gainesville.

45. *St. Petersburg Times,* July 26 and 31, 1964; *Florida Flambeau,* July 31, 1964.

46. *Tampa Tribune,* September 11, 1964.

47. Robert Kleidman, *Organizing for Peace: Neutrality, the Test Ban, and the Freeze* (Syracuse, N.Y.: Syracuse University Press, 1993), 91–113.

48. Memo, CNVA Walk Team, September 18, 1963, Papers of Barbara Deming, box 9, Schlesinger Library, Harvard University, Cambridge, Massachusetts.

49. Neil Haworth memo, November 26, 1963, Deming Papers, box 9.

50. A. J. Muste, "The Meaning of Albany," n.d., Deming Papers, box 9.

51. *Florida Flambeau,* February 24, 1964.

52. FLIC, "Background Information on Walk for Peace," February 1, 1964, FLIC Records, box 1.

53. FLIC staff report #16, April 10, 1964, FLIC Records, box 1.

54. Lawrence Rice to John Evans, April 3, 1964, FLIC Records, box 1.

55. *Orlando Sentinel,* May 30, 1964.

56. *Tampa Tribune,* September 11, 1964.

57. Paul Willis, Associated Press, September 30, 1964.

58. FLIC, *Racial and Civil Disorders in St. Augustine* (Tallahassee, February 1965), 1–4.

59. Ibid., 8, 13, 15–16 (emphasis in original).

60. "Martin Luther King," in *Racial and Civil Disorders in St. Augustine,* 3, 5.

61. Mary Stanton, *From Selma to Sorrow: The Life and Death of Viola Liuzzo* (Athens: University of Georgia Press, 1998), 53, 55.

62. Dan T. Carter, *The Politics of Rage: George Wallace, the Origins of the New Conservatism, and the Transformation of American Politics* (Baton Rouge: Louisiana State University Press, 2000), 259.

63. Robert M. Mikell, *Selma* (Charlotte, N.C.: Citadel Press, 1965).

64. Albert C. Parsons, *The True Selma Story: Sex and Civil Rights* (Birmingham, Ala.: Esco Publishers, 1965), 2–11.

65. Ibid., 15, 27.

66. *St. Petersburg Times,* February 26, 1965.

67. David Farber and Jeff Roche, introduction to *The Conservative Sixties* (New York: Peter Lang, 2003).

Joan Little and the Triumph of Testimony

Danielle L. McGuire

In the quiet darkness just before daybreak on August 27, 1974, Sergeant Jerry Helms ambled into the Beaufort County jail in Washington, North Carolina. Escorting a drunken prisoner, he walked through the double doors and down the carpeted stairs to the basement, then turned left toward the women's section of the small but clean jailhouse. Poking out of the cell of the sole female prisoner was a pair of shoeless feet covered in brown socks. Moving closer, Helms saw that the feet belonged to Clarence Alligood, the burly, sixty-two-year-old white jailer, whose lifeless torso slumped over his thighs. Except for the socks, Alligood was naked from the waist down. Blood stained his yellow and white plaid shirt, and a thin line of semen stretched from his penis to his leg. His right hand loosely held an ice pick, and his left arm, dangling lifeless toward the floor, clutched his pants. Blood pooled on the linoleum tiles next to a woman's nightgown. A bra hung on the cell door. Joan Little, the petite twenty-year-old black woman who had occupied that cell for two months, was gone.[1]

Helms and the Beaufort County police immediately began a search for Little, whom they believed had murdered Alligood as part of an elaborate plan to escape. Armed with service dogs and "high-powered rifles," police combed through the dusty streets of "Back of Town," the black community in Washington, going door-to-door inquiring about Little's whereabouts. The police declared Little an "outlaw" and issued "shoot on sight" orders. Ernest "Paps" Barnes, a neighbor whose tiny, run-down shack was known as a "liquor house," granted Little shelter after she told him that Alligood "got naked with her in that cell, tried to make her suck him, and she killed him with an ice pick."[2] Little eluded police for more than a week by hiding beneath one of Barnes's old feather mattresses.[3] After four nerve-wracking police searches of the house, Little decided to yield. Marjorie Wright, Little's childhood friend and sympathetic ally, and Jerry Paul, a white civil rights attorney, spirited Little out of the county in the middle of the night

191

and helped her surrender to the State Bureau of Investigation (SBI) in Chapel Hill.[4] On September 7 Charles Dunn, head of the SBI, arrested Joan Little for first-degree murder. Two days later a grand jury indicted her. If found guilty, Little would receive the death penalty and would be executed in the state's gas chamber.[5]

In the year between Little's arrest and her murder trial, a broad coalition of activists rallied to her defense. The Free Joan Little campaign, as it became known, drew national and international attention to the long history of sexualized violence against black women and sparked spirited debates about a woman's right to self-defense. The campaign to free Joan Little is often portrayed as the product of second-wave feminism, which finally enabled women to break the code of silence surrounding sexual violence and "speak out" against rape.[6] According to many histories of the women's movement, survivors of sexual violence held their tongues until January 24, 1971, when the New York Radical Feminists held the first public "speak-out" at St. Clements Episcopal Church in Manhattan, freeing women from a past of silence and shame.[7] This event may have been the catalyst for white, middle-class feminists who became active in the antirape movement that emerged after the 1971 speak-out, but African American women had been speaking out and organizing politically against sexual violence and rape for more than a century.[8]

African American women used their voices to launch the first public attack on sexual violence as a "systemic abuse of women" in response to slavery and the wave of lynchings in the postemancipation South.[9] Slave narratives offer stark testimony about the brutal sexual exploitation bondswomen faced. For example, Harriet Jacobs detailed her master's lechery, among other things, in an effort to "arouse the women of the North" and "convince the people of the Free States what Slavery really is."[10] When black clubwomen began to organize antilynching campaigns during the late nineteenth century, they "called up this history of rape under slavery and rape as a weapon of terror after slavery."[11]

On October 5, 1892, hundreds of black women converged on Lyric Hall in New York City to hear Ida B. Wells speak out against "Lynch Law." While black men were being accused of ravishing white women, she argued, "the rape of helpless Negro girls, which began in slavery days, still continues without reproof from church, state or press."[12] At the 1893 World's Fair in Chicago, Fannie Barrier Williams told an audience of black and white clubwomen, "It is a significant and shameful fact that I am constantly in receipt of letters from the still unprotected women of the

Joan Little, February 3, 1975. (Courtesy of the North Carolina State Archives. Reprinted with permission of the *Raleigh News and Observer.*)

South." Anna Julia Cooper, an educator, author, and respected clubwoman from Washington, D.C., echoed Williams's testimony. Black women, she told the crowd, were engaged in "painful, patient, and silent toil . . . to gain title to the bodies of their daughters."[13]

The right to bodily integrity required that clubwomen counter the demeaning sexual stereotypes white men used to justify attacks on black women. Darlene Clark Hine argues that respectability and proper deportment negated negative sexual images of black women and ought to be seen as active resistance to sexual violence.[14] The public defense of black women's integrity opened other political possibilities as well. Nannie Helen Burroughs, a cofounder of the National Association of Colored Women, argued that only the vote would protect black women. When a black woman goes to court "in defense of her virtue," Burroughs argued in *Crisis* in 1915, "she is looked upon with contempt. She needs the ballot to reckon with men who place no value upon her virtue and to mould healthy sentiment in favor of her own protection."[15] By simultaneously challenging white stereotypes of the black beast rapist and wanton jezebel, clubwomen used the antilynching campaign and the emerging suffrage struggle as a way to gain citizenship *and* protect their bodily integrity.

Considering the long history of black women's public protests of sexual violence and their politicization of rape, radical white feminists jumped on the antirape bandwagon relatively late, raising questions about the origins of antirape activism within second-wave feminism. Indeed, I argue that antirape activism was rooted in African Americans' struggle for human dignity and constituted a crucial part of the modern civil rights movement. From the slave narratives of Harriet Jacobs to the fiery orations of Ida B. Wells to Fannie Lou Hamer's stark public testimony about a forced hysterectomy and brutal sexualized beating in 1963, many black women refused to remain silent about sexual violence. Instead, they organized public protests, testified about their brutal assaults, and used their voices as weapons in the long struggle for freedom and respect.[16]

A number of high-profile cases after World War II serve as potent examples. In 1944 African Americans launched a nationwide campaign to defend Recy Taylor, an African American sharecropper and mother who had been gang-raped by a group of white men in Abbeville, Alabama. Led by black women in the Southern Negro Youth Congress and the Montgomery, Alabama, branch of the NAACP, the Committee for Equal Justice for Mrs. Recy Taylor created what the *Chicago Defender* called the "strongest campaign for equal justice to be seen in a decade."[17] Seven years later the NAACP, the Civil Rights Congress, and the Sojourners for Truth and Justice, a black women's organization founded in 1951, launched a national and international campaign to free Rosa Lee Ingram, a black sharecropper and mother of twelve who had been sentenced to death in the self-defense slaying of a white man in Ellaville, Georgia, in 1947.[18]

Mainstream black activists and ministers in Montgomery, Alabama, such as E. D. Nixon, Rosa Parks, Rufus Lewis, and the Reverend Solomon Seay Sr., organized campaigns to protect African American women from sexual violence in the years leading up to the 1955 bus boycott. In 1949 Nixon and Seay led a campaign to defend Gertrude Perkins, an African American woman who had been abducted and raped by two white policemen. Their protests exposed the long-standing practice of white police officers sexually assaulting black women in Montgomery, forced a grand jury hearing, and brought the city's disparate black ministers together for the first time.[19] The militant Women's Political Council (WPC) may have been involved, since one of its early goals was to "come to the defense of women who had been victimized by rape and other physical assaults."[20] In 1951 Lewis teamed up with Nixon and others to boycott a grocery store owned by Sam Green, a white man who had raped a black teenager. Since the courts denied the rape victim a victory, they used the boycott to put Green out of business.[21] Their successful protest set a precedent and established the boycott as a potent weapon. In 1954 Jo Ann Robinson, leader of the WPC, threatened a mass boycott of the city's buses after scores of black women complained of sexual harassment and racial and sexualized violence by bus drivers and police officers.[22]

Montgomery wasn't the only place where sexual violence sparked protests. In 1959 Florida A&M University students rallied around classmate Betty Jean Owens after four white men kidnapped and brutally raped her. The arrest, trial, and conviction of Owens's assailants hinged on her willingness to testify publicly about the harrowing assault.[23] In each case described here and in countless others, black women's testimony served as the catalyst for larger campaigns for civil and human rights. In 1974 Joan Little became the symbol of a similar campaign to defend black womanhood and call attention to the sexualized racial violence that still existed, even though much of the legal infrastructure of Jim Crow had fallen.

The Free Joan Little movement brought disparate activists and organizations, each with its own resources and agenda, into a loose coalition. Feminists and women's liberation organizations spoke out against sexual violence and advocated a woman's right to self-defense; civil rights and Black Power groups saw the Little case as another example of police brutality and southern injustice; opponents of the death penalty and prison reformers hoped the case would draw attention to their emerging campaigns. Ultimately, as Karen Galloway, one of Little's attorneys, put it, the case became a test of whether an African American woman "finally had a right to defend herself against a white man's sexual assault."[24] The Free Joan Little coalition helped draw attention to the case, but the final outcome would pivot on Little's testimony about what happened that night in the Beaufort County jail.

Little's murder trial came a decade after the 1965 Voting Rights Act, but African Americans still struggled for social, political, and economic equality.[25] In 1966 Martin Luther King Jr. argued that a "tragic gulf" existed between the promises of civil rights legislation and their fulfillment.[26] For example, federal civil rights legislation did little to remedy the de facto segregation, squalid housing conditions, chronic unemployment, police brutality, and lack of educational opportunity for blacks in northern cities. For three "long hot summers" after the Selma-to-Montgomery march, riots engulfed cities throughout the country. The uprisings exposed and expressed the seething anger and betrayal felt by many African Americans due to the failure to remedy racial and economic oppression. In 1966 alone, thirty-eight riots erupted in cities from San Francisco to Providence, Rhode Island. In 1967 Detroit exploded; 43 people were killed, 2,000 were wounded, and more than 5,000 were burned out of their homes.[27] By the end of the decade half a million blacks in more than 300 cities had witnessed violent uprisings in which 250 people died, 8,000 were injured, and more than 50,000 were arrested.[28]

In North Carolina murderous violence met African Americans' efforts to integrate public schools and gain full citizenship. Events in two cities provide the most gripping examples. In May 1970 African Americans in Oxford torched the town's tobacco warehouses after three white men brutally murdered Henry Marrow in broad daylight. Marrow, an African American soldier and young father, had apparently talked disrespectfully to a white woman. Afterward, a siege mentality set in among whites, who defended the murderers and targeted blacks for violent reprisal.[29]

In the spring of 1971 Wilmington, like Oxford, "hovered on the edge of racial cataclysm" as the controversy over school desegregation, "discrimination against black students, the closing of cherished black institutions, and the demotions and dismissals of black principals and black teachers" stirred deep resentment among African Americans.[30] Fueling this resentment was the Rights of White People, a white supremacist organization that terrorized blacks, incited violence, and made the Ku Klux Klan seem friendly by comparison.[31] Throughout Wilmington white racists and black militants exchanged fire, and black snipers fired at police officers—most of whom were members of the Ku Klux Klan. The National Guard patrolled the streets, and storefronts and businesses regularly went up in flames.[32] Accused of arson, but primarily guilty of leading a militant movement for "black power," Ben Chavis was a field organizer for the United Church of Christ's Commission for Racial Justice. Chavis and nine others implicated in the racial conflagration were sentenced to prison, and they became known as the "Wilmington Ten."[33] Angela Davis, the "most popular female icon of the Black Power era," and the organization she cofounded, the National Alliance against Racist and Political Repression, launched a campaign to defend them.[34]

Race relations were just as volatile in the small towns and hamlets of Beaufort County, which witnessed police killings as well as Klan burnings and bomb threats in an effort to thwart integration.[35] Thus, when the *Washington Daily News* broke the story about the murder of Clarence Alligood, which it characterized as the "most brutal ever to happen in this county," it practically invited reprisal. As if he were a soldier killed in action in Vietnam, the paper eulogized Alligood's service to the county, stating that he "gave his life in the line of duty."[36] The newspaper failed to report the small detail that Alligood had been found naked from the waist down. Once word got out that the medical examiner found semen on his thighs and that his "urethral fluid was loaded with spermatozoa," evidence that he died at the moment of sexual climax, Joan Little's claim of sexual assault gained credibility. However, since many whites still did not believe that a black woman could be raped, they fell back on old stereotypes to explain the unusual circumstances of Alligood's death.

Casual conversations among whites in Washington pegged Little as a stereotypical jezebel, and rumors about her respectability, or lack thereof, spread through town. Little, some whites argued, had seduced Alligood, lured him into her cell, and killed him so she could escape. For the local car dealer, this scenario made perfect sense. "Hell, to them fucking is like saying good morning, or having a Pepsi-Cola," he snorted. Henry Hardy, a textile executive, agreed. "I'll tell you one thing," he said, "she didn't lose her honor in that cell. She lost that years ago at Camp Lejeune," a Marine Corps base outside of town. Hardy obviously believed the rumor that Little was a budding madam who "ferried her girlfriends to the base for prostitution."[37] The manager at the Coca-Cola plant knew Alligood well and found it hard to believe he had a sexual encounter with a black woman. Alligood, he said, "was so racially biased that he wouldn't want a colored woman." Sheriff Jack O. Harris sided with the plant manager but wondered why, if Alligood was going to break down and integrate, he would choose Little, "all eat up with syphilis like she was."[38]

Jerry Paul, Little's primary defense attorney and a veteran civil rights lawyer, knew that many white men still believed black women existed "somewhere between the animal and the human." He was not surprised by rumors that Little was a prostitute with venereal disease. Having been born and raised in Washington, North Carolina, he knew that interracial liaisons between white men and black women, whether coerced or consensual, had a long history and, among white men at least, were "completely accepted." "I used to hear 'em in the workplaces," Paul explained, "bragging about how they got some pussy the night before, and always the question would come up, 'Was it white or black?'" Invariably, someone would say, "Oh, it was black . . . I picked up this nigger walking on the road." Local whites sympathized with Alligood, Paul explained. "They're programmed to believe that she lured him in there," he said. "And if she didn't . . . then he went back there to have a little fun [and] that's okay too. That's expected." The mistake Alligood made was "*getting caught* back there."[39]

With no eyewitnesses and only circumstantial evidence available to pin a first-degree murder charge on the young black woman, Paul expected the prosecution to fall back on these timeworn stereotypes to win its case. He also expected the prosecutors to bring up Little's dysfunctional family history and her criminal record—which was relatively long, considering her age—to paint a picture of a sexually deviant delinquent who murdered Alligood in cold blood.[40]

Such an argument would play well locally—and not just among whites. Many African Americans in Washington did not think Joan Little was a respectable young woman either. Maggie Buck, a white beautician at the Cinderella Beauty Salon, told a reporter that even "her black maid didn't sympathize with Joan Little." Little was so mean, Buck recalled, "she stole her own aunt's color TV." Buck's maid may not have been completely forthright with her employer on issues regarding race, but other African Americans shared the same opinion. Golden Frinks, perhaps the most well-known civil rights leader in North Carolina, argued that prominent members of the black community in Washington "had rejected" and "ostracized" Little because she was a "wayward girl" who had "led a fast life." Little's behavior "was not up to the general moral standard of the community," he said. After hearing about Little's escape and subsequent arrest, Frinks went to Mount Hebron Baptist Church, where Little's family were registered members, hoping to organize a campaign for her defense. They turned him away. "You see," Frinks recalled, "the community had moved thumbs down on Little because of her previous record [and] her breaking and entering into a mobile home of a black person."[41]

Respectability mattered, but not as much as it had in previous decades. Back in 1955, respectability was the defining issue that made Rosa Parks the symbol of wronged black womanhood rather than Claudette Colvin, an unwed pregnant teenager arrested for failing to abide by Jim Crow on a city bus. The two decades between the Montgomery bus boycott and Joan Little's trial had witnessed enormous social, political, and economic changes that permanently altered the American landscape. The civil rights movement and the women's movement drew attention to and helped free African Americans and women from the strict racial and sexual codes that had been inscribed in the social and legal bedrock of the United States for centuries. Certainly civil rights and Black Power activists' exposure of police brutality, institutional racism, and the violent practices of white supremacists in the 1960s and early 1970s played a role in challenging the importance of respectability and innocence.

By the mid-1970s the National Organization for Women had made tremendous legal and political inroads. The equal rights amendment was fiercely debated across the country and had been ratified by more than thirty states. The Supreme Court gave women power over their own reproductive choices in 1973 in the landmark *Roe v. Wade* decision. Women's liberation groups had "revolutionized the common understanding of rape and domestic violence" and had "forced law enforcement agencies to stop blaming rape and battering victims."[42] As noted earlier, radical feminists in New York held a speak-out in 1971, and subsequent organizing led to the creation of rape crisis centers.[43] In 1973 the National Organization for Women formed the NOW Rape Task Force to investigate rape laws around the country. Over the next few years, rape crisis centers and rape hotlines sprang up throughout the country, radical feminists held conferences dedicated to discussing sexual violence, and a wave of public speak-outs put rape on the national political agenda.[44]

Maggie Buck, the white beautician in Washington, seemed to grasp these historic changes when she told a reporter, "Even if a girl has loose morals, she should be able to pick the man she wants to be raped by."[45] Buck's bizarre understanding of a woman's right to choose her sexual partners indicated that Little might garner sympathy among women, regardless of race. Their views on gender and sexuality had been influenced by the women's rights movement, even if they were not feminists.

However, Joan Little would not be the only one on trial. If the prosecution was going to draw on racial stereotypes of wanton women and blacks' tendency toward criminality, Little's defense attorneys would counter by painting a picture of North Carolina mired in a "Tobacco Road" past, where ignorant and cruel rednecks lorded over innocent and defenseless blacks.[46] This strategy would hurt the state's image and, given the sweeping social changes, might even gain an acquittal. Indeed, violent clashes over school desegregation made North Carolina the focal point of national news stories throughout the 1970s, seriously damaging the state's "progressive mystique."[47] The *New York Times* reported the "growing concern" of state officials, who feared losing tourists and big industry to other Sun Belt states in the South. They feared that "national attention . . . [will hurt] the state's already battered image of racial moderation." Governor James E. Holshouser was especially "sensitive to the critical publicity the state has been receiving lately."[48] "They know they're racists," attorney Paul quipped, "but in 1975, it may not be a good thing to admit you're a racist—they think that the nation comes down on you if you're that way and you won't get industry in your town."[49]

In the year leading up to Little's trial, Paul presented her to the public as a poor but brave black woman who defended herself and her dignity from a lecherous racist and was being railroaded into the gas chamber by a Jim Crow justice system. Paul pounced on state prosecutors every time they said or did something that even hinted of racial prejudice, citing it as proof that they were stuck in an Old South mind-set. David Milligan, editor of the *Beaufort-Hyde News,* resented Paul's strategy because, he complained, the northern press eagerly lapped it up and spit it out in caricature: "This is the South. Here's a rinky-dink town with its shacks and shanties. You've got this old redneck sheriff and this old redneck jailer and this pore little ole colored gal. She's there in jail, so defenseless, so innocent, and she gets raped and ravaged by this gross jailer and all of a sudden, out of nowhere, she struck out, trying to defend herself. She had to kill the jailer and now those ignorant rednecks are gonna get their revenge on her. They're gonna make her pay for it with her life."[50]

Paul couldn't have said it better himself. He and a coterie of supporters spent ten months repeating that story, or versions of it, at rallies and media events, whipping up support for Little throughout the country. This was more than a canny legal strategy; Paul realized that Little's story would resonate with feminist and antirape organizations as well as with large swaths of the black public, especially civil rights activists, who had intimate knowledge of Jim Crow justice. He teamed up with Karen Galloway, one of the first African American women to graduate from Duke Law School. Together they traveled to Washington, D.C., to speak to women's organizations. They "sold the Joan Little case," Paul said later, "and all the women's groups started to pick it up."[51]

Underground magazines and newsletters, such as the feminist periodical *Off Our Backs,* helped spread Little's story through feminist circles before the mainstream media picked it up.[52] Angela Davis's article in *Ms.* magazine brought prominent attention to the trial and introduced thousands of activists and institutions across the nation to Little's plight and to black women's long history of fighting against sexual violence. "All people who see themselves as members of the existing community of struggle for justice, equality, and progress," Davis argued, "have a responsibility to fulfill toward Joan Little."[53] The Southern Poverty Law Center (SPLC), founded by civil rights lawyers Morris Dees and Joe Levin in 1971 to test the new civil rights laws, signed on as well. They used Dees's publishing and direct-mail expertise to solicit funds from people across the nation. Dees and Julian Bond, the SPLC's first president, wrote a letter and mailed it to a quarter of a million people; in it, they claimed that Little's case represented the "most shocking and outrageous example of injustice against women on record."[54]

As word of Little's defiant stand against sexual violence spread, national feminist groups and civil rights organizations rallied behind her. The Women's Legal Defense Fund, the Feminist Alliance against Rape, the Rape Crisis Center, the National Black Feminist Organization, and the National Organization for Women, which was struggling to appeal to women of color, joined the fund-raising effort and mobilized nationwide support.[55] Although the national NAACP did not get involved, local branches indicated a willingness to help raise money for Little's defense.[56]

In an article for the *Black Scholar,* Maulana Ron Karenga, a Black Power advocate, cultural nationalist, and founder of the U.S. Organization and Kwanzaa, called on African Americans to "accept and support [Little's] account of what actually happened and to reject . . . the version offered by the oppressor." Karenga placed the attack on Little in the long

Black and white women assert their right to self-defense outside the Joan Little trial, August 17, 1975. (Courtesy of the North Carolina State Archives. Reprinted with permission of the *Raleigh News and Observer*.)

history of "personal and political terrorism directed against black women and the black community since slavery." Her willingness to resist Alligood's advances, he argued, proved that even though "the movement was at a lull, our people were still in motion, still resisting."[57] Little's decision to fight back became a catalyst for a much larger struggle.

Rosa Parks, who had been an antirape activist since the 1940s, helped found a local branch of the Joanne Little Legal Defense Committee in Detroit, where Parks fled after the Montgomery bus boycott.[58] In a press release issued on March 12, 1975, the committee announced a student rally at the University of Detroit, a march to be held April 18, and a massive fund-raising drive to defend Little "all the way to the Supreme Court if necessary." We hope "Miss Little will be acquitted of the charge of first degree murder," the press release stated, "but, also, that the question, 'should a woman defend herself against a rapist?' will be decided in the affirmative." Within a month the committee had secured local speakers and entertainment for the April rally, sent 500 solicitations for donations, and called on Detroit citizens to rally to Little's defense on local television and radio programs.[59] Similar chapters emerged throughout the country.

Bernice Johnson Reagon, founder of the a cappella group Sweet Honey in the Rock, was a former Student Nonviolent Coordinating Committee activist who had worked closely with Fannie Lou Hamer the summer after her brutal assault by police in the Winona, Mississippi, jail. Reagon saw Joan Little as a kind of everywoman trapped by a racist and sexist society, and her song "Joanne Little" became the anthem for the Free Joan Little movement. Its refrain, "Joanne is you, Joanne is me, our prison is this whole society," rallied Little's diverse supporters.[60]

The Southern Christian Leadership Conference (SCLC), founded by Martin Luther King Jr., supported Little and demanded protection for black womanhood. The Reverend Ralph Abernathy, King's handpicked successor, joined Frinks to headline a protest at the Beaufort County courthouse. "Here is a young Black woman locked in jail," Abernathy shouted, "sexually assaulted [and] charged with first degree murder, simply because she protected herself from being raped by a white barbarian."[61] It was perhaps the SCLC's most outspoken statement in defense of black women's bodily integrity.

At the grassroots level, African American women in North Carolina—who were, as historian Christina Greene put it, "often unrecognized and largely out of the limelight—set about doing what needed to be done." They drew from deep wells of experience fighting racial injustice and sexual abuse; in 1975 a number of them joined hands across the state to form Concerned Women for Justice and Fairness to Joan Little (later known as just the Concerned Women for Justice, or CWJ).[62] Christine Strudwick, a veteran of the Durham, North Carolina, freedom struggle, became CWJ's second vice president and recalled that she "felt like Joan could have been one of my daughters and was caught up in a situation, that she really had no control."[63] Strudwick cultivated local support and introduced Little's attorneys to black churchwomen at the Union Baptist Church, which had served as the organizational base for civil rights activists in the 1950s and 1960s. By calling on the churchwomen at Union Baptist, Strudwick placed Little's case in the hands of experienced activists who understood black women's long history of racial and sexual abuse. Together they helped raise money, provided moral support, and offered assistance to Little's mother, Jessie Williams.[64]

The Durham branch of the Joan Little Defense Fund Inc. served as the home base for state and national organizing. Originally founded by Little's attorneys to help raise funds for her defense, it was run on a day-to-day basis primarily by black female college students. Yvonne Davis, a student at the University of North Carolina at Chapel Hill, "traveled making talks and arranging publicity . . . for little or no pay." She was also responsible for keeping in contact with groups around the country. Alexis Randolph "kept [the Joan Little Defense Fund] going almost single-handed." Vivian Grimes, a secretary in Paul's law firm, "spent numerous hours working on the case, on and off the job." Tyree Barnes, a student at Guilford College, was in charge of a survey from which a special venire was drawn and, according to a committee newsletter, "has on many occasions taken it upon herself to carry out many of the things that needed doing." Nancy Mills helped set up the first rally in Washington, D.C.; Celene Chernier, a prison reform activist and representative of the North Carolina Alliance against Racial and Political Repression, helped nurture relationships in like-minded organizations; and Larry Little, head of the Winston-Salem Black Panther Party, secured support from Black Power advocates. Their efforts, along with those of the SPLC, raised approximately $250,000 for Little's defense.[65]

Months before Joan Little's trial began, her supporters in Durham and throughout the country had already decided she was innocent. Five hundred supporters—carrying "Free Joan Little" and "Defend Black Womanhood" signs and chanting "One, two, three. Joan must be set free. Four, five, six. Power to the ice pick"—rallied outside the Wake County court-

Demonstrators demand "Justice for Joanne" outside the Wake County courthouse. (Courtesy of the North Carolina State Archives. Reprinted with permission of the *Raleigh News and Observer.*)

house on July 15, 1975, as what the *Chicago Tribune* called the "trial of the decade" began.[66] Inside, Little sat quietly in a pink and blue dress as her attorneys and the prosecutors squared off over potential jurors and tested their competing narratives. William Griffin, the "boyish-looking" thirty-one-year-old prosecutor, presented Little as a seductive and calculating killer who had murdered Alligood as part of a plot to escape. She deserved the death penalty, he claimed, and looked for potential jurors who supported it.[67]

The *New York Times* reported that the defense "made clear today that they were putting the southern system of justice on trial as much as defending a young black woman accused of first-degree murder."[68] Indeed, when assistant prosecutor Lester Chalmers dismissed the first black prospective juror, Paul, hewing to this strategy, yelled, "I object! He's excusing them because they're black." In the end, the jury consisted of six African Americans and six whites. Nine of the twelve were women, and all but five were younger than forty years old.[69]

As prosecutors struggled to present a case based on circumstantial evidence, defense attorneys placed the case in its historical context and argued that southern police officers had a long history of assaulting and sexually harassing black women in their custody.[70] In the Beaufort County jail, black women were wholly unprotected. For example, officers kept a camera trained on female prisoners at all times, watching them—or "peeping at them," as Paul put it—while they showered, changed clothes, and went to the bathroom. Little testified that when she tried to "tie up a blanket to block the TV monitor" and protect her privacy when she was naked, officers took her blanket away. She also described how she "had to call the jailer and have him turn the water on" when she wanted to take a shower. Then he would stand outside her cell and watch, she said.[71]

Little was not the only victim of sexual abuse in the Beaufort County jail, Galloway told the jury. She was one of many black women routinely harassed by the white officers. Galloway summoned a stream of black women to the stand to testify about their experiences. Rosa Ida Mae Roberson, a "hefty black woman who was jailed for twenty-one days for making threatening phone calls," told the jury that Alligood propositioned her "seven to ten times" while she was incarcerated. He told her that she had been "confined so long [she] needed sex." When Roberson warned the wizened jailer that she "would kill him if he entered her cell," he backed off. Phyllis Ann Moore, a nineteen-year-old black woman, testified that during her short stay she witnessed Alligood sexually harass Little by repeatedly asking her if she "missed her man."[72] Little ignored the sexual innuendo, Moore said, and once "turned away in disgust and muttered that she'd report the jailer if he said it again." It was the last witness, however, who "seemed to command the closest attention of the jury." Jurors sat "on the edge of their seats" as Galloway questioned Anne Marie Gardner, a twenty-six-year-old black woman who said that Alligood made repeated sexual advances toward her. "Alligood came to the female section just about every night," she said, "to offer her sandwiches, sometimes awakening her to hand over the un-requested snacks." When she scrubbed the floors, Alligood shuffled along behind her, attempting to pinch and fondle her breasts. "I'd knock his hand away," she said.[73] On cross-examination, Chalmers sharply asked Gardner why she had not reported the behavior, and someone in the audience balked, saying, "Come on, mister." Emboldened by the spectator, Gardner snapped back, "I wanted to forget it."[74]

By presenting multiple victims of Alligood's lust, the defense readied the jurors for Little's testimony. Paul had prepared her for this moment and had spent months training her in the art of respectability. She had to assert her dignity and personhood without being too brash, and she had to appear reputable without being too demure. It was a difficult task, since Little had a "negative side" her attorneys did not want to slip out. "She's not an honest person," Paul admitted later. "She's not a kind person. She's a violent person. That doesn't mean she committed this crime," he explained, "it only means she's a product of her environment."[75] If she had said, "I did a brave thing, I killed the old lecher and I'm glad of it," Paul argued, she would have "blown it."[76] Paul taught Little how to behave in a way that made the jury believe she was an honorable and decent young woman and that any allusions the prosecutors made to her criminal or sexual history were signs of their own racism, not her moral shortcomings.

Paul helped create an image of respectability by pairing Little with her attorney, Karen Galloway. As a recent graduate of Duke Law School, Galloway was everything Little was not: middle class, educated, poised, well spoken, and respectable. "To be really good on the stand," Paul told a journalist later, "the client must be an extension of her lawyer. The client literally must *be* her lawyer." Paul realized that Galloway commanded respect when she spoke to the jurors, and white women in particular responded to her grace and self-assuredness. "I figure if they'll accept Karen . . . she'll drag Joan along with her. They'll never look at Joan." Galloway's presence provided jurors with "an image of what Joan can be . . . and maybe is."[77]

By the time Little testified on her own behalf, the prosecution's case had been severely weakened. On August 6 Judge Hamilton Hobgood reduced the charge against her to second-degree murder because the "state had failed to offer sufficient evidence that she had planned the killing."[78] As prosecutors lost legal ground, they increasingly relied on racial and sexual stereotypes to make their case. This was most clear when Little, after sitting expressionless for nearly three weeks, finally took the stand.

Wearing a peach pullover and checkered slacks, the petite woman testified that she had killed Clarence Alligood in self-defense after he forced his way into her cell. She spoke so softly at times that jurors and spectators leaned forward, straining to hear the details of what had happened almost a year earlier.[79] "Choking back a sob," Little told the jury how Alligood had often brought her sandwiches and snacks late at night, without her asking. After about three weeks in jail, she said, Alligood started making passes at her, "talking about how nice I looked in my gown and that he wanted me to you know, have sex with him." "Well, what did you say?" Paul asked. "I told him to leave and that if he didn't I was gonna tell."[80] When prosecutor Griffin asked her why she hadn't followed through on the threat to report

Alligood, Little told the court that "coming up as a black woman, it's a difficult thing . . . it's a question of your word against a white person."[81]

Alligood's late-night visits and the snacks and sandwiches were just a ploy, the defense claimed, to manipulate Little into having sex with him. When he walked into her cell in the early-morning hours of August 27, 1974, he had a "silly grin on his face, a weird look," Little testified. "He said that he had been nice to me and it was time I be nice to him." Holding back tears, Little told the jury she rebuffed Alligood and told him that she "wasn't gonna be nice to him."[82] Undeterred by her apparent rebuke, Alligood slipped his shoes off, walked into the cell, and started to fondle her breasts. "You might as well [tell]," Alligood said as he "started to feel all over [her]," because the other police officers "aren't going to believe you anyway." Little, her voice barely audible in the courtroom, told the jury she began to cry when Alligood stepped closer, pulled her nightgown up over her head, and "stuck his left hand in between my legs." With his right hand he grabbed her neck and growled, "give me some pussy."[83] "I was scared so I just let him do that."[84]

"You never screamed?" Griffin asked on cross-examination. "No, I just stood there," Little said quietly. "You just stood there," Griffin said incredulously. "You didn't slap his hands away from you, you didn't push him away from you?" "No sir," Little replied. Clearly exasperated, Griffin raised his voice. "You never hollered, shouted, pushed him away, struck him or anything?" Calm and composed, Little told him she did not resist because she was afraid. "He had not threatened you at that point, had he?" Griffin argued. "He was bigger than me," she said, pointing out that the jailer was over 200 pounds and she was half that size. "But you didn't fight him off, is that right?" Griffin bullied her until she finally broke down. Instead of losing her cool, however, she turned the tables and gracefully upbraided him. "If you had been a woman," Little said, "you wouldn't have known what to do either, you probably wouldn't have screamed . . . because you wouldn't have known what he would have done to you."[85]

Little continued with her raw testimony, which no amount of planning or prepping by Paul could have produced. She described how the jailer removed his pants, forced her to her knees, and then, ice pick in hand, pushed her head down between his legs and told her to "suck him." "I didn't know whether he was going to kill me or what," she said, trembling. She wept as she described how she grabbed the ice pick when his grip loosened. "I reached for it and it fell," she said, her voice cracking. "He grabbed for it . . . I grabbed for it," she said, burying her face into a handkerchief. She looked at the jury, her eyes red and puffy from sobbing, and told them that she "got to the ice pick first [and] struck at him each time he came at me." In the struggle, she said, she lashed out at Alligood after he grabbed her wrists and ran when he finally fell down.[86] Little's heart-wrenching testimony touched a raw nerve among the black women jurors, especially Cora Judkins and Pecola Jones, who "wept softly" as Little dried her eyes and prepared for Griffin's cross-examination.

The *New York Times* reported that three hours of "wheedling and battering" by Griffin "failed to evoke any anger from the young black woman." Griffin's cross-examination followed what *Times* reporter Wayne King called "the classic courtroom pattern where allegations of rape are made—an attempt to impeach the accuser's reputation and/or force her into a contradiction through anger or simple repetition of the facts."[87] On the latter point, Griffin and his assistant prosecutors failed miserably. By making Little repeat answers to their questions and retell the more brutal aspects of her struggle, they appeared insensitive at best. It did not help that Griffin used a sharp, sarcastic voice when he demanded to know why Little did not scream or physically resist Alligood's sexual attack.

When prosecutors could not rattle Little, they attacked her credibility and portrayed her as a prostitute. Griffin asked Little if she ever gave a bondsman sexual favors in return for a loan to get out of jail, if another woman was her lesbian lover while she awaited trial in the woman's prison, if she had a venereal disease, and if she ferried women to Jacksonville, North Carolina, as part of a prostitution ring. To all but one question, Paul objected and Judge Hobgood overruled. Little calmly defended herself, maintaining her composure and her dignity.[88]

Griffin and his fellow prosecutors followed this strategy during their closing arguments. They berated Little for not resisting and suggested that she actually wanted to have sex with Alligood. Just because there was "sexual activity underway" does not "give her the right to kill this man," Griffin argued. He suggested that not only did Little have consensual sex with the jailer; *she* seduced *him*. What else could explain Alligood's erection, Griffin asked. "[It's] strange to me that a man with rape on his mind would go in without an erection. That's strange to me. Does that make any sense at all? A man with rape on his mind?" Finally, Griffin described Little as a "calculating criminal, who, bent on escape, lured the jailer into her cell with a promise of sexual favors" and then, "at the moment of ecstasy, she let him have it." She "stabbed a man all over his body—directed at his heart . . . how else would a man sit there and take those kind of wounds? How else?"[89]

Defense attorneys painted a different picture in their closing statements. Wearing the same color as her client and sporting a similar short
Afro, Karen Galloway taped off a four- by seven-foot box on the courtroom floor and stood inside it, inviting the jurors to put themselves in Joan
Little's shoes. Galloway skillfully transported the jurors to the Beaufort
County jail on the night of the crime. Imagine a "young black woman
whose white jailer had come to her cell demanding sex," she said. "Imagine Alligood's power and Miss Little's sense of fear."[90] Here is a "two
hundred pound man sitting on the bunk, you on your knees on the floor,"
Galloway said, adroitly re-creating the physical sense of powerlessness
Little must have felt. The young attorney then "described in stark language
the sexual assault," the *New York Times* reported, "weaving into the account over and over again, the power of the jailer." Alligood was a "man
of position, of authority," she argued. Little ran, she argued, because white
men in the South could do anything to black women and get away with it.
She ran to save her own life. And then, pointing to the white male prosecutors as if they too were guilty, she said disgustedly, "They suggest that she
enjoyed it."[91] As a respectable black woman, Galloway's condemnation of
white men's lawlessness and indifference toward black women's bodily
integrity was a powerful indictment. Indeed, Galloway's ability to make
Alligood's power and perversion real enabled the jury to gain a sense of
Little's "defenselessness, paralysis, [and] violation." Her performance reduced the jurors to tears.[92]

The defense team could have rested after Galloway's wrenching closing argument, but Paul wanted the jury to understand that Little's story
fit into a long and painful history. Taking the jury back to Jim Crow, Paul
opened his dog-eared copy of Gerda Lerner's *Black Women in White
America* and read a long passage from an essay written in 1902 by an
anonymous African American woman. The essay denounced white men
for defiling black womanhood. The author prayed that "someone will arise
who will champion [black women's] cause and compel the world to see
that we deserve justice, as other heroes compelled it to see that we deserved freedom."[93] Paul argued that that someone was Joan Little.

"God chose Joan Little," Paul insisted, "like he chose Rosa Parks" to
end the "domination of southern black women by white males."[94] "And
that is what this case is all about. This case compels the world to see that
women, black women, deserve justice; that women are victims of rape and
that rape is not a sex crime and that they do not lure men into raping them.
It is a crime of violence, of hatred, of humiliation." He then put the entire

Joan Little (left) with attorney Karen Galloway, July 14, 1975. (Courtesy of the North Carolina State Archives. Reprinted with permission of the *Raleigh News and Observer.*)

history of the South's racial and sexual subjugation on trial and asked the jury to decide whether it wanted to continue to live in a world dominated by white supremacy. "Whose word do you believe," he asked, "the history of whiteness on a pedestal, white southern womanhood on the pedestal, righteousness, purity, or do you believe the black woman who has a history of being lower than the prostitute?"[95]

After deliberating for seventy-eight minutes, the jury unanimously voted to acquit Joan Little.[96] As jury foreman Mark Neilson read the verdict, Little "broke into sobs at the defense table as her lawyers clustered around her." Wiping the tears away, she said, "It feels good to be free."[97] News of the victory quickly spread to the crowd of 100 supporters outside. When Little emerged, the throng erupted into cheers and chanted, "Freedom! Freedom! Freedom!"[98] At a press conference in the green and yellow lobby of the Lemon Tree Inn in Raleigh later that day, Little told reporters that she "always had confidence in the people" and felt she received a fair trial, despite the fact that the prosecutors were more "interested in sending black women to the gas chamber than the truth." Standing next to Galloway, Little told the crowd of television reporters and journalists that she hoped her experience might help women who "go through the same kinds of abuse."[99]

According to Michael Coakley, a *Chicago Tribune* reporter who sat through the five-week trial, Little's case provided a national airing of issues that plagued the country, particularly "racism, sexism, and prison reform" and "the whole question of self-defense against rape."[100] The case helped fuel a public debate about the prosecution of sex crimes and aided feminist efforts to redefine rape as a crime of violence, aggression, and humiliation that had little if anything to do with sex. Additionally, by constantly challenging prosecutors' implied arguments that Little could not have been raped because she was not respectable, she and her attorneys helped dispel stereotypes of black women as jezebels who could not be "legitimate" victims of rape. The fact that these arguments were seen as racist attempts to smear the victim indicated that a New South could emerge from the ruins of the old. "I like to think we at least made a beginning," Galloway said later. "Maybe now rape victims won't have to take the witness stand and become the defendant."[101]

The Joan Little case proved that respectability mattered, but only to a degree. Despite Paul's comparison of Little to Rosa Parks, she was *nothing* like the heroine of the Montgomery bus boycott. By 1975 respectability was no longer the defining personality trait supporters needed to rally to the cause. Everyone knew from the beginning that Little had been incarcerated for committing a crime, but that did not stop supporters from insisting that she still had a right to bodily integrity and deserved to be treated with respect. Certainly the modern civil rights movement, which forced the nation to recognize African Americans as citizens and as human beings—at least legally—had something to do with the change. When Paul told the jury that "there is no human being on the face of the earth" who has the right to violate or abuse another person, "no matter who you are or where you think you come from or whatever possession or control you have," he reflected those changes.[102]

Although the verdict in the Little case highlighted these breaks with the past, there was much continuity. The trial drew national and international attention, and a broad coalition of supporters rallied in defense of Little's womanhood and her right to self-defense. The widespread support Little engendered among leftist and liberal organizations mirrored the nationwide coalitions that had formed to demand justice for Recy Taylor in 1944 and Rosa Lee Ingram in 1947. Like the Committee for Equal Justice for Mrs. Recy Taylor and the Sojourners for Truth and Justice, the Free

Joan Little campaign, led primarily by African American women, helped mobilize support on behalf of black womanhood and served as a catalyst for larger struggles. The Little trial also drew attention to the long history of sexualized violence against African American women.

When Paul read to the jury from a 1902 essay decrying the lack of protection for black women and their special vulnerability in a system where white men could abuse them with impunity, he bore witness not only to black women's decades of abuse during slavery and Jim Crow but also to their long history of speaking out against it. Even though Paul highlighted this history and helped it find a broader audience, it was African American women who bore the ultimate burden of testimony.

Speaking out was never easy. It was emotionally trying and frightening. Joan Little told reporters shortly after her trial that the "toughest thing" about the entire ordeal was testifying. "I spent many months trying to force it from the bottom of me, to try to tell people what happened. I knew people would think that I must have enticed him," she said. "I don't think any woman enjoys talking about being sexually attacked."[103] For African American women who were raped or sexually harassed in the segregated South or anywhere their bodies were not their own, speaking out was downright dangerous. As a result, testimony must be seen as a form of direct action and radical protest against the social and sexual status quo. Indeed, the willingness of African American women to testify about the crimes committed against their bodies and their personhood reflected their enormous courage and strength and indicated their understanding that the "personal is political."

Notes

This essay is adapted from Danielle L. McGuire, *At the Dark End of the Street: Black Women, Rape and Resistance—A New History of the Civil Rights Movement from Rosa Parks to the Rise of Black Power* (New York: Knopf, 2010). Copyright 2010 by Danielle L. McGuire. Reprinted by permission of Knopf.

A hearty thanks to John Dittmer, Christina Greene, Nancy Hewitt, Steven Lawson, Jeanne Theoharis, Tim Tyson, and Craig Werner, all of whom read various versions of this essay. I am also grateful to my colleagues and friends from Rutgers and Wayne State University, who have invariably made me a better scholar and teacher. And of course, none of my work is possible without the love and support of Adam, Ruby, and Rhys Rosh.

1. Joan's name has been spelled multiple ways, but it is always pronounced Jo-Ann. See "Exhibit A," Medical Examiner's Report, folder 4, box 4, Hamilton

Hobgood Papers, Southern Historical Collection, Manuscript Department, Wilson Library, University of North Carolina, Chapel Hill; James Reston Jr., *The Innocence of Joan Little: A Southern Mystery* (New York: Times Books, 1977), 9–11. Little had received a seven- to ten-year sentence for larceny and breaking and entering, which she began serving on June 6, 1974. See James Reston Jr., "The Joan Little Case," *New York Times Magazine,* April 6, 1975.

2. Reston, *Innocence of Joan Little,* 37.

3. Joan Little with Rebecca Ranson, "I Am Joan," *Southern Exposure* 6, no. 1 (1978): 46.

4. Marjorie Wright, interview by James Reston, audiocassette, James Reston Collection, Southern Historical Collection, Manuscripts Department, Wilson Library, University of North Carolina, Chapel Hill.

5. Little with Ransom, "I Am Joan," 47.

6. In her authoritative study of the Little case, Genna Rae McNeil credits "sisterhood" as the catalyst for the organizing to defend Joan Little, rather than the long history of black women's testimony and organized resistance to sexual violence. See Genna Rae McNeil, "'Joanne Is You and Joanne Is Me': A Consideration of African American Women and the 'Free Joan Little' Movement, 1974–75," in *Sisters in the Struggle: African American Women in the Civil Rights–Black Power Movement,* ed. Bettye Collier-Thomas and V. P. Franklin (New York: New York University Press, 2001), 259–79. See also Ruth Rosen, *The World Split Open: How the Modern Women's Movement Changed America* (New York: Viking, 2000), 183.

7. Maria Bevacqua, *Rape on the Public Agenda: Feminism and the Politics of Sexual Assault* (Boston: Northeastern University Press, 2000), 56. Bevacqua argues that this event served as a catalyst for the antirape movement. See also Flora Davis, *Moving the Mountain: The Women's Movement in America since 1960* (New York: Prentice Hall, 1991), 310–11; Rosen, *World Split Open,* 181–83; Estelle B. Freedman, *No Turning Back: The History of Feminism and the Future of Women* (New York: Ballantine Books, 2002), 282–87.

8. For more on the history of antirape organizing, see Bevacqua, *Rape.*

9. Bevacqua, *Rape,* 21.

10. Linda Brent, "Incidents in the Life of a Slave Girl," in *The Classic Slave Narratives,* ed. Henry Louis Gates Jr. (New York: Penguin, 1987), 335.

11. Bevacqua, *Rape,* 24.

12. Paula Giddings, *When and Where I Enter: The Impact of Black Women on Race and Sex in America* (New York: Morrow, 1984), 31.

13. Ibid., 86–87.

14. Darlene Clark Hine, "Rape and the Inner Lives of Black Women in the Middle West: Preliminary Thoughts on the Culture of Dissemblance," *Signs* 14 (summer 1989): 918.

15. Giddings, *When and Where I Enter,* 121.

16. On Fannie Lou Hamer's testimony, see Chana Kai Lee, *For Freedom's*

Sake: The Life of Fannie Lou Hamer (Urbana: University of Illinois Press, 1999), 54, 59, 79, 80–81, 89, 196n2.

17. Fred Atwater, "$600 to Rape Wife? Alabama Whites Make Offer to Recy Taylor Mate," *Chicago Defender,* January 27, 1945, 1.

18. For more on the Ingram case, see Charles H. Martin, "Race, Gender, and Southern Justice: The Rosa Lee Ingram Case," *American Journal of Legal History* 29, no. 3 (July 1985): 251–68; Virginia Shadron, "Popular Protest and Legal Authority in Post–World War II Georgia: Race, Class, and Gender Politics in the Rosa Lee Ingram Case" (PhD diss., Emory University, 1991).

19. The Gertrude Perkins case received sustained attention in Montgomery's white daily newspaper, the *Montgomery Advertiser.* See "Racial Discord Is Promoted by NAACP, Says Mayor," *Montgomery Advertiser,* April 15, 1949, and the following editions of the *Montgomery Advertiser:* April 5, 1949, 8A; April 6, 1949, 1B; April 7, 1949, 2A; April 15, 1949, 8A; April 17, 1949, 3A; April 20, 1949, 3A; April 21, 1949, last page; May 3, 1949, 1A; May 21, 1949, 1A; May 27, 1949, 12A. See also S. S. Seay, *I Was There by the Grace of God* (Montgomery, Ala.: New South Books, 1990), 130–31; "Rape Cry against Dixie Cops Fall on Deaf Ears," *Baltimore Afro American,* April 9, 1949, 1; J. Mills Thornton, *Dividing Lines: Municipal Politics and the Struggle for Civil Rights in Montgomery, Birmingham, and Selma* (Tuscaloosa: University of Alabama Press, 2002), 33, 591n28. On police brutality in Montgomery, see Thornton, *Dividing Lines,* 33–36.

20. Lamont H. Yeakey, "The Montgomery, Alabama Bus Boycott, 1955–1956" (PhD diss., Columbia University, 1979), 152; Stewart Burns, ed., *Daybreak of Freedom: The Montgomery Bus Boycott* (Chapel Hill: University of North Carolina Press, 1997), 7.

21. Case 2, folder IV, box 30, p. 14, Martin Luther King Papers, Boston University. According to these documents, victim Flossie Hardman died of shock five years after her attack. Her mother claimed Flossie's death "was caused by her never recovering from the ordeal she went through." Townsend Davis, *Weary Feet, Rested Souls: A Guided History of the Civil Rights Movement* (New York: Norton, 1998), 34; Yeakey, "Montgomery Bus Boycott," 85.

22. Jo Ann Gibson Robinson, *The Montgomery Bus Boycott and the Women Who Started It* (Knoxville: University of Tennessee Press, 1987), 21, 22. Robinson notes that there were at least thirty complaints of abusive treatment on the buses in 1953 alone; see also Yeakey, "Montgomery Bus Boycott," 9–13. Yeakey notes that even a "cursory survey of those who had run-ins with bus drivers reveals a preponderance of women involved in such incidents" (226).

23. Danielle L. McGuire, "'It Was Like All of Us Had Been Raped': Sexualized Violence, Community Mobilization and the African American Freedom Struggle," *Journal of American History* 91 (December 2004): 906–31.

24. Quoted in Anne Blythe, "Role of Women in the Civil Rights Plight," *Raleigh News and Observer,* July 23, 2005.

25. Steven F. Lawson, *Running for Freedom: Civil Rights and Black Politics in America since 1941* (New York: McGraw-Hill, 1991), 111. According to Lawson, four years after the passage of the Voting Rights Act, about three-fifths of southern black adults had registered to vote. In Mississippi alone, black registration jumped from 6.7 percent in 1964 to 59.4 percent in 1968. In Alabama, black registration increased from 23 to 53 percent.

26. Peniel E. Joseph, *Waiting 'til the Midnight Hour: A Narrative History of Black Power in America* (New York: Henry Holt, 2006), 157.

27. Steve M. Gillon and Cathy D. Matson, *The American Experiment: A History of the United States,* vol. 2 (Boston: Houghton Mifflin, 2002), 1155; Lawson, *Running for Freedom,* 127.

28. Lawson, *Running for Freedom,* 127. For more on urban riots during the 1960s, see Thomas J. Sugrue, *The Origins of Urban Crisis: Race and Inequality in Postwar Detroit* (Princeton, N.J.: Princeton University Press, 1996).

29. Timothy B. Tyson, *Blood Done Sign My Name: A True Story* (New York: Random House, 2004), 118–29.

30. Ibid., 257.

31. Ibid., 258.

32. Ibid., 258, 268–69. Tyson says the New Hanover County Sheriff's Department was "heavily infiltrated by the Ku Klux Klan" and notes that Sheriff Marion Millis admitted as much in the *Raleigh News and Observer,* October 27, 1965 (ibid., 342).

33. Chavis drew a thirty-five-year prison sentence. The Wilmington Ten garnered massive media attention, and in 1977 Amnesty International launched a campaign to have them declared "political prisoners." In 1980 a federal court reversed the verdicts after discovering that "the prosecution's tactics had worked hand in glove with the FBI's COINTELPRO (Counter Intelligence Program) operation to shut down the black freedom movement." Tyson, *Blood Done Sign My Name,* 270. For more on the Wilmington Ten, see Bud Schulz and Ruth Schulz, *It Did Happen Here: Recollections of Political Repression in America* (Berkeley: University of California Press, 1989), 195–212; Larry Reni Thomas, *The True Story behind the Wilmington Ten* (Chapel Hill: University of North Carolina Press, 1980); Ben Chavis, *Wilmington 10: Editorials and Cartoons* (New York: United Church of Christ, 1977).

34. Angela Davis, "The Struggle of Ben Chavis and the Wilmington 10," *Black Scholar,* April 1975, 29–31. It was because of her involvement with the Wilmington Ten that Davis first heard about Joan Little. See Joseph, *Waiting 'til the Midnight Hour,* 241–75.

35. Reston, *Innocence of Joan Little,* 28. In Ayden, North Carolina, twenty-five miles west of Washington, white students bombed the high school bathroom, and months of turmoil followed the murder of a black laborer by a white policeman. In Williamston, twenty miles to the north, Golden Frinks, SCLC field secre-

tary, led the Williamston freedom movement from 1963 to 1965. National leaders in the SCLC eyed Williamston for a national campaign in 1965 because it had a vibrant black community that was well organized and a violent white leadership connected to an active Ku Klux Klan that eagerly resisted black freedom. According to David Cecelski, the SCLC ultimately chose Selma instead of the "small Tobacco Belt" town to make a national stand. "Bloody Sunday," Cecelski notes, "would become world famous; Williamston and Frinks, thus far, historical footnotes." David Cecelski, *Along Freedom Road: Hyde County, North Carolina and the Fate of Black Schools in the South* (Chapel Hill: University of North Carolina Press, 1994), 82–85.

36. Reston, *Innocence of Joan Little,* 22.

37. Ibid., 6, 176.

38. Ibid., 14.

39. Ibid., 73; Reston, "Joan Little Case." See also Jerry Paul and Joan Little, interview by James Reston, audiocassette, Reston Collection.

40. See Reston, *Innocence of Joan Little,* 284–89; Little interview by Reston. In Jacksonville, North Carolina, police charged Little with possession of stolen goods and a sawed-off shotgun; on January 3, 1974, police in Washington, North Carolina, arrested her for shoplifting, but the charge was dismissed. Six days later she was arrested again for shoplifting, this time drawing a suspended sentence. Less than a week passed before Little was arrested again and charged with three separate felonies: breaking, entering, and larceny. A grand jury indicted Little on March 15, 1974, and on June 4, 1974, she was sentenced to seven to ten years.

41. Golden Frinks, interview by James Reston, audiocassette, Reston Collection.

42. Rosalyn Baxandall and Linda Gordon, "Second Wave Feminism," in *Blackwell's Companion to American Women's History,* ed. Nancy A. Hewitt (Oxford: Blackwell Publishing, 2005), 417. For more on the women's movement, see Rosalyn Baxandall and Linda Gordon, eds., *Dear Sisters: Dispatches from the Women's Liberation Movement* (New York: Basic Books, 2000); Sara M. Evans, *Tidal Wave: How Women Changed America at Century's End* (New York: Vintage, 2003); Rosen, *World Split Open.*

43. New York Women against Rape (NYWAR) founded the first rape crisis center in October 1971. Bevacqua, *Rape,* 33.

44. The Crenshaw Women's Center in Los Angeles organized an "anti-rape squad" and created a rape hotline; in Berkeley, California, women organized the Bay Area Women against Rape; in Washington, D.C., women's rights activists created a rape crisis center; and in Chicago, Women against Rape organized a conference dedicated to rape. Bevacqua, *Rape,* 33, 36.

45. Reston, *Innocence of Joan Little,* 7.

46. Erskine Caldwell, *Tobacco Road* (New York: First Edition Library, 1932).

47. For more on the "progressive mystique," see William H. Chafe, *Civilities*

and Civil Rights: Greensboro, North Carolina and the Black Struggle for Freedom (New York: Oxford University Press, 1981).

48. "Justice in North Carolina: Once More Old South," *New York Times,* March 9, 1975, B5E.

49. Reston, *Innocence of Joan Little,* 77.

50. Ibid., 13.

51. James Reston, "The Innocence of Joan Little," *Southern Exposure* 6, no. 1 (1978): 37.

52. "Joanne Little: No Escape Yet," *Off Our Backs,* January 1975, folder 3, box 4, Hobgood Papers.

53. Angela Davis, "Forum: Joanne Little: The Dialectics of Rape," *Ms.* 3, no. 12 (June 1975): 74–77.

54. Julian Bond's letter soliciting funds, n.d., folder 3, box 4, Hobgood Papers.

55. Reston, "Joan Little Case."

56. The file on Joan Little in the NAACP Legal Defense and Educational Fund Papers contains few documents. They consist mainly of letters to constituents indicating that the NAACP stood ready to support Little if she asked it to do so, but in the meantime, it deferred to the Southern Poverty Law Center. See "Memorandum to Mabel Smith from Mildred Bond," February 5, 1975; Nathanial R. Jones to Alfred Baker Lewis, March 11, 1975; and Charles E. Carter to Ms. L. Wailes, April 22, 1975, folder 2, part V, 1911, NAACP Papers, Manuscripts Reading Room, Library of Congress, Washington, D.C. A draft of a memo to Joan Little offering the NAACP's assistance was crossed out, and "not sent" was written on the top.

57. Maulana Ron Karenga, "In Defense of Sister Joanne: For Ourselves and History," *Black Scholar,* July–August 1975, 40, 42.

58. For more on Rosa Parks's history as an antirape activist, see Danielle L. McGuire, *At the Dark End of the Street: Black Women, Rape and Resistance—A New History of the Civil Rights Movement from Rosa Parks to the Rise of Black Power* (New York: Knopf, 2010).

59. "Minutes of the Joanne Little Defense Committee," folder 1, box 3, Rosa L. Parks Collection, Archives of Labor and Urban Affairs, Walter P. Reuther Library, Wayne State University, Detroit, Michigan. Thanks to William LeFevre for sending me these documents and to Jeanne Theoharis, who shared her find with me.

60. McNeil, "Joanne Is You and Joanne Is Me," 271.

61. Christina Greene, *Our Separate Ways: Women and the Black Freedom Movement in Durham, North Carolina* (Chapel Hill: University of North Carolina Press, 2005), 225.

62. Ibid., 225–26.

63. McNeil, "Joanne Is You and Joanne Is Me," 270.

64. Ibid.

65. Newsletter, n.d., box 1, "Southern Poverty Law Center," and "Funds Sought for Miss Little's Defense," *Durham Morning Herald,* n.d., box 1, "Ann and Raymond Cobb," Joann Little Papers, 1973–1975 and n.d., Rare Book, Manuscript, and Special Collections Library, Duke University, Durham, North Carolina.

66. Ginny Carroll, "500 Stage Courthouse Rally," *Raleigh News and Observer,* July 15, 1975, 1; Michael Coakley, "The Joan Little Trial Is Over, but the Issues Remain," *Chicago Tribune,* August 24, 1975, B1. The rally included members of the National Organization for Women, the National Black Feminist Organization, the Black Panther Party, and local members of the Free Joanne Little Defense Fund Inc., as well as other individuals and groups.

67. Rick Nichols, "Stage Set to Weigh a Killing," *Raleigh News and Observer,* July 27, 1965, 1.

68. Wayne King, "Jury Selection Challenged by Joan Little's Lawyers," *New York Times,* July 15, 1975, 20.

69. "Jury Seated in Murder Trial of Joan Little," *Raleigh News and Observer,* July 24, 1975, 1. The *Raleigh News and Observer* featured pictures of the jurors after the trial. "Jurors Say Evidence Too Thin to Convict," *Raleigh News and Observer,* August 16, 1975, 1, 5B.

70. The defense exploited the lax practices of small-town southern policemen, their lack of education and experience, and their careless collection of evidence, creating the perception that the police had bungled the investigation from the start. The state's witnesses only added to the impression that the investigation had been bungled. For example, "the local detective could produce no identifiable fingerprint from the bars or the bed or the sink or the clothes or the ice pick. The SBI chemist's test of Joan Little's scarf, found underneath Alligood's body, was inconclusive." Photographs were splattered with developing chemicals, making it impossible to tell the difference between blood spatters and chemical dots. Worse, "from the technical legal standpoint," the prosecution could not even establish Little's presence in the jail cell where Alligood was murdered. See Reston, *Innocence of Joan Little,* 259, 260–76.

71. Testimony of Joan Little, transcript, folder 2, box 1, Reston Collection.

72. Frances B. Kent, "Joan Little's Lawyers to Show Jailer Made Frequent Sexual Advances," *Los Angeles Times,* August 8, 1975, B20.

73. "Ex-Inmates Testify in Little Case," *Raleigh News and Observer,* August 8, 1975, 1.

74. Ibid.

75. Reston, *Innocence of Joan Little,* 113.

76. Ibid., 114.

77. Reston, "Innocence of Joan Little," 36.

78. Rick Nichols, "Charge Is Reduced in Joan Little Trial," *Raleigh News and Observer,* August 7, 1975, 1.

79. "Little Says She Stabbed Jailer," *New York Times,* August 12, 1975.

80. Testimony of Joan Little, trial transcript, folder 2, box 1, Hobgood Papers.

81. Rick Nichols, "Testifies at Trial," *Raleigh News and Observer,* August 12, 1975, 1.

82. Testimony of Joan Little, trial transcript, folder 2, box 1.

83. Ibid. Little used the word *sex* at first and admitted that Alligood had actually said *pussy* only after Griffin harassed her. "Is that what you said yesterday? What did you say he said yesterday? Did he say sex or use some other term?" Little replied calmly, "I am using the word sex because I don't want to use any other word because it's still embarrassing to me." Griffin's point was to raise the question that if Alligood wanted to "get some pussy," why did he accept oral sex instead? At best, this line of questioning made Griffin appear to be subjecting Little to unnecessary harassment. Worse, it forced Griffin to admit that Alligood had asked for sex—what kind of sex didn't matter.

84. Ibid.; Michael Coakley, "Admits She Stabbed Him," *Chicago Tribune,* August 12, 1975, 1.

85. Testimony of Joan Little, trial transcript, folder 2, box 1.

86. Ibid.; Coakley, "Admits She Stabbed Him," 1; Nichols, "Testifies at Trial," 1.

87. Wayne King, "Defense Closes for Joan Little," *New York Times,* August 13, 1975, 68.

88. Hobgood ruled that the question about whether she had a sexually transmitted disease was "irrelevant." Testimony of Joan Little, trial transcript; "Defense Closes," *New York Times,* August 13, 1975, 68. John A. Wilkinson, who had been retained by the Alligood family members to act in their interests, also gave a closing statement in which he argued that oral sex, or "unnatural sex," was not rape. "It is a detestable, horrible thing, but it's not the statutory crime of rape, and it's not punishable by death." Wilkinson argued that what Alligood had allegedly done to Little was only "mistreatment," for which he did not deserve to be murdered. See "Jury Argument of John A. Wilkinson," trial transcript, folder 10, box 2, Reston Collection.

89. "Joan Little Case Goes to Trial Today," *Los Angeles Times,* August 15, 1975, B5; "Mr. Griffin's Argument to the Jury," trial transcript, folder 8, box 2, Hobgood Papers.

90. "Final Arguments Heard in Trial of Joanne Little," n.d., clipping, folder 12, box 3, Hobgood Papers.

91. "Prosecutor and Defense Present Final Arguments in Joan Little Case," *New York Times,* August 15, 1975; "Final Arguments Heard in Trial of Joanne Little."

92. Reston, *Innocence of Joan Little,* 320–21. There is no transcript of Galloway's closing argument in the Hobgood Papers or the Reston Collection. It is interesting that of all the people Reston interviewed for his book, he did not speak to Karen Galloway, the one black woman who could have shed the most light on the racial and sexual dynamics of the Little trial. When Reston refers to Galloway in his book, it is only in passing.

93. "Mr. Paul's Argument to the Jury," trial transcript, folder 9, box 2, Reston Collection. See also Gerda Lerner, ed., *Black Women in White America: A Documentary History* (New York: Pantheon Books, 1972), 166–69.

94. "Final Arguments Heard in Trial of Joanne Little." Paul's portrayal of Little as a civil rights heroine was a stretch, but it helped counter the negative images the prosecution presented to the jury. It also set up expectations that Little could not meet. Supporters hoped Little would become a political activist, and she often pledged to fight racism, sexual violence, and prison abuse. Instead, in the months and years after her acquittal, she was in and out of prison. In December 1975 she missed a court date, and a warrant was issued for her arrest. She then served twenty-one months in prison for the original breaking and entering charge. In October 1977 she escaped from prison and was captured in Brooklyn two months later. Little refused to return to North Carolina until the Supreme Court ordered her to do so. Beginning in February 1979 she served four months in the women's prison in Raleigh, North Carolina. She was arrested again ten years later in New York for driving a car with a stolen license plate and possession of an illegal weapon. See Melynn Glusman, "Forgetting Joan Little: The Rise and Fall of a Mythical Black Woman" (unpublished paper in the author's possession).

95. "Mr. Paul's Argument to the Jury."

96. Wayne King, "Joan Little Acquitted in Jailer's Slaying," *New York Times,* August 16, 1975, 49.

97. Ibid.

98. Rick Nichols, "Wake Jury Acquits Joan Little, Says State Didn't Prove Its Case," *News and Observer,* August 16, 1975, 1.

99. "Joan Little Says Jurors Just," *Raleigh News and Observer,* August 16, 1975, 5B.

100. Coakley, "Little Trial Is Over, but Issues Remain," B1.

101. Ibid.

102. "Mr. Paul's Argument to the Jury."

103. "Little Says Jurors Just," 5B.

Gender, Jazz, and Justice in Cold War Freedom Movements

Jacqueline Castledine

> I am told that Lionel Hampton, the little orchestra leader who keeps our feet tapping with his drums and xylophones, has developed a new thing in jazz—a theme based on the beat of the tom toms of Africa. . . . If our young maestro captures this "freedom theme" with his drums, he will be making still another contribution to the cause of civil rights.
>
> —Mary McLeod Bethune

> Since the early fifties jazz in South Africa has been threatening to burst the very seams of apartheid.
>
> —Lewis Nkosi

As it flowed across boundaries and borders of the African diaspora in the postwar period, jazz music moved through spaces denied to black bodies because of economic oppression, government repression, banishment, or self-imposed exile. In its travels it carried not only overt messages of political resistance but also covert messages about the subversive possibilities implicit in interracial sexuality, ideas that challenged white supremacy. The music's potential to confuse racial boundaries by attracting mixed race and mixed gender audiences—and especially the possibility of hybridity resulting from interracial pairings—combined with the more obvious threat to social order posed by the politically charged lyrics of protest songs, made jazz a powerful vernacular of postwar freedom movements. As the opening quotations suggest, figures as diverse as African American educator Mary McLeod Bethune and South African journalist Lewis Nkosi saw in jazz the potential to break down racial barriers and further the goals of black liberation. Whether Bethune and Nkosi also perceived the ways the "beat of the tom toms of Africa" intersected with gender and, in particular, the ways gender helped shape our understandings of race is less clear.[1]

The field of diaspora studies has recently produced an interdisciplinary body of literature exploring the relationship between the U.S. civil rights and the South African antiapartheid movements, yet it has only begun to examine the significance of gender to these causes. Historian Pamela Brooks points out that the Cold War produced "a world in which the racial and colonial balance was under siege," destabilizing social and political order while at the same time creating spaces for women's resistance.[2] Sociologist M. Bahati Kuumba adds that exploitation of black labor, political disenfranchisement, and systems of social oppression and segregation resulting from European colonialism closely linked the experiences of black women globally.[3] This scholarship demonstrates that even when women have been excluded by men from formal leadership positions, their work in liberation movements has made them central to diasporic exchange.[4]

Not surprisingly, given its Cold War context, black women's activism drew the attention and concern of governments. Attempts to suppress their work centered not only on women's organizational resistance to white supremacy, led by such groups as the African National Congress Women's League and the radical African American Sojourners for Truth and Justice (STJ), but also on mid-twentieth-century *cultural* resistance to colonialism, evident in the work of such South African and U.S. jazz artists as Miriam Makeba, Dorothy Masuka, Sophie Mgcina, Abbey Lincoln, and Nina Simone.[5] Their shared experiences of racism, sexism, decolonization, and exile contributed to the development of a unique articulation of anticolonial activism. This essay examines similarities as well as points of departure in the contributions of women jazz artists to freedom movements, particularly the role that gender and sexual expression played in shaping their resistance to colonial oppression.

Overlapping Diasporas

In the immediate postwar years South African apartheid and U.S. Jim Crow came under increasing attack on opposite sides of the Atlantic. In the aftermath of the war both countries experienced racial unrest attributable to a legacy of white supremacy combined with such economic difficulties as black unemployment, growing inflation, and housing shortages.[6] It is easy to draw parallels between the social and legal status of blacks in the United States and blacks in South Africa during this period, yet important distinctions complicate facile comparisons. Perhaps most important, African Americans remained a numerical minority in the United States, while black and "colored" South Africans were the overwhelming majority. In the words of jazz artist Sathima Bea Benjamin, South Africans "weren't ripped away from our continent, but our continent was ripped away from us."[7] The Supreme Court's 1954 *Brown v. Board of Education* ruling that overturned the doctrine of "separate but equal" also created the wedge needed to begin a legal dismantling of white supremacy in the United States; at the same time, white supremacy was being rigidly codified in South African law. For these reasons, historian Earl Lewis's concept of "overlapping diasporas" resulting from many points of social, cultural, and political intersection provides the best framework for understanding the relationship between the United States and South Africa following World War II.[8]

The history of racial segregation in South Africa can be traced to the 1652 founding at Cape Town of the Dutch East India Company. Apartheid law built on this long history and on such twentieth-century legislation as the Natives Land Act (1913), which set aside 7 percent of the country's land for black occupancy, leaving 83 percent for the whites who made up approximately a fifth of the population. Following the 1948 election of Nationalist Party candidate and Afrikaner partisan Daniel Malan as prime minister, his government passed several laws in quick succession intended to designate and separate races. The Population Registration Act established racial classifications, and the Group Areas Act designated geographic zones where each race would be permitted to live and work. Passed that same year, the Bantu Self-Government and Bantu Authorities Acts created homelands, or Bantustans, and directed tribal groups to govern black South Africans, denying them participation in the national government. Laws prohibiting mixed marriages, reserving professional jobs for whites, and outlawing opposition to the government ensured that white supremacy would regulate every aspect of South African life.

From the 1920s through the 1960s black South African women's resistance to white supremacy included sporadic demonstrations against legislation proposing that they be required, as black men were, to carry passes or identification papers meant to regulate their movement. Many African American women fighting Jim Crow in the South were aware of these protests. Above all, they were impressed by the attention the anti–pass law movement brought to the discussion of colonialism's effects on women. Acutely attuned to the significance of gender in their activism, radical African American women in groups such as the STJ viewed anticolonial movements of the 1950s as opportunities to achieve not only black liberation but also, in the words of one U.S. activist, "the complete emancipation of women throughout the world."[9]

Some Americans—especially those on the political Left—made known their concerns about the overt racism of South Africa's Nationalist Party. The Communist Party–aligned Council on African Affairs (CAA) chronicled the construction of apartheid law and other violence occurring in Cold War Africa until the council disbanded in 1955 under intense government harassment. For U.S. groups like the CAA, the fight against the Malan government offered yet another opportunity to draw embarrassing parallels between apartheid and Jim Crow in their demand for racial equality at home. Nonetheless, South Africa's vast reserves of the uranium required to produce nuclear weapons, coupled with U.S. fears of Soviet expansion, created a strong alliance between the governments of Daniel Malan and President Harry Truman.[10]

Intersections: Gender and Jazz

One response to the appallingly harsh living conditions endured by black South Africans was the popularity of township jazz, which was, in the words of one African musician, "taken from American Negro jazz and hammered out on the anvil of the South African experience."[11] Since its creation at the turn of the twentieth century, jazz was notable for its blend of African and European influences. African roots were easily discernible in the syncopated melodies of black spirituals and in the call-and-response of the blues, both of which helped form the foundation of jass (later jazz) music. From the spirituals and blues of post–Civil War America through the World War II period, jazz evolved from turn-of-the-century ragtime and New Orleans Dixieland to the swing and big band music of the 1930s and 1940s to the bebop, cool, and hard bop of the postwar era, a period also straddled by "free" and "avant-garde" jazz. Throughout this evolution, jazz was characterized by a tendency toward spontaneity, improvisation, collectivism, and struggle—characteristics that also describe black liberation movements. Heavily influenced by U.S. bands of the 1930s and 1940s, artists from South Africa built on urban sounds produced by blacks who had been forced from their rural homes in search of work—the sounds of townships such as Soweto and Sophiatown—to create a unique working-class music.[12] A product of overlapping diasporas, African jazz reflected the music resulting not only from forced black migration to the United States but also from forced migration within South Africa.

With razor-sharp language, songs written and performed by U.S. and South African jazz women employed common themes to critique a legacy of colonialism. Perhaps no performer influenced more female artists in both these nations than Billie Holiday. Scholar-activist Angela Davis writes that Holiday's songs often represented a form of resistance, rejecting European-American culture and U.S. government oppression while providing "a site where women could articulate and communicate their protests against male dominance."[13] Her 1939 recording of Lewis Allen's "Strange Fruit" challenged the white government's inaction on the issue of racial violence, graphically depicting lynching at a time when African Americans continued to lobby the Roosevelt administration to support decades-old antilynching legislation.[14] "Strange Fruit" was, in the words of Davis, "an undisguised rallying cry against the state."[15] In such clubs as New York's Café Society, Holiday sang:

Southern trees bear strange fruit,
Blood on the leaves and blood at the root,
Black bodies swinging in the southern breeze,
Strange fruit hanging from the poplar trees.

Pastoral scene of the gallant south,
The bulging eyes and the twisted mouth,
Scent of magnolias, sweet and fresh,
Then the sudden smell of burning flesh.[16]

Performing with "fervor and smoldering hatred in her eyes," Holiday gave voice to the growing anger and frustration that would help fuel the modern civil rights movement.[17] By addressing what critics would later identify as "institutional racism," Holiday, in both her popularity and her song lyrics, challenged the dominance of male jazz artists, who well into the postwar period epitomized what jazz historian Burton Peretti terms "the Cold War's spirit of machismo."[18]

The influence of American artists of the 1930s and 1940s on a cohort of female South African singers and songwriters who rose to popularity performing township jazz in the 1950s and early 1960s is apparent. For South African artists, the appropriation of African American music served more than merely aesthetic purposes. Social anthropologist Ulf Hannerz writes that "accepting New York could be a way of rejecting Pretoria, to refuse the cultural entailments" of apartheid law.[19] Before apartheid governments took control of South African radio, Holiday, as well as Sarah Vaughn, Dinah Washington, and Ella Fitzgerald, could regularly be heard on the nation's radio programs. Future artists Miriam Makeba, Dorothy Masuka, and Sophie Mgcina credited American jazz women with inspiring their careers.[20]

African American singer Abbey Lincoln was among those who shared with her South African counterparts an appreciation for Holiday, whose recordings were the first she remembers hearing as a child. Born in Chicago and raised on a farm in Michigan, Lincoln left home for California in 1949 to launch a career as a nightclub singer. Changing her given name of Anna Marie Woodridge several times to satisfy the whims of various club owners, she finally settled on Abbey Lincoln at the suggestion of lyricist Bob Russell. Russell reportedly recognized in her a growing race consciousness that the surname Lincoln, the president who freed the slaves, might embody. Her first album was released in 1956, the same year she earned a singing part in the Jayne Mansfield film *The Girl Can't Help It*. Reviews of both these projects often focused as much on Lincoln's appearance as on her other talents. Even liner notes for the album *Abbey Lincoln's Affair . . . A Story of a Girl in Love* addressed her image and not "her style of singing, her choice of lyric or of the musicians who accompany her."[21] It was not until she left California for New York that Lincoln began a fruitful and historic collaboration with many of the leading jazz figures of the civil rights movement.

When she arrived in New York, Lincoln was best known as a West Coast club singer, a label that did not place her in high esteem among jazz artists. That the cover of her first album had her lying seductively in a low-cut dress did little to dispel the notion that Lincoln was, like Lena Horne and Dorothy Dandridge before her, "poised to inherit the mantle of black sex symbol."[22] But under the guidance of drummer Max Roach, whom she married in 1962, Lincoln met and collaborated with some of the most respected jazz musicians of the era, including Thelonious Monk, Dizzy Gillespie, and Charles Mingus. Her performance on Roach's 1960 landmark civil rights album *We Insist! Max Roach's Freedom Now Suite* would establish her as a serious artist.

Roach's album grew out of a collaboration with lyricist and fellow activist Oscar Brown Jr., and it keenly reflects the historical moment of its creation. With great attention to detail, the album's cover reenacts newspaper photographs depicting the lunch counter protests under way in cities across the South, and upon its release in 1961 the *Pittsburgh Courier* declared the record "a 'boost' for the sit-ins."[23] Such song titles as "Driva Man," "Freedom Day," and "Tears for Johannesburg" suggest why the South African government banned the album's sale in 1962, concerned about its potential for far-reaching influence.[24] Lincoln's vocal performance, especially one minute and twenty seconds of "stylized screaming" on the composition "Triptych: Prayer/Protest/Peace," earned her mixed reviews.[25] Yet given Lincoln's growing militancy, response to her artistic expression on *We Insist!* was undoubtedly seen as an opportunity to critique her politics.

Indeed, Lincoln's voice matches the combative lyrics of Brown's "Driva Man," recounting the history of U.S. plantation slavery:

Driva man the kind of boss,
ride a man and lead a horse.
When his cat-o'-nine-tail fly,
you'll be happy just to die.
Run away and you'll be found,
by his big ole red boned hound.[26]

By juxtaposing "Driva Man" with the wordless "Tears for Johannesburg," a condemnation of the murder of sixty-nine antiapartheid protesters in the recent Sharpeville massacre, *We Insist!* provided a critique of white supremacy that placed Lincoln in a camp of militant civil rights activists.

Although U.S. and South African jazz women were clearly influenced by the giants of postwar jazz—both male and female—other strong female figures were essential to their artistic and political development. Lincoln credits her mother with instilling in her an appreciation of her heritage. Using the West African term for a "praise singer," she describes her mother as the family *griot,* who made it a point to teach her children the history of their ancestors.[27]

Likewise, South African singer Miriam Makeba's mother taught her important lessons about the corrosive effect of apartheid on the fabric of black community life. Makeba's mother's arrest for dealing in *umqombothi,* a home-brewed beer commonly sold by South African women (even though doing so was illegal), ushered her daughter into the world of white supremacy when she was a newborn in 1932.[28] Her father's inability to pay the small fine required for her mother's release resulted in eighteen-day-old Miriam spending the next several months in jail with her mother. Though far too young to remember the event, the significance of her mother's resistance of a colonial government policy intended to limit black women to low-paying domestic work was not lost on Makeba.[29] Singing in her church choir as an adolescent led to a career as a jazz artist, performing with the popular South African groups the Manhattan Brothers and the all-female Skylarks, and finally to the attention of U.S. performer Harry Belafonte, whom she met in London. With Belafonte's help, including joint concert appearances, Makeba earned an RCA recording contract.

As she performed on international stages throughout her career, Makeba carried with her the knowledge that the intersection of gender and colonial politics circumscribes lives from their earliest moments. Her childhood and adolescent memories illustrate how white supremacy creates hardships for women that both distinguish them from and bind them to black men in their liberation struggles. In her later years she recalled: "I was a nanny once, I looked after some white little babies. And you know, you take that baby, put it on your back and it feels the warmth of your back and you hold it. And the child really becomes like yours. And then that very child, as it grows up, it's told that you are different and you must be treated different. And this is the child that will grow up and call you names."[30] The experience of nurturing a white child and having it join one's oppressors was common to African and African-descended women across time and place. Understandably, sixteen-year-old Makeba viewed the 1948 election of Daniel Malan and his implementation of the policy of "apartness" as an effort to make her and other blacks even more invisible to white South Africans.

As it did for their U.S. counterparts, the opportunity to challenge a government built on white supremacy fueled the protest songs of South African women. Lyrics of songs such as *"uDr. Malan Unomthetho Onzima"* (Dr. Malan Has Made a Terrible Law) circulated through the diaspora, documenting the brutality of South African colonial rule.[31] "Dr. Malan has got very strange rules; he is stopping me from doing that and this and the other, in my own land," sang songwriter Dorothy Masuka, who left her home in Southern Rhodesia (now Zimbabwe) as a teenager to pursue a music career in South Africa.[32] Makeba's best-selling recording of Masuka's popular song "Pata Pata," named for a sensual urban dance, would help make both women international stars and enduring friends. Still, it was her songs that targeted the institution of apartheid that brought Masuka to the attention of the South African government. "In this world we are having problems, black people are sorrowful," Masuka wrote, suggesting why she earned a reputation as the most political of the era's South African women performers.[33] For obvious reasons, the matter of how to solve the problems of black people is not directly addressed in many protest songs. Yet the government fully understood that the debate of issues raised by this music, and the global attention to them, might incite activism. Thus, although the banning of songs such as "Dr. Malan" became regular policy, the lyrics were well known in South African townships.

In addition to attacks on important government figures, antiapartheid protest music reached beyond policy makers like Malan to include the everyday acts of ordinary South Africans. The lyrics of Sophie Mgcina's "Madam Please" illustrate that common daily interactions were as instrumental in perpetuating apartheid as was the draconian legislation passed by government officials. Movingly depicting the inequality inherent in the relationship between a black domestic worker and her white employer, Mgcina sang:

Madam please, before you shout about your broken plate,
ask me what my family ate.
Madam please, before you laugh at your servant's English,
try to speak to him in his Zulu language.
Madam please, before you complain your servant stinks,
try washing your clothes in Soweto zinc [a washtub].
Madam please, before you ask me if your children are fine,
ask me when I lost all mine.[34]

The power of Mgcina's lyrics lies in their ability to put a human face on the cruelty of apartheid, lifting the veil of invisibility that concealed the exploitation of domestic workers and allowing black women to confront their white "sisters." Her words reflect the sentiments of those in both South Africa and the United States who felt the sting of racism resulting from the acts of whites, whether influential government figures or middle-class women and children.

American singer-songwriter Nina Simone similarly explored the intersections of race and class in women's labor through her adaptation of the Kurt Weill and Bertolt Brecht song "Pirate Jenny."[35] Simone's version of this *Threepenny Opera* number expands the critique of class relations central to the 1928 original to include the issue of race, transforming the character of Jenny from a white Victorian-era London prostitute to a black woman in the southern United States. The anger of Simone's Jenny suggests a fomenting black rebellion:

You people can watch while I'm scrubbing these floors,
and I'm scrubbing the floors while you're gawking.
Maybe once you'll tip me and it makes you feel swell,
in this crummy southern town in this crummy old hotel.
But you'll never guess to who you're talking.

The sweet justice of revenge that is central to the original remains a focus of this adaptation, as Jenny fantasizes about the destruction of the town, except for the hotel where she works. "You gentlemen can wipe that smile off your face," she sings. "This whole frickin' place will be down to the ground."[36] Commenting on the significance of Jenny, historian Ruth Feldstein suggests that Simone's fictional character represents a "point of entry" for the "singer's discussion of socioeconomic and gendered dimensions of racism." Both critics and the sympathetic Feldstein note the "rage" evident in Simone's lyrics and voice.[37]

But whereas Mgcina "could identify" with the work of Billie Holiday because she "felt her anger," Simone rejected the suggestion that bitterness or anger inspired her art.[38] Perhaps leery of being stereotyped as "an angry black woman," she conceded that while "anger has its place," "intelligence" was at the heart of her thirty-year effort to "defend the rights of American blacks and third world people." Education, or making an audience "conscious of what has been done to my people around the world," was Simone's goal.[39] Her 1963 "Mississippi Goddam," which she wrote to protest the bombing of Sixteenth Street Baptist Church in Birmingham, Alabama, and the assassination of Mississippi NAACP leader Medgar Evers, became a civil rights anthem precisely because it graphically educated white America about the violence undergirding white supremacy.

Simone's background as the daughter of a Methodist minister and a student of classical music who later attended the Julliard School of Music may also account for her reticence to characterize her work as "angry." Her 1958 recording of Gershwin's "I Loves You, Porgy," popularized earlier by Holiday, had made the top-forty charts. And like artists of an earlier era, her recordings reached eager African ears. In the early 1960s Miriam Makeba confided to Simone that since first hearing her records played in South Africa, she had hoped for an opportunity to meet.[40] A shared vision for black liberation; Simone's friendship with Makeba's future husband, Black Nationalist Stokely Carmichael; and joint appearances in such venues as Carnegie Hall helped cement a meaningful, decades-long personal and professional relationship based on their mutual commitment to issues of gender, jazz, and justice.

Intersections: Jazz and Sexuality

By the late 1950s Miriam Makeba enjoyed increasing popularity as an international star, performing in films, on the London stage, and in concert. While she was traveling overseas in 1959, however, the South African government revoked her passport and refused to let her reenter the country. This separated Makeba from the things that were most important to her: family and homeland. What would become a thirty-year exile resulted from Makeba's appearances in the antiapartheid films *Come Back Africa* and *King Kong,* offering stark depictions of black South African life.[41] Forced to make a life for herself outside her native land, Makeba continued her singing career in Europe and the United States. In addition to having a strong and captivating voice, Makeba was a natural beauty with a sensual stage presence. She glamorized the short-cropped Afro hairstyle for women as a symbol of their African roots, and she firmly established her sensuality with her rhythmic performances of such songs as "Pata Pata" in concert and on television. But despite being labeled a political threat by the South African government, Makeba appeared to be uncomfortable with media depictions of her politics. When American journalists asked in 1959 about her association with African nationalist movements, she said, "I am not a politician or a diplomat . . . I am just a singer."[42] Her introduction that year to American television audiences illustrates how entwined singing, sexuality, and racial politics were in this phase of Makeba's career.

When she appeared in December 1959 on the *Steve Allen Show,* a *New York Times* reviewer drew parallels, beginning with their shared initials, between Miriam Makeba and actress Marilyn Monroe.[43] In an equally telling comparison a year later, another reviewer described Makeba's performance of an African folk song as "a primitive equivalent of" Billie Holiday's "My Man."[44] And in 1961 *New York Times* reviewer Robert Shelton wrote of Makeba's performance, "Stalking about the stage like a tiger on the prowl, she sang in a fluid, sinuous, sensual voice that ranged freely in a manner not unlike Ella Fitzgerald's."[45] Thus, even favorable comparisons to her childhood idols reminded Western audiences of her "exotic" and "primitive" homeland. Though often condescending, comments about Makeba's appearance suggest the success of her efforts to overcome apartheid's power to make black South Africans, and women in particular, invisible. Indeed, she deftly exploited attention to her appearance and her vocal gifts, using interest in her music for political ends.

Makeba may have initially gained notice because of her prominent display of her sexuality, but once she had their attention, Makeba reminded U.S. and European audiences in countless interviews about the political difficulties of blacks in South Africa. This same approach was employed by other antiapartheid activists who sang African songs in English to gain the support of the English-speaking world. In 1953, at age eighteen, Dorothy Masuka had earned the title "Miss Bulawayo" in a beauty contest. Despite her reputation as the most political songwriter of the apartheid period, her introduction for a BBC interview nearly fifty years later still included a description of Masuka as a 1950s "pin up girl."[46] The enduring title reflected Masuka's commitment to the cultivation of her image, especially an ongoing association between her politics and her sexuality.

As anticolonial activists like Makeba and Masuka constructed messages for both black and white Western audiences, their understanding of protest music did not always coincide with that of Western observers. Asked by an interviewer in 2002 why, given the potential danger, she had written political songs during the apartheid era, Masuka appeared reluctant to describe her work as political. She explained: "I don't know why, whoever found the name politics, what the person thought about. What they call politics, to me, it's the truth. They should have called politics the truth. Because . . . you are actually asking, why is this thing? You see it's wrong, you know, and you ask why you are doing this? And then the person turns it around and says you shouldn't ask that. And you ask yourself why shouldn't I ask?"[47] Even after the demise of apartheid in the early 1990s, Masuka insisted on discussing "the truth" as she understood it and distancing herself from the world of politics.

Masuka's presenting herself as a sexual object and framing her work as a nonpolitical exploration for "truth" (similar to Makeba's claim to be a singer, not a diplomat) suggests a culture of dissemblance strategically employed to shield herself from retribution for her political activism.[48] Yet Makeba's performance of Masuka's "Khawuleza" reveals how cultural production, even when not explicitly political, was employed to expose the injustices of apartheid. Makeba would introduce the song to U.S. audiences by explaining: "Khawuleza is a South African song. It comes from the townships, locations, reservations, whichever, near the cities of South Africa where all the black South Africans live. The children shout from the streets as they see police cars coming to raid their homes for one thing or another. They say, 'Khawuleza Mama!' which simply means 'Hurry Mama, please don't let them catch you!'"[49]

Likewise, politically committed African American artist (and Makeba mentor) Harry Belafonte acknowledges attempts to conceal his radical political leanings, including deep admiration for leftists Paul Robeson and W. E. B. Du Bois. Yet in contrast to jazz women, Belafonte consciously diverted attention from his politics by taking advantage of many white Americans' belief that he looked "close to white" and, rather than overtly sexual, like "the kind of Negro I'd like my daughter to date."[50] Educating white audiences about black liberation movements sometimes required differing strategies, based on the audience's understanding of gender.

Sexuality also figured prominently in the performances of U.S. jazz women, who saw in jazz's fluidity and malleability a unique opportunity for political expression in the civil rights era. Between the late 1950s and early 1960s, Abbey Lincoln set out to redefine on her own terms her sexuality and its relationship to her politics. Historian Brian Ward notes that for a decade following the mid-1950s Montgomery bus boycott, "there were distinct signs of jazz's growing identification with the formal Movement and its goals."[51] During this period both Lincoln and Makeba performed regularly at the Village Gate, a prominent jazz club in New York's Greenwich Village. They also donated their talents to various civil rights fundraisers and appeared together on the bill of a "Giant 12-Hour Civil Rights Rally" held at New York's Polo Grounds just days before the historic 1963 March on Washington.[52] In the late 1950s Lincoln had adopted a short Afro hairstyle, which, as it had for Makeba, garnered a great deal of comment in the press. That Lincoln felt a need to defend the unprocessed look (called at the time *au naturel*)— commenting that her husband, Max Roach, found it beautiful—suggests how radical her new style seemed to some.[53]

The public's reaction to Lincoln's change of style (both hair and dress) is perhaps understandable, considering that early in her career she, like Makeba, had been compared with the reigning international sex symbol of the day, Marilyn Monroe. In fact, Lincoln's revealing red dress in *The Girl Can't Help It* had first been worn by Monroe in *Gentlemen Prefer Blondes*. The singer later recalled, "I didn't realize at the time the dress was such a powerful symbol."[54] Lincoln's inexperience may have obscured the reality that the dress carried one meaning when worn by a white woman (whose shrewd use of sexuality in Cold War America was later emulated by, among others, the singer Madonna) and another meaning when worn by her. Although she donned it again for an *Ebony* magazine cover, Lincoln was increasingly uncomfortable with the image the dress represented. Perhaps believing that, by wearing it, she embodied the trope of the hypersexualized black body, Lincoln burned the dress soon after and adopted Africa-inspired fashions.[55]

Commenting on this period, scholar Linda F. Williams writes that Lincoln began a transformation in which her "onstage sexuality was eventually replaced by her commitment to voicing a political and social conscience."[56] Whether leading protests through formal organizations or through musical collaboration with artists such as Max Roach and Oscar Brown Jr., Lincoln's was a steadfast voice in the fight against white supremacy. Her dramatic makeover from sex symbol to civil rights icon, however, might also be understood not as a rejection or replacement of her sexuality but as a redefining of it. Eschewing chemically straightened hair, provocative dress, nightclub performing, and suggestive film roles in favor of more militant civil rights projects allowed Lincoln to help define what *sexy* meant to African American women—and men—in the years immediately preceding the Black Power movement. Her vocal contributions to *We Insist!* would mark an important milestone in her efforts to build cultural connections between jazz and freedom movements.

Jazz Women in Exile

At the same time that editors of the African American newspaper the *Daily Defender* described Lincoln as "a staunch advocate of Negro womanhood," *New York Times* reporter Peter Kihss concluded that she was among a growing group of "Negro extremists" affiliated with nationalist causes. Lincoln earned the appellation in a spring 1961 article as a result of her founding of the Cultural Association for Women of African Heritage (CAWAH), an organization that had recently taken part in a silent demonstration at the United Nations to protest the assassination of Patrice Lumumba. Because of Lumumba's importance as the first prime minister of Congo and a leader of the anticolonial movement, his death became a rallying cry for U.S. activists, who compared it to the Mississippi lynching of fourteen-year-old Emmett Till six years earlier.[57] There were false reports that the protest had gotten out of hand, with demonstrators clutching chains and brass knuckles, which only exaggerated the supposed radicalism of Lincoln and the CAWAH. Decades later Lincoln characterized the goal of CAWAH, whose members included authors Maya Angelou and Rosa Guy, as an effort to "explore our culture, our African ancestors."[58] Yet in the eyes of some in the white liberal press, she joined the ranks of the leaders of the Nation of Islam, the Liberation Committee for Africa, and the Communist Party USA, each described by the *New York Times* as organizations "seeking to rouse American Negroes to a more militant attitude in their efforts to obtain equality."[59] Shortly thereafter, following the release of her solo album *Straight Ahead,* music critic Ira Gitler accused Lincoln of "becoming a professional Negro" and advised her that "pride in one's heritage is one thing, but we don't need the Elijah Muhammed [*sic*] type of thinking in jazz."[60] Lincoln's status as a female singer made her uniquely vulnerable to attack from critics like Gitler, who by and large placed a much higher value on the work of male instrumentalist jazz artists.

In response to the increasingly harsh reception of her work in the United States, and following a painful divorce from Roach, Lincoln traveled throughout Africa in the early 1970s. She was accompanied by Makeba, who, after her 1968 marriage to Stokely Carmichael, had settled in Guinea to avoid ongoing harassment by the U.S. government. During her travels, Guinea's president Sekou Toure gave Lincoln the name Aminata, while Zairian prime minister Mobutu called her Moseka. For Lincoln, as for other jazz women, travel in Africa became not only a symbol of racial pride but also an opportunity for healing. After returning to the United States she sometimes performed under the name Aminata Moseka, and in the late 1970s and 1980s Lincoln reestablished her singing career. Until her death in August 2010 she continued to earn critical praise for club performances and recordings.

At the same time, Nina Simone also began a self-imposed exile. Deeply troubled by the assassination of Martin Luther King, battles with the Internal Revenue Service, and disputes with her record company over the increasingly controversial themes of her music, Simone fled to Barbados in the early 1970s. Later Simone was encouraged by her friend Makeba (who, for a while, moved between Guinea and Liberia) to join her in Liberia.[61] Simone eventually settled in France, but for a short time, Africa offered her a peace she could not find in the country of her birth.

The politics of apartheid perpetuated the dispersal of Africans from their native homelands, whether they were living abroad due to government action or self-imposed exile. Government bans based on the 1950 Suppression of Communism Act were often the reason behind South African artists' exile. Under the act, anyone perceived as being a potential threat to the social order, and especially to white-black relations, was confined to his or her home and, with the exception of family members, was not allowed to speak with more than one person at a time. In addition, banned persons could not speak publically or be quoted in any publication. Upon release of the song "Lumumba," Dorothy Masuka's 1961 tribute to the slain leader, she was banned by the South African government, which moved quickly to contain the song's message. Masuka joined notable South Africans Miriam Makeba, jazz trumpeter Hugh Masekela (one of Makeba's four husbands), pianist Abdullah Abraham, and countless others in exile. Ironically, an unintended consequence of increased global exposure to songs of protest was that although certain artists could no longer travel through South Africa, their songs did.

In a 2000 interview Masekela explained the significance of this diasporic exchange and his former wife's influence on U.S. audiences, crediting Makeba with bringing to light the injustices of apartheid in the early Cold War period. Masekela explained:

> I think that there is nobody in Africa who made the world more aware of what was happening in South Africa than Miriam Makeba. . . . By the time I got to the States, Miriam had educated, unwittingly, African-American and other artists like Bing Crosby, even Frank Sinatra. . . . And then in 1963 [she] addressed the [United Nations] General Assembly and for the first time the world became aware of what was happening in this country. . . . From that point the West looked at her as an enemy, at the time when she was at the most lucrative stage in her career.[62]

Makeba's marriage to Carmichael, who had rejected nonviolence when he joined the Black Panther Party in 1967, further antagonized Cold War Western governments.

Intersections: Nationalism and Feminism

Placing the work of Cold War jazz women on the continuum of black women's activism is a complicated endeavor. At her 2008 passing, music lovers and social activists across the globe mourned the loss of Miriam Makeba. From Johannesburg to London, Lagos to New York City, Makeba was remembered for the way she combined political and artistic passions to inspire movements for black liberation throughout the African diaspora. Citing the honorary titles "Mama Afrika" and "Female Mandela," writers paid tribute to her nearly sixty years as a performer and spokesperson for Pan-African movements. Less attention was paid to the skill with which she had used music to successfully maneuver through traditionally male spaces and challenge gendered assumptions about women's political activism.

Observers' reluctance to consider Makeba's activism as feminist is supported by her very public rejection of the U.S. women's liberation movement of the 1970s, which she described as "just a product of [women] not having more important things to do, too much luxury."[63] Makeba's critique of the "second wave" of Western liberal feminism was well developed and shared by women of color the world over, including Abbey Lincoln. Echoing decades-long debates that have defined women's movements, Lincoln once characterized feminists as women whose primary concern was that they "didn't get mine yet" and suggested that they take more responsibility for their lives.[64]

Cheryl Johnson-Odim's comment that, historically, "Black women's theories regarding women's liberation [have] focused on racism, poverty, and imperialism as much as on sexism" keenly reflects Makeba's and Lincoln's sentiments about the limited focus of many feminist movements led by white, liberal women.[65] Makeba's belief that "the South African woman has always been in the front if not by the side of her man in the struggle for liberation" suggests a significant relationship between women's causes and the nationalist causes Makeba championed.[66] Her rejection of women's liberation was based not on blindness to colonial systems' unique ways of oppressing women but on the blindness of many women's liberationists to the significant ways that race and class shape gender oppression.

African and African-descended women's criticism of feminism follows a long tradition of black women challenging social injustice out of concern for family and community, as well as gender equality.[67] Indeed, although Lincoln refused to consider herself a feminist, by the late 1960s she had begun to voice her disapproval of the lyrics of many classic blues and jazz songs that depict abusive relationships between men and women, and she refused to sing them. Thus the goals of jazz women, though always balanced with goals for their race, were often shared by white women doing the work of feminism. Linda Williams suggests that generational issues may help explain the attitudes of some black women toward feminist movements. Williams writes that although many African American women born between 1945 and 1965 "regard race and gender as comparable arenas for advocacy," those born before that period often "emphasize the prioritization of racial empowerment over sexual liberation," viewing feminism as "an inverted form of white patriarchy."[68] If a generational divide does in fact help explain jazz women's perceptions of women's movements, it reflects what Earl Lewis terms the "multipositionality" of women within the diaspora, who see race as one of several important factors that inform their identity.[69]

Makeba, Lincoln, and others like them chose not to identify themselves with a feminist movement, but they supported many of the same causes as those who did. Their comments about the narrow focus of women's liberation attest to the fact that, like many other women, both black and white, they were critical of a movement rooted in liberal concepts of individual rights. Their work reflected a concern for the global black community across the diaspora, a concern that balanced nationalist and women's goals in the struggle for black liberation.

Considered on their own, the contributions of U.S. women jazz singers to postwar freedom movements were significant. Often drawing parallels between men's domination of women and colonial powers' social, political, and economic domination of native populations, artists such as Abbey Lincoln and Nina Simone challenged white supremacy through their songwriting, performance, sexual expression, and support of liberation movements. Placed within a larger framework of overlapping diasporas characterized by significant social, political, and cultural intersections, these contributions take on deeper meaning. The broad influence of American Billie Holiday and South African Miriam Makeba provides perhaps the best example of the dialectic between diaspora and homeland—illustrating how lives, like the diasporas that shape them, overlap.

Heavily influenced by African rhythms, Holiday's music was deeply indebted to a "homeland" that she never saw. Nonetheless, her work had a profound impact on young female artists in Africa, including Makeba; these women found inspiration not only in Holiday's vocal talent but also in her commitment to freedom. In turn, the exiled Makeba nurtured the talent and race consciousness of such U.S. artists as Lincoln. The diasporic flow back and forth across the Atlantic—a movement of not only music but also the notion of freedom embedded in it—fueled liberation movements in the United States, South Africa, and other decolonizing nations around the globe. The significance of this exchange does not fit well into a paradigm of neat parallel progressions; attention must be paid to the overlapping diasporas of African peoples, including an examination of the cultural memories of those who produced jazz music and helped inspire African and African American liberation.

Notes

For their helpful comments and encouragement, I am grateful to those who attended presentations of earlier versions of this essay at the Transnational Feminisms Conference, University of Manchester, Manchester, England, December 4, 2009; the Boston Seminar Series on the History of Women and Gender, Boston, Massachusetts, April 16, 2009; and the Institute for Democracy in South Africa, Cape Town, South Africa, November 2, 2010. I am especially thankful to Karen Garner, Christopher Whann, Margaret Burnham, Robin Henry, Danielle McGuire, and John Dittmer for their close reading of and generous comments on earlier drafts.

Epigraphs: Mary McLeod Bethune, "Lionel Hampton Beats Out New Rhythm for Civil Rights," *Chicago Defender,* February 4, 1950, 6; Lewis Nkosi, "Jazz in Exile," *Transition* 24 (1966): 36.

1. The U.S. government was also attuned to the subversive possibilities of jazz early in the Cold War. To that end, in 1956 the State Department initiated a program to send abroad delegations of jazz artists, especially black artists, to Cold War hot spots, such as the Middle East. This was an effort to discount Soviet "propaganda" about the poor treatment African Americans received in the United States. See Ingrid Monson, *Freedom Sounds: Civil Rights Call out to Jazz and Africa* (New York: Oxford University Press, 2007), and Penny Von Eschen, *Sachmo Blows up the World: Jazz Ambassadors Play the Cold War* (Cambridge, Mass.: Harvard University Press, 2004).

2. Pamela E. Brooks, *Boycotts, Buses, and Passes: Black Women's Resistance in the U.S. South and South Africa* (Amherst: University of Massachusetts Press, 2008), 2.

3. M. Bahati Kuumba, *Gender and Social Movements* (Walnut Creek, Calif.: AltaMira Press, 2001), 3.

4. The research of Kuumba and Brooks builds on the important work of such scholars as George Fredrickson and Stanley Greenberg. See George Fredrickson, *White Supremacy: A Comparative Study in American and South African History* (New York: Oxford University Press, 1981); George Fredrickson, *Black Liberation: A Comparative History of Black Ideologies in the United States and South Africa* (New York: Oxford University Press, 1995); Stanley B. Greenberg, *Race and State in Capitalist Development: South Africa in Comparative Perspective* (Johannesburg: Raven Press, 1980).

5. For more on the Sojourners for Truth and Justice, see Jacqueline Castledine, "'In a Solid Bond of Unity': Anticolonial Feminism in the Age of McCarthy," *Journal of Women's History* 20, no. 4 (winter 2008): 57–81, and Erik

McDuffie, "A 'New Freedom Movement of Negro Women': Sojourning for Truth, Justice, and Human Rights during the Early Cold War," *Radical History Review* 101 (spring 2008): 85–106.

6. See Cherryl Walker, *Women and Resistance in South Africa* (London: Onyx Press, 1982), 72.

7. Quoted in Carol Muller, "Capturing the 'Spirit of Africa' in the Jazz Singing of South African–Born Sathima Bea Benjamin," *Research in African Literatures* 32 no. 2 (2001): 140.

8. Earl Lewis, "To Turn as on a Pivot: Writing African Americans into a History of Overlapping Diasporas," *American Historical Review* 100, no. 3 (1995): 765–87.

9. Quoted in Castledine, "'In a Solid Bond of Unity,'" 2.

10. See Thomas Borstelmann, *Apartheid's Reluctant Uncle: The United States and Southern Africa in the Early Cold War* (New York: Oxford University Press, 1993), 96.

11. Es'kia Mphahlele quoted in Ulf Hannerz, "Sophiatown: The View from Afar," *Journal of Southern African Studies* 20, no. 2 (June 1994): 189.

12. For a discussion of the origin of South African jazz, see David B. Coplan, *In Township Tonight! South Africa's Black City Music and Theatre* (London: Longman Group, 1985), and Gwen Ansell, *Soweto Blues: Jazz, Popular Music and Politics in South Africa* (London: Continuum, 2004).

13. Angela Y. Davis, *Blues Legacies and Black Feminism* (New York: Vintage Books, 1998), 128. On black women and the blues, see also Hazel Carby, "'It Jus Be's Dat Way Sometime': The Sexual Politics of Women's Blues," in *Unequal Sisters: A Multicultural Reader in U.S. History,* 2nd ed., ed. Ellen DuBois and Vicki Ruiz (New York: Routledge, 1990), 330–41.

14. Lewis Allen was the pseudonym of Abel Meeropol, a well-known leftist. He and his wife adopted and raised the sons of Julius and Ethel Rosenberg following their executions. For more on Lewis and the cultural significance of "Strange Fruit," see David Margolick, *Strange Fruit: Billie Holiday, Café Society, and an Early Cry for Civil Rights* (Philadelphia: Running Press, 2000).

15. Davis, *Blues Legacies,* 191–92.

16. *OAH Magazine of History* 18, no. 2 (January 2004): 55.

17. "Billie Holiday Tells Story of Plantation Club Jim Crow," *Chicago Defender,* December 30, 1944, 13.

18. Quoted in Muller, "Capturing the 'Spirit of Africa,'" 143.

19. Hannerz, "Sophiatown," 192.

20. Muller, "Capturing the 'Spirit of Africa,'" 139.

21. Farah Jasmine Griffin, *If You Can't Be Free, Be a Mystery* (New York: Free Press, 2001), 164.

22. Ibid.

23. "Max Roach Album Is Boost for Sit-Ins!" *Pittsburgh Courier,* February 25, 1961, A22.

24. Monson, *Freedom Sounds,* 172–78.

25. Ibid., 177–78.

26. Kevin Whitehead, "The Musical Is the Political," *Emusic,* http://www .emusic.com/ features/ spotlight/291_200610.html (accessed January 25, 2011).

27. Lisa Jones, "'Late Bloomer' in Her Prime," *New York Times,* August 4, 1991, H22.

28. Kuumba argues that women's home brewing can be understood as "an act of cultural resistance." Kuumba, *Gender and Social Movements,* 12.

29. Miriam Makeba, *My Story* (New York: NAL Books, 1987).

30. *Amandla! A Revolution in Four-Part Harmony,* director Lee Hirsch, producer Sherry Simpson (Kwela Productions, 2002).

31. Title translation from Ama Ata Aidoo, *No Sweetness Here* (London: Longman, 1988), 38.

32. National Public Radio, *Mandela: An Audio History,* part 1, "The Birth of Apartheid (1944–1960)," April 26, 2004, http://www.npr.org/templates/story/ story.php?storyId=1851882 (accessed January 21, 2011).

33. Quoted in Lara Allen, "Commerce, Politics, and Musical Hybridity: Vocalizing Urban Black South African Identity during the 1950s," *Ethnomusicology* 47, no. 2 (spring–summer 2003): 235.

34. See Ansell, *Soweto Blues,* 145; *Amandla!*

35. For an insightful discussion of Simone's interpretation of "Pirate Jenny," see Ruth Feldstein, "'I Don't Trust You Anymore': Nina Simone, Culture, and Black Activism in the 1960s," *Journal of American History* 91, no. 4 (March 2005): 1363–64.

36. Kurt Weill and Bertolt Brecht, "Pirate Jenny," performed by Nina Simone (1964), *In Concert—I Put a Spell on You;* Kurt Weill and Bertolt Brecht, *The Threepenny Opera* (1928), English adaptation by Marc Blitzstein (1954) (CD, 2000).

37. Feldstein, "'I Don't Trust You,'" 1363.

38. "Message of Condolence by Pallo Jordan, Minister of Arts and Culture on the Death of Sophie Mgcina," *South African Government Information,* December 4, 2005, http://www.info.gov.za/speeches/2005/05120814451001.htm (accessed June 30, 2010).

39. Interview with Nina Simone, British Broadcasting Company, "Hard Talk" (video), n.d., http://www.youtube.com/watch?v=9IFWgK046jU (accessed March 13, 2009).

40. Nina Simone, *I Put a Spell on You: The Autobiography of Nina Simone* (New York: Da Capo Press, 1993), 98.

41. A popular stage musical and film, *King Kong* tells the real-life story of former heavyweight boxer Ezekiel Dlamini, imprisoned for killing his female companion.

42. Makeba, *My Story,* 103.

43. "Steve Allen Show Has Everything But What's Needed: Entertainment," *New York Times,* December 3, 1959, 20.

44. Milton Bracker, "Xhosa Songstress," *New York Times Magazine,* February 28, 1960, 32.

45. Robert Shelton, "Miriam Makeba in Song Program," *New York Times,* October 16, 1961, 33.

46. *Woman's Hour,* BBC Radio interview with Dorothy Masuka, December 9, 2002, http://www.bbc.co.uk/radi04/womanshour/2002_50_mon_02.shtml (accessed January 21, 2011).

47. Ibid.

48. In her seminal essay on resistance, Darlene Clark Hine introduces the concept of a culture of dissemblance to describe attempts by black women to "shield the truth of their inner lives from their oppressors." Darlene Clark Hine, "Rape and the Inner Lives of Black Women in the Middle West: Preliminary Thoughts on the Culture of Dissemblance," *Signs* 14 (summer 1989): 912–20. I argue here that anticolonial feminists engaged in dissembling to shield the truth of their *public* lives from their oppressors.

49. "Khawuleza" (video, 1966), YouTube (accessed October 23, 2010).

50. Michael Eldridge and Harry Belafonte, "Remains of the Day-O," *Transition* 92 (2002): 122.

51. Brian Ward, *Just My Soul Responding: Rhythm and Blues, Black Consciousness, and Race Relations* (Berkeley: University of California Press, 1998), 305.

52. See Monson, *Freedom Sounds,* 165–67.

53. Bob Hunter, "Abbey Is 'Swingingest' of All the Lincolns," *Daily Defender,* November 13, 1962, 16.

54. Jones, "'Late Bloomer.'"

55. Griffin, *If You Can't Be Free,* 163–64.

56. Linda F. Williams, "Black Women, Jazz, and Feminism," in *Black Women and Music: More than the Blues,* ed. Eileen M. Haynes and Linda F. Williams (Urbana: University of Illinois Press, 2007), 127.

57. See John Henrik Clark, "The New Afro American Nationalism," *Freedomways* 1, no. 4 (fall 1961): 285–95.

58. Monson, *Freedom Sounds,* 245–46.

59. Peter Kihss, "Negro Extremist Groups Step up Nationalist Drive," *New York Times,* March 1, 1961, 1.

60. Quoted in Monson, *Freedom Sounds,* 239.

61. Simone, *I Put a Spell on You,* 137–54.

62. Interview cited in Ansell, *Soweto Blues,* 226.

63. Bonnie Schultz, "Women and the African Liberation—Miriam Makeba," *Africa Report* 22, no. 1 (January–February 1977): 14.

64. Lara Pellegrinelli interview with Abbey Lincoln, "A Woman Speaking Her Mind," May 10, 2002, http://www.newmusicbox.org/38/interview_lincoln.pdf (accessed January 22, 2011).

65. Cheryl Johnson-Odim, "Mirror Images and Shared Standpoint: Black Women in Africa and in the African Diaspora," *Issue: A Journal of Opinion* 24, no. 2 (1996): 18–22.

66. Schultz, "Women and the African Liberation," 13.

67. Works central to the discussion of black feminism include Alice Walker, *In Search of Our Mothers' Gardens: Womanist Prose* (San Diego: Harcourt Brace, 1983); Cherríe Moraga and Gloria E. Anzaldúa, eds., *This Bridge Called My Back: Writings by Radical Women of Color* (Watertown, Mass.: Persephone Press, 1981); Patricia Hill Collins, *Black Feminist Thought: Knowledge, Consciousness and the Politics of Empowerment* (New York: Routledge, 2000); Beverly Guy-Sheftall, "African American Women: The Legacy of Black Feminism," in *Sisterhood Is Forever: The Women's Anthology for a New Millennium,* ed. Robin Morgan (New York: Washington Square Press, 2003); Beverly Guy-Sheftall, *Words of Fire: An Anthology of African American Feminist Thought* (New York: New Press, 1995); Robin D. G. Kelley, *Freedom Dreams* (Boston: Beacon Press, 2002); Ula Y. Taylor, "Making Waves: The Theory and Practice of Black Feminism," *Black Scholar* 28, no. 2 (summer 1988): 18–28; and Becky Thompson, "Multiracial Feminism: Recasting the Chronology of Second Wave Feminism," *Feminist Studies* 28, no. 2 (summer 2002): 337–60.

68. Williams, "Black Women, Jazz, and Feminism," 120–23.

69. Lewis, "To Turn as on a Pivot," 783.

EEOC Politics and Limits on Reagan's Civil Rights Legacy

Emily Zuckerman

In 1981 future chief justice of the Supreme Court John Roberts was a twenty-six-year-old special assistant to the attorney general at the Justice Department. He spent much of his time drafting memos, op-ed articles, and talking points in support of President Ronald Reagan's opposition to the renewal of the Voting Rights Act of 1965. "This is an exciting time to be at the Justice Department," Roberts wrote to a mentor. "So much that has been taken for granted for so long is being seriously reconsidered." He responded to complaints from enraged civil rights groups, arguing that a bill recently passed by the House of Representatives would "establish a quota system for electoral politics," and he prepared Attorney General William French Smith for a White House meeting, saying that the president's position "is a very positive one and should be put in that light."[1]

This was a dramatic change from civil rights policies of the past. Elected in a rising conservative climate, Reagan sought to weaken civil rights policy. However, a variety of factors combined to ensure that not all was lost during his presidency. The slow pace of governmental change, the dedication of career attorneys, a solid legal foundation established over fifteen years of enforcement, and resistance from within the administration, particularly at the Equal Employment Opportunity Commission (EEOC), all limited, if not prevented, the complete overhaul of affirmative action policy that Reagan desired. Although enforcement slowed, the EEOC and even its conservative chair, Clarence Thomas, at times stood strong against attempts to weaken civil rights, ensuring that policy and enforcement structures remained to be revived by a more favorable administration.

Beginning with the passage of major civil rights legislation in the mid-1960s, Republican and Democratic administrations accepted the same definitions of affirmative action and equal employment opportunity. They agreed the laws were intended to integrate minorities into the workplace and correct past discrimination, even if some administrations were more proactive than others in implementing them.

Although racial concerns were far from his top priority, President Richard Nixon accepted the existence of the new civil rights laws and the EEOC, a new federal agency established in the mid-1960s to help implement and enforce the Civil Rights Act of 1964. Nixon, Hugh Davis Graham notes, "confirmed the Kennedy-Johnson legacy in civil rights law in much the same way that Eisenhower had confirmed the New Deal—not by embracing it, but by accommodating to it on the margins in a way that guaranteed its legitimacy and secured its permanence in the federal establishment."[2] Beyond accepting existing polices, Nixon actually helped advance civil rights, albeit for political reasons rather than out of concern for racial justice. He enforced court orders that desegregated southern schools, tried to revoke tax-exempt status for segregated private schools, and gave the EEOC increased authority.[3] One administration member described the "pattern of civil rights enforcement" during Nixon's first term as "operationally progressive but obscured by clouds of retrogressive rhetoric."[4]

Moreover, Nixon's EEOC chair actively tried to make the semiautonomous federal agency stronger and more independent. In 1969 Nixon chose Bill Brown, a Republican African American attorney who had been appointed to the commission by President Lyndon Johnson, to be chair.[5] Brown had a mixed relationship with the Nixon administration. He bolstered his argument that the government should ensure that African Americans had good jobs with benefits by appealing to Nixon's desire to decrease the welfare rolls. Congress regularly cut the EEOC's funding, so Brown relied on his friend Len Garment, Nixon's counsel and the token liberal in the White House, to help restore it. Brown asserted the agency's independence by refusing to ask permission before initiating an unprecedented suit against corporate giant AT&T and by using Congress's 1972 grant of powers to sue employers directly to broaden the commission's authority.[6] He reorganized the commission to focus on broad-based systemic discrimination rather than individual charges of discrimination (or complaints filed with the agency) by creating the National Programs Division (NPD), under the control of one of the star attorneys from the AT&T team. Brown allocated 60 percent of the EEOC's resources to investigate large cases against nationwide employers (referred to as "Track 1" cases); the rest went to individual cases and regional offices to handle local "Track 2" cases.[7]

After considering the number of discrimination charges filed against them and the size, revenue, and number of workers at several of the nation's largest corporations, in September 1973 the NPD filed Commissioner's Charges against General Motors, General Electric, Ford, and Sears.[8] Although the Departments of Labor and Defense had already given "clean bills of health" to the affirmative action efforts of some of these companies, the young EEOC asserted itself as the main antidiscrimination agency.[9] It spent several years during the 1970s meticulously investigating and building cases against these Track 1 companies. Brown's tenure at the EEOC helped establish it as a relatively independent federal agency, which made later attempts to dismantle the commission more difficult.

Brown also insisted on total settlements from the corporations he pursued. Whereas the Departments of Labor and Justice might be willing to accept a mere promise to stop discriminating based on race or a small payment to an individual claimant, Brown pressed for large settlements covering the entire class of workers involved. He also insisted on back-pay awards for all the years the company had discriminated—at a high cost to the company—as opposed to a simple "slap on the wrist." Brown's position put him at odds with his successor, John Powell, the former general counsel of the Civil Rights Commission (CRC). Before he was even confirmed, Powell made efforts, behind Brown's back, to settle a large discrimination action brought by the EEOC and other agencies against the steel industry. Brown stood up to Powell and undermined—at least temporarily—his willingness to accept a weak settlement, declaring that the EEOC would pursue the steel industry regardless of any other settlement reached.[10] Once confirmed, Powell ran the commission as less of an independent agency than it had been under Brown, settling with the steel industry in April 1974 without back pay, and giving up the units Brown had put in place, although the Track 1 company investigations continued.[11]

Nixon's administration and Brown's EEOC tenure demonstrated that political party mattered little in the early years of equal employment opportunity and affirmative action enforcement. The EEOC often asserted its independence and refused to follow the administration. The EEOC faced a lot of ups and downs in the early 1970s. It successfully settled its major race and sex discrimination case with AT&T, but it spent most of the rest of the decade enforcing the consent decree when the company failed to make the required progress in affirmative action.[12] By the end of the Ford administration the commission was at a low point, plagued by a huge backlog of charges, which affected its credibility; management problems;

high turnover, which left the commission without a full panel of members; low morale; and eroding gains due to the recession.[13] Nevertheless, Nixon himself accepted the existence of the new civil rights laws and the EEOC, allowing large cases against AT&T and the steel industry to continue. Brown, a Republican originally appointed by a Democratic president, acted independently of the Nixon administration when he deemed it necessary.[14] The EEOC's position as a semi-independent agency created a constant tension between it and the administration—a tension that did not exist between the administration and the Justice Department. As Graham notes, the EEOC was "the era's fragile infant among regulatory boards"—an independent agency with career service employees who tried to enforce the old policy.[15] This early precedent of limited independence and acceptance of the terms of the affirmative action debate ensured that later attempts to completely change the agency and civil rights policy would be less than wholly successful.

With the election of President Jimmy Carter in 1976, conflict between the EEOC and the administration eased, allowing the EEOC to consolidate its power, strengthen operations, and accumulate several more years of case law addressing employment discrimination. Despite the low morale and disorganization of the EEOC at the end of the Ford administration, things began to improve with Carter's nomination of Eleanor Holmes Norton as EEOC chair in March 1977.[16] The product of a segregated high school and civil rights protests in college, Norton was remembered by Yale Law School classmates as a brilliant student who talked "about using the law as an instrument for social change." Soon after finishing law school, Norton helped write the brief for the Mississippi Freedom Democratic Party, the African American group that forced the national Democratic Party to reform its delegate selection system in 1964. She worked on First Amendment issues for the American Civil Liberties Union, even representing George Wallace and the National States Rights Party before the Supreme Court.[17] In 1970 Norton became chair of the New York City Commission on Human Rights, which served as the model for other government employment agencies, including the EEOC.[18] Her success at the New York City Commission became the blueprint for her EEOC job.[19] She promised to control the backlog, speed up complaint processing, and improve management.[20]

Norton faced a number of challenges and critics in Washington, D.C. Republicans had harshly criticized Democrats about the EEOC's inefficiency, and it was now up to Norton to fix it. She inherited a commission with damaged credibility. Despite its new power to sue employers, the EEOC still took years to dispose of cases. Staff members did not communicate effectively; investigators recommended cases to pursue, and then the attorneys rejected them because the investigators had not gathered adequate evidence. The agency still lacked a strong systemic program, which many believed was the only way to eliminate discrimination.[21] The wage gap between the sexes had not narrowed, and women remained in low-paying, female-dominated jobs.[22] Furthermore, Norton had to deal with Carter's own ineffectiveness. Although being an outsider had helped him get elected after the tawdry politics of the Nixon administration and Watergate, Carter's outsider status compromised his ability to govern effectively. He focused too much on detail, did not advance major reforms, and lost control of his administration.[23] He was not a savvy politician and did not satisfy Democrats, blacks, Hispanics, women, or the poor on issues related to affirmative action.[24] The economy further threatened the long-standing Democratic Party coalition, and the rise in conservatism forced Carter to move farther to the Right, making his job more difficult and his tenure just a brief interlude in an increasingly conservative political landscape.[25] Observers on the Left criticized the EEOC for not going far enough and for being useless during such difficult economic times, while those on the Right resisted increased regulation of businesses. No one was satisfied.

Nevertheless, Norton's reorganization of the EEOC was considered a success. Her employees described Norton as a committed and politically brilliant civil rights lawyer who thought about every angle and knew all the key players of the racial justice and women's rights movements. She brought in talented people, turned the EEOC's procedures upside down, and instituted a rapid charge-processing system.[26] She used "common-sense tactics" for quickly handling cases that needed more attention and significantly reduced the backlog and shortened the average conciliation time from two years to sixty-five days.[27] Since passage of the Civil Rights Act of 1964, the *Washington Post* argued, Title VII, which prohibited employment discrimination based on certain protected classifications such as race and sex, had become the act's central section, and access to jobs and income had become the most important civil rights issue of the 1970s. The EEOC received more than 85,000 complaints a year, and the courts and the executive branch had become involved in defining equal employment opportunity. Employers were finally on notice that they would be forced to change.[28] Norton did what Democrats had asked, reorganizing the agency, speeding up complaint processing, improving management, and restoring its respect, although focusing so closely on individual charges in order to clean up the backlog left little time for broader systemic cases.[29]

Norton cemented several years of developing case law and agency guidance on discrimination issues, and in March 1978 the commission issued internal guidelines for charging employers with race and sex discrimination.[30] At the end of the year Norton confirmed that the commission would emphasize broad patterns of discrimination over individual complaints, using class-action lawsuits, back-pay awards, loss of government contracts, and an improved settlement process.[31] Norton also resolved several cases initiated almost a decade earlier by Bill Brown. She presided over the end of AT&T's consent decree in January 1979, marking the end of "a pioneering chapter in the history of employees' civil rights" in which affirmative action plans had become "a fixture of the corporate scene."[32] In June 1978 Norton settled a Track 1 race and sex discrimination case against General Electric, which agreed—in lieu of "becoming engaged in lengthy adversary proceedings"—to spend $31.9 million for training, back pay, affirmative action programs, and bonuses for past discrimination; to implement numerical goals for hiring and promoting women and minorities; and to submit to five years of monitoring.[33] In November 1980 the EEOC settled its discrimination case with Ford Motor Company in exchange for $23 million in training and back pay, thus ending "longstanding areas of disagreement between [the company] and government agencies" and avoiding "prolonged litigation."[34] And in 1979 Norton decided to file five separate race and sex discrimination lawsuits against another Track 1 company, Sears, Roebuck & Co., based on four years of investigation by the EEOC. Regardless of recent debates, affirmative action and the EEOC had enough legitimacy to convince some of the nation's largest employers that it was better to settle than to endure a long litigation process.[35] In 1980 Norton's EEOC issued the first guidelines making sexual harassment a form of sex discrimination under the Civil Rights Act.[36] Although some employers claimed that sexual harassment was not a real problem, the EEOC's announcement that they had a duty to eliminate harassment, would be liable for supervisors who harassed others, and might be subject to lawsuits motivated organizations to educate themselves.[37]

Norton herself strongly believed that the law was now so well established that changing political moods could not reverse it. At her farewell party soon after President Reagan's inauguration in January 1981, the former chair was confident that affirmative action would survive. The field was "very stable" after ten years of "extraordinary and deep court cases to build the law. . . . Even if they disbanded the EEOC tomorrow . . . there would still be thousands of court cases presented each year based on precedent."[38] Nor did Norton have any doubts about the commission's future, since "they would have to amend Title VII, and nobody's going to do that." History was on their side: "affirmative action . . . was made after a large, nonviolent civil rights movement, and . . . responded to a 200-year history of intentional discrimination against women and minorities. And the decision is vindicated. Every federal court has sanctioned these remedies."[39] Even after she left the EEOC, Norton continued to believe that the next administration would have a limited effect on the system she had helped establish. Commission policy was settled enough to withstand a chair with different beliefs: "Thousands of decisions mandate the direction of the agency, many of them settled long ago, with even conservative courts embracing both discrimination remedies and affirmative action."[40]

Moreover, future changes would be limited by the slow pace of bureaucratic change in the federal government and the dedication of career staff members at the EEOC. As Graham notes, although presidents come and go, administrative agencies stay and try to enforce the laws in a day-to-day manner; thus, an administration is made up of not just political appointees but also the "permanent government . . . the career civil servants in the semi-independent mission agencies and their sub-baronies in departments like Labor."[41] The next administration tried to mount a counterrevolution but found a "formidable barrier to change" in Congress, the federal courts, and the administrative apparatus of government.[42]

Indeed, Nancy MacLean has shown that advances for minorities and women were not reversed during this period because of the unstoppable tide of change in the workplace, led by activists without regard to whether they could rely on the government as an ally.[43] The same was true of government policy and civil rights case law—a solid framework was in place, and fifteen years of enforcement could not be completely erased. Norton's years of strong enforcement, major advancements in establishing guidelines and developing case law, and the hiring of committed staff members who would remain after she left made it difficult for the next administration to emasculate the EEOC and its policies, but it certainly tried.

In 1980 Ronald Reagan was elected president on a wave of conservative sentiment and a promise to fundamentally alter the civil rights policy of the previous twenty years, sending a message to the EEOC that things would soon be changing. Despite the history of Republican and Democratic administrations accepting the same definition of equal employment opportunity and agreeing that remedies should be implemented to integrate minorities into the workplace, Reagan promised to eliminate "quotas" (numerical goals and timetables for hiring and promotion), affirmative action, and busing. From the outset, his transition team recommended major changes: dropping the requirement that employers adopt affirmative action plans, requiring proof that a company intended to discriminate rather than just employed few minorities, cutting the EEOC's budget, barring new guidelines and lawsuits for a year, and taking away the commission's role as the lead enforcement agency.[44] Norton resigned soon after Reagan's inauguration. The *Washington Post* described her farewell party as a "somber affair" where civil rights workers reassessed strategies to prevent the inevitable cutbacks.[45]

Reagan's primary architect for redefining civil rights policy was William Bradford Reynolds, the new head of the Civil Rights Division at the Justice Department. Reynolds came from a wealthy family, had attended elite schools, had worked for the solicitor general of the United States, and later became a partner at a large D.C. law firm.[46] As assistant attorney general, Reynolds clashed with the 150 career attorneys he supervised as he worked to "review and modify [their] legal briefs . . . , making sure that 'equal rights' had not been twisted into 'special preferences.'"[47] Reagan and Reynolds saw themselves not as opponents of civil rights but as strict constructionists who were concerned that the original meaning of the Civil Rights Act of 1964 had been distorted. They argued that the law intended to provide equal opportunity regardless of race, not guarantee equal results. For example, blacks should have the same opportunity to apply for a particular position as whites. In reality, however, that rarely increased the number of minorities in a particular field; other factors played a role in keeping them out, such as discrimination by the interviewer or a lack of educational and training opportunities that qualified minority applicants for the job. Reagan argued that any attempt to require equal results—that more blacks be hired—constituted preferential treatment of minorities and discrimination against whites.[48] The administration wanted to require a higher standard of proof to show that a company intended to discriminate, not just that it employed few women or minorities. It also wanted to ban broad-based settlements that ordered employers to hire or promote more minorities in general, preferring the narrower remedy of compensating an individual who had been denied a job.[49] Reagan and Reynolds claimed to be in favor of equality, but they were against the traditional remedies, such as busing and affirmative action, needed to bring it about.[50]

It was an unusual approach. Reagan was the first president to have an assistant attorney general for civil rights who was actually *against* everything *civil rights* had meant up until then. It was the first major departure in civil rights policy. Reagan succeeded by boldly insisting that he was committed to civil rights while taking contrary positions, confusing the general public's understanding of affirmative action, setting equal employment opportunity on its head, and turning *quota* into a bad word.[51] Reagan couched bigotry in the language of color blindness and nondiscrimination for everyone, making it possible for him to take previously unthinkable positions. For example, he opposed renewing the Voting Rights Act of 1965, supported tax-exempt status for private schools that discriminated based on race, and favored overturning voluntary affirmative action programs between employers and unions.[52] He protected not those who were supposed to benefit from civil rights remedies but rather white men, arguing that they suffered "reverse discrimination" when "special preferences" were given to minorities. Even Norton acknowledged that the administration was winning the public relations war by confusing people: "Affirmative action is not a gratuity . . . but a legal remedy established by the courts after . . . evidence" of discrimination. "We need to find a way to better explain these remedies."[53] Reagan built a new political coalition, using social issues such as "law and order," abortion, "forced busing," and fear of racial quotas to appeal to millions of working-class whites who had previously been loyal Democrats.[54] The key to his political success, according to black activist Roger Wilkins, was that he "found a way to make racism palatable and politically potent again."[55] As Terry Anderson notes, Reagan's main success in advancing his agenda was promoting the idea that affirmative action equaled quotas, which led to declining public support for affirmative action programs despite the fact that most people supported civil rights generally.[56]

The administration attacked affirmative action plans that had been widely accepted and endorsed by the courts. In 1984 the Justice Department declared victory when the Supreme Court reversed the layoff of three whites who had seniority over black Memphis firefighters hired under a court-approved affirmative action plan. The justices ruled that courts may not interfere with seniority systems when layoffs are necessary. Reynolds broadly interpreted the decision as an "unequivocal" statement that court-ordered quotas were illegal, and he pledged to reevaluate all prior agreements and ban the EEOC from using quotas in new agreements. Civil rights attorneys worried that the case would invalidate existing affirmative action agreements and other previously imposed remedies, including the ten-year-old steel industry settlement, and make employers more reluctant to settle complaints.[57]

The administration also tried to cut the budgets of agencies enforcing civil rights laws and reduce governmental regulation of corporations overall, shifting policy decisions from civil rights experts to those focused on the cost of new regulations and back-pay awards at the White House Office of Management and Budget.[58] Reynolds tried to change regulations that required federal contractors with at least fifty employees and contracts totaling $50,000 to implement affirmative action plans when they employed few women and minorities. He claimed such a disparity was not necessarily due to discrimination and sought to raise the thresholds to cover fewer employers.[59] The administration also sought to change EEOC regulations on employee screening tests; require employers only to make reasonable efforts to attract women and minorities, rather than impose hiring quotas; and centralize enforcement at the Justice Department, while weakening or abolishing other civil rights agencies.[60]

Reagan's main deputy at the EEOC was Clarence Thomas, a thirty-three-year-old conservative attorney who had attended segregated schools in Georgia and faced derisive comments at a religious seminary where he was the only African American student. In college he participated in black student protests to change grade requirements but soon came to believe that many blacks were at the bottom of the class for reasons that "had less to do with the college than with the students." Thomas felt victimized by affirmative action because whites assumed he succeeded only because of racial quotas. After graduating from Yale Law School, Thomas avoided jobs dealing with racial issues until friends persuaded him to accept a position as assistant secretary of education for civil rights in 1981, reminding him that his view of blacks' "path to progress" was different from that of civil rights groups.[61] At the Education Department, Thomas faced a court-imposed timetable for processing school desegregation enforcement complaints, which were being handled too slowly.[62] In February 1982, after his first choice was publicly defeated, Reagan nominated Thomas to head the EEOC.[63]

Once confirmed, Thomas ran the EEOC quite differently from Norton. Although he promised to "press hard to process . . . complaints," he was "skeptical" of the commission's efforts to challenge patterns of industry-wide discrimination in court.[64] He changed Norton's processing system to emphasize speed and efficiency in resolving charges, at the expense of a careful review and remedy of alleged discriminatory conduct. As a result, between 1980 and 1983 the EEOC determined that an increasing number of new charges were unfounded and settled fewer charges. It filed half as many lawsuits, including an 80 percent drop in cases attacking broad-based discriminatory patterns. Simply put, Thomas's EEOC was less aggressive in pursuing companies that discriminated and in seeking substantial awards. EEOC attorneys argued that this was due to a new incentive to quickly dispose of cases rather than closely examine them.[65] In February 1984 the commission's own general counsel criticized Thomas to staff attorneys, alleging that thousands of cases had been "curtailed [and] . . . settled prematurely and for inadequate relief" because of his new system. Attorneys were required to report the average time spent on each case, which encouraged them to close cases regardless of their complexity or merits.[66]

Thomas agreed with the administration that remedies for discrimination should be limited to actual victims and should not include numerical goals and timetables for hiring greater numbers of minorities.[67] He believed statistics were "terribly overused" because they assumed that any disparity in hiring was due to discrimination rather than historical and cultural factors, and he preferred evidence of actual conduct, such as witnesses testifying about discrimination or company policies that excluded women and minorities.[68] Of course, after the early 1970s most companies had changed explicitly discriminatory policies, so the EEOC needed to address more subtle forms of prejudice. Thomas saw equality of opportunity rather than proportional representation or a rigid quota system as the proper remedy for racial discrimination.[69]

At the end of 1984 Thomas testified before a House subcommittee on the misuse of statistics. Thomas proffered a misleading analogy, arguing that having an all-black basketball team at a predominantly white school such as Georgetown University was not the result of discrimination but rather of "a whole range of considerations other than race," such as being taller than five feet eight inches, aggressive on defense, and a disciplined and exemplary student. One congressman likened statistics to smoke before the fire—a sign that discrimination might exist—thus shifting the burden to the employer to prove it was not true. The EEOC's job was to look behind a disparity to determine whether the charge of discrimination was justified. Committee chair Augustus Hawkins could barely contain his hostility during Thomas's testimony. Hawkins said, "I don't think we understand each other very well. . . . You disagree with the courts, you disagree with Title VII which prohibits bias in employment, you disagree with every opinion ever written, so I don't know whom you're in step with except possibly Justice Rehnquist . . . and on that basis you are talking about changing federal policies?" Thomas insisted that just as Georgetown might not be discriminating, others might not be discriminating either, continuing, "it cuts both ways. Someone may have a great representation of minorities in their work force, and we may go behind that and find evidence of discrimination." He followed Reagan's lead in distorting the previously settled and commonsense conclusion that a company that employed very few minorities was more likely discriminating than one that employed many minorities. Hawkins responded, "If your views ever become universal in this country, God help us . . . you simply want to emasculate all progress we've made in the last 50 years."[70]

Civil rights observers saw both the Reagan administration and Thomas's EEOC as reversing the progress of civil rights policy, halting enforcement, giving up its role as the lead civil rights agency to the Justice Department, neglecting class-action lawsuits in favor of individual claims, slowing litigation to a crawl, and paralyzing the agency by discouraging lawyers from filing cases that politically appointed commissioners would not support.[71] One activist thought it would be impossible to underestimate Thomas's impact. It was, Anne Ladky said, a "180-degree" turn from Norton.[72] Changes at the EEOC reflected broader political changes at the time. In the early 1970s the civil rights and women's movements had enjoyed a string of successes in pressuring employers to change their practices, helping the EEOC win major settlements from AT&T and the steel industry for discriminating against women and minorities. Reagan's election signaled a new era of greater protection for big business. Large class-action lawsuits and the use of statistical evidence fell out of favor. By the mid-1980s the Justice Department had stopped seeking consent decrees that established goals and timetables.[73] As enforcement slowed, the laws became empty promises, and civil rights agencies became more irrelevant.[74] Historians began to see Ronald Reagan's presidency as a substantial regression in civil rights policy as it had existed up to that point.

However, not all was lost. In fact, most of the EEOC's policies were not fundamentally changed, and progress continued to be made in remedying discrimination. The commission even continued to assert its independence through the 1970s and into the 1980s. For example, after Norton resigned only two commissioners remained, and Reagan, for whom civil rights policy was a low priority, was in no rush to nominate replacements.[75] In 1981 he made J. Clay Smith, a Republican African American appointed to the commission by President Carter in 1978, acting chair and authorized him to make decisions when the commission lacked a quorum. Therefore, the agency continued to act, often against Reagan's stated policies. Smith immediately distributed documents in Congress arguing that the administration's transition report—which recommended ending affirmative action plans, cutting the EEOC's budget, barring new lawsuits, and eliminating the commission's role as the lead enforcement agency—demonstrated ignorance of the law, disregarded Supreme Court decisions, and evidenced a desire to make the EEOC a political arm of the White House with no independent power to protect minorities.[76]

When he was finally ready to fill high-level civil rights jobs, Reagan faced problems. Several lawyers turned down the "once coveted" position of assistant attorney general for civil rights in the Justice Department, and it remained empty for almost four months before Reynolds took it. Even if black Republicans disagreed with "some aspects" of affirmative action policies, no one wanted to preside "over the dismantling of the civil rights enforcement machinery of the country."[77] In June 1981 Reagan chose William Bell to head the EEOC, but his nomination quickly ran into trouble. Civil rights groups and senators argued that Bell had never held a steady job, having worked as an insurance agent, real estate salesman, magazine distributor, investment consultant, and president of a sham minority recruiting firm. In addition, Bell had run unsuccessfully for the Michigan senate, Detroit city council, chair of the Republican Thirteenth Congressional District committee, and House of Representatives. He also would have been the first chair who did not graduate from law school. Bell had attended the University of Detroit Law School but did not graduate because he "didn't care for it and . . . wasn't very successful at it." Opponents charged that Bell was unqualified to run an agency with a $140 million annual budget, 3,000 employees, 50,000 cases, and 400 lawyers.[78] By mid-November an embarrassed administration dropped the nomination amid signs that there were enough votes to defeat it.[79] Having spent a great deal of energy fighting Bell, civil rights groups and legislators saw Reagan's next nominee—Thomas—as generally qualified to run the EEOC, and his nomination engendered little enthusiasm or resistance.[80]

Even when Reagan's nominees succeeded, they did not always agree with him. In 1982 Clarence Pendleton, a conservative African American

Reagan appointed to chair the CRC, complained that the administration's 1983 budget was "a new low point in a disturbing trend of declining support for civil rights enforcement."[81] Although Pendleton did not personally believe the proposed cutbacks demonstrated a lack of commitment to civil rights, he acknowledged that such a widespread perception existed and publicly called on the president to send a "clear signal" of his commitment.[82] In 1983 the CRC declared that two years of fiscal austerity and staff reductions had seriously eroded civil rights enforcement.[83] The next year the CRC suddenly found itself unable to obtain information from the White House and federal agencies. One editorial called Pendleton's complaints of a "lack of cooperation . . . [that was] undermining [their] ability" to monitor enforcement a blow to ideological efforts to change civil rights.[84]

Beyond nominations, the Reagan administration had widely disparate levels of success in changing the three main executive agencies that enforced civil rights laws, which often pursued different policies and made conflicting statements. The administration had the most control over the Justice Department, which publicly rejected numerical goals and timetables for hiring. It had somewhat less control over the Department of Labor, which wanted to use goals and timetables as tools of affirmative action but reduce the amount of regulation and paperwork imposed on federal contractors. Change came last to the EEOC, where policy continued basically unchanged during Reagan's first year in office, and acting chair J. Clay Smith openly advocated affirmative action, including setting goals and timetables.[85] Under Smith, the EEOC resisted the Department of Labor's attempts to exclude more federal contractors from affirmative action reporting requirements. In what the *New York Times* called an unusual "public breach" and the "first major rift . . . within the Administration over the handling of civil rights and job discrimination cases," the EEOC refused to approve Labor's 1981 proposal to exclude more federal contractors from affirmative action reporting requirements; this stalled the regulations for more than two years, by which time the administration was trying to "mend fences" with women and minorities.[86] Smith left the commission after only a year because his views on equal employment opportunity differed from the president's. Looking back on his EEOC tenure, Smith was proud to be the first Republican in the Reagan administration to testify before Congress in support of affirmative action and the commission's sexual harassment guidelines, and he was proud of successfully fighting a $17 million budget cut that would have closed district offices and laid off hundreds of employees.[87] Thus, Reagan's efforts were resisted by some Republicans and by some of his own appointees.

Even Clarence Thomas challenged some of the administration's civil rights policies and made enemies among those who wanted "to slow down the civil rights enforcement machinery."[88] Although Thomas had hedged throughout his career on whether he supported goals and timetables, during his early years at the agency he demonstrated some independence by resisting the administration's "avowed goal" to "eliminate all quota-based settlements" because doing so would throw existing consent decrees and conciliation agreements into "chaos."[89] In June 1983 he promised to insist on an enforcement provision in new government contractor rules: "Voluntarism," he said, "should be continued, but there have to be sanctions and disincentives to those who refuse to do what is right."[90]

In August 1983 Thomas appeared on a National Urban League panel with William Bradford Reynolds and Mary Frances Berry, a CRC member and black activist who had been fired by Reagan that year and later sued successfully to be reinstated. Reynolds claimed his civil rights efforts had been "vigorous and uncompromising" and the administration's enforcement "unprecedented."[91] Thomas, however, offered little support for the administration, saying it could not effectively enforce antidiscrimination laws until it got "its own house in order" and complied with the laws and policies it imposed on private employers. He openly disputed Reynolds's claim that Justice was vigorously enforcing the law, stating, "We cannot allow important matters of national policy to be reduced to simple matters of political posturing. . . . The issues we face are clearly too complex to be tossed around as oversimplified campaign slogans which inflame more than inform. . . . Our personal views on the laws we enforce are, at most, inconsequential. We have sworn to uphold the law."[92] Rather than carrying out Reagan's policy changes unquestioningly, Thomas contradicted Reynolds and criticized the administration.

At times, Thomas's EEOC even defied the administration through litigation. In 1981 the NAACP settled a case with the New Orleans police department in exchange for an agreement to promote one black employee for every white one until supervisory positions were 50 percent black. Although courts had upheld similar settlements, in early 1983 the Justice Department challenged such quotas as unconstitutionally broad because they hurt innocent nonminorities and rewarded blacks who were not victims of discrimination. In response, the EEOC unanimously approved a brief criticizing Justice's position as being without legal merit, "prohibit[ing] . . .

any prospective race-conscious 'affirmative action' or employment goals," and undermining years of progress in remedying discrimination. Thomas wrote to Attorney General William French Smith that the commission would file its brief because of Justice's "dramatic departure" from established policy, which could nullify many existing agreements and consent decrees and prevent courts from addressing even a proven "long-continued and egregious pattern of discrimination."[93]

The White House called Thomas to a meeting with Attorney General Smith, Reynolds, and other advisers to pressure the EEOC to withdraw its brief. Justice Department representatives told Thomas the commission lacked the legal authority to express independent views in such cases and that opposition to quotas was "explicitly" laid out in the Republican Party platform. Smith said the government "should speak with one voice," and it would damage Justice's position to mention a contrary viewpoint with no legal standing.[94] The CRC supported the EEOC, urging Reagan to allow the brief because the commission's "expert opinions on . . . affirmative action . . . should be publicly aired even when they conflict" with Justice.[95] Nevertheless, the EEOC bowed to the pressure and voted four to one not to submit the brief, announcing that it was not in the public interest to submit views that conflicted with those of the Justice Department. However, Thomas still urged Smith to reconsider Justice's position or at least acknowledge the EEOC's opinion. The failure to consult, according to the *New York Times,* was "a sharp departure from acceptable standards of inter-agency protocol" and a breach of the EEOC's role as "the chief interpreter" of the laws against employment discrimination.[96] Thomas noted, "We were created to take the lead responsibility in setting civil rights policy in court but we are in the executive branch which has its own opinions. So there is a contradiction there that has to be ironed out . . . this commission should be independent and this case clearly shows why."[97] Finally, lawyers from the Center for National Policy Review at Catholic University Law School attached the commission's brief to their own, ensuring that its criticism of the administration would be heard after all.[98] This represented just one of several internal skirmishes and turf wars over civil rights that threatened to embarrass the administration and echoed the constant question of how independent the commission should be.

The EEOC also clashed with the administration over executive agencies' internal affirmative action policy. In 1981 the commission asked federal agencies to report how many women and minorities they employed and to set out five-year affirmative action plans to address discrimination.

Reynolds refused to comply for the Justice Department, saying the EEOC had no authority to require goals and timetables. The EEOC replied that it had clear legal authority but thanked Reynolds for "informing us of your views."[99] By mid-1983 Justice had submitted only a plan regarding disabled individuals, but the EEOC sent it back because it lacked goals for hiring, earlier figures for comparison, and data on recruitment and access to department buildings. One Justice official cryptically said that instead of setting goals, they "insure that the recruitment process includes a representative sample of all groups, and then . . . make sure the selection process is based solely on merit."[100] The EEOC responded that the goals were flexible, and everyone faced objectives and timetables for reaching them; even reporters worked on a deadline.[101] In July 1983 Attorney General Smith escalated the battle by submitting a plan for women and minorities—a year and a half late—but again refused to set numerical targets. He told the heads of each unit to make every effort to hire more women and minorities but to rely on recruiting rather than quotas. He wrote to Thomas, who had inherited this battle when he became chair, that his department was committed to "equality of employment opportunity," but hiring goals can become quotas by giving preferences based on race, sex, religion, or handicap: "That is discrimination and that is wrong."[102]

The administration wanted the EEOC to be satisfied with a pledge not to discriminate and voluntary compliance with nondiscrimination laws, rather than measuring progress through numbers.[103] However, Thomas insisted the EEOC needed numbers "to fulfill our responsibilities . . . to report to Congress on progress in the executive branch. . . . We don't think that there's any way we can report to Congress accurately if we don't know where an agency is today, where it plans to be five or six years from now, and where it is in terms of progress based on that plan. . . . Justice seems to think that they don't need those numbers. We disagree." Thomas compared the EEOC's need for statistics to measure progress with companies reporting to the Environmental Protection Agency on hazardous emissions.[104] In September 1983 the EEOC again rejected Justice's affirmative action plan for its failure to include goals and timetables, reflecting the "philosophical confrontation" between the two enforcement agencies. As the EEOC and Justice sparred over the plan, Thomas wrote to the attorney general, "Use of goals in federal employment is presently required, has been required for some time and is necessary for this commission to carry out its responsibilities." Without them, there was no way to determine whether increases in female and minority employees reflected an improvement or simply the addition of more women and minorities in jobs where they were already represented.[105] Thus, the EEOC continued to clash with the administration well into Reagan's first term. Although this could be attributable to civil service employees held over from Norton's tenure, even Reagan appointee Thomas at times took his job to enforce civil rights—or at least uphold the existing law—seriously and publicly resisted the administration.

Despite administration efforts, Justice's attitude toward affirmative action was far from universal. Of 110 agencies required to submit hiring plans in 1983, only three others failed to do so.[106] The next year the National Endowment for the Humanities (NEH) followed Justice's lead and announced it would not set numerical goals, a position chairman William Bennett believed he was authorized to take "by the rights of man, the moral teaching of generations, the ancient founding faith of this country, constitutional principle and the determination of the Justice Department."[107] Thomas reasserted the commission's "statutory authority and obligations," despite his agreement that color-consciousness and goals were morally wrong and unjust.[108] He appeared to be committed to upholding the law even if he did not agree with it. Again in 1984 all but three agencies complied, and even those three submitted plans that included race, sex, and disability breakdowns; they just refused to estimate how many women and minorities they would hire and when they would do so.[109] Although the administration could control the Justice Department, it could not necessarily control the other agencies. The fact that so few agencies followed its lead, and that it took several years to get those few on board, demonstrates that Reagan could not make all the drastic changes he promised. As Anderson notes, despite his strong rhetoric and Reynolds's efforts, Reagan's actions early in the administration were "awkward and contradictory," and he never signed an executive order to abolish affirmative action, choosing to fight small battles rather than risk alienating women and minorities and causing a split within his own administration.[110] His reluctance was no doubt partly due to the stubborn if not passionate resistance of career officials and even political appointees, making his desired changes slow in coming and far from complete.

Thomas's resistance to the administration appeared to be rooted in part in a desire to protect his own power. He was sensitive to a perceived lack of respect from whatever quarter and expressed bitterness toward African Americans for not currying favor with him. In 1984 he protested that although blacks complained about Reagan, in more than three years no major leader had sought to take advantage of his influence with the administration. They had chosen, as he put it, to "bitch, bitch, bitch, moan and moan, whine and whine" rather than reshape administration policies. It was an affront to Thomas's authority that his own constituency would rather shun political power: "It's a basic law of politics that you should always have access to people in power. . . . [Y]ou don't call the banker reviewing your loan application a fool."[111] Thomas failed to see that blacks felt he had little to offer them. "Is it that black people are so dumb," Carl T. Rowan responded angrily, "or that they simply know who their enemy is?" According to Rowan, Thomas was frustrated because he got no respect but had to "face the reality" that his EEOC predecessors were "held in the highest esteem" by blacks and whites alike. Blacks had survived slavery, Jim Crow, and the Ku Klux Klan; they could endure four more years of Reagan and Thomas.[112] At times, Thomas resisted the administration because he resented its incursions into his area of authority; then the turf battle and pride trumped his views on affirmative action. Similarly, Reagan may have appointed Thomas to eviscerate the EEOC, but Thomas resisted destroying or undermining his own agency.

In another sign that Reagan's efforts were not as far-reaching as they appeared, the EEOC continued to pursue and settle cases with large employers. In 1982 Eastern Airlines settled a 1979 suit—"putting [it] to rest as quickly and quietly as possible"—by paying $65,000 to 23 women who claimed they had not been hired as flight attendants because of their age.[113] Dean Witter Reynolds agreed to pay $2 million to 4,000 women and minorities who had been denied employment or promotion between 1976 and 1981 and to set up a $3 million affirmative action program.[114] In 1983 General Motors settled its Track 1 case initiated by Bill Brown in the early 1970s by agreeing to a five-year plan to pay $42.5 million to 100,000 employees, to establish hiring and promotion goals, and to spend $15 million on educational opportunities for employees and their families. The company decided to settle because it would "be good for our women and minority employees and good for the company."[115] The agreement did not include back pay, in part because it would be difficult to track down people who had not been hired many years earlier; however, the commission promised to continue to seek back pay "in appropriate cases." Also, the goals were delayed because the company had 61,000 workers on indefinite layoff, making the settlement "more prospective than retrospective."[116] Despite administration policy, the GM settlement set numerical goals, the Reagan-appointed commissioners unanimously approved it, and Thomas hailed it as a "significant achievement." Such settlements continued to illustrate the existence of real disagreement among civil rights agencies and resistance within the administration.[117] Despite Reagan's efforts, many of the cases initiated in the early 1970s were still being settled in the late 1970s and early 1980s with major awards.

Moreover, the EEOC continued to fund major litigation. During Thomas's tenure the commission was preparing its Track 1 lawsuit against Sears, Roebuck & Co. In 1984 a House subcommittee accused Thomas of criticizing his own agency's case and wanting it to fail.[118] Nevertheless, as the *Sears* case dragged on for years and career attorneys handling the litigation requested more and more money for ballooning budgets, Thomas's commission continued to fund the case with little resistance. Some observers, such as EEOC expert witness Alice Kessler-Harris, complained that the EEOC abandoned the case against Sears or that the case continued only because it was pushed along by a few dedicated career attorneys.[119] To the contrary, it was by far the largest case the EEOC had ever taken on. High-level authorities repeatedly approved growing budgets for items such as huge expert witness fees. Rather than "slipping through the cracks," this case received more attention and funding than any previous EEOC case. In fact, those who knew it best—the career attorneys trying it—had no complaints about the commission's level of support.[120] Despite the conservative climate, changes at the top, and Reagan's attempts to alter the meaning of affirmative action, his changes were limited, and gains continued to be made in EEOC cases in the early 1980s.

Beyond the precedent for a semi-independent EEOC, the work of established career staff members, and a strong legal foundation built during the 1970s, even political appointees like Thomas sometimes took seriously the EEOC's independent role and the importance of upholding the law, regardless of personal views. It is hard to give too much credit to Thomas, who could scarcely be called a civil rights advocate, or to underestimate the effect of Reagan's judicial appointments in ultimately undermining affirmative action through the courts.[121] However, if there was this level of resistance within Reagan's own administration and from his own appointees, there must have been a lot more in other sectors, and the state of civil rights policy may not have been as bad as previously thought.

Although much has been made of Reagan's negative impact on affirmative action, he could not automatically or completely reverse the gains of the prior two decades. Changes under Reagan were limited, if not prevented, by the EEOC's constant struggle for independence, by the work of staff members held over from Norton's tenure, and by the solid civil rights legal framework that could not be destroyed. Indeed, four years after Norton left the EEOC, she continued to downplay the administration's impact. In a speech celebrating the twentieth anniversary of the 1964 Civil Rights Act, she cited only one official, Reynolds, as creating confusion, saying he "used his federal office to escalate the drumbeat" against affirmative action. She painted a positive picture of civil rights policy, saying that more Americans opposed race discrimination in 1984 than in 1965. American businesses had not attacked affirmative action and "deserve[d] some praise" for abiding by it. Any new controversy did "not emanate from the American people" but from "a few politically motivated politicians who . . . preferred to exploit the existing puzzlement and concern over affirmative action."[122]

And from the perspective of several more decades, Norton's view was correct. Reagan's influence came last to the EEOC, which, despite growing constraints, retained some independence and, particularly during Reagan's first term, limited the extent of change. For various reasons, there was a counterforce at the commission, which was often criticized for lacking power, and it was quite different from what existed under Reynolds at Justice. Enforcement may have become dormant, but not all was lost. Reagan's civil rights changes were less than complete, some progress continued to be made, major cases and settlements continued without complaint from the attorneys litigating them, and the basic civil rights machinery remained to be revived by the more favorable Clinton administration. Reagan's changes, particularly at the EEOC, pushed back but did not halt the progress of civil rights. They were just an ebb in a period of continual, if gradual, improvement.

Notes

I would like to thank John Dittmer and Danielle McGuire for inviting me to contribute to this collection and for their crucial comments on this essay. I would also like to thank the participants at the October 2010 "Bending toward Justice" conference at Rutgers University for their important insights. Finally, I thank Steven Lawson for his caring mentorship and guidance.

1. Robin Toner and Jonathan D. Glater, "Roberts Helped to Shape 80's Civil Rights Debate," *New York Times,* August 4, 2005.

2. Hugh Davis Graham, *The Civil Rights Era: Origins and Development of National Policy, 1960–1972* (New York: Oxford University Press, 1990), 4; Terry H. Anderson, *The Pursuit of Fairness: A History of Affirmative Action* (New York: Oxford University Press, 2004), 157.

3. Leonard Garment, *Crazy Rhythm: My Journey from Brooklyn, Jazz, and Wall Street to Nixon's White House, Watergate, and Beyond* (New York: Times Books, Random House, 1997), 203–19; Dean J. Kotlowski, *Nixon's Civil Rights: Politics, Principle, and Policy* (Cambridge, Mass.: Harvard University Press, 2001); William C. Berman, *America's Right Turn: From Nixon to Bush* (Baltimore: Johns Hopkins University Press, 1994), 11; Anderson, *Pursuit of Fairness,* chap. 3.

4. Garment, *Crazy Rhythm,* 220.

5. Bill Brown, telephone interview by the author, February 26, 2004.

6. Ibid.; Peter Masley, "Bias Complaints; U.S. Agencies Lag in Resolving Charges of Discrimination," *Washington Post,* September 28, 1977.

7. Brown interview; Marjorie A. Stockford, *The Bellwomen: The Story of the Landmark AT&T Sex Discrimination Case* (New Brunswick, N.J.: Rutgers University Press, 2004), 209.

8. Philip Shabecoff, "A Full Right to Fairness," *New York Times,* September 23, 1973.

9. Philip Shabecoff, "Rulings on Job Bias Vary among Agencies," *New York Times,* September 30, 1973.

10. Brown interview; Kotlowski, *Nixon's Civil Rights;* Garment, *Crazy Rhythm,* 220; Philip Shabecoff, "Job Equality Pact in Steel Industry Being Negotiated," *New York Times,* December 5, 1973.

11. Brown interview.

12. Georgette Jasen, "Ma Bell's Daughters: Women Got Big Gains in '73 AT&T Job Pact, But Sexism Cry Persists," *Wall Street Journal,* February 28, 1978; Jack Egan, "Changes May Be Needed in AT&T Hiring Program," *Washington Post,* July 4, 1978; Eileen Shanahan, "AT&T Is Penalized Anew for Job Bias; $2.5 Million Will Be Paid for Violations," *New York Times,* May 14, 1975.

13. Lynne Darcy, "Can Congress Roll the Backlog?" *NOW Compliance Newsletter* 14 (November 1974): 7, box 3, in folder 1, Papers of NOW Chicago, 78–034, University of Illinois at Chicago Special Collections; William Chapman, "An Agency in Shambles; The EEOC 11 Years Later: An 'Unbelievable Morass,'" *Washington Post,* February 6, 1977; Ernest Holsendolph, "General Accounting Office Reports that Progress of Equal Employment Commission Is 'Limited,'" *New York Times,* September 30, 1976; "Chairman to Leave Panel on Job Rights," *New York Times,* March 19, 1975; Staff Reporter, "EEOC Chairman's Resignation Poses Problem for Ford," *Wall Street Journal,* April 14, 1976; Charlayne Hunter, "Economist Finds Widening in Black-White Income Gap," *New York Times,* November 29, 1975. The commission postponed guidelines that would protect women and minorities from disproportionate layoffs through rotated furloughs and work sharing. Ernest Holsendolph, "Equal Employment Guideline on Layoffs Delayed," *New York Times,* April 16, 1975.

14. Kotlowski, *Nixon's Civil Rights;* Garment, *Crazy Rhythm,* chap. 8.

15. Graham, *Civil Rights Era,* 5, 7.

16. Gary M. Fink and Hugh Davis Graham, eds., *The Carter Presidency: Policy Choices in the Post–New Deal Era* (Lawrence: University Press of Kansas, 1998), 3 (internal citations omitted). See, generally, Susan M. Hartmann, "Feminism, Public Policy, and the Carter Administration," in Fink and Graham, *Carter Presidency,* chap. 11.

17. Jacqueline Trescott, "Eleanor Norton: A Fighter in the EEOC Chair," *Washington Post,* June 22, 1977.

18. Paul D. Moreno, *From Direct Action to Affirmative Action: Fair Employment Law and Policy in America, 1933–1972* (Baton Rouge: Louisiana State University Press, 1997), chaps. 5, 6; Anderson, *Pursuit of Fairness,* 47.

19. Trescott, "Eleanor Norton."

20. Ibid.; Staff Reporter, "EEOC Adopts System to Speed Case-Handling," *Wall Street Journal,* July 21, 1977; Walter Mossberg, "Wary Watchdogs: Besieged by Criticism, Job-Bias Agencies Seek to Bolster Programs," *Wall Street Journal,* August 26, 1977.

21. Peter Milius, "Jobs Become Leading Rights Issue," *Washington Post,* July 24, 1979.

22. Leslie Bennetts, "The Equal Pay Issue: Focusing on 'Comparable Worth'; 'Occupational Segregation,'" *New York Times,* October 26, 1979.

23. Joseph A. Califano Jr., *Governing America: An Insider's Report from the White House and the Cabinet* (New York: Simon and Schuster, 1981).

24. William E. Leuchtenburg, "Jimmy Carter and the Post–New Deal Presidency," in Fink and Graham, *Carter Presidency,* chap. 1; Mike Causey, "Hispanic Group Targets 3 Agencies," *Washington Post,* May 11, 1979.

25. Fink and Graham, *Carter Presidency,* 3–4. See also Steve Fraser and Gary Gerstle, eds., *The Rise and Fall of the New Deal Order, 1930–1980* (Princeton, N.J.: Princeton University Press, 1989), pt. 2; Berman, *America's Right Turn,* 11, 43, 45, 52, 55; John Yemma, "Public-Interest Law Firms Struggle as Apathy Dries up Fund Sources," *Christian Science Monitor,* January 21, 1980.

26. Jane Dolkart, interview by the author, July 16, 2004, Dallas, Texas.

27. JoAnn Lublin, "Guideline-Happy at the EEOC?" *Wall Street Journal,* August 28, 1980; Nathaniel Sheppard, "Fair-Employment Agency Cleans up Its Backlog," *New York Times,* February 24, 1979.

28. Milius, "Jobs Become Leading Rights Issue."

29. David Copus, interview by the author, November 13, 2003, Washington, D.C.; Lublin, "Guideline-Happy at the EEOC?"

30. Robert Reinhold, "U.S. Equal Opportunity Agency Lists Criteria for Prosecution," *New York Times,* March 21, 1978.

31. Ibid.; "Equal-Employment Unit to Stress Bias Patterns," *New York Times,* December 3, 1978; Jerry M. Flint, "Washington Plans Affirmative Action Push in '79," *New York Times,* December 24, 1978.

32. Bradley Graham, "AT&T Found in Compliance on Ending Job Bias,"

Washington Post, January 18, 1979; Staff Reporter, "AT&T Has Complied with Antibias Decree, U.S. Attorneys Say," *Wall Street Journal,* January 18, 1979.

33. "GE to Spend $31.9 Million in Bias Accord," *Washington Post,* June 16, 1978.

34. Warren Brown, "Ford Agrees to $23 Million Settlement of Sex, Race Discrimination Complaint," *Washington Post,* November 26, 1980; Ernest Holsendolph, "Ford Motor to Spend $23 Million to Settle Bias Case," *New York Times,* November 26, 1980.

35. Many companies, eager to avoid AT&T's fate, chose to settle old claims rather than let them drag out. Stockford, *Bellwomen,* 209–11.

36. Staff Reporter, "EEOC Devises Rules Defining On-the-Job Sexual Harassment," *Wall Street Journal,* March 12, 1980; Ruth Walker, ed., "Legal Barriers Placed around Sexual Harassment," *Christian Science Monitor,* March 13, 1980.

37. Georgia Dullea, "Sexual Harassment at Work: A Sensitive and Confusing Issue," *New York Times,* October 24, 1980.

38. Cass Peterson, "EEOC Chief Norton to Resign Feb. 21 to Smooth Way for Successor," *Washington Post,* January 23, 1981; Jacqueline Trescott, "Much Adieu about Norton," *Washington Post,* February 20, 1981; Deborah Churchman, "Eleanor Norton Reflects on Equal-Employment Successes," *Christian Science Monitor,* March 3, 1981.

39. Churchman, "Eleanor Norton Reflects on Equal-Employment Successes."

40. Ernest Holsendolph, "Skills, Not Bias, Seen as Key for Jobs," *New York Times,* July 3, 1982.

41. Graham, *Civil Rights Era,* 5, 7.

42. Ibid.

43. Nancy MacLean, *Freedom Is Not Enough: The Opening of the American Workplace* (New York: Russell Sage Foundation; Cambridge, Mass.: Harvard University Press, 2006).

44. See, for example, Spencer Rich, "Reagan Panel, Citing 'New Racism,' Urges Easing of EEOC Rules," *Washington Post,* January 30, 1981.

45. Peterson, "EEOC Chief Norton to Resign"; Trescott, "Much Adieu about Norton."

46. Raymond Wolters, *Right Turn: William Bradford Reynolds, the Reagan Administration, and Black Civil Rights* (New Brunswick, N.J.: Transaction Publishers, 1996), 6–7.

47. Ibid., 7, 9.

48. Ibid., introduction.

49. Robert Pear, "U.S. Agencies Vary on Rights Policy," *New York Times,* November 16, 1981.

50. Howell Raines, "Blacks Shift to Sharper Criticism on Civil Rights," *New York Times,* July 26, 1981; Pear, "U.S. Agencies Vary on Rights Policy"; Julia Malone, "Black Conservatives Like 'Jay' Parkers Step into Reagan Limelight," *Christian Science Monitor,* February 11, 1981.

51. Leslie Maitland Werner, "Justice Dept. Files a Plan for Minority Hiring," *New York Times,* July 22, 1983.

52. Tom Wicker, "'Working on' Blacks," *New York Times,* February 16, 1982; Toner and Glater, "Roberts Helped Shape 80's Civil Rights Debate"; Fred Barbash and Juan Williams, "Administration Prods EEOC on Quotas Brief," *Washington Post,* April 7, 1983; Anderson, *Pursuit of Fairness,* 173–75.

53. Karlyn Barker, "Dole Tells Lawyer Group that GOP Is Concerned about Civil Rights Issues," *Washington Post,* September 28, 1983.

54. Wolters, *Right Turn,* 5.

55. Ibid., 2–3 (citing Roger Wilkins; internal citations omitted).

56. Anderson, *Pursuit of Fairness,* 197, 216.

57. Fred Barbash and Kathy Sawyer, "Justice Dept. Declares Win over Quotas," *Washington Post,* June 14, 1984; *Firefighters Local Union No. 1784 v. Stotts,* 467 U.S. 561 (1984).

58. Raines, "Blacks Shift to Sharper Criticism on Civil Rights"; Rich, "Reagan Panel."

59. Felicity Barringer and Kathy Sawyer, "Job Bias: Easing Rules Anything But Easy," *Washington Post,* June 29, 1981; Kathy Sawyer, "Plan to Ease Job Bias Rules Announced," *Washington Post,* August 25, 1981; Marjorie Hunter, "Plan to Ease Fight on Jobs Criticized," *New York Times,* October 8, 1981; Kathy Sawyer, "Labor's Embattled Bias Proposals Advance," *Washington Post,* July 27, 1983; Felicity Barringer, "EEOC Withholds Seal of Approval," *Washington Post,* August 24, 1981; Pear, "U.S. Agencies Vary on Rights Policy."

60. Robert Pear, "Changes Weighed in Federal Rules on Discrimination," *New York Times,* December 3, 1984; Felicity Barringer, "Job Bias Debate Is Reopened," *Washington Post,* August 14, 1981. See, for example, Rich, "Reagan Panel." Critics protested it was easier to enforce a numerical quota than to determine whether hiring was done in good faith. The *Washington Post* called the decision to no longer impose quotas an improvement "if it can . . . be made to produce real job gains for the victims of discrimination." But a policy is only as strong as its enforcement, and a voluntary policy is effective only if employers comply. Editorial, "Affirmative Action," *Washington Post,* October 10, 1981; Mary Thornton, "Shifts Eyed for Rights Enforcers," *Washington Post,* November 12, 1981.

61. Herbert H. Denton, "Reagan Picks Black Lawyer for EEOC," *Washington Post,* February 13, 1982.

62. Charles R. Babcock, "Contempt Ruling Sought against EEOC Nominee," *Washington Post,* March 12, 1982; Steven R. Weisman, "Reagan Rescinds Rights Nomination in Wake of Outcry," *New York Times,* February 13, 1982.

63. Weisman, "Reagan Rescinds Rights Nomination."

64. Holsendolph, "Skills, Not Bias, Seen as Key for Jobs."

65. Felicity Barringer, "EEOC's Two-Part Mission Pulling Its Employees in Opposing Directions," *Washington Post,* March 12, 1984.

66. Ibid.; Juan Williams, "Improper Handling of EEOC Cases Charged," *Washington Post,* February 8, 1984; Cass Peterson and Christine Russell, "Feud Defused at EEOC," *Washington Post,* June 26, 1984.

67. Juan Williams, "EEOC Chief Cites Abuse of Racial Bias Criteria," *Washington Post,* December 4, 1984.

68. Pear, "Changes Weighed in Federal Rules on Discrimination."

69. Holsendolph, "Skills, Not Bias, Seen as Key for Jobs"; Denton, "Reagan Picks Black Lawyer for EEOC."

70. Juan Williams, "Chairman of EEOC Tells Panel Statistics Misused to Prove Bias; Example of Georgetown Basketball Team Bandied," *Washington Post,* December 15, 1984. See also Pear, "Changes Weighed in Federal Rules on Discrimination."

71. Bill McAllister, "Under Thomas, EEOC Relinquished Rights Role," *Washington Post,* September 10, 1991.

72. Anne Ladky, telephone interview by author, March 20, 2002.

73. Pear, "U.S. Agencies Vary on Rights Policy."

74. Howell Raines, "Blacks Shift to Sharper Criticism on Civil Rights," *New York Times,* July 26, 1981; Pear, "U.S. Agencies Vary on Rights Policy"; Malone, "Black Conservatives Like 'Jay' Parkers."

75. David Shribman, "Study Finds Women Are Systematically Underpaid," *New York Times,* September 2, 1981.

76. Sara Fitzgerald, "The Federal Report; Executive Notes," *Washington Post,* October 1, 1981; Rich, "Reagan Panel."

77. Nina Totenberg, "The Government Jobs No One Wants," *Christian Science Monitor,* May 6, 1981.

78. Herbert H. Denton, "Hill Unit Postpones Vote on Nominee to EEOC Job," *Washington Post,* November 13, 1981; Herbert H. Denton, "Reagan Nominee under Attack," *Washington Post,* November 4, 1981; Marjorie Hunter, "Reagan Defending Nominee to Lead Job Fairness Agency," *New York Times,* November 5, 1981; Iver Peterson, "Reagan Job Rights Nominee Arouses Dispute," *New York Times,* November 13, 1981.

79. Editorial, "Reconsider the Choice for EEOC," *Washington Post,* November 12, 1981; Pear, "U.S. Agencies Vary on Rights Policy"; Denton, "Hill Unit Postpones Vote." Reagan also bowed to pressure to drop his nominee for the Civil Rights Commission chair in February 1982. Steven R. Weisman, "President Drops Nominee for Post on a Rights Panel," *New York Times,* February 27, 1982.

80. Weisman, "Reagan Rescinds Rights Nomination."

81. Robert Pear, "Rights Panel Says Reagan Officials Hamper Its Work," *New York Times,* March 20, 1983.

82. Robert Pear, "Rights Unit Says Budget Cuts Imperil Move to Curb Racism," *New York Times,* May 28, 1982.

83. Robert Pear, "Cutbacks Weaken Rights Policies, U.S. Panel Says," *New York Times,* October 11, 1983.

84. Pear, "Rights Panel Says Reagan Officials Hamper Its Work"; editorial, "Hiding the Bad News," *Washington Post,* March 26, 1983.

85. Pear, "U.S. Agencies Vary on Rights Policy."

86. Hunter, "Plan to Ease Fight on Jobs Criticized." See also Barringer and Sawyer, "Job Bias"; Sawyer, "Plan to Ease Job Bias Rules Announced"; Sawyer, "Labor's Embattled Bias Proposals Advance"; Barringer, "EEOC Withholds Seal of Approval."

87. "A Letter from J. Clay Smith," EEOC History: 35th Anniversary: 1965–2000, http://www.eeoc.gov/eeoc/history/35th/voices/smith.html.

88. "Two Jobs for the EEOC," *Washington Post,* March 14, 1984.

89. McAllister, "Under Thomas, EEOC Relinquished Rights Role"; Ladky interview.

90. Milton R. Benjamin and Sara Fitzgerald, "EEOC Chairman Vows Enforcement of Job Bias Rules for Contractors," *Washington Post,* June 9, 1983.

91. Carlyle C. Douglas, Caroline Rand Herron, and Michael Wright, "Administration Grinds Its Gears on Rights Issues," *New York Times,* August 7, 1983; Sheila Rule, "Debate Continues on Rights Policies," *New York Times,* August 3, 1983; Juan Williams, "EEOC Chief Faults Administration on Curbing Bias," *Washington Post,* August 3, 1983.

92. Williams, "EEOC Chief Faults Administration"; Juan Williams, "New Poverty Rationale May Be Emerging," *Washington Post,* August 13, 1983.

93. United Press International, "Pressure Seen in Vote to Withdraw Brief on Quotas," *New York Times,* April 8, 1983; Fred Barbash, "Private Groups Plead Case for Stifled EEOC," *Washington Post,* April 28, 1983; Barbash and Williams, "Administration Prods EEOC on Quotas Brief"; McAllister, "Under Thomas, EEOC Relinquished Rights Role."

94. Barbash and Williams, "Administration Prods EEOC on Quotas Brief"; United Press International, "Pressure Seen in Vote to Withdraw Brief on Quotas."

95. Fred Barbash and Pete Earley, "Civil Rights Unit Supports EEOC on Race Quota Case," *Washington Post,* April 15, 1983. Chairman Pendleton, however, said, "Like you, I support affirmative action, but oppose quotas" (ibid.). See also Associated Press, "Action Is Sought on Bias Pact," *New York Times,* April 16, 1983.

96. Barbash and Williams, "Administration Prods EEOC on Quotas Brief"; United Press International, "Pressure Seen in Vote to Withdraw Brief on Quotas." See also Anderson, *Pursuit of Fairness,* 178.

97. Juan Williams, "Lawmaker Urges EEOC Not to Quit Rights Case," *Washington Post,* April 10, 1983.

98. Barbash, "Private Groups Plead Case for Stifled EEOC."

99. Pear, "U.S. Agencies Vary on Rights Policy"; Associated Press, "3 U.S. Agencies Facing Action over Hiring Goals," *New York Times,* August 22, 1984.

100. Werner, "Justice Dept. Files Plan for Minority Hiring"; William Raspberry, "Fill in the Numbers, Please," *Washington Post,* July 15, 1983.

101. Felicity Barringer, "EEOC's Bielan Feeds on Plans, Goals, Timetables—and Paper," *Washington Post,* August 4, 1983.

102. Werner, "Justice Dept. Files Plan for Minority Hiring"; Felicity Barringer, "EEOC Chief Criticizes Justice Dept. Job Plan," *Washington Post,* September 7, 1983; "Attorney General Resubmits Equal Opportunity Proposal," *Washington Post,* July 22, 1983.

103. Deborah Churchman, "Affirmative Action: The Struggle Goes on for Parity in the Workplace," *Christian Science Monitor,* August 24, 1983.

104. Raspberry, "Fill in the Numbers."

105. Barringer, "EEOC Chief Criticizes Justice Dept. Job Plan."

106. Werner, "Justice Dept. Files Plan for Minority Hiring."

107. Phil McCombs, "NEH Chief Rejects Job Rules: Bennett Balks at Goals on Women, Minorities Job Rules," *Washington Post,* January 19, 1984.

108. Myron Struck, "3 Agencies Won't Supply EEOC with Hiring Data," *Washington Post,* August 9, 1984.

109. Bosko Jaksic, "Three Agencies Facing Crackdown," *Washington Post,* August 22, 1984; Struck, "3 Agencies Won't Supply EEOC with Hiring Data"; Associated Press, "3 U.S. Agencies Facing Action over Hiring Goals," *New York Times,* August 22, 1984.

110. Anderson, *Pursuit of Fairness,* 168–69, 173, 176, 187–88.

111. Juan Williams, "EEOC Chairman Blasts Black Leaders," *Washington Post,* October 25, 1984.

112. Carl T. Rowan, "The Real Shame," *Washington Post,* October 30, 1984.

113. United Press International, "$65,000 Payment in Bias Suit Agreed to by Eastern Airlines," *New York Times,* April 18, 1982.

114. Thomas W. Lippman, "Broker to Pay $2 Million to End Bias Suit," *Washington Post,* May 7, 1982.

115. Kathy Sawyer, "Job Bias Claim Settled by GM for $42 Million," *Washington Post,* October 19, 1983.

116. Ibid.; Robert Pear, "G.M. Agrees to Pay $42 Million to End Case on Job Bias," *New York Times,* October 19, 1983.

117. Robert Pear, "G.M. Settlement and Reagan Tenets," *New York Times,* October 21, 1983.

118. U.S. House of Representatives Subcommittee on Employment Opportunities of the Committee on Education and Labor, *Oversight Hearing on the EEOC's Enforcement Policies,* 98th Cong., 2nd sess., December 14, 1984, 11.

119. Alice Kessler-Harris, interview by the author, November 12, 2003, New York, N.Y.

120. Dolkart interview; Gerald Letwin, interview by the author, July 9, 2004, Washington, D.C.

121. Anderson, *Pursuit of Fairness,* 197, 216.

122. Juan Williams, "Former EEOC Head Defends Use of Affirmative Action," *Washington Post,* December 13, 1984. See also Anderson, *Pursuit of Fairness,* 175–76 (discussing the momentum of affirmative action and companies' willingness to comply with it to show they were not discriminating).

Race and Partisanship in Criminal Disfranchisement Laws

Pippa Holloway

In 2000 America woke up to the issue of felon disfranchisement. That year George W. Bush won the presidential election by carrying the state of Florida by 537 votes. However, close to 10 percent of Florida's voting-age population had been unable to vote due to a state law permanently disfranchising anyone with a felony conviction unless pardoned by the governor. In addition, many individuals who did not have prior felony convictions were wrongly purged from registration lists and prevented from voting. Many argued that because the individuals legally disfranchised, as well as those mistakenly barred from voting, were disproportionately African American—a population that votes for the Democratic Party by wide margins—felon disfranchisement in Florida benefited the Republican Party and gave the presidency to Bush. This election, and subsequent publicity about the impact of similar laws in other states, convinced many Americans of the potential electoral impact of such laws.

Laws that disfranchise because of criminal convictions are the primary means of excluding adult citizens from suffrage in the United States today. In 2010 approximately 5.3 million people could not vote due to criminal convictions. Only about one-fourth of these disfranchised individuals are incarcerated; the majority either are under correctional supervision (probation or parole) or have fully completed their sentences but remain disfranchised under state laws. The disproportionate racial impact of these laws is startling. Due to racial disparities in the criminal justice system, African Americans are disfranchised at seven times the national average. As a result, one out of every eight adult black males is disfranchised due to a prior criminal conviction.

The racial effect of these laws is no coincidence. Although disfranchisement for crime has a long history rooted in Anglo-European legal traditions, laws were modified in the nineteenth century and enforced with the intent of denying the vote to the newly enfranchised former slaves.[1] For

277

many decades disfranchisement for crime took a backseat to other means of restricting the African American vote, including literacy tests, poll taxes, and registration laws. The Voting Rights Act and the Twenty-Fourth Amendment put a stop to most such tactics, but federal courts have upheld many state laws that disfranchise for crime. Most significant was the 1974 *Richardson v. Ramirez* decision, in which the U.S. Supreme Court upheld a California law disfranchising ex-felons. In a six-to-three decision, the majority of the justices construed section 2 of the amendment as granting states an "affirmative sanction" to disfranchise ex-felons, thus exempting such laws from strict scrutiny.[2] This decision protected most state laws disfranchising for crime, despite their disproportionate impact on the African American population.

Since other techniques did the lion's share of the work of disfranchisement in the late nineteenth and early twentieth centuries, they were the focus of the earliest organized efforts to challenge racial discrimination in access to suffrage. Although civil rights organizations paid scant attention to laws disfranchising for crime in this period, individual black citizens challenged such laws when they felt unfairly excluded from suffrage. This essay considers court cases initiated by three African American men between 1914 and 1916. None of these plaintiffs claimed discrimination based on race, and neither national nor local civil rights groups were involved in the cases. Nonetheless, these cases represent some of the first court challenges by African Americans—or any individuals disfranchised for crime—to the enforcement of laws that disfranchise based on crime. And the efforts of these three men were connected to and inform our understanding of the black freedom movement and the struggle for African American civil rights.

Cornelius "Canary" Curtis was disfranchised in Knoxville, Tennessee, for a 1907 larceny conviction. In 1914 Curtis petitioned for the restoration of his rights of citizenship and was denied twice by the local courts. He brought his case to the Tennessee Court of Civil Appeals, which ruled in his favor. The Tennessee Supreme Court affirmed the appeals court's judgment in 1915. The other two cases involved voting in the 1916 presidential election in St. Louis, Missouri. Democratic Party operatives in the city coordinated efforts to target African American voters that year—many of whom had recently migrated to Missouri from southern states—with stepped-up and arguably fraudulent enforcement of laws disfranchising for crime. After the election Henry Lucas and Johns Sullivan, two of the voters who were wrongfully disfranchised owing to false accusations of prior criminal convictions, initiated individual civil suits against Democratic Party leaders.

These cases in Knoxville and St. Louis originated in border states, where African Americans were not entirely excluded from citizenship and electoral participation. But the relatively peaceful racial climate in both locales was threatened at the time. In St. Louis white Democrats feared that African American migrants from the South were "colonizing" the city on behalf of the Republican Party.[3] Republicans, in turn, accused Democrats of "southernizing" elections—manipulating election practices, including disfranchisement laws, to target African American voters.[4] Knoxville, in eastern Tennessee, had less racial tension and violence than cities in the western part of the state, particularly Memphis. But problems were escalating there, too, where a race riot and a near lynching occurred in 1919.[5] In both Knoxville and St. Louis the degenerating racial climate and challenges to African American citizenship were reflected in general assaults on African American civil rights, as well as these specific incidents involving disfranchisement for criminal convictions. And in both cities, African Americans turned to the courts when their right to vote came under attack.

These events occurred not only in pivotal locations but also at a critical time in the context of the black freedom movement nationally. What historian Rayford Logan calls the "nadir" of African American history had come to an end, although this was not clear at the time.[6] After a series of defeats—twelve in a row—for African American voting rights in federal courts between 1890 and 1908, the NAACP eked out a slow pattern of victories that would escalate over the next several decades.[7] When Curtis filed his appeal, the landmark case challenging Oklahoma's "grandfather clause," *Guinn v. United States,* had been argued before the U.S. Supreme Court but had not been decided.[8] The two St. Louis cases were filed just a year after the remarkable victory in *Guinn* that overturned these laws. Although there is no evidence that the NAACP or any other activist groups had any connection to these cases in Tennessee and Missouri or that the national movement inspired these actions, it is striking that these three African American men were moved at this precise historical moment to go to court to challenge those who sought to disfranchise them.

In December 1907 a Knox County court convicted Cornelius Curtis of larceny for stealing money that had been left in an office on Prince Street, in downtown Knoxville, where he worked as a janitor. The judge sentenced twenty-three-year-old Curtis to five years in prison and judged him "infamous" due to the larceny conviction. *Infamy* was a term in Tennessee

law that dated back to 1829, when the legislature established a legal definition of infamy, categorized a number of criminal offenses as "infamous,"
and barred infamous individuals from testifying in court.[9] After serving
about three and a half years Curtis was pardoned for good behavior in
March 1911. Following his release from prison Curtis resumed working as
a janitor for various Knoxville businesses.[10]

As a result of the infamy judgment, Curtis became disfranchised and
was disqualified from testifying in court (except in his own criminal case).
This loss of citizenship rights was the result of a number of constitutional
and legislative developments dating back to the early days of the state.
Tennessee's disqualification of infamous individuals from testifying in
court was similar to the laws of many other states in this period, as was a
clause in its 1835 constitution authorizing the legislature to exclude these
individuals from suffrage.[11] In 1851 the legislature established a process
by which infamous individuals might have their civil rights restored by
petitioning the circuit court.[12]

In November 1914 Curtis filed a petition in the Knox County circuit
court to restore his rights of citizenship. He had good reason to believe his
request would be granted. Petitions for restoration of citizenship rights
were fairly common in Tennessee in the late nineteenth and early twentieth centuries. The Knox County court had restored citizenship rights to
twenty-nine individuals in the previous two decades.[13] Nor did Curtis have
any reason to be particularly concerned that his race would be a barrier to
the restoration of his citizenship. Alfred Easley and Zack Hale, who were
identified in the court records as African American, successfully applied
for restoration of citizenship in 1901 and 1902, respectively. But Easley
and Hale may have been the last African American men whose petitions
were approved by the county court for some time. In the two decades after
Curtis's case, I found no petitions from African American citizens, successful or unsuccessful, in the Knox County records. This absence suggests that African American residents of Knoxville understood that the
local court would be inimical to their petitions, based on Curtis's experience there.[14]

Successful applications for the restoration of citizenship rights were
relatively common for both black and white Tennesseans in these decades.
In Giles County, a midstate county with a relatively large African American population, twenty-nine infamous men sought the removal of their
infamy judgments at the circuit court in Pulaski between 1885 and 1920.
Sixteen of these petitions came from individuals identified as African

American, and all but one were successful. The court records from Maury, Crocket, and Hayward counties reveal successful petitions from African American men as well.

African American men in other southern states had mixed success in getting their citizenship rights restored following criminal convictions in this period.[15] Those in Tennessee, though, seemed to face the fewest obstacles—at least until the Curtis case. This is partly because Tennessee did not have the same historical commitment to black disfranchisement that other southern states did. Political machines dominated Tennessee politics in this period, and rival factions sometimes sought black votes to tip close races in their favor. In Knoxville, where the Republican Party controlled local politics, competing candidates sometimes sought the support of African American voters. The city's relatively small African American population meant that black voting would never threaten white political dominance, but it could be important in close races. Although African American electoral participation dropped in the 1890s following the enactment of voter registration and secret ballot laws and a poll tax, it recovered somewhat in subsequent decades.[16]

The process for restoring citizenship rights in Tennessee varied little from county to county, and court records indicate that Curtis's application followed the standard procedure. Individuals had to demonstrate to the circuit court that they had "sustained the character of a person of honesty, respectability, and veracity."[17] The most common way to demonstrate such character was to present a signed petition attesting to it. Such petitions generally stated the date of the infamy judgment and the crime that provoked it, verified the petitioner's residence in the county, and attested to the petitioner's good character. Signatories usually included neighbors, employers, local businessmen, and sometimes individuals connected to the criminal justice system, such as the judge, prosecutor, or court clerk.

Most individuals seeking restoration of citizenship waited one to three years to petition the court, as this would support their claim of "sustained" good character. However, some successful petitions were submitted within months of the petitioner's release from prison.[18] Curtis applied for the restoration of his citizenship rights about three and a half years after his release from prison, putting him well within the average bounds of such petitions. The obstacles Curtis faced apparently were not due to his failure to follow standard procedure.

The court notified the district attorney of Curtis's filing ten days before the hearing, as prescribed by Tennessee law, and he declined to challenge it. On the day of the hearing, four witnesses accompanied Curtis to court and testified as to his good character. These witnesses were present and former employers, some of whom had known Curtis for many years, even before his conviction and incarceration. All were among the white elite of Knox County—two prominent lawyers, a deputy sheriff and secretary of the Knoxville Board of Commerce, and a court reporter. These men testified that Curtis had been a "trusted, faithful servant"; they "had trusted him in their houses and were willing to trust him again." Curtis, they assured the court, was an "honest and faithful colored man."[19]

Like many of the African Americans who petitioned to restore their citizenship, Curtis was not a wealthy man. Successful petitions from illiterate individuals and landless tenant farmers can also be found in Tennessee court records, despite the financial and logistical challenges such individuals faced. But thanks to his employment in downtown Knoxville, Curtis had connections among the city's white business elite that proved useful. Among his duties was cleaning the Women's Building on Main Street, and according to one story, Curtis had identified the cause of the Christmas Eve 1906 fire that destroyed the building. After the fire, he found the remains of a firecracker in the back alley. Curtis was clearly a well-known figure in the downtown area.[20]

The presence of witnesses at the court hearing was the only irregularity I found in Curtis's case. Signatures on the petition ordinarily sufficed as evidence, and witnesses for the petitioner rarely appeared. The fact that Curtis's witnesses testified at court suggests that he may have anticipated opposition to his petition. Given the prominence of these men in the local community, he must have assumed they would be particularly helpful should the judge be inclined to question his application.

Though the image of white southern men supporting their African American employee's efforts to regain the rights of citizenship might seem anomalous, this was not uncommon.[21] For example, in Georgia in 1897 John W. Arnow Jr. wrote to Governor William Atkinson to recommend the restoration of citizenship rights for his two African American farmhands. Arnow wrote, "Allonzo Jones and Robert Cowan lived with me for the last 5 years and have been good faithful servants and had no trouble and I think they deserve a pardon." Jones and Cowan signed the document with "X," indicating they were illiterate.[22]

A similar example occurred in Alabama in 1886. Two African American men, Daniel Butler and Elias Peavy, petitioned Governor Edward O'Neal for citizenship rights they had lost after being convicted of grand larceny. In addition to a petition signed by twelve people, recommending both men for citizenship, each sent a letter from his employer. Peavy's employer, William Gaddis, told the governor that he and Peavy had a long history of business transactions. Peavy had bought land from him after renting the property for several years. Gaddis wrote, "He has made an uncommonly good citizen for a colored man, and the petition he will offer will show you in what estimation he is held by his white neighbors." Butler offered a letter from the man he had been convicted of stealing cotton from twelve years earlier. Edmund Williams wrote that Butler had "resided on my place" much of the time since his release from prison and that "his conduct has been entirely exemplary and honorable."[23]

The letters from Arnow, Gaddis, and Williams indicate the complex intersection of social structures and personal relationships that marked southern life in the late nineteenth and early twentieth centuries. White men of property were on occasion willing to use their social status to assist African American employees and acquaintances in their efforts to regain citizenship. White men were the gatekeepers of citizenship, but in some circumstances they were willing to open those gates to African American men they knew and respected. Such respect might even transcend prior animosity—Williams was willing to advocate for an African American man he had accused of criminal conduct in the past.[24]

Such participation and assistance by white men reaffirmed their status as guardians of citizenship. Benevolence can function as a means of articulating and even strengthening social hierarchies. By extending assistance to poor African American men, Arnow, Gaddis, and Williams confirmed their own standing in the social and political hierarchy of their community. Similarly, the assistance Curtis received from his white employers may have been based on genuine friendship and affection, but Curtis's relationship to them was nonetheless grounded in hierarchies—the occupational hierarchy of employer and employee and the social hierarchy of race. Helping their African American janitor with a legal problem was a way to highlight the benevolence of paternalism, thereby obfuscating the unequal power relations and violence endemic to such a system.

Electoral politics may well have been a factor in both his employers' support and the opposition to Curtis's claim. It was an election year in Knoxville, and voters would soon select a new mayor, Democrat John E. McMillan. McMillan had spoken out against the Ku Klux Klan and had solicited votes from the city's black population, even dispatching operatives to African American neighborhoods to distribute blank poll tax receipts.

There is no direct evidence connecting Curtis to McMillan's campaign, but African American votes were valuable in Knoxville in 1915.[25] Curtis may have been using this situation to get his citizenship rights restored; his advocates may have been hoping to gain a vote for McMillan; and, in refusing the petition, Judge Von A. Huffaker may have been seeking to deter those who supported McMillan.

Black voters in other states had been able, on occasion, to use their political allegiance to secure the restoration of citizenship rights. For example, Alabama governor Rufus Cobb restored an African American man's citizenship in 1880 after being assured that the petitioner "is a colored man but votes the Democratic ticket all the time."[26] In 1894 the mayor of Milner, Georgia, wrote to Governor Atkinson asking for a pardon for Berry Burt, an African American man, so he could vote in the next election: "Enclosed I send petition from Berry Burt . . . could get more signatures to petition by having more time but our election for county offices is next Wednesday and we have not got time to wait."[27]

Following the testimony by the witnesses, Curtis took the stand and was questioned by the judge. Curtis described his prior offense and told of his release for good behavior. He said he had not had any legal trouble since leaving prison, although he had been accused of stealing keys from "Mr. Turner." More questioning of Curtis and the witnesses clarified that no one believed he had been involved in the theft of Turner's keys. In fact, a cook in the Turner household admitted to misplacing the keys and locating them a few hours later.[28]

Despite the testimony of prominent witnesses in Curtis's favor, Judge Huffaker refused to grant him restoration. Huffaker dismissed Curtis's petition and charged him a court fee. Curtis was not willing to abandon the quest for the restoration of his citizenship rights and applied for a rehearing the following January. Again the judge heard the petition, again the district attorney failed to appear to contest the petition, and again the judge dismissed the case and charged Curtis another fee.[29]

Still undaunted, Curtis decided to file an appeal. At some point in the process he secured legal representation from prominent Knoxville attorney Malcolm McDermott, dean of the University of Tennessee Law School and future president of the Tennessee Bar Association.[30] One must assume that McDermott's involvement came through Curtis's professional connections. Curtis needed money to pursue an appeal because the court required the appellant to obtain an appeal bond, which was basically a prepayment of the court costs. Such bonds could be paid in either cash or property, but Curtis offered neither. Instead, he filed a "pauper's oath," which allowed him to avoid paying the bond. Filing an appeal and applying for a pauper's bond would have required an extensive knowledge of the workings of the criminal justice system, making legal advice or assistance invaluable.

The Tennessee Court of Civil Appeals heard the case in 1915. At the hearing, the counsel for the attorney general contested Curtis's claim on several counts. First, he contested the appeals court's jurisdiction on the matter, claiming that such petitions could be heard only in circuit court. Second, the attorney general's counsel asserted that Curtis had lost his citizenship upon being declared infamous and therefore was not eligible to file as a pauper. According to this argument, Curtis's infamy made him incompetent to testify in court and therefore incompetent to take the pauper's oath.

The court sided with Curtis in all these matters. First, it claimed appellate jurisdiction on all judgments of the circuit court, including petitions for restoration of citizenship. In other words, the Court of Civil Appeals asserted its right to overturn a circuit court's judgment on such matters. It also upheld Curtis's right to apply for a pauper's oath. The court found that since infamous individuals could testify on their own behalf in criminal cases, they should also be able to make affidavits on their own behalf to appeal judgments against them. Although the court recognized that infamous individuals were not citizens, it found that they were state residents and were therefore entitled to make such affidavits. Finally, the court ruled that the controversy over the missing keys did not amount to a reason to deny his petition. "This record satisfies us that the petitioner had nothing to do with the loss of those keys, and the circuit court should have . . . granted him the relief sought in his petition." Curtis's citizenship rights were restored, and he was charged for the costs of the court proceedings. A few months later the Tennessee Supreme Court affirmed the judgment.[31]

Canary Curtis used his personal and professional connections to navigate the legal process, scoring a victory in the Tennessee Court of Civil Appeals. The historical record does not indicate why his original petition was denied in the circuit court. Presumably, the missing keys were not the real issue, but it is unclear why the circuit court twice refused to grant his petition. Race and politics were likely the main issue, although it may have been something else entirely. Whatever the reasons for the initial refusal at the circuit court level, the appeals court found the local court's reasoning inadequate and granted Canary Curtis full citizenship rights.

A year after Curtis's victory in Tennessee, a dispute over the enforcement of disfranchisement laws brought two African American men to court in Missouri. That state's 1875 constitution disfranchised individuals convicted of felonies or infamous crimes.[32] A 1909 statute also denied such individuals the ability to run for office or serve on juries.[33] Then in 1912 a state supreme court decision held that the civil disabilities incurred for felony grand larceny should also be assigned to those convicted of misdemeanor petit larceny.[34] These developments expanded the collateral consequences of criminal conviction and helped set the stage for a controversy that unfolded in 1916 in St. Louis.

The 1916 election was important because it occurred during a shift in the balance of political power in the city. St. Louis was an important destination in the Great Migration, and the growing black population enhanced the political power of the Republican Party there. In 1910 St. Louis had 43,960 African American residents; this number climbed to 69,854 by 1920, a 58 percent increase. In comparison, the white population of the city increased only 9.4 percent during this period.[35] Voting by the new migrants helped put the GOP in control of city politics until the 1930s.[36] Democrats, in this time of social and political transition, sought to limit the electoral impact of the new southern migrants in various ways.

The suggestion that criminality offered a reason to disfranchise these new black migrants from the South first surfaced in St. Louis during a hotly contested election for state superintendent of public schools. Democrat Howard A. Gass filed a court challenge to the victory of Republican William P. Evans. Gass claimed that 1,100 black votes had been cast illegally for the Republican candidate. These illegal votes, Gass said, had come from recent migrants who had been improperly registered. Many had listed their residences as lodging houses or boardinghouses in African American neighborhoods, and multiple individuals claimed to live at the same address. Gass suggested that those who listed temporary addresses did not really live there and were engaged in election fraud. Furthermore, Gass pointed out, individuals who did live in such "disreputable" residences should not be able to vote. He argued that these votes should be stripped from Evans's total, which would give Gass the victory.[37]

The court responded to these arguments by defending black voters and taking issue with allegations of African American immorality and criminality. First, the court explained why African Americans tended to live in temporary residences in segregated neighborhoods: "prevailing social conditions irresistibly drive negroes to herd together." So the court rejected

Gass's claim that the presence of numerous African American voters living in the same or adjacent residences was irregular or suspicious. Furthermore, the court pointed out that these new migrants moved frequently, so the fact that many voters could not be located weeks or months after the election was no surprise and did not prove electoral corruption.[38] As for the claim that African American voters, by virtue of their residence in disreputable locations, should be disfranchised, the court responded this way: "Exconvicts [*sic*], unpardoned, may be disfranchised; but up to this time technical or actual sexual morality is not made a statutory test of a voter by the Missouri lawmaker. When that day comes, if ever, there will be fine grinding in the mill—but no matter about that. As the law now stands, we do not understand it would avail contestant aught to show that all or any of those negroes were ethically incorrect."[39]

The tactics used by Democrats to dispute black votes failed in 1910, but with partisan and racial tensions escalating in 1916, some party leaders tried again. In March of that year St. Louis held a special election to consider a residential segregation ordinance, and it passed by a large majority. Despite the new law's title, "An Ordinance to Prevent Ill Feeling, Conflict and Collisions between the White and Colored Races, and to Preserve the Public Peace," its passage indicated an escalation in racial tensions.[40] That fall's presidential election was closely contested, and many correctly predicted that Missouri would be a key battleground. Democrats hoped the state would go to Woodrow Wilson, while Republicans hoped to put the state's electoral votes in Charles Evans Hughes's column. The result in densely populated St. Louis was critical to both sides.

In the weeks before Election Day a group of Missouri Democrats came up with a plan. In charge of the effort was Breckenridge Long, who would later serve as Woodrow Wilson's assistant secretary of the navy and Franklin Roosevelt's ambassador to Italy. Long is also remembered as a key player in the Roosevelt administration's decision not to relax immigration laws and allow Jewish refugees from the Holocaust to enter the United States.[41] Long later testified that the Election Day plan had been hatched by Edward A. Glenn, a longtime Democratic Party activist.[42] First, Long dispatched about twenty young attorneys to comb the criminal court records and compile lists of African American voters who had been convicted of crimes.[43] This research produced a list of approximately 3,000 names, or about 25 percent of the registered African American voters in the city.[44] Democrats would use these lists to challenge African American voters at the polls.

Long and his allies used their influence over the Police Board (which was run by Democrats) to undermine the authority of the Election Commission (which was run by Republicans). The Election Commission had ordered that police officers be "shifted"—moved around town to different neighborhoods—on Election Day, arguing that officers who worked in particular neighborhoods had built connections with local citizens and thus might be more inclined toward corruption. Thus, on Election Day, the police department was supposed to transfer officers to different districts for the day, with the hope that they would enforce the laws more fairly. Long, however, asked his allies on the Police Board to refuse to comply with this plan.[45]

The day before the election, the *St. Louis Republic* published a statement by Long warning African American voters: "Democratic challengers in every affected precinct in the sixteen wards have been given a precinct list of the negroes who have registered illegally. AS RAPIDLY AS THEY ARRIVE AT THE POLLS THEY WILL BE CHALLENGED. IF THEY INSIST ON CASTING THEIR BALLOTS AND START TO SWEAR IN THEIR VOTE, THEY WILL BE ARRESTED AT ONCE, CHARGED WITH PERJURY."[46] The police geared up to help. Chief of Police William Young instructed his officers that election laws should be "rigidly enforced."[47] Republicans responded by publishing a notice in the local African American newspaper, the *St. Louis Argus,* reassuring their supporters. Voters who were properly registered "need not fear any man," and free legal counsel would be available for those that needed it.[48]

Motivating the Democrats was the specter of "negro colonization." Democrats claimed that Republicans intentionally brought African Americans from the South and registered them to vote in an attempt to boost Republican ballots. The *Republic* asserted that Republicans had "colonized" 3,000 illegal voters in St. Louis. Fred English, a former Democratic candidate for Congress, claimed to have personally witnessed this importation of voters:

On October 19 I went to Union Station to take a train to Maysville, KY . . . I saw a Mobile & Ohio train come into Union Station with fifteen coaches full of negroes. There were so many negroes on the train that they blocked up the midway of Union Station. I questioned about twenty of the negroes as to their reason for coming and they said that they had come from Mississippi on a $3 excursion, but nearly all of them stated that they intended to stay in this part of the country for a few weeks. This sort of thing

went on in several of the States bordering Missouri in an attempt
to swing the election, and the committee finding this out began
the investigation which resulted in the uncovering of about 3,000
illegally registered negroes in this city.[49]

Police Chief Young fanned the flames, claiming, "Thousands of negroes
in the south were . . . invading St. Louis, East St. Louis and other northern
cities in an effort to carry close states for the Republican party."[50]

Highlighting "colonization" and tying migration to political corruption would offer an excuse to disfranchise black voters while energizing
the Democratic base. A similar set of circumstances was unfolding across
the river in East St. Louis, Illinois. The "colonization conspiracy" there
has received more historical attention because accusations of crime and
electoral manipulation by recent black migrants escalated racial tensions,
culminating in the East St. Louis race riot.[51] Whereas Democrats claimed
that black southerners were entering the city to aid Republicans, Republicans suggested that voter suppression tactics from the South had come to
the city instead. The St. Louis Argus reported, "This effort on the part of St.
Louis Democracy is an effort to Southernize the ballot."[52]

On Election Day in St. Louis, Democrats dispatched workers to precincts in black neighborhoods. These "challengers" had lists of African
Americans in each precinct identified by Long's men as having prior,
disfranchising convictions. When an African American man tried to vote,
challengers would consult their lists to determine whether that voter had
been tagged as having a prior conviction.[53] Newspaper accounts disagree
as to what information the challengers possessed. One challenger claimed
that his list included full names and addresses of targeted voters.[54] However, in a statement released ten days after the election, the city's election
commissioner, a Democrat, said that challengers confronted any black voters whose last name matched one on their lists, regardless of the address.[55]
In fact, the techniques of challengers may have varied from precinct to
precinct. Court records did not list addresses, so it is unclear how such
information, if it existed, had been gathered.[56]

When men whose names appeared on the lists attempted to vote, the
challengers would step forward and dispute their right to do so. At this
point, apparently, some individuals gave up and left without voting. However, others contested the challenge. According to protocol, when this happened, the election judges at the precinct would decide how to proceed.
Each precinct had four judges—two Democrats and two Republicans—

charged with assessing the qualifications of each voter. In the event of a challenge, the judges would ask the voter to swear he had never been arrested or convicted and ask the challenger to swear to the challenge. Then the four judges had to decide between these two conflicting stories. Generally, they voted along party lines—two to admit the challenged vote and two to reject it. This split decision resulted in the voter being allowed to vote, but the ballot was placed in a separate envelope for "rejected ballots." The legitimacy of the vote would be assessed later.

A variety of scenarios unfolded across the city. At each of the city's 500 polling places, police officers were stationed inside. In some precincts, according to reports, officers arrested African American voters immediately after they were challenged. In other instances they waited until the judges had allowed the individual to vote and then arrested him. Police escorted others out of the polling place without arresting them but prevented them from voting. The St. Louis Argus reported that some individuals simply left without voting, "refus[ing] to be humiliated."[57] By noon eighty-nine African American men had been arrested at polling places.[58] According to the final count, police arrested ninety-six African American men and two white men on allegations of trying to vote with prior, disfranchising convictions.[59]

As word of the proceedings spread, Republican leaders sought to halt these tactics. By 9:30 A.M. a group that included Republican city committee chair John Schmoll and Republican mayor Henry Kiel arrived at city hall, seeking intervention. They met with the Board of Police Commissioners, which agreed to tell officers to stop arresting voters based solely on the accusations of challengers; three of the four precinct judges had to request the arrest for the police to act. The Board of Election Commissioners issued an order that challengers had to have personal knowledge of the people they challenged; they could not simply read names from a list.

At midday, circuit court judge Karl Kimmel, a Republican, issued an injunction to restrain police from intimidating voters.[60] This slowed the arrests, but Democrats continued to use other tactics to suppress Republican votes throughout the rest of the day. Democratic operatives continued to challenge African American voters with allegations of prior convictions. As noted earlier, in the case of a split decision by the judges, the ballot would be placed in a separate envelope for challenged ballots.[61] Judges rejected about 1,000 votes in this manner.[62]

The Seventeenth Ward saw the largest number of challenged voters.[63] For example, when Matthew Bell, a forty-one-year-old black fireman, tried to vote, he was challenged by Democrat John McFadden. Bell was allowed to vote, but judges placed his ballot in the provisional ballot envelope. When Joseph P. Crofts, a thirty-six-year-old porter, tried to vote in another Seventeenth Ward precinct, Democrat Michael Weisman challenged him. The judges allowed Crofts to vote, but then police arrested him. Events like this took place all over the city.[64]

On Election Day the Republican Party did its best to protect black voters, using the parts of the city government that were under its control. Republicans held the majority of the seats on the Election Commission, and Mayor Henry Kiel was a Republican as well.[65] Bondsmen hired by the party waited at the police stations to free arrested men as soon as possible. Judge Kimmel and another Republican circuit court judge, Calvin Miller, signed bonds so that arrested individuals would be released immediately. Then Republican Party workers would drive them back to the precincts to try to vote again. For example, when William Baker tried to vote that morning in the Fourth Ward, he was arrested. When he was released on bond later in the day, he returned to the polling place, but election officers still refused to let him vote.[66]

Democrats used their power in the police department to try to block the participation of African American voters while Republican leaders tried, in kind, to protect these voters. African American Democrats, however, were not so lucky. Police mistakenly arrested a Democrat named Frank Edge, along with a number of other African American men. Edge's vocal insistence that his arrest was a mistake led Republicans to realize that he was a Democrat, and they refused to bail him out with the others. All the Republicans were freed, but Edge remained in jail for the rest of the day.[67]

An important side effect of all this controversy was a significant delay for voters, particularly at precincts in African American neighborhoods.[68] A Republican Party official told the press that in some precincts there was a two-hour wait to vote while challengers and judges interrogated the voters.[69] In a precinct on Laclede Avenue, according to another Republican leader, sixty voters waited for two hours, but only eight were allowed to vote.

Several voters used their professional connections to protect them or to aid their efforts to vote. When James Cole tried to vote, a challenger claimed he had served a term in the county workhouse in 1905. Cole was exceptionally well known and well respected locally. He had, according to the *Argus,* "served in some of the fashionable and well-known families in St. Louis for nearly fifty years at various functions." He was also personally acquainted with all the judges, who therefore allowed him to vote.[70] Police also arrested two men who worked as janitors in the Municipal Court Building, as well as the porter of the former mayor and the chauffeur of an Election Board member. Their arrests were highlighted in reports to the press.[71] Julius S. Walsh Jr., the industrial commissioner of the Wabash Railroad, protested when his stableman, James Siler, and his butler, George Miller, were threatened and intimidated when they tried to vote. Walsh insisted that these men led crime-free lives and had valid registrations.[72] A subsequent newspaper article confirmed that "businessmen and others, whose employees had been arrested without cause, protested against this action."[73]

The day after the election, the *St. Louis Daily Globe Democrat* published a list of arrested voters in an article titled "GOP Voters Arrested in Police Intimidation." The article chronicled the experiences of forty-nine individuals arrested on Election Day. All but two of these men were African American, and most had tried to vote in the Seventeenth or Sixth Wards. Averaging just over forty years of age, these men worked in a variety of professions, including as porters, laborers, waiters, firemen, barbers, teamsters, cooks, and drivers.[74]

Three days after the election, Judge Miller discharged the cases against all the men arrested at the polls that day.[75] The police insisted they had done nothing wrong. In an angry rebuttal, Chief Young told his officers to assist fully with the prosecution of "all negro criminals who voted or attempted to vote last Tuesday."[76]

Republican leaders also sought to prevent Democrats from using such tactics again. The Election Board met and voted to revise the challenger statutes.[77] The *St. Louis Argus* supported this plan, editorializing that the law gave "judges of election booths arbitrary power to reject ballots of challenged voters."[78] A grand jury investigated, calling members of the Election Board to testify. The grand jury retained a special prosecutor and made plans to work with the U.S. district attorney.[79] Although the grand jury indicted several election officials working in the Sixth and Seventeenth Wards for feloniously hindering voters, I found no evidence that these cases actually went to trial.[80] A group of individuals formed the Citizens Nonpartisan Committee, aimed at prosecuting all cases of election fraud, but again, I found no evidence that their work had much impact.[81]

The most dramatic outcome of the events on Election Day were two lawsuits filed by African American men who had been refused the right to vote. The first to file was Henry Lucas, a thirty-two-year-old teamster and Missouri native. Lucas had been arrested in the Fifth Precinct of the Eighth Ward following an accusation from Democratic challenger Theodore Sandman that he had spent time in prison for a grand larceny conviction in 1906.[82] The arresting officer, James. E. Sullivan, later testified that Sandman requested the arrest. Sullivan explained, "I said to Lucas: 'This man accuses you of illegal voting and orders you arrested.' Lucas said 'I am not guilty. I was never arrested before in my life.' We stood there awhile, and then Sandman said: 'Let's go up to the station with him.'"[83] When the three arrived at the Soulard Street station, Captain George T. McNamee asked why Lucas had been arrested. Sandman said that Lucas was guilty of fraudulent voting and claimed to have a "slip of paper" with Lucas's name on it. Later Sandman said that a man named "Briney" Kennedy had given him the paper. The police kept Lucas in jail for two and a half hours until Republican Party workers bailed him out.[84]

Lucas sued Sandman, Breckenridge Long, and John J. Kennedy, the Democratic city committeeman in the Eighth Precinct. He asked for $5,000 in actual damages, $5,000 in punitive damages, and court costs.[85] Lucas had significant backing from the local Republican establishment and was represented in court by a prominent St. Louis law firm, Ferris and Rosskopf, which had close connections to the Republican Party.[86] This support from the party was obviously useful in obtaining counsel and, most likely, in paying the court costs, which amounted to $251.85. Records from the trial indicate that Lucas had been required to give a bond or deposit security in advance to cover these costs, and he opted to deposit cash.[87]

A few weeks into the trial Lucas chose to drop the suit against Long and focus on Sandman and Kennedy.[88] Then the judge upheld a motion for an "involuntary non suit" against Kennedy, effectively dismissing that case.[89] Sandman was now the sole defendant. Lucas's attorneys took depositions from police officers, precinct workers, and Democratic Party officials.[90] The suit accused Sandman of causing Lucas to be wrongfully arrested and detained in an attempt to intimidate him, "disgrace" him, and "deprive him of his liberty."[91] Sandman replied that he had the right under the law to challenge voters. Sandman maintained that the decision by the police to arrest Lucas was not his fault; he did not have the power or the authority to arrest anyone.[92] The suit dragged on until 1920, when the jury ultimately found in favor of Lucas and awarded him $250 in actual damages and $50 in punitive damages. Lucas received full payment of the judgment.[93] Sandman moved for a new trial, but the judge refused his request.[94] Lucas had won.

Another disfranchised African American voter, John L. Sullivan, filed suit shortly after Lucas. Sullivan claimed that he had been prevented from voting when a Democratic challenger asserted he had been convicted of petit larceny in 1896 and served a forty-one-day sentence in the work-house. Sullivan said he had never been in the workhouse and had not been arrested or convicted anywhere. He had not even been living in St. Louis in 1896, having moved there in 1910.[95] Sullivan was freed on bond after about two hours and returned to the polling place to try again to cast his ballot. The Democratic precinct judge again refused him, saying he had already voted. When Sullivan continued to argue, the judge finally gave him a ballot but warned him it would be put in the "rejected" envelope.[96]

Sullivan's $11,000 claim—$1,000 in actual damages and $10,000 in punitive damages—charged a large group of individuals with intimidating him on Election Day. Sullivan, who was represented by attorney Taylor R. Young, identified a total of twenty people in his suit, including Long, four members of the Police Board, Police Chief William Young, George War-ner (whom he identified as "president of the Democratic machine" of the Sixth Ward), the two Democratic precinct judges, members of the Demo-cratic Central Committee, the local police captain, and the two police of-ficers who arrested him. Finally he named Horace Rumsey, "a Democrat and anxious and willing to assist in the perpetration of the fraud herein mentioned."[97] Sullivan's agenda was grander than Lucas's. Whereas Lucas had simply sued those who tried to block him from voting, Sullivan more ambitiously hoped to reach further into the police force and the larger Democratic establishment, essentially claiming a conspiracy. He sued not just on his own behalf but also on behalf of the black community, asserting that the twenty defendants had conspired together to "concoct a scheme to prevent the plaintiff and thousands of other people of his color" from voting. He also claimed that the defendants had "employed a number of young lawyers" to search criminal records and compile a list of disfran-chised voters. Then these lists were used to target the plaintiff and "voters of his color."[98]

Sullivan had a much harder time paying the court costs than Lucas had. This was due in part to the large number of defendants. About fifty people were subpoenaed and deposed in preparation for the trial, for a total cost (according to a defense motion) of about $700.[99] Court documents indicate multiple requests for dismissal by the defense due to Sullivan's failure to pay the costs. On February 17 Sullivan deposited $50 with the clerk, with the agreement that he would pay another $50 in thirty days.[100]

A motion to dismiss was set aside when Sullivan paid another $50 on March 30, 1918.[101] However, the records cease at that point, and it appears that the case was never heard in court.[102]

Lucas and Sullivan undertook their efforts without help from the small but growing movement to secure civil rights through legal challenges. The NAACP was active in St. Louis, and it was organizing protests and challenges to the residential segregation ordinance; however, there is no indication that it responded to the events on Election Day or supported these two lawsuits. The articulated strategy of the group was to take cases "which show actual discrimination because of color" and those that "test broad principles."[103] The cases of Sullivan and Lucas did not fit the bill. They were not incidents of *clear* racial discrimination by the standards of the day—certainly not as clear as a racially restrictive residential segregation ordinance or Oklahoma's grandfather clause, for example.

The cases of Lucas and Sullivan illustrate the shortcomings resulting from a lack of coordination in legal strategy, a coordination the NAACP would bring to civil rights cases in years to come. Although it is possible that there was an agreement that Lucas would pursue a narrow claim and Sullivan a broader one, this is unlikely, and there is no evidence of it. I can think of no other reasonable explanation for why the two men would pursue separate claims. Their duplication of effort was costly and inefficient, and it must have reduced the impact of their assertions. In particular, Sullivan's claim that Long and others conspired to disfranchise a wide swath of the black population certainly would have been bolstered by more plaintiffs.

The difficulties all three plaintiffs faced in financing their lawsuits underscore the significance of the NAACP's contribution to the black freedom movement. Claims backed by the national organization would have better financial resources and lawyers who were well versed in making arguments for civil rights and against racial discrimination. Their efforts would be better coordinated—unlike Lucas's and Sullivan's chaotic, self-guided efforts. Lack of financial resources proved to be a challenge to Curtis and an insurmountable obstacle to Sullivan, because filing civil suits cost money. With the help of the dean of the University of Tennessee Law School, Curtis solved the problem by filing a pauper's oath. Lucas, too, received assistance from white allies, albeit allies with an explicitly partisan agenda. Sullivan may have had help from Republican allies as well, but not enough to pursue his case to the finish.

White attorneys stood up for these black plaintiffs in the courts, but

African American forerunners and community members also made their victories possible. Curtis was following in the footsteps of other African American men who had succeeded in getting voting rights in Knox County and elsewhere in Tennessee. His sense of entitlement to those rights clearly motivated his claim and stemmed at least in part from the fact that many other black men had petitioned for and received their voting rights in Tennessee courts. Reaching back even further into history demonstrates that both these victories were due to the fact that African Americans had obtained the right to equal standing in court during the Reconstruction years, a critical element of citizenship and a right that is essential to the defense of other rights.[104]

Although Lucas and Sullivan were the only men to take St. Louis officials and local Democratic operatives to court, a collective outrage in the African American community must have encouraged them to pursue their cases. Many of those who faced obstacles on Election Day confronted their accusers, challenged their assertions, and demanded the right to vote. Many who were arrested returned to the polls to try again. Dozens told their tales to the newspapers.[105] When Lucas and Sullivan went to court, they spoke for all disfranchised African American voters in the city.

However, neither individual efforts nor collective outrage would be as significant as partisanship in enfranchising St. Louis's African American population. A growing tide of Republican power in St. Louis meant that the party would strive to protect the political rights of its voters in the coming decade. Black southern migrants to St. Louis would find a new political landscape where their votes counted, unlike the one they left behind.

In Tennessee, *In re: Curtis* set two important precedents for convicted individuals. First, this case determined that individuals whose civil rights had been denied due to prior convictions could still file a pauper's oath. Second, the court held that Curtis had the right to restoration of his citizenship because he had demonstrated that he was a respected citizen. The court's decision set a significant precedent, rejecting restoration as a kind of favor handed out when judges felt benevolent. Rather, the court saw citizenship restoration as a right—a convicted individual who behaves well and has several "unimpeachable" citizens who will testify on his or her behalf is "entitled to be restored to his rights as a citizen."[106] Curtis proved that former convicts could and would demand their legal rights.

Curtis's triumph did not lead to successful petitions by other African American men in Knoxville. Records indicate that he was the last African American man to be restored to citizenship in the city for at least several decades. Perhaps sensing the degenerating racial environment in the city or concerned about negative responses to his legal victory, Curtis and his family moved away. In the 1920 census he is listed as living in Belmont, Ohio, and working as a laborer in a steel mill; ten years later the family had settled in Cleveland, where Curtis was employed as a janitor.[107]

The 1916 election in St. Louis was neither the first nor the last in which allegations of prior convictions were used to disfranchise African American voters. The Election Day events in St. Louis paralleled a similar incident in Richmond, Virginia, in 1888. There, Democratic challengers stationed at precincts in African American neighborhoods delayed the votes of African American men by asking them many questions, including about their prior criminal activity. They used accusations of prior convictions, as well as other issues, both to dissuade individual voters and to slow the electoral procedure so that many African Americans were unable to vote before the polls closed.[108]

These elections also foreshadowed recent contests in the United States, most famously in 2000. In Florida, African American voters were disproportionately affected by false accusations of prior disfranchising convictions. Long lines formed at the polls in St. Louis, too, that year, due in part to controversies and delays over the removal of certain names from the voter registration lists; as a result, a judge ordered that the polls remain open three hours past their normal closing time. The 2004 election in Ohio offered similar stories—long lines of voters in predominantly Democratic and African American precincts. There, many claimed that the Republican secretary of state had intentionally undersupplied African American neighborhoods with voting machines. Intimidation and delay are two tactics that have been used repeatedly in history to disfranchise African American voters and achieve a partisan agenda.[109]

Although the victories of Lucas and Curtis were limited, they were achieved by mobilizing personal resources, forming alliances, and doggedly pursuing legal action in times and places where the odds were stacked against them and a national consensus on African American voting rights had yet to be reached. Despite the fact that Curtis, Lucas, and Sullivan all acted independently of the NAACP and that none claimed to be the victim of racial discrimination, their insistence on their right to vote at this critical moment in history was part of African Americans' larger struggle for the rights of citizenship. Beyond the key court battles fought by the NAACP, and beyond the organized civil rights movement, were disorganized acts of protest that stoked the fire of resistance. African Americans challenged laws and practices that denied them access to the ballot box in diverse settings. Recognizing this history of African American resistance to laws that disfranchise based on criminal conviction helps underscore the fact that these laws have made a unique contribution to white supremacy that continues to this day.

Notes

The research for this essay was supported by a grant from the Open Society Institute's Soros Justice Fund and a Middle Tennessee State University Faculty Research and Creative Activity Award. Michael Everman and the staff at the Missouri State Archives–St. Louis provided valuable research assistance.

1. On crime-based disfranchisement laws passed in the aftermath of Reconstruction in the South, see Pippa Holloway, "'A Chicken-Stealer Shall Lose His Vote': Disfranchisement for Larceny in the South, 1874–1890," *Journal of Southern History* 75, no. 4 (November 2009): 931–62. On the racial intent of such laws passed at southern constitutional conventions in the 1890s, see Alec C. Ewald, "Civil Death: The Ideological Paradox of Criminal Disenfranchisement Law in the United States," *Wisconsin Law Review* (2002): 1045–138; Angela Behrens, Christopher Uggen, and Jeff Manza, "Ballot Manipulation and the 'Menace of Negro Domination': Racial Threat and Felon Disenfranchisement in the United States, 1850–2002," *American Journal of Sociology* 109, no. 3 (November 2003): 559–605.

2. *Richardson v. Ramirez,* 418 U.S. 24 (1974).

3. "Statements Made by Democrats on Vote Controversy," *St. Louis Star,* n.d., Tuskegee Institute News Clippings File.

4. "Bring the Vote Thieves to Judgment," *St. Louis Argus,* November 10, 1916.

5. Matthew Lakin, "'A Dark Night': The Knoxville Race Riot of 1919," *Journal of East Tennessee History* 72 (2000): 1–29.

6. Rayford Logan, *The Negro in American Life and Thought: The Nadir, 1877–1901* (New York: Collier Books, 1965).

7. On legal defeats for black voting rights activists in this earlier period, see R. Volney Riser, *Defying Disfranchisement: Black Voting Rights Activism in the Jim Crow South, 1890–1908* (Baton Rouge: Louisiana State University Press, 2010).

8. *Guinn v. United States,* 238 U.S. 347 (1915).

9. *Tennessee Acts of 1829,* chap. 23, sec. 71.

10. *In re: Curtis,* 6 Tenn. Civ. App. (1915); "Grand Jury Didn't Finish," *Daily Journal and Tribune* (Knoxville, Tenn.), December 21, 1907, 8; Knox County Criminal Court Minute Books, vol. 53, pp. 234–35, December 19, 1907; vol. 53,

p. 243, December 20, 1907; vol. 57, p. 335, April 20, 1910, East Tennessee Historical Society, Knoxville. Curtis is listed as a prisoner at Brushy Mountain Penitentiary in the 1910 census.

11. Tennessee Constitution of 1834, art. IV, sec. 2; Alexander Keyssar, *The Right to Vote: The Contested History of Democracy in the United States* (New York: Basic Books, 2000), 61–63.

12. *Tennessee Acts of 1851–1852,* chap. 30, sec. 1. The 1858 Tennessee Code added the penalty of disfranchisement for infamy, as required by the 1834 constitution, stipulating that infamous individuals lost the vote for the remainder of their lives unless they petitioned the court for restoration. *Tennessee Code of 1858,* sec. 834, 5226.

13. I found seventy-six petitions for restoration in the Knox County court minutes between 1881 and 1940.

14. Knox County court records continued to identify petitioners by race in this period. These records indicate two more rejected petitions in the years after the Curtis case, but both were submitted by white men, and both appear to have been rejected on reasonable grounds. One man's petition was dismissed because he failed to appear at his own court hearing, and the other's petition was denied because the court determined that crime he had been convicted of—violation of the age of consent laws—was not an infamous offense. Petition of L. C. Lovett, Knox County Circuit Court Minutes, roll I-39, p. 310, November 29, 1926; petition of Ben Carroll, Knox County Circuit Court Minutes, roll I-47, p. 396, September 6, 1938.

15. I have surveyed pardon records and petitions for the restoration of citizenship in Virginia, South Carolina, North Carolina, Georgia, Alabama, and Mississippi. The results of this more extensive survey will be published elsewhere.

16. Frederic D. Ogden, *The Poll Tax in the South* (Tuscaloosa: University of Alabama Press, 1958), 96–98; Joseph H. Cartwright, *The Triumph of Jim Crow: Tennessee Race Relations in the 1880's* (Knoxville: University of Tennessee Press, 1976), 242–50; V. O. Key, *Southern Politics in State and Nation* (New York: Alfred A. Knopf, 1949), 74–75; J. Morgan Kousser, *The Shaping of Southern Politics: Suffrage Restriction and the Establishment of the One-Party South, 1880–1910* (New Haven, Conn.: Yale University Press, 1974), 104–23.

17. The phrase "honesty, respectability, and veracity" comes from the statute. *Tennessee Acts of 1851–1852,* chap. 30, sec. 1.

18. In 1915 Roscoe Eakes of Giles County had served nearly a year of a three- to five-year sentence for unlawful carnal knowledge when Governor Tom Rye pardoned him; eight months later he filed successfully for restoration. Anderson County's Bruce Pemberton worked even faster. Rendered infamous in January 1933 on an arson charge (he and two accomplices were accused of setting fire to three automobiles and a barn belonging to one of the three for an insurance claim), he was sentenced to a year in prison but successfully petitioned for a suspended sentence. His rights were restored five months later. Giles County Circuit Court,

Criminal Minutes, roll A-1411, vol. 12, p. 335 (criminal case); Giles County Circuit Court, Civil Minutes, roll A-1419, vol. 14, p. 354, October 19, 1915 (restoration); Anderson County Circuit Court Criminal Minutes, roll A-4095, vol. 3, pp. 138–40, 308–9 (criminal case), Tennessee State Library and Archives, Nashville.

19. *In re: Curtis.*

20. Jack Neely, "The Chill in the Air: One Century Ago, the Traditional Christmas Disaster," *Metro Pulse* (Knoxville, Tenn.), December 21, 2006, http://www.metropulse.com/news/2006/Dec/21/secret_history-2006-51/ (accessed February 18, 2010).

21. Vivien M. L. Miller finds that African American men serving prison sentences often sought assistance from white men—including former employers—in seeking pardons and gaining release from incarceration. She notes, "Race, gender, and class relations were marked by personal, interclass, and interracial ties which could be paternalistic and patronizing, but which at the same time could yield the desired outcome for social inferiors and offenders. Indifference or hostility was exhibited toward assertive and threatening black and lower-class white men and women, but paternalism was demonstrated toward 'good negroes' and 'model prisoners' of both races." Vivien M. L. Miller, *Crime, Sexual Violence and Clemency: Florida's Pardon Board and Penal System in the Progressive Era* (Gainesville: University Press of Florida, 2000), 159.

22. Petition of Allonzo Jones, Convict and Fugitive Records—Applications for Clemency, 1858–1942, RCB 10008, C 181566, Georgia Archives, Morrow.

23. Alabama Board of Pardons, Applications for Pardons, Paroles, or Remission of Fines 1846–1915, box SG 10274, Alabama Department of Archives and History, Montgomery.

24. On the social and personal ties between African Americans and whites in the rural South, see Mark Schultz, *The Rural Face of White Supremacy: Beyond Jim Crow* (Urbana: University of Illinois Press, 2005).

25. On the 1915 election in Knoxville, see Lakin, "'A Dark Night,'" 1–29.

26. Letter from Governor Cobb to A. G. Gordon, July 20, 1880, Alabama Board of Pardons, Applications for Pardons, Paroles, or Remission of Fines, 1846–1915, box SG 10311.

27. Letter to Governor from J. E. Gardner, December 28, 1894, Convict and Fugitive Records—Applications for Clemency, 1858–1942, RCB 30680, C 177525, Georgia Archives.

28. *In re: Curtis.*

29. Ibid.

30. On McDermott, see *Law Notes* (Long Island, N.Y.: Edward Thompson, 1921), 96.

31. *In re: Curtis.*

32. Missouri Constitution of 1820, sec. 14, art. 3; Missouri Constitution of 1865, sec. 26, art. 2; Missouri Constitution of 1875, art. 8, sec. 10.

33. Missouri Revised Statutes 1909, sec. 4925: "Any person who shall be convicted of arson, burglary, robbery or larceny, in any degree, in this article specified shall be incompetent to serve as a juror in any cause, and shall be forever disqualified from voting at any election or holding any office of honor, trust or profit within this state."

34. *Hartwig v. Hartwig,* 160 Mo. App. 284 (1912).

35. Chicago Commission on Race Relations, *The Negro in Chicago: A Study of Race Relations and a Race Riot* (Chicago: University of Chicago Press, 1922), 80.

36. Lana Stein, *St. Louis Politics: The Triumph of Tradition* (St. Louis: Missouri Historical Society Press, 2002), 13–20.

37. *Gass v. Evans,* 244 Mo. 329 (1912).

38. Ibid.

39. Ibid.

40. Stephen Grant Meyer, *As Long as They Don't Move Next Door: Segregation and Racial Conflict in American Neighborhoods* (Lanham, Md.: Rowman and Littlefield, 2000), 20–22.

41. Richard Breitman and Alan M. Kraut, *American Refugee Policy and European Jewry, 1933–1945* (Bloomington: Indiana University Press, 1988), 126–45.

42. "Long Declares Glenn Planned Wholesale Arrest of Negroes," *St. Louis Daily Globe Democrat* (hereafter *DGD*), December 3, 1916.

43. "Injunctions to Stop Arrest of Negroes Refused," *St. Louis Post Dispatch* (hereafter *PD*), November 7, 1916; "Long Declares Glenn Planned Wholesale Arrest of Negroes."

44. "Election Board Admits Wholesale Fraud in St. Louis," *DGD,* November 17, 1916; "Lawyers Say They Gave Lists to Long in Election Probe," *DGD,* November 24, 1916. Later, press accounts of this controversy emphasized that the Democrats collected only the names of African Americans.

45. "Election Board Admits Wholesale Fraud."

46. "Intimidated Voter Files $10,000 Suit against Democrats," *DGD,* November 18, 1916.

47. William Young, General Order No. 228, November 2, 1916, reprinted in *St. Louis Police Journal* 5, no. 32 (November 4, 1916): 1, 8 (this was the official organ of the Board of Police Commissioners and the Police Department of St. Louis).

48. "Warning to Negro Voters," *St. Louis Argus,* November 3, 1916.

49. "Statements Made by Democrats on Vote Controversy," *St. Louis Star,* n.d., Tuskegee Institute News Clippings File.

50. "Circuit Attorney to Prosecute," *St. Louis Police Journal* 5, no. 3 (November 1916): 3.

51. Elliott M. Rudwick, *Race Riot at East St. Louis* (Carbondale: Southern Illinois University Press, 1964).

52. "Bring the Vote Thieves to Judgment," *St. Louis Argus,* November 10, 1916, 4.

53. "Police Keep 3000 Voters from Polls," *DGD,* November 8, 1916, 2, 8.

54. "Officer Tells of Arrest of Man at Polls," *DGD,* November 23, 1916, 2.

55. Steps to Contest the Election of Gardner Taken," *PD,* November 17, 1916, 3.

56. "Checking Registration Laws," *DGD,* December 3, 1916, 12. This article also supported the contention that challengers merely used last names to match convicts to voters.

57. "Against Rejected St. Louis Ballots," *St. Louis Argus,* November 24, 1916, Tuskegee Institute News Clippings File.

58. "Injunctions to Stop Arrest of Negroes Refused"; "Negroes Arrested on Election Day Are All Discharged," *PD,* November 10, 1916.

59. "Grand Jury Has Kiel and Election Board Summoned," *PD,* November 24, 1916.

60. "Police Keep 3000 Voters from Polls."

61. "Election Board Admits Wholesale Fraud."

62. "Grand Jury Has Kiel and Election Board Summoned."

63. "Intimidation Charge False, Says Democrats," *St. Louis Star,* n.d., Tuskegee Institute News Clippings File.

64. "Police Keep 3000 Voters from Polls."

65. In St. Louis the majority of the Police Board members are appointed by the governor, so the city police are effectively under state, not local, control. This was true in 1916 and remains true today.

66. "Police Keep 3000 Voters from Polls."

67. "Negro Democrat Is Arrested by Mistake," *DGD,* November 8, 1916.

68. "Injunctions to Stop Arrest of Negroes Refused."

69. "Police Keep 3000 Voters from Polls."

70. "Intimidated Voter Files $10,000 Suit."

71. "Injunctions to Stop Arrest of Negroes Refused."

72. "Police Keep 3000 Voters from Polls."

73. "Three Indicted after Election Fraud Inquiry," *DGD,* December 3, 1916.

74. Ages and occupations were listed for most but not all of the arrested men. "GOP Voters Arrested in Police Intimidation," *DGD,* November 8, 1916.

75. "Negroes Arrested on Election Day Are All Discharged."

76. "Circuit Attorney to Prosecute," 3.

77. "Move Started to Get Election Law Amended," *PD,* November 22, 1916.

78. "Against Rejected St. Louis Ballots."

79. "Grand Jury Has Kiel and Election Board Summoned."

80. "Indictments Returned in Vote Inquiry," *DGD,* November 30, 1916, 1; "Three Indicted after Election Fraud Inquiry."

81. "Nonpartisan Committee Urges Co-operation to Punish Frauds," *DGD,* November 26, 1916.

82. For the age and occupation of Lucas, see Register of Voters, Record Retention, Office of the Comptroller, Microfilm DA 581, St. Louis City Hall, St. Louis, Missouri.

83. "Officer Tells of Arrest of Man at Polls."

84. Ibid.

85. Plaintiff's petition, case file for *Henry Lucas v. Theodore Sandman et al.*, December 1916, Case File 6916, Circuit Court Case Files, Office of the Circuit Clerk–St. Louis, Missouri State Archives–St. Louis, Office of the Secretary of State; hereafter *Lucas v. Sandman* case file.

86. Ibid. On Ferris and Rosskpof, see Walter B. Stevens, *Centennial History of Missouri (the Center State): One Hundred Years in the Union, 1820–1921* (St. Louis: Clarke Publishing, 1921), 201.

87. List of witnesses and charges, April 7, 1920, *Lucas v. Sandman* case file; minutes of proceedings 1916–1919, *Lucas v. Sandman* case file.

88. Memorandum for clerk, March 10, 1920, *Lucas v. Sandman* case file.

89. Ibid.

90. "Intimidated Voter Files $10,000 Suit."

91. Plaintiff's petition, *Lucas v. Sandman* case file.

92. "Second Amended Answer" of the defendant, *Lucas v. Sandman* case file.

93. Handwritten jury verdict, *Lucas v. Sandman* case file.

94. Minutes of proceedings 1916–1919, *Lucas v. Sandman* case file.

95. "Intimidated Voter Files $10,000 Suit."

96. "Negro Files $11,000 Damage Suit against Democratic Officials," *DGD*, November 29, 1916; "Indictments Returned in Vote Inquiry."

97. Amended petition, case file for *John L. Sullivan v. Breckenridge Long et al.*, December 1916, Case Number 7075, Circuit Court Case Files, Office of the Circuit Clerk–St. Louis, Missouri State Archives–St. Louis, Office of the Secretary of State; hereafter *Sullivan v. Long* case file.

98. "Officer Tells of Arrest of Man at Polls," 2; amended petition, *Sullivan v. Long* case file.

99. Motion for security for costs, January 1917, *Sullivan v. Long* case file.

100. Memorandum for clerk, February 17, 1917, *Sullivan v. Long* case file.

101. Motion to dismiss, February 1918, *Sullivan v. Long* case file; memorandum for clerk, March 30, 1918, *Sullivan v. Long* case file.

102. Minutes of proceedings, *Sullivan v. Long* case file.

103. Report of Chair of Board of Directors, 1916, NAACP Papers, quoted in Susan D. Carle, "Race, Class, and Legal Ethics in the Early NAACP (1910–1920)," *Law and History Review* 20, no. 97 (2002): 118.

104. Eric Foner writes that most states had eliminated bans on court testimony by 1867, although they did this reluctantly and primarily to return such cases to local jurisdiction and out of Freedmen's Bureau control. See Eric Foner, *Reconstruction: America's Unfinished Revolution* (New York: Harper and Row, 1988), 149, 204.

105. "GOP Voters Arrested in Police Intimidation"; "Police Keep 3000 Voters from Polls."

106. *In re: Curtis.*

107. 1920 Census manuscript, Belmont, Ohio, sheet 10, enumeration district 16; 1930 Census manuscript, Cleveland, Ohio, sheet 8, enumeration district 18–346.

108. *House Reports,* 51st Cong., 1st sess., no. 1182 (pt. 1): *Edmund Waddill v. George D. Wise* (Serial 2810, Washington, D.C., 1890), 1–4; Holloway, "'Chicken-Stealer Shall Lose His Vote,'" 952–54.

109. John Hardin Young, Sara L. Dubois, and Rachel Steinberg, "Lessons Learned from the 2000 and 2004 Presidential Elections," in *America Votes! A Guide to Modern Election Law and Voting Rights,* ed. Benjamin E. Griffith (Chicago: ABA Publishing, 2008), 1–18; Tracy Campbell, *Deliver the Vote: A History of Election Fraud, an American Political Tradition—1742–2004* (New York: Carroll and Graff, 2005), 292–340.

"The Community Don't Know What's Good for Them"

Local Politics in the Alabama Black Belt during the Post–Civil Rights Era

George Derek Musgrove and Hasan Kwame Jeffries

Very few residents of Perry County, a majority black, desperately poor rural county in the heart of Alabama, wanted to have anything to do with storing the 3 million cubic yards of arsenic-laced coal ash from a spill that had occurred at a Tennessee power plant in December 2008, but they had little choice in the matter. The county's political leaders, almost all of whom were African American, had agreed to accept the toxic waste for a "host fee" of $3 million, which was more than half the county government's annual budget. "This gives us an opportunity to fund our schools, to help build our roads, to create some things in Perry County that will enhance the lives of individuals," said black county commissioner Fairest Cureton.[1] The financial windfall, however, was of little consolation to residents. "Money ain't worth everything," said Mary Gibson Holley, a retired teacher. "In the long run, they ain't looking [at] what this could do to the community if something goes wrong."[2] Black elected officials, however, dismissed the concerns of their black constituents. Johnny Flowers, a former county commissioner who had helped bring the coal ash to the county, put it bluntly: "The community don't know what's good for them."[3]

The incredibly low regard Perry County's black elected officials had for the thoughts and opinions of their constituents reflected developments in black politics that voting rights activists in the 1960s and 1970s had worked hard to avoid. In the wake of the 1965 Voting Rights Act, which enabled African Americans throughout the South to register en masse, two national civil rights organizations, the Southern Christian Leadership Conference (SCLC) and the Student Nonviolent Coordinating Committee

305

(SNCC), developed voter projects in the Alabama Black Belt, a string of seventeen rural counties with rich black clay soil and majority black populations that extends east to west across the south-central part of the state. The organizations were drawn to the area partly because of the extreme nature of the political exclusion there. At the start of 1965 only a couple of counties in the Black Belt had more than a few dozen African Americans on the voter registration rolls, and some counties, such as Lowndes, did not have any registered African American voters at all. The two groups also focused on the Black Belt because they had organizing assets in the area, having developed desegregation and voting rights projects in Perry, Dallas, Wilcox, and Lowndes counties. In addition, Alabama's Democratic primary was scheduled for May 3, 1966, making it the first election in which newly enfranchised black southerners could participate.[4]

The presence of the SCLC and SNCC in the Alabama Black Belt transformed the region into ground zero for the struggle to define the form and function of black political participation. The work of the two groups also proved critical to the development of politics in the region. While working in the Black Belt, both organizations created new models for engaging in electoral politics that were based on their experiences in the movement. Although these models differed in their degree of democratic engagement, each was a far cry from the kind of politics the region's white oligarchs had developed, which revolved around exclusivity in political participation and decision making.

This essay explores the changing nature of black politics in the Alabama Black Belt, from the passage of the Voting Rights Act through the present, using a series of joint state and federal voter fraud investigations that occurred between 1984 and 2005 as prisms through which to examine key developments. These investigations illuminate the obstacles black political activists had to overcome to gain control of local governments; the response of local whites to the loss of political power; the role of state and federal Republicans in black voter suppression; and the evolution of the exercise of black political power, including the slow embrace of undemocratic forms of political engagement. We begin, though, with a look at the models of black political practice that SNCC and the SCLC developed in the wake of the Voting Rights Act, models that served as the baseline for black politics for the next several decades.

Two weeks after the Voting Rights Act became law, SNCC field secretary Stokely Carmichael, who had been organizing in Lowndes County for nearly six months, suggested that the leaders of the burgeoning local movement form their own political party to challenge white Democrats for control of the county government. "It is not enough to add more and more people to the voter rolls and then send them into the old 'do-nothing,' compromise-oriented political parties," he explained. "Those new voters will only become frustrated and alienated." Besides, he said, "there's no room for Negroes in the same party as [Alabama governor George] Wallace."[5]

Carmichael's suggestion struck a responsive chord with the leaders of the Lowndes movement. "It didn't make sense for us to go join the Democrat party, when they were the people who had done the killing in the county and had beat our heads," explained Frank Miles Jr., a founding member of the Lowndes County Christian Movement for Human Rights.[6] Convinced that independent politics was the best way to give meaning to black votes, local movement leaders formed the Lowndes County Freedom Organization (LCFO), an all-black, countywide third party whose ballot symbol was a snarling black panther.

SNCC organizers played a leading role in the development of the LCFO. In February 1966, shortly after local leaders announced the formation of the party, the young activists began holding biweekly political education workshops across the county, where they explained Alabama election law and the duties of elected officials. At all times they stressed the right of ordinary people to make decisions about their own lives, which, they insisted, was "the most fundamental right that a member of a democratic society can have."[7] In this way, they wove into the fabric of the embryonic party a commitment to the democratic principles that were at SNCC's core. As a result, LCFO supporters rejected the undemocratic traditions that defined American politics and embraced a new kind of politics—freedom politics—which coupled SNCC's egalitarian organizing methods with local people's movement goals. Thus, rather than promote the interests of the socioeconomic elite, draw candidates exclusively from the ranks of the propertied and the privileged, or limit decision making to a select few individuals, LCFO supporters adopted a platform that touted basic civil and human rights, selected candidates from the poor and working class, and practiced democratic decision making.[8]

While SNCC organizers were helping African Americans in Lowndes and several other Black Belt counties build their own parties, SCLC activists were busy generating support for the candidates they favored in the May 3, 1966, Democratic primary. Unlike their SNCC counterparts, SCLC organizers, who had built strong bonds of trust with local people in

Dallas, Perry, and Wilcox counties, believed that the best way for African Americans to transform black votes into political power was to join the Democratic Party. "We must let the Negro vote hang there like a ripe fruit, and whoever is willing to give the Negro the most freedom can pick it," explained Hosea Williams, SCLC's Alabama director of voter registration and political education. "We may not be able to elect a black man, but God knows we can say what white man."[9] Toward this end, SCLC activists launched a statewide voter registration drive, believing, as Williams put it, that "the person who register[s] [black voters] controls them."[10] To coordinate this effort, they formed the Confederation of Alabama Political Organizations, which Williams promised would be able to deliver black votes to white candidates in exchange for political spoils that could be redistributed to loyalists at the county level. "We've been selling our vote all along," he argued. "Now we've got to sell it for freedom."[11]

Although SCLC activists shared SNCC organizers' commitment to using the ballot to transform the Black Belt, their approach to electoral politics replicated many of the undemocratic political traditions that had dominated the region for generations. Most notably, they engaged in a kind of politics that curtailed the ability of ordinary people, particularly the poor and those with limited education, to make the political decisions that impacted their lives. Thus, rather than equipping newly registered black voters with the knowledge they needed to decide who ought to represent them in public office, the SCLC simply told them who to vote for. This top-down approach to politics, which was reminiscent of the SCLC's approach to movement organizing, contrasted sharply with SNCC's bottom-up efforts, creating a palpable tension that permeated the region's local movements.

Regardless of the organizing method they used, African Americans in the Black Belt had limited success electing black candidates to positions in county and local government. Prior to 1978 only Greene County, which was 80 percent African American, had a majority black government. Black electoral struggles were a direct result of successful attempts by local whites to curtail black political participation. White election officials led this effort by intimidating African Americans seeking to register, purging voter rolls, and locating polling places in remote areas or all-white spaces. White employers, meanwhile, refused to grant African Americans time off to vote on Election Day or offered them overtime to keep them away from the polls. Others bribed economically vulnerable African Americans to vote for white candidates or paid them not to vote at all.[12] Each of these activities helped stem the tide of black political power, but none was as effective as the fraudulent use of absentee ballots.

Long before passage of the Voting Rights Act, it was not uncommon for large numbers of Black Belt whites to cast absentee ballots, partly because many were elderly and lacked high levels of formal education, but also because quite a few worked far from home because of the scarcity of nonagricultural jobs in the region. Black political mobilization, however, prompted white elites to use the absentee ballot to marshal every legal white vote possible, and when that failed to stave off the black insurgency, they manufactured white votes.

In Sumter County, for example, whites appealed directly to former residents to cast absentee ballots in the 1976 general election. "Your name still appears on the registered voters list of Sumter County. Therefore, you remain eligible to vote absentee in the coming November General Election," read a letter sent by the Concerned Citizens of Sumter County, a white political organization, to white former residents of the county. The group made no secret of the reason for the solicitation. "Being a former resident of this county, we feel sure that you are aware of the delicate political situation that exists in our county. Certain individuals and groups of individuals are making a concerted effort to seize control in this election." Thus, the letter "urgently" requested that the recipients complete the enclosed absentee ballot request forms and return them to election officials immediately.[13]

Whites also used their influence over elderly, economically vulnerable, and less well-educated blacks to get them to file absentee ballots and vote for favored white candidates. In 1976 Lowndes County voters cast some 350 absentee ballots, nearly twice as many as in any previous election and second only to Jefferson County, which included Birmingham, a city with fifty times as many people. "It really looks suspicious," said John Hulett, a movement veteran and the county's first black sheriff. "Some of these people are getting them because they say they will be out of town on Election Day. I know that's not so in some of the cases." He claimed that many of the applicants were black senior citizens with poor reading skills whom whites had persuaded to fill out absentee ballots. "A white person is picking them up and taking them to the registrar's home," Hulett noted. "White people have never tried to help blacks vote before," so "you have to wonder why they're taking this effort to provide free transportation now for blacks."[14]

African Americans did not stand idly by as whites manipulated the absentee ballot system. Throughout the Black Belt they filed election challenges based on absentee ballot abuse. They also implored federal officials in the Carter administration to look into the problem. "I wrote, telephoned, and even went to Washington to try to persuade people in the Department of Justice to investigate the absentee-ballot situation in the Black Belt," recalled Dallas County attorney and voting rights activist J. L. Chestnut. "They listened and sympathized, but said that fraud in a county or state election was a state matter." Federal officials did offer Chestnut one piece of advice: "They told me that with so many black people in these counties, we shouldn't be leaning on Washington. We should master the absentee system ourselves." Chestnut and others took this suggestion seriously. "By the late seventies, each of the little black county organizations had two or three people in charge of nothing but absentee ballots," explained Chestnut, who provided legal counsel to many of these organizations. "They learned the process and requirements, and usually one of them became a notary public. They went to the old black folk in nursing homes and out in the country. They learned whose kids were away at college and who worked out of the county and got them to vote absentee."[15] The operation was extremely complex and time-consuming. "You got to know the laws, you got to have dedication," explained Albert Turner Sr., president of the Perry County Civic League and a veteran SCLC activist. "You've got to get up off your ass and get out there and go to them folks' houses. This ain't no playtime."[16]

These efforts proved decisive. Between 1978 and 1982, with black voter turnout reaching 80 percent in some counties, African Americans retained majority control of Greene County; elected a majority of the countywide officeholders in Perry, Lowndes, Wilcox, and Sumter counties; gained seats on two previously all-white county commissions; and elected Jenkins Bryant and James Thomas to the state house of representatives. And one year later, following court-ordered redistricting, Lucius Black joined Bryant and Thomas in the Alabama house, and Hank Sanders went to the state senate. For the first time since Reconstruction, the Black Belt had African American representatives in the statehouse and in every county courthouse.[17]

It took a decade and a half after passage of the Voting Rights Act for African Americans to supplant whites in a majority of elected offices in the Black Belt. During that time the SCLC's brand of top-down politics gained more traction than SNCC's freedom politics, largely because the momentum that had given rise to freedom politics had dissipated. Telling people who to vote for required less time, energy, and commitment to democracy than convening mass meetings, holding political education workshops, and canvassing door-to-door—the hallmarks of freedom politics. Although the decline of freedom politics was not inevitable, it was somewhat predictable due to the difficulty of sustaining social and political movements for long periods. People still believed in freedom politics, but the number who organized around it was dwindling rapidly. In addition, its adherents included only a handful of the black candidates elected at this time, which increased the possibility that black political leaders would embrace more undemocratic political practices.

White elites who refused to accept the loss of political power turned to the courts and to the white members of the state legislature to invalidate black electoral victories and prevent future victories from occurring. Between 1978 and 1981 the region's white district attorneys brought voter fraud cases against black absentee ballot organizers, and legislators passed re-registration bills that purged the voter rolls. Their actions, however, were in vain.[18]

Unable to stop the wave of black political success, which reached new heights in 1982, local white district attorneys Roy Johnson and Nathan Watkins initiated the most far-reaching voter fraud investigations to date. These investigations revolved around allegations that black political activists operating in counties where whites had lost power had coerced elderly and illiterate African Americans into casting absentee ballots for slates of black candidates and that they had altered absentee ballots without the permission of voters. The district attorneys' efforts, however, did not lead to any indictments, let alone convictions, because they failed to convince grand juries composed mostly of African Americans that fraud had been committed. Undeterred, Johnson and Watkins appealed to the federal government for help, and unlike Chestnut, they were not turned away.[19]

In the four years since Chestnut had traveled to Washington, things had changed dramatically in the nation's capital. Above all else, Democrats no longer controlled the White House. In 1980 conservative Republican Ronald Reagan won the presidency, and immediately upon taking the oath of office, he acted on his campaign promise to scale back civil rights and voting rights enforcement, which fell under the jurisdiction of the Justice Department. Also, there had been a series of federal court rulings expanding the right of federal investigators to get involved in state and local election fraud cases.[20] Consequently, when Johnson and Watkins brought their case to the U.S. attorney for the Southern District of Alabama, Jefferson Sessions—a racial conservative who strongly believed in the ideological precepts of Reaganism—he took up their cause. The irony of the federal government's newfound interest and involvement in voting fraud was not lost on civil rights attorney Lani Guinier. "Whereas the Justice Department under President Carter had dismissed years of complaints from blacks about white use of the absentee process," she writes, "under Ronald Reagan it seized the very first opportunity to investigate the absentee ballot process when called upon to do so by whites who had long held power."[21]

During the summer of 1984 Sessions helped lead a joint federal and state investigation of voting fraud in Greene, Lowndes, Perry, Sumter, and Wilcox counties—the same counties where African Americans had recently secured majority control of the local government. Working with white district attorneys and county registrars, many of whom were known to have manipulated absentee ballots in the past, investigators placed black political organizations, such as the Perry County Civic League, under surveillance, tracking its members as they handled secretly coded absentee ballots. At the same time, they turned a blind eye to ongoing malfeasance by white political organizations. They also pressed the issue with black voters in an intimidating manner, declaring in press releases that they intended to prosecute fully anyone accused of voting fraud and announcing at public forums that anyone who voted in the most recent primary or in the upcoming general election could be called to testify before a grand jury. In addition, the FBI conducted home interrogations of more than a thousand African Americans, most of whom were elderly and had used absentee ballots to vote for black candidates in recent elections. Many of those questioned were photographed, fingerprinted, and required to submit writing samples, and more than a hundred were bused to Montgomery, Birmingham, and Mobile to testify before grand juries.[22]

These investigative tactics conjured bad memories for many of the people questioned. Less than twenty years earlier, white authorities had denied many of these same people the right to vote using eerily similar methods. But a small number refused to be intimidated. "Those FBI men showed me their badges and told me didn't I know it was wrong to vote absentee, but I knew I hadn't done anything wrong," said sixty-five-year-old Mamie Speight. "I've voted every year I've had the opportunity and I'm not going to give it up now."[23] Not all of Speight's neighbors were as defiant. The vast majority were shaken by the experience. When asked under oath if her 1984 absentee ballot was the first one she had submitted,

Fannie May Williams, an elderly Perry County resident, replied, "Uh-huh. First and the last."[24]

Although very well resourced, the investigation produced only eight indictments. In Perry County, SCLC organizers Albert and Evelyn Turner Sr., along with voting rights activist Spencer Hogue, were charged with 87 counts of violating state and federal law. And in Greene County, five activists and elected officials were charged with 138 counts of criminal activity.

Supporters of the "Greene County Five" and the "Marion Three," led by African American state senator Hank Sanders and former movement activist and newspaper publisher John Zippert, mounted a vigorous defense. They assembled a veritable who's who defense team that included Lani Guinier and Duval Patrick of the NAACP Legal Defense Fund, and they created the Black Belt Defense Fund to help cover legal costs. They also raised national awareness of the defense effort by holding support rallies and registering new black voters throughout the Black Belt. In addition, they convinced members of the Judiciary Committee of the U.S. House of Representatives to hold hearings on the activities of Alabama's U.S. attorneys.[25]

The trial of the Marion Three began on June 17, 1985. Prosecutors alleged that the defendants had marked absentee ballots for voters, which, they argued, constituted voting twice in a single election. They also contended that it did not matter whether the defendants had the consent of the voters whose ballots they marked. The defense countered by saying that the accused had simply helped marginalized citizens—namely, the elderly, the infirm, and migrant workers—participate in the political process. While the prosecution's theory stretched reasonable definitions of voting fraud, the defense's argument blurred the lines of legality, ignoring the very real possibility that those who marked ballots for others could easily coerce them into voting for candidates not of their choosing. This was already a concern for some African American activists in counties such as Lowndes, where black bosses were beginning to emerge.[26]

In the end, the evidence did not support the fraud allegations. Of the 200 African Americans interviewed by the FBI in Perry County, only 17 provided information that could have been interpreted as evidence of wrongdoing, and their testimony fell apart under close scrutiny. These witnesses also expressed tremendous affection for the defendants, as well as full faith in their character, which further undermined the prosecution's case. "I been knowin' Albert [Turner] all my life," said one witness under oath. "I know his daddy. I know his mama and that's his little brother sittin' there beside him. Albert's been pickin' my ballot for sixteen years."[27] Such testimony by the prosecution's own witnesses swayed the jurors, who found the defendants not guilty on all counts.

Prosecutors made similar arguments later that year in the trials of the Greene County Five, with nearly the same result. Majority-white and all-white juries in Tuscaloosa and Birmingham acquitted the defendants on almost all charges, finding only Eutaw city councilman Spiver Gordon guilty of two counts of mail fraud and two counts of providing false information to an election official. Gordon's conviction was eventually overturned by an appellate court, which found that the U.S. attorney had violated Gordon's right to a jury of his peers by striking all African Americans from the jury pool.[28]

The attempt by Black Belt whites to reverse their political fortunes failed miserably. Rather than suppress the black vote, their efforts actually energized black voters, who saw the selective prosecutions by conservative federal officials for what they were—attempts by whites to regain political power in the Black Belt at the expense of their democratically elected representatives. It also strengthened the standing of African American elected officials in the region, who were viewed by most black voters as being fully committed to practicing a kind of politics that was significantly more democratic than traditional American politics.

Following the 1984–1985 voting fraud investigations, African American political activists in the Black Belt, particularly those associated with the upstart Alabama New South Coalition, worked to expand earlier electoral gains. New South maintained close ties with the SCLC and sought to position the Black Belt, as opposed to Birmingham, as the center of black political power in the state. Central to this effort were absentee ballots, which the activists used to turn out high percentages of black voters on Election Day. As a result, by the 1990s, New South activists had emerged as the most powerful political faction in the region. But their fiercely guarded control of county courthouses, combined with their inability to solve the devastating financial crisis facing Black Belt counties, stimulated black political opposition. At the same time, local whites who were eager to regain control of local governments, and state Republicans who were equally anxious to gain control of the state government as well as federal offices, exploited the political rift in the black community by initiating another wave of voting fraud investigations. These developments were most starkly evident in Greene County.

By the mid-1990s Greene County faced a financial crisis brought about by a rapidly eroding tax base and the ever-increasing costs for maintaining public services and infrastructure, a crisis that eventually forced the all-black county commission to declare bankruptcy.[29] Greene County tax assessor John Kennard insisted that mismanagement on the part of the New South politicos running the government was to blame, leading him and three other African Americans to challenge them in 1994 for control of the local government. To bolster their chances of victory, they accepted the help of Citizens for a Better Greene County (CBGC), a white-dominated political organization of approximately 600 local residents who had joined forces over the issues of fiscal responsibility in government and honesty in elections.[30]

During the 1994 election both sides engaged in bitter fighting and used absentee ballots to increase the turnout for their respective candidates. Their combined efforts pushed the number of absentee ballots cast to approximately 30 percent of all votes, up from 16 percent in the 1992 election. With its older and better-established operation, New South easily outpaced the biracial coalition in the race for absentee ballots, claiming two-thirds of the total number.[31] At the same time, the white leaders of the CBGC tried to suppress the turnout of New South supporters by launching a localized version of the national Republican Party's "ballot integrity" program. Like Republicans elsewhere, CBGC cofounder Pam Montgomery sent letters to black residents on the eve of the election, threatening to investigate any and all allegations of voting fraud. And on Election Day she helped videotape African Americans entering and exiting the polls, while others photographed absentee ballots that had been mailed in by New South organizers. In the end, though, New South partisans prevailed, sweeping nearly every electoral contest.[32]

After the election the biracial coalition alleged that New South organizers had engaged in widespread voting fraud. To make their case, they pointed to the disproportionately high number of absentee ballots cast as prima facie evidence of wrongdoing. White candidates in neighboring Black Belt counties who lost to established black politicians, most of whom were affiliated with New South, made similar claims. These charges, however, obscured the fact that in Greene County, at least, candidates favored by the opposition coalition received approximately 30 percent of the absentee ballots cast.[33]

The white district attorney in charge of Hale, Wilcox, and Lowndes counties was willing to entertain these politically motivated allegations of fraud and convened grand juries to investigate. In Greene County, however, things had changed. In 1992 African Americans in Greene, Sumter, and Marengo counties had elected Barron Lankster as district attorney, making him the first black district attorney in the history of the Alabama Black Belt. Members of the CBGC petitioned Lankster to investigate the fraud allegations, but he found their evidence weak and declined to impanel a grand jury. Undeterred, the CBGC circumvented Lankster, taking its case to Jefferson Sessions, Alabama's newly elected attorney general.[34]

Since the earlier voting fraud investigations, Sessions had emerged as a popular figure in the state Republican Party, which was still establishing itself as the heir to conservative southern Democrats. In 1994 he was the top statewide vote-getter among a tremendously successful slate of Republican candidates. Looking ahead to the 1996 election, though, Sessions understood that Republican success was not a foregone conclusion. And he knew that investigating alleged voting fraud among Democrats would further diminish the luster of the Democratic Party in the eyes of conservative whites, thereby bolstering the Republican Party's chances of electoral success.[35]

Sessions coordinated the voting fraud investigations with characteristic zeal. He worked closely with the district attorney representing Hale, Wilcox, and Lowndes counties to support that investigation. Lankster continued to refuse to investigate allegations of fraud in Greene County, so Sessions worked around him, partnering with the U.S. attorney for the Northern District of Alabama to launch a joint state and federal investigation. Very soon, agents from the FBI and the Alabama Bureau of Investigation (ABI) were crisscrossing the Black Belt, reviewing election records and interviewing voters.[36]

The latest round of investigations once again focused exclusively on black voters and black political organizers, specifically those affiliated with New South. In Greene County, investigators interviewed only African Americans who had voted for candidates backed by New South. They also looked at only the roughly 1,000 absentee ballots New South candidates had received, out of the 1,400 absentee ballots cast.[37] At the same time, they ignored strong evidence of voter intimidation and ballot fraud committed by white members of the biracial coalition. The lead attorneys for the investigation, however, denied that they were engaging in selective prosecution, telling U.S. magistrate Michael Putnam that more indictments, ostensibly of white political operatives who had also misused the absentee ballot system, were forthcoming. Putnam accepted this claim. "What today may seem like defendants being singled out for prosecution may later be nothing more than the first of many prosecutions," he explained. But in February 1998, when indictments were handed down for marking and mishandling ballots during the 1994 general election and for attempting to coerce a single voter during that same election, the nine people charged were African American, and no other indictments followed.[38]

Sanders and Zippert once again took up the cause of those who had been indicted. On the eve of the 1998 primary elections, Sanders brought volunteers from the Kentucky Alliance, the Southern Organizing Committee, the Southern Regional Council, and his wife Rose's 21st Century Youth Leadership Movement into Greene County to canvass and conduct voter registration. Later that month the SCLC organized a "voting rights caravan" through the Black Belt led by Martin Luther King III. But Sanders and Zippert were unable to generate the same kind of enthusiasm they had garnered a decade and a half earlier. Part of the problem was that John Kennard, the African American leader of the biracial coalition, publicly declared that those who had been indicted were guilty as charged, sowing doubt among African Americans that they were being prosecuted solely because of their race or because of their democratic impulse. The national SCLC and others, he said, had "fallen for the propaganda that a few crooks are putting out." He even went so far as to claim that "for years, it has been dishonest black politicians who have been cheating us, their own people into selling or giving away our ballots," which belied the area's history. But it was statements like these that gave people pause.[39] In addition, some of those who had been indicted admitted to committing technical violations of absentee ballot law when they applied for and filled out ballots for other people. "I made mistakes but they were honest mistakes," said Connie Tyree, who faced several criminal counts for mishandling ballots.[40] These mistakes may have been honest, but they still violated the law, raising the possibility that the more serious allegations of marking ballots without the voters' expressed permission were true.

The first defendants to go on trial, Connie Tyree and Frank Smith, were found guilty of thirteen counts of voting fraud and were given sentences of thirty-three months. Fearing a similar fate, the remaining defendants entered into single-count plea agreements with the prosecution that involved sentences ranging from probation, fines, and resigning from public office to six months in prison.[41]

These investigations had an adverse impact on African American political organizing and voting behavior in the Black Belt. The impact was especially severe in Greene County, which had once been a beacon of black political power. In 1994 there were 1,463 absentee ballots cast in the county's general election, representing 30 percent of the total vote. Four years later the number of absentee ballots had dropped to 147. The precipitous decline stemmed from the fact that African Americans who usually voted by absentee ballot stopped participating in the political process. Not only were they no longer using absentee ballots; they were no longer voting at all.[42] This was partly a matter of inconvenience, as no one was coming around to pick up their ballots. At the same time, however, the actions of those who had been convicted dampened a lot of people's interest in voting.

The void created by the absence of traditional absentee voters, along with the disruption of New South's political operation, was a boon to Greene County's biracial coalition, which quickly secured a majority of the seats on the county commission. It also enabled the white members of the coalition to regain a toehold in the government. The elevation of white Republican Chip Beeker to chair of the county commission and Lankster's defeat by white Democrat Nathan Watkins reflected their newfound political clout.[43]

Attorney general Sessions and the state Republican Party also benefited tremendously from the investigations and convictions. From the outset, Republicans pointed to the investigations as evidence that the state's Democrats were "liars, cheaters, stealers, [and] immoral," as one Republican strategist put it, which helped erode the standing of white Democrats in the minds of white voters. Republicans reinforced this impression on the eve of the 1996 election by pushing a bill through the legislature that more closely regulated absentee ballot voting. Although the Justice Department denied the state's request to allow implementation of the new law in time for the 1996 election, the measure had the intended political effect. In 1996 Republicans unseated Democrats as the state's ruling party, sweeping every contested statewide and federal contest. Sessions was among the victors, winning an open seat in the U.S. Senate.[44]

A new generation of black political activists came of age between the first and second voting fraud trials. Too young to have participated in the civil rights struggles of the 1960s or the electoral struggles of the 1970s, their political loyalty was up for grabs. Some gravitated toward old guard activists, such as the New South politicos who had wielded power in the Black

Belt since the early 1980s. Those who chose this route inherited the old guard's absentee ballot operations. The use and misuse of absentee ballots had been slowed by the most recent voting fraud investigation, especially in Greene County. But even there, these operations remained functional, and in the surrounding counties they continued to play a pivotal role in elections. It was impossible, however, for the new generation to inherit the old guard's experiential understanding of how the bonds of trust between political activists and voters were essential to the success of absentee ballot programs, not only because these bonds ensured access to voters but also because they kept activists from crossing the line into fraud. Other members of the younger generation forged alliances with white political groups. They had grown tired of the old guard's inability to govern effectively—to deal directly with the crippling issues of poverty, unemployment, and poorly resourced schools—and had become frustrated by persistent allegations of fraud that, upon close scrutiny, appeared to have merit. These developments played out most clearly in Perry and Hale counties.

The Perry County Civic Association (PCCA) was the dominant old guard political organization there. Albert Turner Sr., former director of SCLC operations in Alabama, had led the organization for several decades until his death in 2000. At that time his son, Albert Turner Jr., inherited leadership of the PCCA. Turner Jr., who had formed his own multicounty political organization, Campaign 2000 & Beyond, also assumed his father's seat on the Perry County commission.[45]

In a series of regular and special elections in 2004 and 2005, Turner Jr. used his new political clout to bolster support for local candidates endorsed by Campaign 2000. He did so by tapping into his father's absentee ballot network, which in most cases provided his candidates with the edge they needed to win. Turner Jr., however, did not fare as well as his political comrades. Despite receiving the vast majority of absentee ballots in the three counties that covered his district, he lost his bid for a seat in the state house of representatives.[46]

The grossly disproportionate number of absentee ballots cast in favor of Campaign 2000 candidates raised the ire of politically active whites. At the beginning of 2005 whites in Hale County formed the Democracy Defense League (DDL) to lobby for strict policing of absentee ballots and for an increase in the penalties for voting fraud, which, according to DDL founder Perry Beasley, was a veritable epidemic that had been "handled with a wink and a nod for years by those in power." The organization's agenda appealed to many people inside and outside of Hale County, and within two years the DDL claimed nearly 1,700 members, most of them white, across the Black Belt.[47]

Intrigued by the possibility that the allegations of systemic voter fraud were true, regional media partnered with the DDL, publishing laudatory profiles of its members, reporting DDL allegations of fraud, and carrying DDL letters to the editor. State Republicans, anxious to find Democrat-directed voter fraud that would justify "voter security" programs and counter-balance Democratic allegations of Republican-directed voter suppression, also embraced the DDL.[48] Two Republicans in particular, Secretary of State Beth Chapman and Attorney General Troy King, took special interest in the group. Chapman lauded the DDL publicly and pointed to the organization as the inspiration for the voter fraud unit she created in 2008. King was just as excited. Shortly after meeting with the group's leaders in 2005 he launched an investigation of voter fraud in Hale County; three years later, ahead of the 2008 general election in which he served as state cochair for John McCain's presidential campaign, he opened another investigation of alleged vote buying in Lowndes, Perry, and Bullock counties.[49]

On the surface, King's probes seemed to mirror the two earlier voting fraud investigations. Like those inquiries, his investigation began in response to allegations of fraud leveled by a handful of whites; it scrutinized the activities of black political organizers and served the political interests of state and national Republicans. But unlike the previous investigations, his neither targeted nor harassed black voters. The ABI agents he sent into the field focused strictly on absentee ballots; they conducted handwriting comparisons between ballot signatures and signatures of the organizers who had submitted them, and they interviewed only the organizers who had collected the ballots, not the voters themselves. King's findings also differed from earlier results. He discovered 22 fraudulent absentee ballots among those cast in a mayoral election in Hale County in 2004, and another 140 that had been recorded as valid even though they had not been filled out properly. Nearly all these ballots favored the candidate endorsed by Turner Jr. and Campaign 2000, compelling a circuit court judge to void the election result and declare the opposition candidate the victor.[50] The investigators also found ballot abuse in a 2004 special election in Hale County in the form of forged affidavits and improper ballot certifications, leading to indictments against two absentee ballot organizers and the county's circuit clerk, all of whom worked closely with Turner Jr. and Campaign 2000.[51]

As in the past, supporters of those under indictment tried to garner attention for their cause by bringing national black political leaders to the

Black Belt. On Sunday, October 2, 2007, the Reverend Al Sharpton spoke in defense of the accused at a support rally at Salem Baptist Church in Hale County.[52] The following Friday, Charles Steele, chairperson of the SCLC, led a similar gathering. These efforts, though, were noticeably different from earlier mobilizations, in that they did not include voter registration activity, and the speakers focused more on past investigations than on the current cases. Steele, for instance, expressed more concern about the fact that "there have been charges of abuse of the election system in Hale County by white people that have never been prosecuted" than about the possibility that the current charges against African Americans might be true.[53] Beyond these rallies, there was little organized support for those facing charges. Personality politics was partially responsible. Turner Jr., for instance, flatly rejected offers of help. He was "a little hot-headed and erratic," explained activist Zippert.[54] More important, black people tended to believe the charges, which turned out to be true. Indeed, everyone who was indicted eventually pled guilty.[55]

The investigations, indictments, and guilty pleas did not dissuade black politicos, who had come to rely on the fraudulent use of absentee ballots, from continuing to engage in misconduct. In 2008 rumors swirled that old-guard black political organizations, led by Turner Jr. and other members of the younger generation of black political activists, were buying votes in Perry, Lowndes, and Bullock counties. After the DDL submitted affidavits from African Americans swearing to this fact, King launched a second voting fraud investigation.[56] Turner Jr. responded by claiming that the investigation was part of a larger Republican scheme to suppress the black vote. "The Republican Party has an unscripted mandate to target Democratic counties, and African Americans in particular," he declared. [57] His claims, though ostensibly true, gained little traction, even among African Americans, because the allegations against him and the PCCA were also true. "I've been standing around when [PCCA representatives] come and do it," Perry County resident Kisha Cole told an investigative reporter from the *New York Times*. "They say, 'I gotcha,' meaning they're going to handle you when you sign your ballot, give you $20–$30." Cole added that this kind of behavior was widespread and widely known. Another Perry County resident, Christopher Collins, added that vote buying had been going on for a number of years. The twenty-three-year-old told the *Times* that he had been paid for his vote every year since becoming eligible to vote. African Americans interviewed by other news agencies shared similar stories of vote buying.[58]

After nearly forty years of allegations of systemic black voter fraud, a core group of black politicians and political organizers had finally crossed the line, turning their backs on the democratic politics that had defined African American political practice in the years following passage of the Voting Rights Act. Instead, they chose to embrace a politics similar to that which had disfranchised so many for so long.

Looking back over time, Albert Turner Jr.'s brand of politics, which involved ballot fraud and led black politicians to ignore the concerns of the black community, is not what civil rights activists had in mind when they began organizing in the Black Belt in the wake of the Voting Rights Act. They envisioned a participatory democracy, one that rejected traditional forms of political engagement. For a while, this kind of politics was popular, but it was hard to sustain. Slowly, over time, the usual forms of political engagement prevailed.

The triumph of "politics as usual" lent credence to allegations of systemic black voter fraud, a charge that had been a staple of white voter suppression from the moment African Americans regained the vote. It also alienated large numbers of African Americans who had invested so much in the promise of electoral politics during and after the civil rights and Black Power eras.

Today, African Americans in the Black Belt find themselves in the untenable position of having to choose between black political groups that practice traditional, undemocratic politics and biracial coalitions that tend to ignore the region's troubled racial past and reject the need for African American self-determination. Hopefully, the next generation of black political activists will look to local history and draw on the models of democratic political engagement that flowered briefly in the rich black soil of the region. If properly tended, these models can flower again.

Notes

This essay would not have been possible without the willingness of countless people in the Alabama Black Belt to sit down with us and share their personal experiences and political insights. We are forever grateful for their kindness and generosity and hope our work does justice to their struggle and sacrifice. We also would like to thank our grandmothers, Frances Cephas and Margaret Wynkoop, who were dear friends long before we were born and whose friendship paved the way for this collaboration.

1. Cureton quoted in "Clash in Alabama over Tennessee Coal Ash," *New York Times,* August 30, 2009.

2. Holley quoted in ibid.

3. Flowers quoted in ibid.

4. Hasan Kwame Jeffries, *Bloody Lowndes: Civil Rights and Black Power in Alabama's Black Belt* (New York: NYU Press, 2009), 39–80, 143–79.

5. For more on the evolution of the Lowndes County Freedom Organization, see Jeffries, *Bloody Lowndes,* chaps. 5, 6; Kwame Ture (formerly known as Stokely Carmichael) and Charles V. Hamilton, *Black Power: The Politics of Liberation* (New York: Vintage Books, 1967, 1992), 181–82; "Interview with New SNCC Chairman," *Militant,* May 23, 1966.

6. Miles quoted in "Lowndes County Freedom Organization Leaders," *Movement,* June 1966.

7. "Snick in Alabama," Student Nonviolent Coordinating Committee Papers, box 47, folder 73, Martin Luther King Jr. Center Archives, Atlanta, Georgia.

8. For an expanded discussion of freedom politics, see Jeffries, *Bloody Lowndes,* chap. 5.

9. Williams quoted in "SCLC Proposes Political Group," *Southern Courier,* March 5–6, 1965.

10. Williams quoted in "Leaders in 15 Counties Meet to Plan Bloc Vote," *Southern Courier,* March 12–13, 1966.

11. Ibid.

12. United States Commission on Civil Rights, *The Voting Rights Act: Unfulfilled Goals* (Washington, D.C.: Government Printing Office, 1981), 22–35.

13. Form letter from the Concerned Citizens of Sumter County to white former residents, September 20, 1976, in Richard Arrington Jr. Investigation Files, file 1935, Department of Archives and Manuscripts, Birmingham Public Library, Birmingham, Alabama. Federal authorities were aware of these letters and the prevalence of absentee ballot fraud in the region as early as 1978. J. L. Chestnut Jr. and Julia Cass, *Black in Selma: The Uncommon Life of J. L. Chestnut, Jr.* (New York: Farrar, Straus and Giroux, 1990), 322; U.S. Commission on Civil Rights, *Voting Rights Act,* 35–36.

14. Hulett quoted in "Blacks May Ask Justice Voting Probe," *Birmingham News,* April 27, 1976.

15. Chestnut and Cass, *Black in Selma,* 322.

16. Turner quoted in Allen Tullos, "Crackdown in the Black Belt: Not So Simple Justice," *Southern Changes* 7, no. 2 (1985).

17. Chestnut and Cass, *Black in Selma,* 311; Lani Guinier, *Lift Every Voice: Turning a Civil Rights Setback into a New Vision of Social Justice* (New York: Simon and Schuster, 1998), 188; "Wilder, Bozeman Go Free," *Montgomery Advertiser,* November 10, 1982.

18. "2 Alabama Rights Workers Are Jailed for Voting Fraud," *New York Times,*

January 12, 1982; "4,000 March for Vote-Fraud Duo's Freedom," *Washington Post*, February 19, 1982; "Justice Department to Check Wilcox Voter Plan," *Montgomery Advertiser*, September 23, 1981; Thomas Bethell, *Sumter County Blues: The Ordeal of the Federation of Southern Cooperative* (Washington, D.C.: National Committee in Support of Community Based Organizations, 1982).

19. U.S. House of Representatives, Committee on the Judiciary, Subcommittee on Civil and Constitutional Rights, *Civil Rights Implications of Federal Voting Fraud Prosecutions: Hearing before the Subcommittee on Civil and Constitutional Rights of the Committee on the Judiciary, House of Representatives, Ninety-Ninth Congress* (Washington, D.C.: Government Printing Office, 1986), 26.

20. For a short description of these changes, see Craig Donsanto, *Federal Prosecution of Election Offenses*, 4th ed. (Washington, D.C.: Department of Justice, Criminal Division, Public Integrity Section, 1984), vii–viii, 7, 17. The Reagan administration appears to have accepted these cases in response to several 1983–1984 voter registration drives designed to add 2 million black and poor voters to the rolls and drive the president from office. See Frances Fox Piven, Lorraine Minnite, and Margaret Groarke, *Keeping Down the Black Vote: Race and the Demobilization of American Voters* (New York: New Press, 2009), 102–9.

21. Guinier, *Lift Every Voice*, xx.

22. U.S. House of Representatives, *Civil Rights Implications of Federal Voting Fraud Prosecutions;* "Election Violators to Be Prosecuted," *Greene County Democrat*, October 10, 1984; "FBI Agents Raid County Office Building," *Greene County Democrat*, October 17, 1984; "U.S. Attorney Addresses Vote Fraud Issue in County," *Greene County Democrat*, October 31, 1984; Randall Williams, "Crackdown in the Black Belt: On to Greene County," *Southern Changes* 7, no. 3 (1985).

23. Speight quoted in "Blacks Charge Bias in Voter Fraud Indictments," *Atlanta Journal Constitution*, June 16, 1985.

24. Williams quoted in Guinier, *Lift Every Voice*, 193.

25. "Black Lawmakers Say Probes Inconsistent," *Selma Times Journal*, May 26, 1985; John Zippert, interview with George Derek Musgrove, August 10, 2001, Eutaw, Alabama; U.S. House of Representatives, *Civil Rights Implications of Federal Voting Fraud Prosecutions*.

26. Jeffries, *Bloody Lowndes*, 239.

27. Witness quoted in Chestnut and Cass, *Black in Selma*, 383; Guinier, *Lift Every Voice*, 211–12.

28. Two members of the Greene County Five, Bessie J. Underwood and James Colvin, fearful of the possibility of going to jail, pled guilty to one misdemeanor count of improperly handling absentee ballots, thereby avoiding a trial. They received fines and probation. "Black Activist Guilty in Alabama Voting Case," *New York Times*, October 17, 1985; "Justice Department Dealt Setbacks in Prosecuting Black Activists," *Washington Post*, July 4, 1987; "All-White Jury Picked to Hear

Alabama Vote Fraud Trial," *Washington Post,* September 26, 1985; *United States v. Gordon,* 817 F.2d 1538, 1540 (11th Cir. 1987).

29. By 1989 Greene County owed $176,000 in back taxes; eight years later the tax debt had ballooned to $508,000. "Politicians Are under Scrutiny over Election Procedures and the Handling of Funds," *Atlanta Journal Constitution,* January 19, 1997.

30. Hans von Spakofsky, *Absentee Ballot Fraud: A Stolen Election in Greene County Alabama,* Legal Memorandum No. 31 (Washington, D.C.: Heritage Foundation, 2008), 4.

31. "Civil Rights Leaders Meet with AG Janet Reno on Voter Persecution in West Alabama," *Greene County Democrat,* June 17, 1998.

32. For a discussion of Republican voter integrity programs as a national phenomenon in the mid-1990s, see People for the American Way and National Association for the Advancement of Colored People, "The Long Shadow of Jim Crow: Voter Intimidation and Suppression in America Today" (October 2004); "Turning Back the Clock on Voting Rights," *Nation,* October 28, 1999; *United States of America v. Frank Smith and Connie Tyree,* No. 98–6121, U.S. Court of Appeals, Eleventh Circuit, October 25, 2000.

33. "Civil Rights Leaders Meet with AG Reno."

34. Ibid.

35. For more on the Republican Party in Alabama during this time, see Alexander P. Lamis, ed., *Southern Politics in the 1990s* (Baton Rouge: Louisiana State University Press, 1999), 235–37.

36. "Blackbelt Defense Committee Reactivated," *Greene County Democrat,* March 20, 1996; "Absentee Ballot Probe Postponed," *Greene County Democrat,* May 29, 1996; "Voters Given Reason for FBI Subpoenas," *Greene County Democrat,* June 19, 1996.

37. Ibid.; "Turning Back the Clock on Voting Rights."

38. *U.S. v. Smith and Tyree;* "Federal Ruling: No Selective Prosecution in Alabama Vote Fraud Case," *Atlanta Journal Constitution,* August 7, 1997; "New Wave of Federal Indictments Add to Atmosphere of Political Terrorism in Greene Co.," *Greene County Democrat,* February 4, 1998.

39. "Activists Come to Greene from Throughout the Nation to Show Support, Get out the Vote," *Greene County Democrat,* May 6, 1998; "Voting Rights Caravan Tours Black Belt," *Greene County Democrat,* May 27, 1988; "Some Blacks Criticize SCLC Vote Campaign," *Atlanta Journal Constitution,* May 20, 1998.

40. *U.S. v. Smith and Tyree;* "Smith, Tyree Given 33 Month Sentences Each; Will Appeal," *Greene County Democrat,* February 4, 1988.

41. "New Wave of Federal Indictments Add to Atmosphere of Political Terrorism"; "Greene County 6 Plead Guilty to One Count Each," *Greene County Democrat,* March 3, 1999; "Three Given Probation in Vote Fraud Cases," *Greene County Democrat,* April 28, 1999; "Feds Indict Three More on Misdemeanor Vote

Irregularities," *Greene County Democrat,* May 5, 1999; "Guilty Pleas End Greene County Vote Fraud Cases," Associated Press, June 15, 1999.

42. Voters in Greene County cast an average of 4,800 votes in 1992 and 1994. In 1996 and 1998 they cast an average of 4,000 votes. "Civil Rights Leaders Meet with AG Reno."

43. "Alabama County Votes for Change; Fund Misuse, Fraud Targeted in Election," *Atlanta Journal Constitution,* June 6, 1998.

44. Lamis, *Southern Politics in the 1990s,* 236.

45. "Albert Turner Is Dead at 64; Strove for Civil Rights in South," *New York Times,* April 15, 2000; "Politics of Color: Who Deserves to Lead," *Birmingham News,* October 13, 2002.

46. "Woman Tells of Being Signed up for Ballot—Questions Surround City's Absentee Ballots," *Mobile Register,* September 6, 2004; "Two Accused of Voter Fraud in Hale County," *Tuscaloosa News,* August 17, 2007; Lorraine Minnite, *The Myth of Voter Fraud* (Ithaca, N.Y.: Cornell University Press, 2010), 163.

47. "2 Accused of Voter Fraud in Hale County," *Tuscaloosa News,* August 18, 2007; "Defending Democracy," *Tuscaloosa News,* August 6, 2007.

48. According to Loraine Minnite, since 2002 Republicans have adopted a strategy of "aggressively investigat[ing] Democrats and their allies for voter fraud on the barest of evidence . . . us[ing] the media to promote the investigations . . . and strategically tim[ing] and keep[ing] those investigations open to influence elections." Critical to this strategy have been Republican attorneys general and secretaries of state, a significant number of whom have made policing voter fraud a priority despite being unable to produce any evidence of its existence. Minnite, *Myth of Voter Fraud,* 4.

49. "Defending Democracy."

50. Minnite, *Myth of Voter Fraud,* 163.

51. "Woman Pleads Guilty to Voter Fraud," *Tuscaloosa News,* September 2, 2009; "Ex-Councilwoman Convicted in Greensboro Voter Fraud, Had Forged Affidavit of Absentee Voter," WHNT-19 News, September 14, 2009; "Former Hale Circuit Clerk Charged in Voter Fraud Probe," *Tuscaloosa News,* March 18, 2008; "Ex-Clerk Guilty of Voter Fraud," *Tuscaloosa News,* September 1, 2010.

52. "Rights Activists Target Hale County," *Tuscaloosa News,* October 8, 2007; *In the matter of Marvin W. Wiggins, Circuit Judge of the Fourth Judicial District of Alabama,* Court of the Judiciary of Alabama, Case No. 37.

53. "Black Leaders to Rally for Voter Fraud Suspects," *Tuscaloosa News,* October 4, 2007.

54. John Zippert, telephone interview with George Derek Musgrove, November 25, 2008.

55. "Woman Pleads Guilty to Voter Fraud"; "Ex-Councilwoman Convicted in Greensboro Voter Fraud."

56. "Officials Investigate 3 Alabama Counties in Voter Fraud Accusations,"

New York Times, June 10, 2008; "Reports of Voter Fraud Continue," press release from the office of Alabama Secretary of State Beth Chapman, June 12, 2008; "New SOS Unit Dedicated to Stop Voter Fraud," press release from the office of Alabama Secretary of State Beth Chapman, June 18, 2008.

   57. "Officials Investigate 3 Alabama Counties."

   58. Ibid.; "Alabama County Accused of Voter Fraud," National Public Radio, July 14, 2008.

"I Want My Country Back, I Want My Dream Back"

Barack Obama and the Appeal of Postracial Fictions

Brian Ward

On August 28, 2008, Illinois' junior senator Barack Obama became the first African American to be nominated as the presidential candidate of a major political party in the United States. That historic day coincided with the forty-fifth anniversary of the March on Washington, when Dr. Martin Luther King delivered his "I Have a Dream" speech from the steps of the Lincoln Memorial. Obama and his campaign team were quick to capitalize on this synchronicity. At the climax of the Democratic Convention at Invesco Field in Denver, the nominee was preceded onto the stage by two of King's children—the Reverend Bernice King and Martin Luther King III—and by veteran activist John Lewis, former chairman of the Student Nonviolent Coordinating Committee and long-serving congressman from Georgia who had shared the podium with King in 1963. Their presence offered personal and rhetorical witness to the continuity between Obama and King and the black struggles of the past. "Tonight," Lewis told millions of Americans, "we have gathered here in this magnificent stadium in Denver because we still have a dream. With the nomination of Senator Barack Obama . . . we are making a down payment on the fulfillment of that dream."[1]

Obama's acceptance speech also harked back to King and the March on Washington, hoping to revive a shared commitment to the sometimes tattered dreams and unfulfilled promises enshrined in the nation's cherished foundational documents: the Declaration of Independence, the Constitution, and the Bill of Rights. It is "that American promise," Obama explained, "that pushes us forward even when the path is uncertain; that binds us together in spite of our differences. . . . And it is that promise that, 45 years ago today, brought Americans from every corner of this land to stand together on a Mall in Washington, before Lincoln's Memorial, and hear a young preacher from Georgia speak of his dream."[2]

This was neither the first nor the last time Obama alluded to King or his dream or expressed his indebtedness to the modern African American civil rights movement of the 1950s and 1960s, with which King has become almost synonymous in popular memory if not necessarily in historical scholarship.[3] While working as a young community organizer in Chicago's benighted South Side, Obama had read *Parting the Waters,* the first volume of Taylor Branch's three-volume history *America in the King Years,* and announced to Jerry Kellman, founder of the Developing Communities Project, "This is my story."[4] As we shall see, on the campaign trail Obama readily acknowledged King's intellectual and moral influence and skillfully mobilized King's posthumous prestige for his own political ends. Obama and his campaign staff were hardly alone in invoking King to contextualize his candidacy. For a while it seemed as if there was barely a commentator, scholar, pundit, cartoonist, poet, or politician—friend or foe, young or old, black or white—who could resist drawing some kind of parallel, connection, or comparison between Obama and King. The sheer ubiquity of this tendency among disparate groups suggests the enormous popular investment in linking the two men. The main concern of this essay is to explore the nature of that investment: to pick away at some of the causes, coordinates, and implications of the widespread impulse to connect Obama to King, and especially to portray his victory as the fulfillment of King's 1963 vision of a redeemed, equalitarian America in which race was no longer an impediment to opportunity and achievement.

Within this broad remit, the essay focuses on three interrelated themes. The first concerns the connections among Obama, King, and ideas of *postracialism,* a term that became ubiquitous in the discourse surrounding Obama's campaign. In fact, the election furnished plenty of evidence of racism in America, and Obama's first two years in office saw so much racist and racially inflected invective directed against the new president from an incensed American right wing that by the time of the November 2010 midterm elections, *postracialism* had virtually disappeared from political discussion and the public imagination. Indeed, one of the main challenges facing future historians will be to take seriously the vogue for postracial rhetoric during the 2008 election cycle. Hindsight and distance are usually the historian's great allies in interpreting the events of the past. But for those trying to understand the 2008 election, knowing what happened next may actually prove as much a hindrance as a help, making it hard to credit that the day after Obama's election a headline in the *Beaumont Enterprise* in Texas could seriously announce, "Race is history."[5]

While postracialism was always a nebulous and ahistorical concept, the argument here is that historians should not underestimate its fleeting power. The beguiling romance of postracial fictions helps explain what Obama represented to many voters and, in part, why he won. Against the odds, against logic, and against the grain of much evidence, the romance of postracial mythologies helped foster a belief, particularly among white voters, that Obama might offer a way to reconnect with America's core civic ideals. Of particular interest here is how Obama used popular understandings of Martin Luther King, an African American leader widely admired across racial lines as emblematic of America's best aspirations, to minimize the potential damage race might inflict on his electoral chances. Careful alignment with certain aspects of King's career helped Obama enjoy the benefits of postracial enthusiasms without ever subscribing to what was, at best, a naïve projection of good intentions, not a reflection of American racial realities, let alone the foundation for a truly progressive politics.

The second theme of the essay concerns an obvious but revealing tension in how Obama was portrayed and sought to portray himself. Obama presented himself as a successor to King and heir to a long African American freedom struggle, while at the same time projecting a new kind of black political persona far removed from the bitter racial hostilities and entrenched identity politics of the past. To some extent, this juggling act depended on Obama's mastery of "dog-whistle" politics, a blend of gesture, style, and rhetoric that quietly affirmed his links to the black community without unduly alarming most white voters. At key junctures in his campaign, however, Obama was willing and sometimes compelled to abandon the stealth strategy of dog-whistle politics and position himself as an overtly black candidate, conspicuously aligned with the ongoing struggle for racial justice. This essay argues that Obama's genius was to do so in ways that made that struggle part of a national—not just a black—narrative of slow, often painful and piecemeal, but relentless progress toward, in the words of both the Constitution and Obama's most important speech, "a more perfect union." It was a mix for which King provided the most compelling model. Before Obama, no one had so brilliantly anchored the quest for racial equality to the foundational beliefs of America's civil religion. Moreover, both men achieved this goal in large measure by co-opting the prestige of Abraham Lincoln, refashioning the nineteenth-century president's commitment to national unity into a far more inclusive call for social justice than the Great Emancipator had ever imagined.

The final major theme of the essay concerns how the use of King's memory to frame Obama's candidacy turned around a very narrow version of what King actually stood for. The mainstream press, sometimes with the connivance of the Obama election team, usually mobilized an image of King "the dreamer," frozen in national consciousness on the steps of the Lincoln Memorial in August 1963. This not only underestimated the radical undercurrents of the "I Have a Dream" speech but also tended to erase the more radical aspects of King's social and political philosophy from popular memory. What made this condition of widespread (but by no means universal) amnesia especially intriguing was that, as Obama's conservative critics never tired of pointing out, there were plenty of clues that Obama identified as much with the King of 1967 and 1968—the antiwar campaigner, democratic socialist, and international humanitarian preoccupied with the relationships among poverty, racism, and militarism—as he did with the dreamer of 1963.

Color and Character:
The National Appeal of Postracial Dreams

Shortly after Barack Obama was elected president, Alan Posner wrote to *Time* magazine from Royal Oak, Michigan, to celebrate that "Americans from Virginia, home of the capital of the Confederacy, to Georgia, voted for a president not on the basis of the color of his skin but on the content of his character. Now we know what King saw from the mountaintop. We have overcome."[6] By explicitly connecting Obama's victory to King's dream of a "color-blind" America that had overcome racial prejudice and discrimination, Posner articulated the predominant theme in popular understandings of the relationship between the two men. On the eve of Obama's nomination by the Democrats, black former Tennessee congressman Harold Ford Jr. had said much the same: "King had a dream, and Barack Obama is part of its fulfillment."[7] The day after Obama's electoral victory, the front page of the *Patriot News* in Harrisburg, Pennsylvania, featured an extract from King's "I Have a Dream" speech alongside Obama's victory speech.[8]

By the time of Obama's inauguration in January 2009, the connections between King and Obama in the public imagination were even more entrenched, with yoked images dominating many of the commemorative magazines published for the occasion. The cover of *Obama: The Dream Fulfilled* featured a small image of King in the background, pointing his finger toward a larger picture of Obama in the foreground, visually suggesting that the president-elect was being anointed by King as the inheritor of his dream of racial reconciliation and national redemption.[9] *Ebony*, for more than sixty years the nation's leading African American–produced and –oriented magazine, used pictures from the March on Washington, as well as testimony from movement veterans, to place Obama's achievements into a historical context similarly dominated by memories of King. One page bearing the headline "Then and Now" featured a picture of King and excerpts from "I Have a Dream" on the left-hand side, while the right-hand side carried a picture of Obama and extracts from his "A More Perfect Union" speech.[10]

On Inauguration Day Birmingham preacher-activist Calvin Woods, a man beaten and jailed for protesting segregation alongside King in 1963, explained how "countless hundreds across this nation are watching a fulfillment of the dream we sacrificed for."[11] Beth Lawrence, an elderly African-American woman from Tallahassee, had also come to witness the momentous events in Washington. "We got to the mountaintop today," she declared. "I am 84 and I have seen the one thing for which I always dreamed, always hoped, but could never expect in my lifetime." Like Posner, Lawrence evoked both "I Have a Dream" and King's last speech, made in very different circumstances in Memphis in April 1968, when he said, "I've been to the mountaintop. . . . And I've looked over. And I've seen the promised land. I may not get there with you. But I want you to know tonight, that we as a people, will get to the promised land."[12] Such sentiments were not limited to civil rights veterans. The *Star-Ledger*, the biggest paper in New Jersey, headlined its election results edition "Obama Reaches the Mountaintop." And at the time of the Democratic National Convention, Adam Zyglis's editorial cartoon for the *Buffalo News* in upstate New York had been captioned, "I've Been to the Mountaintop"; it featured a smiling King looking down from the Rockies as Obama accepted the nomination.[13]

Without laboring the point further, these examples indicate that a diverse range of observers believed that Obama represented the fulfillment of a dream of an equalitarian, redeemed, united, color-blind America that King had invoked in 1963 and could just about glimpse on the eve of his death. For good reason, however, not everyone was so sure the nation had reached anything resembling a postracial Promised Land in 2008. Indeed, not everyone thought it was even a goal worth pursuing, since postracialism implied that only the erasure of a distinctive black identity and denial of the historical particulars of the African American experience could ensure racial amity and justice in the United States. "I don't like that term," complained philosopher and public intellectual Cornel West early in the primary season. "You work through race, you don't deny race. It's the difference between being color-blind and love-struck. You see, if I love you, I don't need to eliminate your whiteness. If you love me, you don't need to eliminate my blackness. You embrace humanity."[14] Political reporter and Washington insider Gwen Ifill agreed. "I do not believe this to be a 'postracial moment,'" she wrote. "After talking to scores of people, I am still not even entirely sure what that term means." In her view, postracial language was often used to avoid confronting the persistence of race-based inequalities in American society. "For those interested in resisting any discussion of racial difference, it is an easy way to embrace the mythic notion of color blindness," she noted. "Why is 'getting past' race considered to be a good thing? Does that make race a bad thing?"[15]

Historian Jacqueline Jones was also skeptical that Obama's victory marked the dawn of a postracial era. After the election the *Boston Globe* invited several leading historians of U.S. race relations and the civil rights movement to imagine themselves reporting back from "the middle of the century . . . on how the emotionally charged event might appear from a cool distance." From her vantage point in the future, Jones recalled how, on "the night of the election, Obama's supporters joyfully celebrated what many considered to be the elimination of racial barriers to black people's full participation in American political and social life." She concluded more soberly, however, "It's clear now that 'race' had little to do with it. Virtually any Democrat who had survived the grueling primary process would have won the presidency in the fall of 2008."[16]

Jones was surely correct in her assessment. Republican chances had been fatally damaged by the choice of Sarah Palin as a highly polarizing vice-presidential candidate, by the association with a severe economic downturn and recession, by the promotion of an increasingly unpopular and costly military involvement in Iraq and Afghanistan, and by a dilatory and inept response to Hurricane Katrina—a disaster that exposed the persistence of acute, racially circumscribed poverty in America. Nevertheless, it is important to consider how history, demographics, and the tactics of the Obama campaign combined to ensure that race, in Jones's words, "had little to do with it"—or, more precisely, to consider how these factors combined to ensure that Obama's skin color did not matter enough to American voters to destroy his chance of winning his party's nomination and eventually the presidency. Paradoxically, the lengths to which Obama sometimes went to avoid being cast as a traditional black candidate with a typically black agenda, struggling beneath the weight of the stereotypes usually heaped on black men by white America, signaled that race still had enormous salience in the election. So, too, did the intense enthusiasm with which substantial white support for Obama was seized on as indicative of a new postracial moment and, therefore, the fulfillment of what was widely perceived to be King's dream.

There was actually plenty of evidence from the campaign trail that racism was alive and well across the nation. It is worth briefly summarizing some of that evidence to emphasize the extraordinary potency of a postracial discourse that, for a while, seemed largely immune to empirical or logical refutation. At the extremist end of the racist spectrum, an unprecedented number of death threats were leveled at Obama, many of them from self-declared white supremacists.[17] The Southern Poverty Law Center cataloged 200 hate-related incidents connected to Obama's election, while the number of documented "hate groups" rose from 888 in 2007 to 926 in 2008.[18] Shortly after the election CBS news reported "cross burning, schoolchildren chanting 'assassinate Obama.' Black figures hung from nooses. Racial epithets scrawled on homes and cars. Incidents around the country referring to President-elect Barack Obama are dampening the postelection glow of racial progress and harmony, highlighting the stubborn racism that remains in America."[19]

Personal threats against Obama increased significantly after Republican candidate John McCain unexpectedly chose Sarah Palin as his running mate, hoping to hold on to the white, often evangelical Christian supporters who had been the bedrock of GOP electoral successes since Richard Nixon mobilized America's "Silent Majority" against the perceived excesses of 1960s liberalism.[20] Palin, the governor of Alaska—demographically, one of the nation's whitest states—spent a lot of time "othering" Obama. Like nationally syndicated conservative talk-radio star Bill Cunningham, Palin repeatedly used his full name, Barack Hussein Obama, as if trying to fashion a subliminal connection in voters' minds between Obama and Saddam Hussein or to stir rumors circulating on the fringes of the right-wing media that he was secretly a Muslim. One voter in Barefoot Bay, Florida, clearly took this message to heart. Andy Lacasse, a Korean War veteran and a registered Democrat until Obama won the party's nomination, put up a large sign in his backyard that read "OBAMA HALF-BREED MUSLIN [*sic*]."[21]

Never overburdened by the demands of logical consistency, Palin stoked rumors of Obama's Islamic connections while also trying to extract the last drop of political capital from his relationship with his former Chicago minister, the outspoken and occasionally intemperate, but always Christian, Jeremiah Wright. In a 2003 sermon Wright had lambasted America's racist past with the words, "Not God bless America. God damn America!" At other times Wright had endorsed the theory that AIDS had been introduced by the U.S. government to wipe out the black population and, echoing Malcolm X's comments after the assassination of President John Kennedy, suggested that the 9/11 terrorist outrages were an example of "America's chickens coming home to roost."[22] Obama rejected many of Wright's more outré ideas and inflammatory language, yet he refused to completely disavow one of his most important spiritual and political mentors.[23]

The connection to Wright offered Republicans an irresistible opportunity to try to figuratively and literally "blacken" Obama's candidacy and counter any political advantage Obama might derive from notions of postracialism. Conservatives worked hard to encourage color-coded doubts about Obama's patriotism, citizenship, religious beliefs, and political ideology. The Internet, Fox News, and conservative talk radio buzzed with attempts to expose Obama's Hawaiian birth certificate as a forgery, claiming it had been fabricated to hide the fact that he was really Kenyan and therefore ineligible to be president. More exotic still were efforts to prove that he was Malcolm X's love child. This was very convenient for those who sought to portray Obama as heir not to the widely revered, nonviolent Baptist preacher and nationally celebrated hero King but to the Muslim Malcolm, who openly advocated armed self-defense for African Americans and wanted the United Nations to intervene to stop the persecution of the black U.S. population. Eventually the Obama campaign set up its own website to counter the unprecedented torrent of disinformation and flagrant lies in circulation.[24]

Republican candidate John McCain generally ignored such conspiracy theories and avoided racially derogatory language. In relative terms he soft-pedaled criticism of Obama's association with Wright, preferring to focus on what he saw as his opponent's dangerously radical social and economic views. McCain even corrected a supporter in Lakeville, Minnesota, who proclaimed that she didn't trust Obama because she thought he was "an Arab."[25] Yet even McCain raised eyebrows when, in the middle of a debate at Belmont University in Nashville in October 2008, he dismissively waved his hand toward his opponent and referred to Obama as "that one."[26] In that moment, rhetoric and gesture combined in a racially inflected attempt to marginalize and diminish Obama in the eyes of American voters. Obama was, McCain appeared to imply, simultaneously insignificant and dangerous; he was an unwelcome alien presence, a black quasi-socialist with connections to bomb-throwing radicals of the late 1960s—notably, to Bill Ayers, a former member of the Weather Underground with whom Obama had worked briefly in Chicago. Somehow this militant black maverick had infiltrated the regular, white, traditionally male business of U.S. presidential politics.

When it came to Election Day, the continuing significance of race was hard to ignore; however, many people, excited by the momentousness of Obama's victory and eager to see it as the realization of King's dream, did their best to do so. "Racial Barrier Falls in Decisive Victory" gushed the *New York Times,* while *USA Today*'s headline insisted that Obama's election "erases a racial barrier."[27] The polling data behind Obama's victory suggested different conclusions. Nationally, white voters delivered substantially fewer votes to Obama than did any other major demographic group. In addition to garnering 95 percent of the black vote, Obama won among women (55 percent), Hispanics (66 percent), and Asians (62 percent) and among every age cohort except those older than sixty-five. Yet only 43 percent of all whites voted for Obama (women, 46 percent; men, 41 percent); 55 percent of white voters went for McCain.[28] Of course, race was not the only issue in play here. Some whites voted for McCain because they sincerely believed that the Republicans better served their economic interests, were more in tune with their social and moral values, and would provide better national security. Still, it is hard to escape the conclusion that racial preferences and aversion to a black candidate affected some whites' votes.

This was true not just among Republicans but also among some erstwhile white Democrats, such as Andy Lacasse in Florida. Labor stalwart Richard Trumka, secretary-general of the AFL-CIO, raised $53.4 million for Obama's campaign, but he told a chastening story about one white Democratic Party member he encountered while campaigning in his hometown of Nemacolin, Pennsylvania. The woman was a Hillary Clinton supporter and told Trumka, "There's no way that I'd ever vote for Obama." When Trumka asked why, she branded Obama a Muslim and then accused him of refusing to wear a patriotic American flag pin on his lapel. When Trumka corrected these fallacies, the woman explained, "Well, I just don't trust him [then lowered her voice] because he's black."[29]

White southerners have often been unfairly and reductively caricatured as the most unregenerate racist cohort in the United States. Still, only about 33 percent of white southerners voted for Obama—roughly 10 percentage points less than whites nationally.[30] In the Deep South the proportion of whites who cast their ballots for the black candidate was closer to 20 percent, with McCain claiming about 90 percent of the white male vote in Alabama and Louisiana.[31] Of the 22 percent of counties in the United States that voted more decisively for Republicans in 2008 than they had in 2004, the vast majority were located in the strongly white-majority districts of Appalachia and the Great Plains.[32] In 1992, 85 percent of voters who told pollsters they believed the economy was in bad shape had voted for Democrat challenger Bill Clinton. In the much bleaker economic circumstances of 2008, only 66 percent of the population who believed the economy was bad cast their vote for Barack Obama.[33]

Cumulatively, these snapshots suggest that, for all the talk of unity and reconciliation associated with the Obama campaign, it was preposterous to think that racism would end with his victory or that his time in office would erase the practical or psychological effects of hundreds of years of racial suspicion, prejudice, discrimination, and inequality. As Jacqueline Jones insisted, race remained a crucial factor in shaping, if never wholly determining, the scope of opportunities and the quality of life for most Americans. "While the symbolism of Obama's election was powerful," Jones wrote to the *Boston Globe* from her imaginary future, "his success at the polls failed to change in any dramatic way the legacy of slavery borne by the nation's impoverished and thus most vulnerable African Americans."[34]

Notwithstanding all these important caveats and cautionary notes, two of the most remarkable things about Obama's victory were the relative lack of success of the "othering" tactics deployed against him and the sheer resilience of the hope that his victory might just herald, or even embody, a postracial moment that was itself redolent of a temporarily rejuvenated sense of national promise. In 2008 it proved extremely difficult to affix threatening "black"—or revolutionary or socialist or Islamic—identities onto Obama and thereby place him beyond the acceptable "norms" of mainstream American politics.

There were several reasons for this. One had to do with demographic shifts that produced a new generation of voters far less concerned than

their parents or grandparents with the racially encoded culture wars unleashed in the 1960s. Obama won overwhelmingly among the 11 percent
of the electorate, 13 million people, voting for the first time. As pollster
Cornell Belcher explained, "The newer, younger voters struggle less with
the racial and cultural ghosts of our country's past."[35] Furthermore, despite
the historical tensions among African Americans, Hispanics, and Asians
that hampered previous attempts at "rainbow" coalition building, Obama
was the beneficiary of demographic transformations whereby nonwhite
voters who were less likely to balk at voting for a nonwhite candidate
wielded more political influence than ever before. Roughly two-thirds of
Asian Americans and Hispanics, the latter constituting the largest minority
group in the United States, cast their votes for Obama.[36]

A second reason why Obama was able to ameliorate the destructive
potential of race was the way he approached the issue during the campaign.
He adopted a breathtaking kind of brinkmanship that sometimes involved
tackling the issue of prejudice and discrimination head-on and sometimes
acting and speaking as if race were wholly irrelevant to his candidacy, if
not to his country's past and present. Unlike previous African American
candidates for the Democratic nomination—Shirley Chisholm, Jesse Jackson, Al Sharpton—Obama generally avoided being pigeonholed as exclusively or even primarily a race leader. He was even able to generate what
Los Angeles Times columnist David Ehrenstein dubbed the "magic Negro"
effect—that is, he made many whites feel comfortable about voting for a
black candidate while simultaneously diminishing any sense of collective
white guilt about the racism that had long stymied African American opportunity and preserved white privilege in the United States.[37]

Some of Obama's capacity to minimize the usual political liabilities
of race and maximize the "American" thrust of his campaign was literally
embodied in his own biography. Many were fascinated by Obama's quest
to reconcile the complex and sometimes conflicted strains of his own bio-
logical identity and cultural lineages. He was born in Hawaii to a white
mother from Kansas and a Kenyan father; he was raised and schooled
in Kansas and Indonesia, attended Occidental College in Los Angeles
and then Harvard Law School, and did a stint as a community organizer
in Chicago before entering state and then national politics. As described
in his memoir-cum-manifesto *The Audacity of Hope* (tellingly subtitled
Thoughts on Reclaiming the American Dream), and as reiterated endlessly
on the campaign trail, Obama's efforts to fashion a coherent identity and
political philosophy from this multiplicity of influences eventually led him

to embrace the core principles of American civil religion, as articulated in its foundational documents and as rearticulated most powerfully by Martin Luther King and Abraham Lincoln.

For some people, this personal and political journey seemed emblematic of America's historical national mission, with its faltering efforts to reconcile increasing diversity with a commitment to a shared set of civic ideals. Obama himself insisted that the "self-evident truths" of the Declaration of Independence "that all men are created equal," repeated so memorably by King in "I Have a Dream," were "our starting points as Americans."[38] The Constitution, meanwhile, serves not to ensure perpetual adherence to any particular law, policy, ideology, or doctrine promulgated several centuries earlier by the founding fathers, as some conservatives and strict-construction jurists would have it; rather, it serves as a living framework for a "deliberative democracy" in which "all citizens are required to engage in a process of testing their ideas against an external reality, persuading others of their point of view, and building shifting alliances of consent." For Obama, the Constitution offers "a road map by which we marry passion to reason, the ideal of individual freedom to the demands of community." And it was Lincoln, Obama explained, "who like no man before or since understood both the deliberative function of our democracy and the limits of such deliberation," ultimately resorting to military force to preserve the integrity of the Union when the political process could no longer ensure that cohesion. But, Obama noted admiringly, Lincoln resisted "the temptation to demonize the fathers and sons who did battle on the other side" in order to reincorporate them into the reborn Union.[39]

Similarly casting himself as a unifier, as a candidate who could transcend or make less destructive the deep fault lines in contemporary American society based on race, class, gender, religion, and ideological zealotry, Obama assumed the symbolic mantle of both Lincoln and King. Like both these iconic figures, Obama implicitly recognized that perhaps the single most important recurring theme in American history has been the attempt to define precisely who is included in what David Hollinger calls "the circle of the 'we'": who in America gets to enjoy the protections and benefits, and bear the responsibilities, associated with citizenship as enshrined in the notion of "we the people."[40] Obama was publicly grappling with this issue as early as the 2004 Democratic National Convention in Boston, where he delivered the keynote address that first brought him to national attention. In this speech Obama focused on the need for America to move beyond the divisiveness that characterized contemporary politics and rededicate itself to the task of reconciling the pull of individual, group, and national needs: "to pursue our individual dreams, yet still come together as a single American family: 'E pluribus unum,' out of many, one."[41]

On the presidential campaign trail, Obama also used popular memories of King as a man dedicated to rallying all Americans in the pursuit of freedom and justice to drive home this message. In January 2008, for example, early in the bruising primary season, Obama visited the Ebenezer Baptist Church in Atlanta, where King had served as co-pastor, to honor King's birthday. Buoyant after his victory in the Iowa caucuses, Obama drew parallels between his own tilt at the White House and what many had once seen as an equally quixotic campaign against entrenched systems of racial oppression in the Jim Crow South. "At a time when many were still doubtful about the possibility of change . . . King inspired with words not of anger, but of an urgency that still speaks to us today: 'Unity is the great need of the hour' is what King said. Unity is how we shall overcome," Obama said. "Instead of having a politics that lives up to King's call for unity," Obama told an audience in Fort Wayne, Indiana, on the fortieth anniversary of King's death, "we've had a politics that's used race to drive us apart, when all this does is feed the forces of division and distraction and stops us from solving our problems."[42]

Obama's King-like calls for unity and emphasis on a shared humanity and commitment to America's civil religion did not imply a rejection of diversity. Perhaps not surprisingly, given his own biography, Obama presented himself as somebody who recognized, respected, and rejoiced in difference and genuinely believed that diversity and honest dissent strengthened the Union. There were echoes of James Madison and *The Federalist Papers* as Obama revisited the virtues of pluralism, not just as a good thing in its own right but as a force that could neutralize or moderate conflicting interests within America.[43] "There's not a liberal America and a conservative America," he insisted, "there's the United States of America. There's not a black America and white America and Latino America and Asian America; there's the United States of America."[44] Without resorting to the simplistic language of postracialism, this kind of rhetoric, emphasizing both the historical diversity of American society and a broadly shared commitment to certain foundational ideals, occupied a similar ideological space and exerted similar appeal. "For all our disagreements," Obama insisted, "we would be hard pressed to find a conservative or liberal in America today, whether Republican or Democrat, academic or layman, who doesn't subscribe to the basic set of individual liberties identified by the Fathers and enshrined in our Constitution and our common law."[45]

In November 2008 the electoral triumph of Obama's inclusive message reflected a new level of comfort with the kind of multicultural hybridity that he personified among more voters of more races and ethnicities than ever before. There was broad agreement among his supporters that the Constitution demanded equal protection of the freedoms and rights of a vast array of individuals and groups in America, many of whom had once been outside the "circle of the 'we.'" Ironically, in this regard, the controversy that erupted concerning his relationship with Jeremiah Wright may have been a proverbial blessing in disguise. It compelled Obama to explicitly confront the issues of diversity and unity and of race and racism. It also required him to define his relationship to the generations of black activists who had joined King in the battle for civil and voting rights in the 1960s and those who had subsequently struggled to turn those legislative victories into instruments of genuine equality.

Some of that older generation, including the Reverend Joseph Lowery, King's former colleague and president of the Southern Christian Leadership Conference, endorsed Obama quickly, as did Al Sharpton in New York and James Clyburn in South Carolina. Other movement veterans, such as John Lewis, took longer, but after much soul-searching they embraced Obama as the voice of the future not just for African Americans but for all Americans. Despite such endorsements, Obama sometimes found himself at odds with older black leaders, including Jesse Jackson, who was overheard on national television saying that he'd like to cut off Obama's "nuts" for being condescending toward or neglectful of poor African Americans. Jackson, along with other black activist-intellectuals such as Cornel West and Julianne Malveaux, was forever cajoling Obama to specifically address black issues and the persistence of white racism, anxious that Obama's need for white approval might push pressing "black" concerns off the agenda.[46]

In Philadelphia on March 18, 2008, Obama argued that such crude differentiations between "black" and "white" problems were unhelpful, counterproductive, and ultimately harmful to the nation. He condemned Wright's inflammatory comments as "not only wrong but divisive, divisive at a time when we need unity; racially charged at a time when we need to come together to solve a set of monumental problems . . . that are neither black or white or Latino or Asian, but rather problems that confront us all." Rather than disavow Wright entirely, however, Obama offered an analysis of the historical roots of the black frustration the preacher articulated. He noted respectfully how Wright's generation had fought to shake off the "inequalities passed on from an earlier generation that suffered under the brutal legacy of slavery and Jim Crow." Many African Americans had succeeded, at least in crude material terms, but, Obama explained, "for all those who scratched and clawed their way to get a piece of the American Dream, there were many who didn't make it. . . . Even for those blacks who did make it, questions of race, and racism, continue to define their worldview in fundamental ways." This generation, he argued, was disillusioned by the false dawn of the civil rights victories of the 1960s: their "anger is real; it is powerful; and to simply wish it away without understanding its roots, only serves to widen the chasm of misunderstanding that exists between the races." Obama then acknowledged that similar anger burned within segments of the white community, poisoning the prospects for any kind of meaningful interracial dialogue and national unity. Most whites, he appreciated, "don't feel they have been particularly privileged by their race." He warned that "to wish away the resentments of white Americans, to label them as misguided or even racist, without recognizing they are grounded in legitimate concerns—this, too, widens the racial divide, and blocks the path to understanding."[47]

Having described the nation's racial impasse, Obama proposed a new progressive politics that might move America beyond the racial antagonisms and intense ideological battle lines of the past. For African Americans, this meant "embracing the burdens of our past without becoming victims of our past . . . to insist on a full measure of justice in every aspect of American life." This call for African Americans to assert their citizenship rights—and embrace their civic responsibilities—echoed King's injunction in 1960, before those rights were fully protected by law, that "the Negro must not be victimized with the delusion of thinking that others should be more concerned than himself about his citizenship rights."[48] Obama also urged whites to recognize legitimate and distinctive black grievances concerning education, housing, health care, employment, and the criminal justice system that required attention for the good of the nation as a whole. Ultimately, Obama insisted, with another rhetorical nod toward King, attainment of that racial peace and national progress "requires all Americans to realize that your dreams do not all have to come at the expense of my dreams. That investing in the health, welfare, and education of black and brown and white children will ultimately help all America prosper."[49]

The "More Perfect Union" speech was classic Obama, with its care-ful blend of sociohistorical analysis, deference to the Constitution, and personal biography ("I will never forget that in no other country on Earth is my story even possible. It is a story that has seared into my genetic makeup the idea that this nation is more than the sum of its parts—that out of many, we are truly one").[50] It was also a major reason why, in the words of black scholar Michael Eric Dyson, Obama "resisted being trapped by narrow definitions of race. . . . It's not that Obama was seeking to escape his Black identity so much as he wanted to leap valiantly past racial lim-its." In celebrating his own mixed heritage without denigrating or evading the importance of his own "blackness" or the history of racial discrimina-tion, Obama presented himself as the embodiment of American ideals. As Dyson notes, the more he was vilified as "a communist, socialist, Marxist, terrorist, traitor and an un-American subversive," the more "Obama an-noyed his critics by becoming ever more American."[51]

These narratives of self-realization, so carefully bound to narratives of unfulfilled yet attainable national promise, were crucial to Obama's ap-peal; they helped assuage doubts about his commitment to the American democratic experiment and stoked the unusual levels of emotional energy, expectation, and hope among his supporters that were the hallmarks of his campaign. Nowhere was this more evident than in the brief biographi-cal film *A Mother's Promise,* shown just before he accepted his party's nomination in Denver. The key scenes in the film, such as those in which Obama eagerly awaits NASA astronauts' return from space, inserted him into the flow of national history and shared memories. "Voters, awash in the complexity of current events, use stories as a means of boiling down complicated realities," observes Evan Cornog in his analysis of how care-fully constructed, emotionally compelling, and conventionally patriotic official biographies have been crucial to the electoral success of presi-dential candidates throughout American history.[52] Obama's personal and political biography was in some ways exotic, but for many voters and com-mentators—and for the candidate and his staff—it was constructed and construed as a quintessentially American tale.

Fist-Bumping with Abraham Lincoln

One of Obama's most important means of becoming "ever more Ameri-can" was invoking either Martin Luther King or King's own favorite secular touchstone, Abraham Lincoln, whenever he wanted to wrap his candidacy within the folds of a traditionally expressed, if less frequently enacted, national commitment to freedom, equality, and justice. There was a certain irony here, given that, in their lifetimes, both Lincoln and King were widely demonized and ultimately murdered for their beliefs. Nonetheless, they—or, more accurately, particular iterations of their political personas in popular memory—are revered by many Americans as personifications of the nation's best hopes and aspirations.

Obama made no secret of his admiration for Lincoln, another Illinois lawyer-turned-politician who made an initially unlikely bid for the White House. It was Lincoln who provided the major point of reference when Obama declared his intention to run for the presidency in February 2007 in Lincoln's hometown of Springfield, Illinois. Announcing his candidacy, Obama channeled Lincoln's "House Divided" speech to the 1858 state Republican convention, where he famously quoted scripture to warn that national unity was imperiled by the spiraling crisis between a slaveholding South and a nonslaveholding North. "A house divided against itself cannot stand," Lincoln had insisted. His presidency was dominated by the Civil War—a military effort to restore the geographic and political cohesion of the nation that Lincoln also framed, perhaps most memorably in the Gettysburg Address, as a mission to restore a shared commitment to the nation's founding principles.[53] Likewise, Obama promised a presidency that would promote unity of purpose and emphasize common values that had been buried beneath a thick crust of ideological, racial, class, religious, and gender factionalism. "This campaign has to be about reclaiming the meaning of citizenship, restoring our common purpose, and realizing that few obstacles can withstand the power of millions of voices calling for change," Obama explained. "Divided, we are bound to fail."[54]

Obama was under no illusions about Lincoln's own racial opinions, refusing to "swallow the whole view of Lincoln as the Great Emancipator. As a law professor and civil rights lawyer and as an African American, I am fully aware of his limited views on race. Anyone who actually reads the Emancipation Proclamation knows it was more a military document than a clarion call for justice."[55] Nevertheless, as president, Obama would have that same proclamation hung proudly in the Oval Office, and throughout his campaign he worked hard and effectively to associate himself with Lincoln in the public consciousness.[56] He was helped in this regard when important commentators drew flattering analogies between the two men, in particular, comparing their powerful rhetorical gifts and dedication to the preservation and perfection of the Union. In the *New York Review of Books,* for example, Garry Wills analyzed Obama's "A More Perfect Union" speech in the context of Lincoln's Cooper Union campaign speech from February 1860. Both speeches were made when the two men were under fire from their political opponents for allegedly associating with or encouraging dangerous extremists who threatened the stability of the nation—militant abolitionists such as John Brown in Lincoln's case, and Jeremiah Wright in Obama's. Like Lincoln, Obama spoke to set the record straight, denounce extremism, and press his claims to be not the destroyer but the savior of the nation. Both men, as Wills put it, "used a campaign occasion to rise to a higher vision of America's future. Both argued intelligently for closer union in the cause of progress."[57] Similarly, Obama's election night victory speech drew heavily on Lincoln's first and second inaugurals and the Gettysburg Address. Obama told his opponents, just as Lincoln had in 1861, "We are not enemies, but friends"; he pledged to unite the country after half a century of culture wars and fierce ideological partisanship, just as Lincoln had promised in 1865 to "bind up the nation's wounds" after four years of bloodshed.[58]

Other commentators, both scholarly and popular, were quick to pick up on Obama's debts, real and imagined, to Lincoln. Some clawed far below the surface of Lincoln's own racial prejudices to stress his underlying vision of a diverse America, reborn in a spirit of genuine freedom and democracy. On the eve of the election, political analyst Harold Fineman told *Newsweek* that it was precisely because of Obama's DNA, his mixed racial and cultural heritage, that he was "the rightful heir to Lincoln's vision and hope" for the nation.[59] Obama's opponents, Democrat as well as Republican, had frequently sought to exploit the notion that, as Hillary Clinton's senior strategist Mark Penn put it, Obama's "roots to basic American values and culture are at best limited."[60] Yet for Fineman, and for a sufficient number of American voters, Obama actually came to embody those "basic American values" associated in the popular consciousness with Lincoln.

One barometer of this association was the ubiquity of editorial cartoons that used Lincoln to situate Obama within a grand narrative of American history. Steve Benson in the *Arizona Republic,* for example, featured a newly elected Obama cozied up to Lincoln among the other stone-hewed presidents of Monument Valley.[61] David Fitzsimmons's cartoon in the *Arizona Daily Star* depicted Lincoln seated in his Memorial—as he was in the vast majority of these images—arms raised aloft in celebration of Obama's victory and unleashing a mighty "Yesssssss." Another Fitzsimmons image had Lincoln weeping tears of joy at the news, as did Jim Morin's cartoon for the *Miami Herald,* where Lincoln proudly sported an Obama campaign "Yes We Can" badge. Jeff Breen's Lincoln in the *San Diego Union Tribune* simply beamed beatifically at the election results. Across the nation, Scott Stantis (*Birmingham News*), John Darkow (*Columbia [Mo.] News Tribune*), Mike Luckovich (*Atlanta Journal Constitution*), and Mike Keefe (*Denver Post*) were among the many artists to feature a jubilant Lincoln giving Obama an approving thumbs-up.

Even more symbolically complex and revealing was Jeff Darcy's cartoon in the *Cleveland Plain Dealer,* in which Lincoln gave Obama a fraternal "fist-bump." This friendly greeting, originally associated with African Americans, caused a stir when Obama and his wife, Michelle, exchanged one in St. Paul, Minnesota, on the evening of June 3, 2008. Hard-right conservatives were quick to cite it as evidence of a sinister, almost gang-like, even alien conspiracy at the heart of Obama's candidacy. Was it "a terrorist fist-jab?" speculated Fox News anchor E. D. Hill, preempting by several months Sarah Palin's condemnation of Obama for "palling around with terrorists who would target their own country."[62] Cartoonist Barry Britt's cover for the *New Yorker* satirized the mix of genuine paranoia, ignorance, and political calculation that motivated such speculation by imagining the fist-bumping Obamas in the Oval Office dressed in Muslim robes. The image of Michelle, replete with gun and ammunition belt, was styled after iconic shots of Black Power–era activist Angela Davis, while in the background Britt included a portrait of an Islamic cleric burning an American flag.[63]

Although Britt intended to mock the way Obama's opponents had desperately seized on the fist-bump as further evidence of his un-Americanism, the candidate's own team was deeply unsettled by the image, fearing that it might somehow be read literally or at least provide more material for right-wing denunciations of Obama's loyalties. In a sense, they were right to worry: reactions to visual cues are inherently more difficult to predict and police than are responses to clearly articulated verbal messages—although words are hardly immune to distortion and misinterpretation. Moreover, the fist-bump was one of many gestures Obama used to maintain contact and credibility with a black constituency, even as he courted cross-racial support. When Obama visited Washington's legendary black diner, Ben's Chili Bowl, and responded to a cashier's inquiry about whether he needed change with a colloquial "Nah, we straight"; when he found time to shoot hoops amid the brutal demands of the campaign trail; when he occasionally adopted an obvious "street lope," a wide, swaggering gait that is culturally marked as being of black origin; or when he lovingly bumped fists with his wife, he was, with varying degrees of calculation, making a visceral appeal to black audiences that was largely independent of the specifics of his political program or the substance of his rhetoric.[64]

Obama was extremely deft in his use of this kind of dog-whistle politics, whereby particular turns of phrase, cadences of speech, and a wide repertoire of nonverbal gestures allowed him to affirm his black identity to black observers in ways that did not particularly alienate or alarm most nonblacks. In this regard he was the beneficiary of the triumph of black-derived trends in speech, dress, and many other aspects of cultural performance in contemporary America. Far from seeming foreign or threatening, Obama's use of such putatively black style markers seemed quite familiar to many Americans. Coming from a smart and erudite black candidate running for the nation's highest public office, Obama's easy nods to black vernacular style conveyed, in the words of linguist John McWhorter, "warmth, authenticity and a touch of seductive danger not only to blacks but many whites, especially ones below about 50."[65]

Darcy's Obama-Lincoln cartoon functioned in a similar way by boldly juxtaposing the fist-bumping and therefore culturally coded "black" Obama with the premier white popular symbol of American national cohesion. In so doing, Darcy placed an African American in the heart of a narrative of national identity and common purpose from which blacks had historically been excluded while simultaneously reimagining Lincoln in an intimate, fraternal, mutually respectful, and supportive relationship with a black man. Darcy and other cartoonists who visually linked Obama and Lincoln—and sometimes included King to complete the trinity (e.g., Nate Beeler's *Washington Examiner* drawing depicted Obama flanked by his two mentors, each resting a tender, supportive hand on his shoulder)—were riffing on, and helping to perpetuate, an important dimension of the 2008 zeitgeist, fusing dreams of racial reconciliation with those of a rejuvenated sense of national mission.

On Inauguration Day it was no accident that Abraham Lincoln cast at least as long a shadow over the official proceedings as did Martin Luther King. Obama's train journey to Washington faithfully followed Lincoln's passage from Philadelphia to the Capitol for his 1861 inauguration; the oath of office was taken on Lincoln's Bible, and the call for "a new birth of freedom" at the heart of the Gettysburg Address provided the overarching theme of Obama's speech. Indeed, a few days before he was sworn in, while still working on his speech, Obama had taken his family to the Lincoln Memorial to reread the Gettysburg Address. The same venue hosted a celebratory preinauguration concert featuring U2, Bruce Springsteen, and Stevie Wonder. It was "the site of the happiest moment of his inaugural celebration," according to journalist Richard Wolffe.[66]

The Lincoln Memorial had long been one of Obama's favorite haunts. It was a place where King and Lincoln, two men who "ultimately laid down their lives in the service of perfecting an imperfect union," came together in his imagination. At the conclusion of *Audacity of Hope,* Obama recalls how as a senator he regularly jogged to the Lincoln Memorial at dusk to read the Gettysburg Address and the second inaugural and to imagine "the crowd stilled by Dr. King's mighty cadence."[67] The placement and the heightened poetic language suggest that this was a passage he particularly wanted his readers to remember. He said as much again at the concert at the memorial, when he invoked the location's and, by extension, Lincoln's special resonance as a symbol of national unity. "What gives me the greatest hope of all is not the stone and marble that surrounds us today, but what fills the spaces in between," he explained. "It is you—Americans of every race and region and station who came here because you believe in what this country can be . . . a belief that if we could just recognize ourselves in one another and bring everyone together—Democrats, Republicans, and Independents; Latino, Asian, and Native American; black and white, gay and straight, disabled and not—then not only would we restore hope and opportunity in places that yearned for both, but maybe, just maybe, we might perfect our union in the process."[68]

Whose Dream, Which King?

Before Barack Obama, no African American leader had been more successful than Martin Luther King at making Abraham Lincoln and the Lincoln Memorial the touchstone of appeals to America's best ideals. King's "I Have a Dream" speech was delivered from the steps of the public monument, which by 1963 had already acquired great significance for the black freedom struggle. As early as 1876, Frederick Douglass had tried to wed Lincoln's prestige as savior of the nation to the ongoing struggle for black rights by calling for the building of a statue dedicated to the "Great Emancipator" in Washington, D.C. The popular association between Lincoln and the cause of civil rights gathered momentum in 1939 when the great African American contralto Marian Anderson sang "My Country 'tis of Thee" from the memorial after being barred from performing at nearby

Constitution Hall. The Anderson concert added new layers of meaning to Lincoln's memory and to the memorial, helping to transform what had primarily been symbols of national unity into emblems of racial justice.[69] King had first spoken there in May 1957, when his "Give Us the Ballot" oration urged federal action to secure black voting rights. Although far less celebrated than "I Have a Dream," and certainly referred to less often in the context of Obama's relationship to the civil rights movement, this hard-nosed call for black political power was an equally significant harbinger of Obama's victory. "Give us the ballot and we will no longer have to worry the federal government about our basic rights," King exhorted. "Give us the ballot and we will fill our legislative halls with men of good will."[70]

At the same venue six years later, in the midst of the Civil War Centennial celebrations, and 100 years after Lincoln's Emancipation Proclamation, King called for a rededication to what he called "the magnificent words of the Constitution and the Declaration of Independence," describing them as "a promissory note to which every American was to fall heir . . . the promise that all men, yes black men as well as white men, would be guaranteed the unalienable rights of life, liberty, and the pursuit of happiness." Delivered at the climax of the "Jobs and Freedom" march, which fused issues of economic and racial justice, "I Have a Dream" was much more militant and rather less optimistic than most popular readings during the 2008 campaign allowed. The specters of Malcolm X, the Nation of Islam, and urban riots stalked the speech in which King offered ominous portents of racial unrest and the rise of much less temperate strains of black activism if his own resolutely nonviolent protests for basic constitutional rights and federal protections were not successful. Angry that America had "defaulted on this promissory note in so far as her citizens of color are concerned," African Americans had marched on Washington "to cash this check, a check that will give us upon demand the riches of freedom and the security of justice." Before moving on to describe his dream, King warned that "the whirlwinds of revolt will continue to shake the foundations of our nation until the bright day of justice emerges."[71]

In his inaugural address, Barack Obama referred to the same "God-given promise that all are equal, all are free, and all deserve a chance to pursue their full measure of happiness." He duly noted that his election was in some ways a measure of the distance come by many African Americans since the 1960s, insofar as "a man whose father less than sixty years ago might not have been served at a local restaurant can now stand before you to take a most sacred oath." In keeping with his most important campaign message, he also cast that achievement as a national and collective triumph, not a black or individual one: "This is the meaning of our liberty and our creed—why men and women and children of every race and every faith can join in celebration across this magnificent mall." Moreover, just as King had called for greater fidelity to the precepts of the nation's founding documents, Obama maintained that America's greatest achievements, past, present, and still to come, were "because We the People have remained faithful to the ideals of our forebears, and true to our founding documents."[72]

And yet, in what was a sober and challenging speech, rather than an uplifting and celebratory one, Obama also emphasized the sense of unfinished business and unfulfilled promise that had animated much of King's 1963 speech. "In reaffirming the greatness of our nation, we understand that greatness is never a given. It must be earned," Obama insisted.[73] Toward the end of his life, King had spent less time affirming the glories of the nation's ideals and foundational documents; he cautioned that it was not enough to pay "blithe lip service to the guarantees of life, liberty and pursuit of happiness" and pointed out that the "fine sentiments . . . embodied in the Declaration of Independence" were "always a declaration of intent rather than reality."[74] In a similar vein, Obama reminded listeners of the continuing gap between aspiration and practice, dream and condition, in American life and urged them to help him fill that gap. "Everywhere we look," Obama noted somberly, "there is work to be done."[75]

Obama had always mixed admiration for the cautiously optimistic and deeply inspirational dreamer of 1963 with an appreciation of the more radical, frustrated, and sometimes disillusioned King in the last year or so of his life. Largely invisible in the annual birthday celebrations that simultaneously reflect and shape popular understandings of King is a man for whom racial justice was only one aspect of a much wider and even more daunting struggle against economic exploitation and militarism, manifested most obviously by what King saw as an unjust, imperialist war in Vietnam. By 1968 King thought of himself, at least in private, as a democratic socialist who was grappling with how to understand, expose, and correct the deep structural impediments to black progress that persisted even after the hard-earned passage of the Civil Rights Act of 1964 and the Voting Rights Act of 1965.

Like Obama, King had to balance racial, national, and global identities and competing loyalties, priorities, and agendas in ways that the relentless emphasis on the magnificent prophetic vision of interracial brotherhood at the end of "I Have Dream" obscured. Indeed, although King's name and his most famous speech were regularly invoked in discussions of Obama's postracialism, there is little to suggest that a world somehow miraculously "beyond race" was really what King had in mind. His conception of freedom, justice, and equality was always based on the affirmation, not the denial, of African American identity. During the Montgomery bus boycott that first brought him to national prominence, King located "a revolutionary change in the Negro's evaluation of himself and of his destiny" at the heart of that protest; at the start of the 1960s he hailed "the rising tide of racial consciousness" with its "new sense of dignity and self-respect" and "self-consciousness" as the sine qua non of a mass black liberation movement; by the end of his life, amid all his reservations about some of the language, tactics, and goals of Black Power, King agreed that it expressed a "legitimate and necessary concern for group unity and black identity." He fully recognized the uniqueness of the historical experiences in which black culture and identity had been forged, finding this racial consciousness and pride perfectly compatible with an unconditional commitment to universal human brotherhood.[76]

Ultimately, King thought of himself not just as a champion of black rights but as somebody working for human rights, for the deliverance from want and fear of all the oppressed, marginalized, and disadvantaged in America and around the world. Just as the 1963 March on Washington had been focused on jobs and freedom, so King's last initiative, the Poor People's Campaign, was an effort to bring the poor and dispossessed of all races to Washington to "demand that the government address itself to the problem of poverty."[77] This attempt to move beyond sectarian racial issues to confront deeper economic inequalities and to see ever more clearly that black and white destinies were inextricably bound together clearly influenced Obama's politics and visions for America. In his Fort Wayne speech on the anniversary of King's death, Obama reminded his listeners that King had been in Memphis to support a strike by fearfully abused sanitation workers. That strike constituted "a struggle for economic justice, for the opportunity that should be available to peoples of all races and all walks of life. Because Dr. King understood that the struggle for economic justice and the struggle for racial justice were really one . . . so long as opportunity was being opened to some but not all—the dream that he spoke of would remain out of reach . . . the struggle for economic justice remains an unfinished part of the Dr. King legacy."[78]

Obama's own readings of American economic and social history, coupled with the dire economic circumstances he had inherited and his pragmatic sense of the art of the possible, meant that he had little problem accepting the idea that the federal government's responsibilities included providing for the basic material needs and well-being of all its citizens and protecting the weak and disadvantaged from the ravages of unfettered capitalism and unregulated market forces. This was an expansive, neo–New Deal notion of government that had been largely absent from the American political landscape since the Great Society experiments of Lyndon Johnson in the 1960s. It was a vision consonant with King's own conception of a federal government proactively committed to extending equal rights, opportunities, and protections to all U.S. citizens, thereby helping to create an environment most conducive to the pursuit of the nation's best ideals of liberty and justice.

Runaway American Dreams

A little more than forty-five years after the March on Washington, one of Barack Obama's most famous supporters, Bruce Springsteen, was among the millions who enthused over the Illinois senator precisely because he seemed to share Martin Luther King's determination to bridge the gap between America's inspirational ideals and its all too often shabby practices. "I spent most of my life as a musician measuring the distance between the American dream and American reality," Springsteen told an audience at an Obama fund-raiser in Cleveland. "For many . . . the distance between that dream and their reality has never been greater or more painful. I believe that Senator Obama has taken the measure of that distance in his own life and work," he continued. "I believe that he understands in his heart the cost of that distance in blood and suffering in the lives of everyday Americans. I believe as president he would work to bring that dream back to life." Springsteen paused for a second before adding, "So I don't know about you, but I want my country back, I want my dream back!"[79]

For many supporters—black, white, Hispanic, and Asian; men and women; gay and straight; old and, especially, young—Obama's appeal was deeply rooted in the same hope that the American dream might yet be redeemed. Obama was elected in 2008 not because he represented the fulfillment of King's vision or the triumph of some dubious form of postracialism but because he had rekindled in many voters the capacity to dream of a more just and equitable America and, in some cases, the energy and courage to work toward that goal. In this formulation, the popular mantra of postracialism became a synecdoche for a wider commitment to a "rebirth of freedom" and to America's core ideals.

This kind of analysis flirts dangerously with traditional narratives of American history that rest on unchallenged claims of exceptionalism and providential destiny that are both historically reductive and usually politically regressive. Yet historians should not shy away from examining the extraordinary excitement and passion associated with the Obama campaign and the way it was so readily connected, by so many supporters and observers in so many contexts, to ideas about reclaiming America's original promise. The vogue for postracialism may have substituted wishful thinking for clear-eyed analysis, turning Obama into a simulacrum, a romantic projection of a better, fairer, more just America, but the very fact that aspirations toward racial reconciliation seemed central to the conception of a healed, purposeful, and morally redeemed America may have been the most potentially radical aspect of the 2008 election.[80]

What happened over the next two years, however, vividly revealed the continuing significance of race and the blight of racism in America. In January 2010 a joint *Washington Post* and ABC News poll revealed that the proportion of Americans who believed Obama's presence in the White House was helping race relations had dropped from 58 percent to 41 percent during his first year in office; the drop in confidence was sharpest—24 percent—among African Americans. Although the poll suggested that "most voters are not judging Obama's presidency based on the color of his skin," it found that the issue "continued to surface . . . with disheartening regularity." Obama's tenure had been "punctuated by racial taunts and innuendos that have slyly, or sometimes blatantly, been circulated on the Internet, in emails and cartoons. The offenses have ranged from crude to subtle, and offenders have ranged from the unknown to elected officials."[81]

Later that same year, when the Republicans reversed the Democrats' majority in the House of Representatives and slashed their Senate majority in the midterm elections, the turnaround was largely due to the economic distress that continued to afflict many Americans. With unemployment exceeding 10 percent, mortgage foreclosures still rampant, and more than one in seven Americans living below the official poverty threshold, Obama got little credit for preventing the recession from developing into a full-blown depression, thanks to his economic stimulus package. The frustration with the slow pace of recovery was real enough; what was revealing in connection to the postracial discourse of 2008, however, was the extent to which those frustrations with Obama and his administration found racialized forms of expression.[82]

Thanks to the Republicans, aided by the Tea Party, Fox News, and other conservative media outlets, the "othering" tactics that had failed to defeat Obama in 2008 worked against him and his party much more effectively in 2010. Fox, in particular, conducted an unremitting campaign of racially inflected criticism of the president's performance, politics, and personality. It continued to stoke doubts about the legitimacy of Obama's birth certificate, his religious affiliations, and the sinister significance of his strange name and youthful experiences outside America. So misleading was its approach to the news that billionaire George Soros gave $1 million to Media Matters for America to expose the network's most egregious distortions of fact.[83] More generally, Obama's conservative opponents worked harder than ever to ensure that he was depicted as a dangerous political radical—in the words of Fox's most bellicose pundit, Glenn Beck, as a black "racist" with a "deep-seated hatred" of white people, and even as a Muslim. The proportion of Americans who believed the falsehood about his Islamic faith rose from 10 percent in 2008 to 20 percent in 2010, reflecting the effectiveness of the conservative media campaign against Obama.[84]

Beck was one of the most influential broadcasters at Fox, a key booster for the Tea Party, and a skilled practitioner of racial innuendo and shrill name-calling. He openly ridiculed Obama's name as un-American, called him a "Marxist," suggested that the president's economic policies were motivated by a desire to secure reparations for African Americans, and argued that slavery had been an "innocent" business that turned bad only when "the government began to regulate things."[85] On August 28, 2010, Beck organized a Washington rally "to restore honor" on the forty-seventh anniversary of the 1963 march and the second anniversary of Obama's nomination by the Democrats. Beck stated that his intention was to "reclaim the civil rights movement" from liberals who had perverted its call for freedom into a socialist exercise in redistributive economics. Aside from location, the event had nothing in common with the original 1963 event, with King's dream, or with the freedom struggle itself, which had always pursued economic justice alongside basic civil and voting rights and had sought federal help to secure those most American of goals.[86]

Beck's popularity indicated that it was not only progressives like Obama and Springsteen who wanted their country back; conservatives also wanted to reclaim America, although they harbored very different ideas of what that country might look like and how it should be governed. When

Tea Party darling and radical libertarian Rand Paul was elected to the Senate from Kentucky in November 2010, he boldly announced, "We've come to take our government back!" A few months earlier Paul had criticized the Civil Rights Act of 1964 as an example of an intrusive federal government imposing its will—in this case, its desire to end racial and other forms of discrimination—on private businesses, which, Paul implied, should be free to discriminate as much as they wished.[87]

Paul subsequently scrambled to nuance his comments and insisted that he abhorred racism, even admitting that in 1964 he would have voted for the act. Nevertheless, this was just one of many examples of how the Tea Party and its supporters, sponsors, and favored Republican candidates became embroiled in racial controversies. In March 2010, at a rally to mark passage of the Healthcare Reform Act, John Lewis was one of several African American congressmen subjected to shouts of "nigger" from the direction of Tea Party demonstrators who were protesting what they saw as an unconstitutional extension of federal power.[88] This was not just a black-white issue. In a midterm season notable for the ubiquity and virulence of negative campaigning by all parties, Sharron Angle, the Tea Party–sponsored Republican candidate for the Senate in Nevada, ran a notorious series of ads depicting waves of sinister immigrants breaching America's borders. One ad showed threatening Hispanic men, some armed and dressed as gang members, transposed against images of anxious white students. The suggestion that illegal immigrants were depriving real—as in white—Americans of educational opportunities tapped into racial stereotypes and prejudices that had clearly survived Obama's election.[89] In more general terms, the Tea Party drew its support overwhelmingly from the kind of white Americans who, research revealed, were far more likely to hold negative views of African Americans than were the rest of the white population. In calling for the Tea Party to denounce its "racist element," NAACP president Benjamin Todd Jealous accused the movement of showing undue "tolerance for bigotry and bigoted statements."[90]

Although the Tea Party attracted people whose opposition to Obama's presidency was grounded in racial as well as political animosity, it would be misleading to suggest that racism was the only, or even the major, source of its appeal. Sentiments against big government and for lower taxes were real enough, as was grassroots anger over high unemployment rates, rampant mortgage foreclosures, and widespread poverty.[91] Moreover, the Tea Party could boast a "rainbow" coalition of its own. In the November 2010 midterm elections the Tea Party helped secure several impressive victories for minority candidates, including Marco Rubio, a charismatic Cuban American son of exiles who was elected to the Senate from Florida; Tim Scott, who became the first African American Republican sent to Congress from South Carolina since Reconstruction; and Nikki Haley, an Indian American businesswoman of Sikh heritage who became the Palmetto State's first female governor.[92]

Ironically, these Republican–Tea Party minority breakthroughs were partially attributable to Obama's own national and cross-racial success, which virtually compelled the GOP to search for minority candidates to compete with the diverse racial and ethnic appeal of the Obama-led Democrats. However, the GOP black, Asian, and Hispanic victories of 2010 were not heralded as evidence of a new era of postracialism. Instead, they were symbols of a rejuvenated right-wing politics that bound frustrated and philosophically like-minded Americans together, at least temporarily, to battle Obama's dangerously radical social and political agenda. There was little reason to think that this multiracial conservative coalition would prove particularly durable or effective when it came to producing better race relations or a more racially just society. One of South Carolina's Republican old guard, state senator Jake Knotts, said of Nikki Haley's candidacy, "We've already got a raghead in the White House, we don't need another in the governor's mansion," suggesting that old prejudices still stalked the GOP, even in places where conservative minority candidates were winning statewide elections with substantial white support.[93] Ultimately, the relatively low levels of minority support for the Republicans, the whiff of racism clinging to the Tea Party, and implacable conservative opposition to the notion that the government might have a legitimate role in ensuring genuine equality of opportunity and guaranteeing minority rights made the GOP–Tea Party axis a highly improbable instrument for the pursuit of racial reconciliation.

By November 2010, then, nothing much was left of the language of postracialism and racial reconciliation that had accompanied Obama's election two years earlier. Despite its naïveté, postracialism's disappearance also diminished the sense of promise, ambition, and optimism, of revived national purpose, inclusiveness, unity, and justice, that had fueled his winning campaign. In 2010 the victories were claimed mostly by those who spoke an intemperate language of rancor, fear, vilification, obstructionism, and divisiveness, replacing the hope that had characterized Obama's election with an almost apocalyptic pessimism and an increasingly desperate hunt for scapegoats to blame for America's woes.

Notes

I wish to thank Canterbury Christ Church University (2009 Martin Luther King Lecture) and the Irish Association for American Studies (2009 Allen Graham Memorial Lecture) for giving me early opportunities to air some of the material on Barack Obama contained in this essay.

1. Lewis quoted in Dave McKinney, "Obama Draws Parallels to Martin Luther King Jr.," *Chicago Sun-Times,* August 29, 2008, http://www.suntimes.com/news/1134541,CST-NWS-dem29.article (accessed December 20, 2008).

2. Barack Obama, "Democratic Party Presidential Nomination Acceptance Speech," August 28, 2008, *New York Times,* August 29, 2008, 1.

3. The disjuncture between mass media representations and public memories of King and historical accounts of his place within the movement and American history is explored in Edward P. Morgan, "The Good, the Bad, and the Forgotten: Media Culture and Public Memory of the Civil Rights Movement," in *The Civil Rights Movement in American Memory,* ed. Renee C. Romano and Leigh Radford (Athens: University of Georgia Press, 2006), 137–66, especially 141–52; and Brian Ward, "Forgotten Wails and Master Narratives: Media, Culture, and Memories of the Modern African American Freedom Struggle," in *Media, Culture, and the Modern African American Freedom Struggle,* ed. Brian Ward (Gainesville: University Press of Florida, 2001), 1–15.

4. Kellman quoted in David Mendell, *Obama: From Promise to Power* (New York: Amistad, 2007), 73. See also Anthony Painter, *Barack Obama: The Movement for Change* (London: Arcadia, 2008), 22.

5. *Beaumont Enterprise,* November 6, 2008, 1.

6. Letter from Alan B. Posner, *Time,* December 1, 2008, 5.

7. Harold Ford Jr., "Go Meet Them Senator," *Newsweek,* June 2, 2008, http://www.newsweek.com/id/138511 (accessed March 30, 2010).

8. *Harrisburg Patriot News*, November 5, 2008, 1.

9. *Obama: The Dream Fulfilled* (Tinton Falls, N.J.: Multi-Media International, 2009).

10. *Ebony Collector's Edition: Mr. President*, January 2009, 83.

11. Woods quoted in *Daily Mirror,* January 21, 2009, 6.

12. Lawrence quoted in ibid.; Martin Luther King Jr., "I See the Promised Land," in *I Have a Dream: Writings and Speeches that Changed the World*, ed. James M. Washington (New York: HarperCollins, 1992), 203.

13. *New Jersey Star-Ledger*, November 5, 2008, 1; Adam Zyglis, *Buffalo News,* August 28, 2008, http://politicalcartoons.com/cartoon/8a5a5e97-e904–4faf-9cb1-cf67ed73a42e.html (accessed April 16, 2010).

14. West quoted in Mark J. Bonham, "Booker Honors History as He Makes It," *Hackensack Chronicle,* February 20, 2008, and cited in Gwen Ifill, *The Breakthrough: Politics and Race in the Age of Obama* (New York: Doubleday, 2009), 167.

15. Ifill, *Breakthrough,* 16–17.

16. Jacqueline Jones, "What It Meant," *Boston Globe*, November 9, 2008, http://www.boston.com/bostonglobe/ideas/articles/2008/11/09/what_it_meant/ (accessed May 13, 2010).

17. Sue Sturgis, "Report Documents Rise in U.S. Hate Groups," *Facing South: A New Voice for a Changing South,* March 18, 2009, http://www.southernstudies .org/2009/03/report-documents-rise-in-us-hate-groups.html (accessed April 16, 2009). See also Mark Potok, "Racist Attacks on Obama Growing More Heated," *Hatewatch,* February 20, 2008, http://www.splcenter.org/blog/2008/02/20/ (accessed April 16, 2010).

18. Sturgis, "Report Documents Rise in U.S. Hate Groups."

19. "Post-Racial USA? Not So Fast," CBS News, http://www.cbsnews.com/ stories/2008/11/15/national/main4607062.shtml?source+related_story (accessed April 23, 2009).

20. For a good journalistic account of the choice of Palin and her influence in the campaign, see John Heilemann and Mark Halperin, *Race of a Lifetime* (London: Penguin, 2010), 358–76, 395–411.

21. "Obama Sign in Yard Stirs up Neighbors," Central Florida News, Channel 13, September 13, 2008, http://www.cfnews13.com/News/Local/2008/9/10/ obama_sign_in_yard_stirs_up_neighbors.html (accessed May 13, 2010).

22. Mark Steyn, "Post Post-Racial Candidate," *National Review,* March 22, 2008, http://article.nationalreview.com/?q=MjExNzMwYzMyMjk0MDY4YzlhO TIwM2YzYWYzNGIyNjU= (accessed May 27, 2009).

23. For Wright's influence, see Barack Obama, *Dreams from My Father* (1995; reprint, New York: Three Rivers Press, 2004), 280–82. For an account of the relationship and the significance of the controversy, see Clarence Walker and Gregory Smitherman, *The Preacher and the Politician: Jeremiah Wright, Barack Obama and Race in America* (Charlottesville: University of Virginia Press, 2009).

24. For more on the rumors and Obama's response, see Max Paul Friedman, "Simulacrobama: The Mediated Election of 2008," *Journal of America Studies* 43, no. 2 (August 2009): 351. See also http://www.fightthesmears.com/ (accessed April 16, 2010).

25. Margaret Talev and William Douglas, "McCain Defends Obama," *Seattle Times,* October 11, 2008, http://seattletimes.nwsource.com/html/nation-world/2008254592_mccain110.html?syndication=rss (accessed May 27, 2009).

26. "Transcript of Second McCain, Obama Debate," October 7, 2008, CNNpolitics.com, http://edition.cnn.com/2008/POLITICS/10/07/presidential .debate.transcript/ (accessed April 16, 2010).

27. *New York Times,* November 5, 2008, 1; *USA Today,* November 5, 2008, 1.

28. *Observer*, November 11, 2008, 21; Jonathan Alter, *The Promise: President Obama, Year One* (London: Simon and Schuster, 2010), 42–43.

29. March Ambinder, "Race Over?" *Atlantic*, January–February 2009, 62–65.

30. Chris Kromm, "A New South Rising," *Southern Exposure: A Journal of Politics and Culture* 36, nos. 3–4 (winter 2008–2009): 2–7.

31. Patrik Jonsson, "After Obama's Win, White Backlash Festers in US," *Christian Science Monitor,* November 17, 2008, http://www.csmonitor.com/USA/Politics/2008/1117/p03s01-uspo.html (accessed June 22, 2010); Alter, *The Promise,* 42.

32. Kromm, "New South Rising."

33. Ambinder, "Race Over?" 65.

34. Jones, "What It Meant."

35. Ambinder, "Race Over?" 65.

36. Hua Hsu, "The End of White America?" *Atlantic,* January–February 2009, 48.

37. David Ehrenstein, "Obama the 'Magic Negro,'" *Los Angeles Times,* March 19, 2007, http://www.latimes.com/news/opinion/la-oe-ehrenstein19mar19,0,5335087.story?coll=la-opinion-center (accessed May 27, 2009).

38. Barack Obama, *The Audacity of Hope: Thoughts on Reclaiming the American Dream* (2006; reprint, Edinburgh: Canongate, 2007), 53.

39. Ibid., 92, 93, 95, 97.

40. David Hollinger, "How Wide the Circle of the 'We'? American Intellectuals and the Problem of Ethnos since World War II," *American Historical Review* 98 (1993): 317–37.

41. Barack Obama, "Keynote Address," Democratic National Convention, Boston, July 27, 2004, *Washington Post,* July 27, 2004, http://www.washingtonpost.com/wp-dyn/articles/A19751–2004Ju127.html (accessed May 28, 2009).

42. Barack Obama, "The Great Need of the Hour," speech, Atlanta, January 20, 2008, http://www.barackobama.com/2008/01/20/remarks_of_senator_barack_obam_40.php (accessed December 20, 2008); Barack Obama, "Remembering Dr. Martin Luther King, Jr.," speech, Fort Wayne, Ind., April 4, 2008, http://www.barackobama.com/2008/04/04/remarks_for_senator_barack_oba_4.php (accessed May 29, 2009).

43. James Madison, "The Federalist No. 10: The Utility of the Union as a Safeguard against Domestic Faction and Insurrection (Continued)," November 22, 1787, in *The Federalist Papers* by Alexander Hamilton, James Madison, and John Jay (New York: Penguin, 1987), 122–28.

44. Obama, "Keynote Address."

45. Obama, *Audacity of Hope,* 86.

46. The generational tensions among African American leaders are nicely summarized in Ifill, *Breakthrough,* 33–50 (Jackson quote, 46). See also David Remnick, *The Bridge: The Life and Rise of Barack Obama* (London: Picador, 2010), 484–95. For more on West's role in the campaign, see Richard Wolffe, *Renegade: The Making of a President* (New York: Crown, 2009), 144–46, 151.

47. Barack Obama, "A More Perfect Union," March 18, 2008, in *Change We*

Can Believe In: Barack Obama's Plan to Renew America's Promise (New York: Three Rivers Press, 2008), 215–32.

48. Ibid.; Martin Luther King, "The Rising Tide of Racial Consciousness," address to National Urban League, 1960, in *A Testament of Hope: The Essential Writings and Speeches of Martin Luther King, Jr.,* ed. James M. Washington (New York: HarperCollins, 1986), 148.

49. Obama, "A More Perfect Union."

50. Ibid.

51. Michael Eric Dyson, "An American Man, an American Moment," *Ebony Collector's Edition,* January 2009, 92.

52. Evan Cornog, *The Power and the Story: How the Crafted Presidential Narrative Has Determined Political Success from George Washington to George W. Bush* (London: Penguin, 2004), 12.

53. Barack Obama, "Declaration of Candidacy," in *Change We Can Believe In*, 193–202; Abraham Lincoln, "House Divided" speech, Springfield, Illinois, June 16, 1858, in *Lincoln: Speeches and Writings, 1832–1858*, ed. Don Edward Fehrenbacher and Alfred Whital (Washington, D.C.: Library of America, 1989), 426–34.

54. Obama, "Declaration of Candidacy," 200–201.

55. Barack Obama, "What I See in Lincoln's Eyes," *Time,* June 26, 2005, http://www.time.com/time/magazine/article/0,9171,1077287,00.html (accessed May 29, 2009).

56. Ericka Blount Danois, "President Obama Puts Emancipation Proclamation in the Oval Office," *Black Voices,* April 19, 2010, http://www.bvblackspin.com/2010/04/19/obama-emancipation-proclamation/ (accessed April 22, 2010).

57. Garry Wills, "Two Speeches on Race," *New York Review of Books,* May 1, 2008, http://www.nybooks.com/articles/21290 (accessed May 29, 2009).

58. Abraham Lincoln, "Inaugural Address," March 4, 1861, in *The Collected Works of Abraham Lincoln,* vol. 4 (New York: H. Wolffe, 1953), 271; Abraham Lincoln, "Second Inaugural Address," March 4, 1865, in Richard Heffner, *A Documentary History of the United States,* 7th ed. (New York: Signet, 2002), 191.

59. Harold Fineman, "Obama and Echoes of Lincoln," *Newsweek,* October 6, 2008.

60. Penn quoted in Wolffe, *Renegade,* 143.

61. Steve Benson, "Rock-O-Bama," *Arizona Republic*, November 6, 2008. All the editorial cartoons relating to Obama and the 2008 election referred to in this essay can be found at Daryl Cagle's Political Cartoonists Index, http://www.cagle.com/politicalcartoons/ (accessed April 21, 1010). See also a smart and funny survey of the Election Day cartoons by freelance writer J. Caleb Mazzocco, "And They'll Never Have to Draw John McCain Again . . . ," *Every Day Is Like Wednesday* (blog), http://everydayislikewednesday.blogspot.com/2008/11/and-theyll-never-have-to-draw-john.html (accessed April 23, 2010).

62. See William Safire, "Fist Bump," *New York Times,* July 6, 2008, http://www.nytimes.com/2008/07/06/magazine/06wwln-safire-t.html?_r=1 (accessed April 22, 2010); Katie Helper, "In Historic Moment, White People Exposed to 'Fist Bump' for First Time," Alternet.org, June 6, 2008, http://www.alternet.org/election08/87230/ (accessed April 22, 2010); Sarah Palin, October 5, 2008, CNN.Politics.com, http://edition.cnn.com/2008/POLITICS/10/04/palin.obama/#cnnSTCVideo (accessed June 17, 2010). Palin's comments referred specifically to Obama's relationship to Bill Ayers.

63. Barry Britt cartoon, *New Yorker,* July 21, 2008, 1.

64. The racial coordinates of—and racially differentiated reactions to—Obama's rhetoric and style politics are discussed in Jack Shafer, "How Obama Does that Thing He Does," *Slate,* February 14, 2008, http://www.slate.com/id/2184480/pagenum/all/#p2 (accessed May 29, 2009); Nia-Malika Henderson, "Blacks, Whites Hear Obama Differently," POLITICO.com, March 3, 2009, http://www.politico.com/news/stories/0309/19538.html (accessed April 20, 2010); C. N., "The Language of Obama and Black Politics," Contexts.org, March 16, 2009, http://contexts.org/colorline/2009/03/16/the-language-of-obama-and-black-politics/ (accessed April 20, 2010).

65. McWhorter quoted in Henderson, "Blacks, Whites Hear Obama Differently."

66. Wolffe, *Renegade,* 306.

67. Obama, *Audacity of Hope,* 361–62.

68. Barack Obama, "Speech at the Lincoln Memorial," January 18, 2010, *New York Times,* January 18, 2010, http://www.nytimes.com/2009/01/18/us/politics/18text-obama.html?_r=1 (accessed April 22, 2010).

69. See Scott Sandage, "A Marble House Divided: The Lincoln Memorial, 1963," *Journal of American History* 80 (1993): 135–67; Raymond Arsenault, *The Sound of Freedom: Marian Anderson, the Lincoln Memorial, and the Concert that Awakened America* (New York: Bloomsbury Press, 2009).

70. Martin Luther King, "Give Us the Ballot—We Will Transform the South," May 17, 1957, in *Testament of Hope,* 198. Preeminent King scholar David J. Garrow makes a similar point about the overlooked significance of this address in "An Unfinished Dream," *Newsweek,* January 21, 2009, http://www.newsweek.com/id/180471 (accessed May 29, 2009).

71. Martin Luther King, "I Have a Dream," Washington, D.C., 1963, in *Testament of Hope,* 217–20.

72. Barack Obama, "Inaugural Address," January 20, 2009, *New York Times,* January 20, 2009, http://www.nytimes.com/2009/01/20/us/politics/20text-obama.html (accessed April 22, 2010).

73. Ibid.

74. Martin Luther King, "A Testament of Hope," 1968, in *Testament of Hope,* 315.

75. Obama, "Inaugural Address."

76. Martin Luther King, "Our Struggle," *Liberation* 1 (April 1956): 3–6, reprinted in *Testament of Hope,* 75–81, quote on 76; King, "Rising Tide of Racial Consciousness," ibid., 145; Martin Luther King, *Where Do We Go from Here: Chaos or Community?* (New York: Harper and Row, 1967), excerpted in ibid., 585.

77. Martin Luther King, "Remaining Awake through a Great Revolution," National Cathedral, Washington, D.C., March 31, 1968, in *Testament of Hope,* 274.

78. Obama, "Remembering Dr. Martin Luther King, Jr."

79. Springsteen quoted in Mark Hagen, "Meet the New Boss," *Observer Music Monthly,* January 2009, 25.

80. For an interesting Baudrillardian analysis of Obama's function as a projection of American postracial hopes, see Friedman, "Simulacrobama," 341–56.

81. Sarah Netter, "Racism in Obama's America One Year Later," ABC News, http://abcnews.go.com/WN/Obama/racism-obamas-america-year/story?id=9638178 (accessed September 27, 2010).

82. Paul Harris, "The American Election," *Observer,* October 31, 2010, 26; Thomas Egan, "How Obama Saved Capitalism and Lost the Midterms," *New York Times,* November 2, 2010, http://opinionator.blogs.nytimes.com/2010/11/02/how-obama-saved-capitalism-and-lost-the-midterms/?partner=rss&emc=rss (accessed November 4, 2010).

83. Chris McGreal, "Sanity or Honour? TV Pundits Invited U.S. Electorate to Choose Sides," *Guardian,* October 26, 2010, 19.

84. "Glenn Beck: Obama Is a Racist," CBS News, July 29, 2009, http://www.cbsnews.com/stories/2009/07/29/politics/main5195604.shtml (accessed November 5, 2010); John Cohen and Michael D. Shear, "Polls Show More Americans Think Obama Is a Muslim," *Washington Post,* August 19, 2010, http://www.washingtonpost.com/wp-dyn/content/article/2010/08/18/AR2010081806913.html (accessed November 5, 2010); Daniel Burke, "Poll: 1 in 10 Think Obama Is a Muslim," *USA Today,* April 1, 2008, http://www.usatoday.com/news/religion/2008-04-01-obama-muslim_N.htm (accessed November 5, 2010).

85. Siddhartha Mahanta, "'Glenn Beck' Greatest Racist Hits," *Mother Jones,* August 26, 2010, http://motherjones.com/print/75146 (accessed October 6, 2010); Michael Sheridan, "Glenn Beck: I Shouldn't Have Called Obama 'Racist,' He's Really Just a Liberation Theology Marxist," *New York Daily News,* August 29, 2010, http://www.nydailynews.com/news/politics/2010/08/29/2010-08-29_glenn_beck_i_shouldnt_have_called_obama_racist_hes_really_just_a_liberation_theo.html (accessed November 5, 2010); *The Glenn Beck Program,* Premier Radio Networks, October 1, 2010, http://mediamatters.org/mmtv/201010010026 (accessed October 6, 2010).

86. Ben Adler, "The Racial Politics of Glenn Beck's March on Washington," *Newsweek,* August 26, 2010, http://www.newsweek.com/blogs/the-gaggle/2010/

08/25/the-racial-politics-of-glenn-beck-s-march-on-washington.html# (accessed October 1, 2010).

87. Krissah Thomspon and Dan Balz, "Rand Paul Comments about Civil Rights Stir Controversy," *Washington Post,* May 21, 2010, http://www.washingtonpost .com/wp-dyn/content/article/2010/05/20/AR2010052003500.html (accessed October 1, 2010); Sam Tanenhaus, "Rand Paul and the Perils of Textbook Libertariansim," *New York Times,* May 22, 2010, http://www.nytimes.com/2010/05/23/ weekinreview/23tanenhaus.html (accessed October 1, 2010).

88. Alter, *The Promise,* 433.

89. Peter Grier, "Sharron Angle Ad: Is It Racist?" *Christian Science Monitor,* October 26, 2010, http://www.cbsnews.com/8301–503544_162–20020926– 503544.html (accessed November 5, 2010); Harris, "American Election," 26.

90. Christopher Parker, "2010 Multi-State Survey of Race & Politics," March 2010, University of Washington Institute for the Study of Ethnicity, Race and Sexuality, http://depts.washington.edu/uwiser/racepolitics.html (accessed October 1, 2010); Jealous quoted in Kathy Kiely, "Black GOPers Defend 'Tea Party' against Racism Charge," *USA Today,* July 16, 2010, http://www.usatoday.com/ news/politics/2010–07–15–1Ateaparty15_ST_N.htm (accessed October 1, 2010). See also Krissah Thompson, "NAACP Watches for 'Tea Party' Racism, Stirs Controversy," *Washington Post,* September 2, 2010, http://www.washingtonpost.com/ wp-dyn/content/article/2010/09/02/AR2010090203169.html (accessed September 27, 2010).

91. Harris, "American Election."

92. Annie Gowan, "Marco Rubio, from Exile to Tea Party Hero," *Washington Post,* November 4, 2010, http://www.washingtonpost.com/wp-dyn/content/ article/2010/11/03/AR2010110308200.html (accessed November 5, 2010); Saurita Chaurey, "Implications Ambiguous for Minority Candidates," *Augusta Chronicle,* November 3, 2010, http://chronicle.augusta.com/news/government/ elections/2010–11–03/implications-ambiguous-minority-candidates (accessed November 5, 2010).

93. Brian Montopoli, "S.C. Lawmaker Refers to Obama and Nikki Haley as 'Raghead,'" CBS News, June 4, 2010, http://www.cbsnews.com/8301– 503544_162–20006815–503544.html (accessed November 5, 2010).

Contributors

Stacy Braukman is a writer and editor at the Georgia Institute of Technology in Atlanta. She coedited *Notable American Women: Completing the Twentieth Century* and coauthored *Gay and Lesbian Atlanta*.

Jacqueline Castledine teaches interdisciplinary studies in the University Without Walls program at the University of Massachusetts–Amherst. She is the coeditor of *Breaking the Wave: Women, Their Organizations, and Feminism, 1945–1985*, and has published in the *Journal of Women's History*, *Women's History Review*, and *Reviews in American History*.

John Dittmer is Professor Emeritus of history at DePauw University. He is the author of *Black Georgia in the Progressive Era, 1900–1920*; *Local People: The Struggle for Civil Rights in Mississippi*, which received the Bancroft Prize and the Lillian Smith Book Award; and *The Good Doctors: The Medical Committee for Human Rights and the Struggle for Social Justice in Health Care*.

Krystal D. Frazier is assistant professor of history at West Virginia University. She is a recipient of the Mustard Seed Foundation's Harvey Fellowship and the Northeast Consortium for Faculty Diversity Visiting Dissertation Scholars Fellowship to the University of Rochester. Frazier is revising a book-length manuscript titled "From the Reunions of Reconstruction to the Reconstruction of Reunions: Extended and Adoptive Kin Traditions among Late-Nineteenth and Twentieth-Century African Americans."

Sara Rzeszutek Haviland is a postdoctoral fellow at the Papers of Elizabeth Cady Stanton and Susan B. Anthony at Rutgers, the State University of New Jersey. Her work has appeared in *American Communist History* and *Red Activists and Black Freedom: James and Esther Jackson and the Long Civil Rights Revolution*.

Pippa Holloway is professor of history at Middle Tennessee State University. She is the author of *Sexuality, Politics, and Social Control in Virginia*,

1920–1945, which was awarded the Willie Lee Rose Prize by the Southern Association of Women's Historians. She is also the editor of *Other Souths: Diversity and Difference in the U.S. South, Reconstruction to Present.* Holloway is currently researching the history of felon disfranchisement in the nineteenth- and early-twentieth-century South.

Hasan Kwame Jeffries is associate professor of African American history in the History Department and at the Kirwan Institute for the Study of Race and Ethnicity at The Ohio State University. He is the author of *Bloody Lowndes: Civil Rights and Black Power in Alabama's Black Belt.*

Steven F. Lawson is Professor Emeritus at Rutgers University and is the author of *Black Ballots: Voting Rights in the South, 1944–1969; In Pursuit of Power: Southern Blacks and Electoral Politics, 1965–1982; Running for Freedom: Civil Rights and Black Politics in America since 1941; Debating the Civil Rights Movement, 1945–1968; To Secure These Rights: The Report of President Harry S. Truman's Committee on Civil Rights; One American in the 21st Century: The Report of President Bill Clinton's Initiative on Race;* and *Civil Rights Crossroads: Nation, Community, and the Black Freedom Struggle.* Lawson has served as an expert witness in several voting rights cases and was an academic adviser to *Eyes on the Prize,* the award-winning PBS documentary on the history of the civil rights movement.

Abigail Sara Lewis is program director of the Athena Scholars Program at the Athena Center for Leadership Studies at Barnard College, Columbia University. She is currently working on a book manuscript titled "'The Barrier-Breaking Love of God': The Multiracial Activism of the Young Women's Christian Association, 1940s–1970s."

Justin T. Lorts teaches courses in race, civil rights, and cultural politics at the Gallatin School of Individualized Study, New York University. He is currently working on a book manuscript that examines the role of African American comedy in the civil rights movement.

Danielle L. McGuire is assistant professor of history at Wayne State University and a distinguished lecturer for the Organization of American Historians (OAH). She is the author of *At the Dark End of the Street: Black Women, Rape and Resistance—A New History of the Civil Rights Move-*

ment from Rosa Parks to the Rise of Black Power, which won the 2011 Frederick Jackson Turner Prize from the OAH and the 2011 Lillian Smith Book Award. Her award-winning essay "It Was Like We Were All Raped: Sexualized Violence, Community Mobilization and the African American Freedom Struggle" was published in the *Journal of American History* and appeared in the OAH's *Best Essays in American History 2006.*

George Derek Musgrove is assistant professor of U.S. history at the University of the District of Columbia. He is the author of *Rumor, Repression, and Racial Politics: The Harassment of Black Elected Officials and the Making of Post–Civil Rights America.*

Brian Ward is professor of American studies at the University of Manchester. His major publications include *Just My Soul Responding: Rhythm and Blues, Black Consciousness and Race Relations,* which won the Organization of American Historians' James A. Rawley Prize and an American Book Award for outstanding literary achievement, and *Radio and the Struggle for Civil Rights in the South,* which earned a CHOICE Outstanding Academic Title Award from the American Library Association and was named best history book of the year by the Association for Education in Journalism and Mass Communication.

Emily Zuckerman has practiced labor and employment law. Her essay "Cooperative Origins of *EEOC v. Sears*" was published in *Feminist Coalitions: Historical Perspectives on Second-Wave Feminism in the United States.* She is currently working on a book manuscript titled "Beyond Dispute: The *Sears* Case, Second-Wave Feminism, and the Legacy of Work-Family Issues."

Index

ABC News, 354
Abernathy, Rev. Ralph David, 143, 147, 185–86, 203
Abraham, Abdullah, 238
absentee ballots, 309–10, 311–22
affirmative action
    enforcement (*see* Equal Employment Opportunity Commission)
    intent of, 247–48
    Reagan's attacks on, 254, 255–56, 261–62
    Reagan's executive agencies and, 262–64
    Clarence Thomas and, 256, 257–58
African American actors and actresses
    complicity in comic stereotyping, 48–49
    criticism of, 49
    response to the NAACP's Hollywood campaigns, 53–54
    response to Walter White's Hollywood Bureau proposal, 55–58
    in 1930s Hollywood, 43–45
    See also "anti-Negro" propaganda
African American children
    as cultural assets, 158n27
    development of political sensibilities in transregional families, 143–50
    interconnections in transregional families and, 141–43
    legacy of Emmett Till's murder, 146, 151–54
African American migrants
    cultural connections through children and child rearing, 141–43

development of political sensibilities in children, 143–50
    disfranchisement controversies in St. Louis, 286–87
    economic interdependence, 141
African American newspapers
    sympathetic coverage of black actors in the 1930s, 44–45
    use of the term "civil rights movement," 24
    voter controversies in St. Louis and, 288, 289, 290, 291, 292
African American sororities, 88
African American veterans, 140
African American women
    activism in Cold War freedom movements, 224, 225–26
    antirape activism, 5, 192, 194–95
    black womanhood and the *St. Louis Woman* controversy, 59
    civil rights community activism and, 20
    clubwomen, 192, 194
    critique of feminism, 239–40
    cultural expectations of black motherhood and, 117, 133n28
    culture of dissemblance concept, 244n48
    importance in the civil rights movement, 27
    jazz artists (*see under* civil rights movement)
    as migrants, 141
    the *St. Louis Woman* controversy and, 59
    supporters of Joan Little, 201, 203–4
    in the YWCA, 76, 92

African National Congress Women's
    League, 224
Alabama, black voter registration in,
    216n25, 305–6
Alabama Black Belt
    absentee ballots controversies,
        309–10, 311–22
    black political gains between 1978
        and 1982, 310
    coal ash controversy, 305
    current political choices of African
        Americans in, 322
    impact of the SNCC and SCLC on
        local politics, 305–8, 310–11
    overview of politics in, 7
    vote buying, 321
    voter registration projects, 305–6
    1984–1985 voting fraud
        investigations, 311–14
    1996–1998 voting fraud
        investigations, 314–18
    2005–2008 voting fraud
        investigations, 318–22
    white efforts to curtail black political
        participation, 308–9
Alabama Bureau of Investigation
    (ABI), 316, 320
Alabama New South Coalition, 314,
    315, 316
Alien Land Law (California), 86–87
Alien Registration Act of 1940, 113
Allen, Lewis, 227, 242n14
Alligood, Clarence, 191, 197, 198,
    206, 207–9, 220n83
Alpha Kappa Alpha, 88
American Association of University
    Women, 88–89, 105–6n137
American Bar Association, 87
American Civil Liberties Union
    (ACLU), 87
American Council of Race Relations,
    85

American Dilemma (Myrdal), 22
American Friends Service Committee
    (AFSC), 108n162
American Red Cross, 86, 87
American Veterinary Association, 87
Amnesty International, 216n33
Amos 'n' Andy (television show), 63
Amsterdam News, 59
Ancient City Gun Club, 176
Anderson, Eddie "Rochester," 44
Anderson, Marian, 39, 349–50
Anderson, Terry, 255
Angelou, Maya, 236
Angle, Sharron, 356
anticommunism
    impact on the civil rights movement,
        3–4, 15–16
    investigations and controversies at
        universities and colleges, 164–66
    in the long civil rights movement
        narrative, 15, 17
    racism and, 113–14
    states outlawing the Communist
        Party in the early 1950s, 113
"anti-Negro" propaganda, black film
    stereotyping and, 47–48
apartheid
    American responses to, 226
    protest music, 230–31, 233–35
    in South Africa, 225
    South African women jazz artists
        and the critique of, 226–28,
        229–31
Arizona Daily Star, 346
Arizona Republic, 346
Armstrong, Louis, 150
Arnall, Ellis, 89
Arnesen, Eric, 16, 17
Arnow, John W., Jr., 282
Ashmore, Harry, 173
Asian exclusion laws, 87
Asian immigration, 87, 104n121

Associated Negro Press, 150
Association of Professional Ball
    Players, 87
Atkinson, William, 282
Atlanta Journal Constitution, 347
AT&T, 248, 252
Audacity of Hope, The (Obama),
    339–40, 349
Ayers, Bill, 337

Baggs, Bill, 173
Bailey, Pearl, 62
Baker, Ella, 29n1
Baker, William, 291
"ballot integrity" program, 315
Baltimore Afro-American, 49, 51, 53,
    119
Bantu Authorities Act (South Africa),
    225
Bantu Self-Government Act (South
    Africa), 225
Bantustans, 225
Barnes, Ernest "Paps," 191
Barnes, Tyree, 204
Baum, Steve, 180
Beasley, Perry, 319
Beaufort-Hyde News, 200
Beaumont Enterprise, 331
Beavers, Louise, 44, 45, 47, 49, 55
Beck, Glenn, 355
Beeker, Chip, 318
Beeler, Nate, 348
Belafonte, Harry, 230, 235
Belcher, Cornell, 338
Bell, Juliet, 82, 83
Bell, Matthew, 290–91
Bell, William, 259
Benchley, Robert, 45
Benjamin, Sathima Bea, 225
Bennett, William, 264
Benson, Steve, 346
Best, Willie, 44

Bethune, Mary McLeod, 223
Bigelow, Albert, 179
Bilbo, Theodore, 20
Bill of Rights, 23
Birmingham News, 347
Birth of a Nation (film), 41, 47
Black, Lucius, 310
Black Belt Defense Fund, 313
Black Belt thesis, 125
black comedians, 44
Black Panthers, 238
Black Power, 25, 26, 196, 204, 352
Black Scholar, 201
Blackwell, Gordon, 178
Black Women in White America
    (Lerner), 210
Bogle, Donald, 43
Bond, Julian, 42, 201
Bontemps, Arna, 58, 60–61
Boozer, Thelma, 60
Boston Globe, 334
boycotts
    in Alabama, 195
    Montgomery bus boycott, 20, 22,
        94, 125, 352
    of the 1930s, 34n40
Boy Scouts, 87, 88
Braden, Carl and Ann, 183
Bradley, Mamie Till, 133n28, 137,
    151, 161n69. *See also* Carthan,
    Mamie; Till-Mobley, Mamie
Branch, Taylor, 330
Brecht, Bertolt, 231
Breen, Jeff, 347
bref durée, 28
Briesemeister, Esther, 74–75, 79, 80,
    99n47
Britt, Barry, 347
Brooklyn Dodgers, 86
Brooks, Pamela, 224
Brotherhood of Sleeping Car Porters,
    17

Brothers under the Skin (McWilliams), 73
Brown, Bill, 248–49, 250
Brown, Claude, 143, 145, 148, 158n17
Brown, Earl, 60
Brown, Linda, 150, 161n66
Brown, Rev. Oliver L., 161n66
Brown, Oscar, Jr., 228, 229
Brown, Sterling, 54
Brown v. Board of Education
  Cold War context and, 18
  dismantling of white supremacy and,
    225
  initiation of the civil rights
    movement and, 21–22
  James Jackson and Henry Winston
    on, 126
  principal plaintiff, 161n66
  Emmett Till's murder and, 150
Bryant, Carolyn, 137
Bryant, Farris, 176
Bryant, Jenkins, 310
Bryant, Roy, 137, 138
Buck, Maggie, 198, 199–200
Buffalo News, 333
Burns, Haydon, 178, 186
Burroughs, Nannie Helen, 194
Burt, Barry, 284
Bush, George W., 277
Butler, Daniel, 282–83

Cabin in the Sky (film), 53, 59
Call, Hal, 173–74
Carmichael, Stokely, 232, 237, 238,
    306–7
Carrier, Virginia, 76
Carter, Ben, 55
Carter, Dan, 184
Carter, Jimmy, 250, 251
Carthan, Alma, 141
Carthan, Mamie, 139. *See also*
    Bradley, Mamie Till; Till-Mobley,
    Mamie

Carthan, Wiley Nash, 139
CBS news, 335
Center for Cold War Education, 167
Center for National Policy Review,
    262
Cha-Jua, Sundiata Keita, 15, 23
Chalmer, Lester, 205, 206
Chapman, Beth, 320
Chavis, Ben, 197, 216n33
Chernier, Celene, 204
Chestnut, J. L., 310
Chicago, 150–51
Chicago Defender, 50, 55, 150,
    194–95
Chicago Tribune, 205, 212
Chinese immigration, 104n121
Citizens for a Better Greene County
    (CBGC), 315, 316
Citizens for Decent Literature (CDL),
    172–73
citizenship rights
  Cornelius Curtis case, 280–85
  political allegiance of black voters in
    the restoration of, 284
  white men as gatekeepers of, 282–83
civil liberties, 23–24, 36n51
Civil Rights Act of 1964
  attacked by Rand Paul, 356
  formation of the EEOC and, 248
  Reagan's attacks on, 254–55
  Title V, 160n43
  Title VII, 251
civil rights bills, 168, 176
Civil Rights Commission, 259–60,
    262
Civil Rights Congress, 195
civil rights movement
  activities in Florida in 1963, 166–67,
    168
  African American women and, 224,
    225–26
  appearance as a term, 24

Birmingham march, 168
central black organizations in, 19
the Communist Party and, 15, 16–17
Esther Cooper Jackson's criticism of
    the FBI, 117–20
debates on the chronology of, 9–12
development in the mid-1950s, 20–21
disfranchisement and, 279, 297–98
grassroots black activism and, 19
growth of student activism in, 164
historical boundaries of, 19–28
"historical ignorance" and, 9, 10
impact of anticommunism on, 3–4,
    15–16
impact of the Cold War on, 3–4,
    15–16, 17–18, 27, 112, 124
impact on America by 1965, 163–64
importance of black community
    organizations in, 22–23
importance of Martin Luther King,
    Jr. to, 24–25, 27–28
importance of transregional families,
    154–55
invocations of Abraham Lincoln and
    the Lincoln Memorial, 349–50
jazz music and, 223
the Joan Little case and, 212
Steven Lawson and the
    historiography of, 1
leftist activism in the early Cold War
    years, 120
links to protests in the pre-1954 era,
    19–20
"lost opportunity thesis," 15–16
master narrative of, 2, 10–11
media representations of African
    Americans and, 42
in the New Deal era, 14–15
opportunities for mass action in the
    mid-1950s, 124–25
short civil rights movement, 21–26,
    27–28

as a social movement, 21
upsurge in activism in 1963, 168–69
violence in 1966, 196
women jazz artists and, 224, 240–41
World War II and, 17, 52
civil rights policy, Reagan's scaling
    back of, 6, 247, 253–56, 311
Clark, Jim, 184
Clark, Kenneth and Mamie, 143
Clark Residence, 80
Claytor, Helen J. Wilkins, 109n174.
    See also Wilkins, Helen J.
Cleveland Day Nursery, 118, 119
Cleveland Indians, 86
Cleveland Plain Dealer, 347
Clyburn, James, 342
Coakley, Michael, 212
coal ash controversy, 305
Coal Black and de Sebben Dwarfs
    (film), 53
Cobb, Rufus, 284
Cold War
    African American women and, 224,
        225–26
    impact on the civil rights movement,
        3–4, 15–16, 17–18, 27, 112, 124
    impact on the Communist Party's
        pursuit of civil rights, 112, 113–14
    jazz music and, 223
    Korean "police action," 114
    women jazz artists and, 224, 240–41
    See also anticommunism
Cole, James, 291–92
Cole, Kisha, 321
Collins, Christopher, 321
Columbia News Tribune, 347
Colvin, Claudette, 199
Colvin, James, 324n28
Come Back Africa (film), 233
Commission on Civil Rights, 86
Committee for a Sane Nuclear Policy
    (SANE), 179

Committee for Equal Justice for Mrs.
    Recy Taylor, 194
Committee for Nonviolent Action
    (CNVA), 178–81
Committee on Civil Rights, 23–24,
    36n51
Communist Party
  Black Belt thesis, 125
  the black freedom struggle and, 15,
      16–17
  boycotts of the 1930s and, 34n40
  concept of long civil rights
      movement and, 12
  Families Committee of Smith Act
      Victims, 116, 119–20
  FBI harassment of Smith Act
      families, 111, 113, 115–16,
      117–20
  impact of McCarthyism on the
      Party's pursuit of civil rights, 112,
      113–14
  James Jackson and (see Jackson,
      James)
  leaders indicted under the Smith
      Act, 112–13, 114
  National Committee to Defend
      Negro Leadership, 120
  "second cadre," 114, 115, 123
  states outlawing in the early 1950s,
      113
  viewed as a threat to American
      universities, 164–65, 166
Concerned Women for Justice (CWJ),
    204
Confederation of Alabama Political
    Organizations, 308
Congregationalist church, 87
Congress of Racial Equality (CORE)
  activities in Florida in 11963, 168
  in the civil rights movement, 21, 22
  collapse of, 26
  founding of, 19

Journey of Reconciliation, 19
  white pacifists in, 34n37
Connor, Bull, 168
Cooper, Anna Julia, 194
Cooper Jackson, Esther, 111–12, 115,
    116–22
Cornog, Evan, 344
Council on African Affairs (CAA),
    226
Cowan, Robert, 282
Cox, Courtland, 143, 144
Cripps, Thomas, 43, 46, 61
Crisis, 45, 46, 51, 56, 194
Crofts, Joseph P., 291
Cullen, Countee, 58, 59, 60, 62
cultural activism, by black leaders, 41
Cultural Association for Women of
    African Heritage (CAWAH),
    236–37
cultural politics, the NAACP and, 40,
    41–42
culture of dissemblance, 244n48
Cunningham, Bill, 335
Curtis, Cornelius "Canary," 278,
    279–85, 295, 296–97

Daily Defender, 236
Daily Tar Heel, 166
Dalfiume, Richard, 11
Darcy, Jeff, 347, 348
Darkow, John, 347
Davidson, Doug, 143, 151
Davis, Angela, 197, 201, 216n34, 227
Davis, Benjamin, Jr., 114, 120
Davis, Yvonne, 204
Dean Witter Reynolds, 265
Declaration of Independence, 340,
    350, 351
Dees, Morris, 201
defense industries, end of
    discrimination in, 39–40
Deming, Barbara, 179

Democracy Defense League (DDL), 319–20, 321
Democratic Party, 286–95, 296
Dennis, Eugene, 114, 122
Dennis, Peggy, 119, 122
Denver Post, 347
de Priest, Oscar, 150
diaspora studies, 224
Dickerson, Earl B., 121
Dickinson, William L., 185
Dietz, Howard, 55
Dillon, Carolyn, 145, 147–48
disfranchisement
    black freedom struggle and, 297–98
    the black freedom struggle and, 279, 297–98
    black voter controversies in St. Louis, 286–95, 296
    black voters in Richmond, Virginia, and, 297
    the Cornelius Curtis case, 278, 279–85, 295, 296–97
    court challenges to, 278–79
    history of, 277–78
    for infamy in Tennessee, 299n12
    NAACP and, 295
    number of people affected by, 277
    precedents from the Curtis case, 296–97
    presidential election of 2000 and, 277
    racial effect of, 277–78
    targeting of African American voters, 6
Dombrowski, James, 183
Dorsey, George, 89
"Double V" campaign, 17, 52, 115
Douglass, Aaron, 60
Douglass, Frederick, 122, 349
"Dr. Malan Has Made a Terrible Law" (song), 230
"Driva Man" (song), 229

Dudziak, Mary, 124
Dunn, Charles, 192
Dutch East India Company, 225
Dyson, Michael Eric, 344

Eagles, Charles, 12
Eakes, Roscoe, 299n18
Easely, Alfred, 280
Eason, Wilma, 142
Eastern Airlines, 265
East St. Louis (Illinois), 289
Ebenezer Baptist Church (Atlanta), 341
Ebony magazine, 77, 90, 150, 236, 333
Edge, Frank, 291
Ehrenstein, David, 339
Ellington, Duke, 54
Emancipation Proclamation, 345
Embree, Edwin, 54
English, Fred, 288–89
Equal Employment Opportunity Commission (EEOC)
    leadership and success in the 1960s and 1970s, 248–53
    leadership in the 1980s, 258–59
    National Programs Division, 248, 249
    Reagan's redefining of civil rights policy and, 247, 253–54, 256, 258
    resistance to Reagan, 6, 259, 260–67
    settlements with large employers in the 1980s, 265–66
    under J. Clay Smith, 259, 260–61
    under Clarence Thomas, 256–58, 259, 261–66
    "Track 1" and "Track 2" cases, 248
Evans, John, 167, 169, 170, 175, 181
Evans, William P., 286
Everett, Anna, 44–45
Executive Order 8802, 39–40
Executive Order 9066, 72–73

Executive Order 9981, 86
Eyes on the Prize (documentary
    series), 28

Fairclough, Adam, 15, 16–17
Fair Employment Practices
    Committee, 19, 84
Fair Play Committee, 57
families
    black migration and, 139–41
    cultural connections through
        children and child rearing, 141–43
    defined, 158n17
    development of political sensibilities
        in children, 143–50
    economic interdependence, 141
    importance to the civil rights
        movement, 154–55
    legacy of Emmett Till's death for
        children, 152–54
Families Committee of Smith Act
    Victims, 116, 119–20
Farmer, James, 19
Federal Bureau of Investigation (FBI)
    assault on Martin Luther King,
        Jr.'s private life and associations,
        177–78
    Esther Cooper Jackson's criticism
        of, 117–20
    harassment of Smith Act families,
        111, 113, 115–16, 117–20
    monitoring of racial unrest in St.
        Augustine, Florida, 167
    the Moore bombing case, 117, 118
    murder of Viola Liuzzo and,
        183–84
    voting fraud investigations in
        Alabama, 312, 316
    the Wilmington Ten and, 216n33
Federal Council of Churches (FCC),
    87, 91
Federalist Papers, The, 341

Feldman, Glenn, 19
Feldstein, Ruth, 116–17, 232
feminism
    antirape activism and, 194
    critiqued by women jazz artists,
        239–40
    support for Joan Little, 192, 201
Feminist Alliance against Rape, 201
Ferris and Rosskopf law firm, 293
Fetchit, Stepin. *See* Perry, Lincoln
Field, Marshall, 54
Fifteenth Amendment, 23
Filipino immigration, 104n121
film industry
    comic black stereotyping, 39, 44,
        45
    films with black characters in a
        central role, 43
    independent black film production,
        51–51
    response to the Hollywood
        campaigns of the NAACP, 40, 53
    response to Walter White's
        Hollywood Bureau proposal, 55
    See also "anti-Negro" propaganda;
        Hollywood
Film Survey, 47–48
Fine, Fred, 114
Fineman, Harold, 346
Fisk University, 77
Fitzsimmons, David, 346
Florida
    civil rights activism in 1963,
        166–67, 168–69
    CNVA "Walk for Peace," 180–81
    disfranchisement and the
        presidential election of 2000, 277,
        297
    1964 NAACP voter registration
        drive, 169
    SCLC's campaign in St. Augustine,
        175–78

Florida A&M University, 168, 195
Florida Children's Commission, 169–70
Florida Legislative Investigation
    Committee. *See* Johns Committee
Florida State University, 168, 169, 178
Flowers, Johnny, 305
Ford, Harold, Jr., 332
Ford, Lucie G., 75–76
Ford Motor Company, 249, 252
Forman, Charles, 178
Forman, James, 29n1, 185
Foster, William Z., 114
Fourteenth Amendment, 23, 36n50,
    86, 87
Fox, Major Matty, 54
Fox News, 355
Fox studios, 44
Freed, Arthur, 58, 59
Freedom Rides, 19
"Freedom Then, Freedom Now"
    (Lawson), 1
Free Joan Little campaign, 192,
    195–96, 201–5, 212–13
Frinks, Golden, 198–99, 216–17n35

Gaddis, William, 283
Galloway, Karen, 196, 201, 206, 207,
    210, 211
Gardner, Anne Marie, 206
Garment, Len, 248
Gass, Howard A., 286
Gates, Henry Louis, Jr., 41
Gates, John, 114
General Electric, 249, 252
General Federation of Women's Clubs,
    87
General Motors, 249, 265
Gershwin, George, 232
Gerson, Deborah, 116
Gerson, Sophie, 119
Gettysburg Address (Lincoln), 345,
    346, 348–49

Gillespie, Dizzy, 228
Gilmore, Glenda, 12
Girl Can't Help It, The (film), 228,
    235
Girl Scouts, 87, 88, 106n141
Gitler, Ira, 237
"Give Us the Ballot" speech (King),
    350
Glenn, Edward A., 287
God Sends Sunday (Bontemps), 58,
    68n62
Gone with the Wind (film), 56
Gordon, Spiver, 314
Graham, Hugh Davis, 248, 250, 253
Graves, Jesse, 55
"Great Migration," 139, 286
Green, Gil, 113, 114, 123
Green, Lillian, 116
Green, Sam, 195
Greenberg, Cheryl, 91
Greene, Christina, 203
Greene County (Alabama), 308, 310,
    313, 314–18, 325n29, 326n42
"Greene County Five," 313, 314,
    324n28
Gregory, James, 139
Griffin, William, 205, 206, 207, 208,
    209, 220n83
Griffith, W. D., 41, 47
Grimes, Vivian, 204
Group Areas Act (South Africa), 225
Guinier, Lani, 312, 313
Guinn v. United States, 279
Guy, Rosa, 236

Hale, Zack, 280
Hale County (Alabama), 319–21
Haley, Nikki, 357
Hall, Gus, 114
Hall, Jacquelyn Dowd, 2, 12, 13, 15,
    25, 31n12
Hall, Prathia, 143–44

Hallelujah! (film), 44
Halliburton, Cecil, 47, 49
Hamer, Fannie Lou, 5, 203
Hampton, Henry, 28
Hannerz, Ulf, 227
Hardman, Flossie, 215n21
Hardwick, Leon, 58, 59
Hardy, Henry, 197
Harlem Liberator, 44
Harlem Renaissance, 41
Harris, Jack O., 198
Hastie, William, 54, 60
Hastings, Frederick C. *See* Winston,
    Henry
Hawes, Mark, 164, 167
Hawkins, Augustus, 257–58
Hayes, Will, 52
Hayling, Robert, 166–67
Hearts in Dixie (film), 44, 45
Height, Dorothy, 77, 83, 90–91
Helms, Jerry, 191
Helms, Jesse, 166
Hicks, James L., 119
Highlander Folk School, 12
Hill, Abe, 59
Hill, E. D., 347
Hill, Ruby, 62
Hine, Darlene Clark, 141, 157n13,
    194, 244n48
Hobgood, Hamilton, 207, 209
Hogue, Spencer, 313
Holiday, Billie, 227, 228, 240
Holley, Mary Gibson, 305
Hollinger, David, 340
Holloway, Karla F. C., 154
Hollywood
    all-black films produced by, 53
    black actors and actresses in the
        1930s, 43–45
    black calls for organized protests or
        boycotts of, 51–52
    black film production, 51–51

response to the NAACP's criticisms
    and requests, 40, 53
response to Walter White's
    Hollywood Bureau proposal, 55
See also film industry
Holshouser, James E., 200
homosexuality, Johns Committee
    report on, 169–72, 173–75
*Homosexuality and Citizenship in
    Florida* (report), 169–72, 173–75
Hoover, J. Edgar, 114, 115, 164, 165,
    177
Horne, Lena, 54, 55, 58–59, 60, 62
Horton, James, 153
"House Divided" speech (Lincoln),
    345
House Un-American Activities
    Committee (HUAC), 165
Houston, Charles, 16, 33n30, 54
Howard University, 20
Huffaker, Von A., 284
Hughes, Langston, 54
Hulett, John, 309
Hunt, Nettie and Nickie, 161n66

Ifill, Gwen, 334
"I Have a Dream" speech (King), 329,
    332, 333, 340, 349, 350
"I Loves You, Porgy" (song), 232
Imitation of Life (film), 45, 47, 56
immigration policy, 87, 104n121
Ingraham, Mary Shotwell, 84–85
Ingram, Rex, 59–60
Ingram, Rosa Lee, 195
International Film and Radio Guild, 58
*Interracial Practices in Community
    YWCAs* (report), 81–82
"I've Been to the Mountaintop" speech
    (King), 333

Jackson, Clara, 116
Jackson, Harriet, 111

Jackson, James
  conviction reversed, 130
  Esther Cooper Jackson on, 121–22
  indictment under the Smith Act,
    112–13
  life underground, 113
  statement at sentencing, 129–30
  surrender of, 129
  work to reinvigorate Communist
    participation in civil rights, 112,
    122–24, 125–29
Jackson, Kathy, 111, 118, 119
Jackson, Marjorie Humber, 109n174
Jackson Daily News, 146
Jacobs, Harriet, 192
Japanese American Citizens League, 91
Japanese American Claims Act of
    1948, 87
Japanese Americans
  forced resettlement and aid from the
    YWCA, 72–77
  reintegration on the West Coast, 77–80
jazz
  Cold War freedom movements and,
    223
  evolution of, 226
  propaganda use of by the U.S.
    government, 241n1
  See also civil rights movement:
    women jazz artists
Jealous, Benjamin Todd, 356
Jefferson County (Alabama), 309
Jenkins, Timothy L., 145, 153,
    159–60n43
Jet magazine, 138, 150
Jezebel character, 59
Jim Clark Story, The (Clark), 184
Jim Crow
  black children in transregional
    families and, 146–48
  federal steps to end, 86
  film portrayal of blacks and, 47

Joan Little Defense Fund Inc., 204
Joanne Little Legal Defense
    Committee, 203
"Jobs and Freedom" march, 350
John Birch Society, 167
Johns, Charley, 163, 164, 181
Johns, Rev. Vernon, 25
Johns Committee
  conservative legacy of, 186–87
  coordination with other
    antisubversive groups, 169
  dissolution of, 186
  investigation of university students,
    164–65, 178
  linking of political and sexual
    deviance by, 163, 164–65, 180,
    182, 184
  monitoring of the Committee for
    Nonviolent Action, 178, 180–81
  overview, 4–5
  primary aim to harass the NAACP,
    163
  1964 promise to investigate internal
    security, 169
  reactionary activities of, 164
  reorganization in 1963, 167
  report on civil rights activism in St.
    Augustine, 181–83
  1964 report on homosexuality,
    169–72, 173–75
  year of creation, 163
Johnson, Charles S., 77, 91
Johnson, Lyndon B., 169, 176
Johnson, Roy, 311–12
Johnson-Odim, Cheryl, 239
Jones, Allonzo, 282
Jones, Jacqueline, 334
Jones, Leo, 181
Jones, Pecola, 209
Joseph, Peniel, 25
Judge Priest (film), 56
Judkins, Cora, 209

Julius Rosenwald Fund, 89–90
Justice Department
  Civil Rights Section, 23, 24,
    35–36n50, 86
  Reagan administration control of, 260
  Reagan's attacks on affirmative
    action and, 254–56, 259, 261–62
  refusal to comply with affirmative
    action policy, 262–64
  voting fraud investigations in
    Alabama, 312–14, 316–17

Karenga, Maulana Ron, 201, 203
Keating, Charles, Jr., 172
Keefe, Mike, 347
Kellman, Jerry, 330
Kennard, John, 315, 317
Kennedy, John F., 168
Kennedy, John J., 293
Kentucky Alliance, 317
Kessler-Harris, Alice, 266
"Khawuleza" (song), 234–35
Kiel, Henry, 290, 291
Kihss, Peter, 236
Kimmel, Karl, 290, 291
King, Rev. Bernice, 329
King, Martin Luther, III, 317, 329
King, Martin Luther, Jr.
  African American identity and, 352
  Birmingham march, 168
  as a democratic socialist, 351–52
  FBI assault on the private life and
    associations of, 177–78
  "Give Us the Ballot" speech, 350
  "I Have a Dream" speech, 329, 332,
    333, 340, 349, 350
  importance to the civil rights
    movement, 24–25, 27–28
  invocations of Abraham Lincoln and
    the Lincoln Memorial, 349–50
  "I've Been to the Mountaintop"
    speech, 333

the Johns Committee's slanted
    biography of, 183
  Montgomery bus boycott and, 125,
    352
  Montgomery speech of 1965, 183
  Barack Obama compared to, 351–52
  Barack Obama's invocations of,
    329–30, 331, 332–33, 340, 341,
    343, 348, 349, 351, 352
  SCLC's St. Augustine campaign
    and, 175
King, Richard, 15
King, Troy, 320, 321
King, Wayne, 209
King Kong (antiapartheid film), 233,
    243n41
"Kitchen Debate," 115
Kluger, Richard, 11
Knotts, Jake, 357
Knoxville (Tennessee), the Cornelius
    Curtis case, 278, 279–85, 295,
    296–97
Koinonia Farm, 180
Korean "police action," 114
Korstad, Robert, 12, 15, 16
Ku Klux Klan
  labor unions and, 16
  murder of Viola Liuzzo, 183–84
  in North Carolina, 197, 216n32,
    217n35
  raid of a Girl Scout camp in
    Alabama, 106n141
  in St. Augustine, Florida, 167, 176
Kuumba, M. Bahati, 224

Labor Department, 260
labor unions
  black civil rights and, 14, 35n50
  Cold War anticommunism and, 16, 17
  demise of, 23
  lack of national charismatic
    leadership, 25

in the long civil rights movement
  concept, 12–13, 17
role of southern white activism in,
  19
Lacasse, Andy, 335–36
Ladner, Joyce, 138, 152–53
LaGuardia, Fiorello, 75
Lang, Clarence, 15, 23
Lankster, Barron, 316, 318
Lawrence, Beth, 333
Lawson, Steven F., 1, 2
Leadership Conference on Civil
  Rights, 18, 26
Lee, Canada, 52
Lee, Ed, 44
Lee, Rev. George, 127
Lerner, Gerda, 210
Levin, Joe, 201
Levinson, Stanley, 178
Lewis, David Levering, 41–42
Lewis, Earl, 158n27, 225
Lewis, John
  childhood "obsession" with the
    North, 144, 147
  cross-regional family of, 158n17
  effect of Emmett Till's murder on,
    153
  Barack Obama and, 329, 342
  racist treatment by the Tea Party,
    356
Lewis, John H., 119
Lewis, Rufus, 195
Liberal Forum, 169
Lichtenstein, Nelson, 15
Lincoln, Abbey, 224, 228–29, 235–37,
  239, 240
Lincoln, Abraham
  Cooper Union campaign speech,
    346
  Gettysburg Address, 345, 346,
    348–49
  "House Divided" speech, 345

invoked by Martin Luther King Jr.
  and the civil rights movement,
  349, 350
Barack Obama's invocations of,
  331–32, 340, 344–46, 347–49
Lincoln Memorial, 39, 329, 330,
  349–50
Lipscomb, Barbara, 145, 147–48
Lipscomb, Mollie, 145
Little, Joan, 193
  acquittal of, 211–12
  criminal convictions, 217n40,
    221n94
  death of Clarence Alligood and, 191,
    207–9
  defense strategy, 200–201
  Free Joan Little campaign, 192,
    195–96, 201–5, 212–13
  on the ordeal of testifying, 213
  racially stereotyped as a wanton
    woman, 197–99
  significance of, 212–13
  "sisterhood" and, 214n6
  support from feminists and civil
    rights groups, 201–5
  surrender and arrest of, 191–92
  trial of, 205–11, 219n70, 220nn83,
    88
Little, Larry, 204
Litwack, Leon, 11–12
Liuzzo, Viola, 183–84
Locke, Alain, 60
Logan, Rayford, 54, 279
Long, Breckenridge, 287, 288, 293
long civil rights movement
  concept of, 2, 12–13
  criticism of, 13–15
  declension narrative of, 17
  Jacquelyn Dowd Hall and, 12, 13,
    31n12
  role of southern white activism in, 19
  second phase of, 15–16

longue durée, 12
Los Angeles (California)
  multiracial coalitions, 107n161
  YWCA, 78–80, 99n55
Los Angeles Times, 339
Louisiana Joint Legislative
  Committee, 183
Lowery, Rev. Joseph, 342
Lowndes County (Alabama), 306–7,
  309
Lowndes County Freedom
  Organization (LCFO), 307
Loyalty Board, 36n51
loyalty oaths, 165
Lucas, Henry, 292–93, 295, 296
Luckovich, Mike, 347
"Lumumba" (song), 238
Lumumba, Patrice, 236
Lynch, Rev. Charles Conley "Connie,"
  176, 177
lynchings, 89
  murder of Emmett Till, 22, 128,
  137–38
Lynn, Susan, 76

MacLean, Nancy, 253
"Madam Please" (song), 231
Madison, James, 341
Magnolia Residence Hall, 78, 79,
  99n55
Makeba, Miriam, 224, 228, 229–30,
  232–34, 235, 237, 238–39
Malan, Daniel, 225, 230
Malcolm X, 336
Malveaux, Julianne, 342
Mammy character, 56
Mann, Charles P. *See* Jackson, James
Manucy, Holstead "Hoss," 176
March on Washington of 1941, 19
March on Washington of 1963, 18, 19
"Marion Three," 313–14
Markham, Pigmeat, 44

Marron, William, 114
Marrow, Henry, 196
Marshall, Thurgood, 60
Masekela, Hugh, 238
Masuka, Dorothy, 224, 228, 230, 234,
  238
Maupin, Armistead, 166
Mayer, Louis, 59
Mays, Benjamin, 54, 85
McAdam, Doug, 18, 21
McCain, John, 335, 336–37
McCarren-Walter Immigration Act of
  1952, 87
McCarthyism
  impact on the black freedom
  struggle, 15
  impact on the Communist Party's
  pursuit of civil rights, 112, 113–14
McDaniel, Hattie, 44, 47, 55–57
McDermott, Malcolm, 284
McFadden, John, 291
McGill, Ralph, 173
McMillan, John, 283–84
McNamee, George T., 293
McWhorter, John, 348
McWilliams, Carey, 73, 85–86
Media Matters for America, 355
Meeropol, Able, 242n14. *See also*
  Allen, Lewis
Meier, August, 14, 15
Methodist church, 87
Mexican Americans, 87, 104n119
Mgcina, Sophie, 224, 228, 231
MGM, 58, 59, 62
Miami Herald, 347
Michaeux, Oscar, 50
migration
  Asian, 87, 104n121
  black experiences in the north, 140
  census figures, 100n67
  forced resettlement of Japanese
  Americans, 72–77

impact on America's racial
    landscape, 71–72, 73, 77
postwar, 139–41
"secondary," 141
"Southern Diaspora," 139
transregional families and, 139–41
during World War I, 139, 286
during World War II, 140
See also African American migration
Mikell, Robert M., 184
Milam, J. W., 137, 138
Miles, Frank, Jr., 307
Miller, Calvin, 291, 292
Miller, George, 292
Miller, Loren, 46, 50, 51
Milligan, David, 200
Millis, Marion, 216n32
Mills, Nancy, 204
Mingus, Charles, 228
Mississippi
    black voter registration in, 216n25
    racial violence in, 127–28, 137–38
"Mississippi Goddam" (song), 232
Mitchell, Charlene, 113
Mitchell, Richard O., 169
Mitchell, Robert, 181
Monk, Thelonious, 228
Monroe, Marilyn, 234, 235
Monroe lynching, 89
Montgomery (Alabama)
    antirape activism in, 195
    bus boycott, 20, 22, 94, 125, 352
Montgomery, Pam, 315
Montgomery Improvement
    Association, 125
Moody, Anne, 152
Moon, Henry, 60
Moore, Amzie, 127, 140
Moore, Harriette, 118
Moore, Harry T., 117, 118
Moore, Phyllis Anne, 206
Moreland, Mantan, 44, 47, 53–54

"More Perfect Union" speech
    (Obama), 342–44, 346
Morin, Jim, 346–47
Morris, Earl, 47, 51–52
Morton, Jelly Roll, 150
Moseka, Aminata, 237. *See also*
    Lincoln, Abbey
Moss, Carlton, 55
Mother's Promise, A (film), 344
Motion Picture Actors Guild, 49
Moton, Leroy, 183–84
Ms. magazine, 201
Muhammad, Askia, 143
Mu'min, Ibrahim, 149
Murphy, Frank, 86–87
Murray, Hugh, 24
Muse, Clarence, 44, 49, 50, 54, 55
Muste, A. J., 179–80
Myrdal, Gunnar, 22

National Alliance against Racist and
    Political Repression, 197
National Association for the
    Advancement of Colored People
    (NAACP)
    affirmative action case with the New
        Orleans police, 261
    Mamie Till Bradley and, 161n69
    civil rights activities in St.
        Augustine, Florida, 166–67
    civil rights efforts following 1968,
        26
    in the civil rights movement, 19, 21,
        22
    Cold War liberalism and, 117
    collaboration with the YWCA, 84
    Committee for Nonviolent Action
        and, 180
    criticism of the FBI in the Moore
        bombing case, 118
    cultural politics and, 2, 40, 41–42
    disfranchisement cases and, 295

National Association for the
Advancement of Colored People (*cont.*)
  effect of the Cold War on, 17, 18
  growth during World War II, 52
  harassment by state governments,
    36n51
  harassment by the Johns Committee,
    163
  Hollywood campaigns:
    disagreements over the
    harmfulness of black comic
    stereotyping, 61; historical
    background, 43–52; legacy of,
    62–63; mixed success of, 2–3,
    43, 61–62; response of black
    actors to, 53–54; response of the
    film industry to, 40, 53; *St. Louis
    Woman* controversy, 58–61, 62;
    tensions limiting the effectiveness
    of, 42–43; treatment of Jews in
    Nazi Germany used as a parallel,
    53, 67n46; Walter White's
    belief in racial justice and, 41;
    Walter White's Hollywood
    Bureau proposal, 42–43, 54–58,
    61–62; Walter White's visits to
    Hollywood, 39, 40, 52–53
  James Jackson and Henry Winston
    on, 126, 127
  the Joan Little case and, 201,
    218n56
  Legal Defense Fund, 313
  March on Washington of 1963 and, 18
  National Emergency Committee
    against Mob Violence, 89
  opposition to black film
    stereotyping, 45–47, 48
  protest against *Amos 'n' Andy*
    television show, 63
  the Recy Taylor case and, 194
  response to Cold War
    anticommunism, 15

  the Rosa Lee Ingram case and, 195
  in 1950s Greensboro, 149
  support for integration of the
    YWCA, 85
  1964 voter registration drive in
    Florida, 169
  Youth Council, 166–67
National Association of Colored
    Graduate Nurses, 88
National Black Feminist Organization,
    201
National Committee to Abolish the
    Poll Tax, 12
National Committee to Defend Negro
    Leadership (NCDNL), 120
National Council for Negro Women
    (NCNW), 91, 92
National Council of Jewish Women,
    91
National Emergency Committee
    against Mob Violence, 89
National Endowment for the
    Humanities (NEH), 264
National Negro Congress, 12
National Organization for Women
    (NOW), 199, 201
national racism, 32n20
National States' Rights Party, 177
National Student Association (NSA),
    159–60n43
National Urban League, 18, 45, 77, 84
Natives Land Act (South Africa), 225
Neblett, Charles, 149
Neilson, Mark, 211
New Deal era, black freedom struggle
    in, 14–15
New Left, 164
"New Negro" image, 41
New Republic, 171, 173
newspapers
  use of the term "civil rights
    movement," 24

See also African American
    newspapers
Newsweek magazine, 346
New York City Commission on
    Human Rights, 250
New York Daily Compass, 119
New Yorker, 347
New York Mirror, 62
New York Radical Feminists, 192
New York Review of Books, 345–46
New York Times, 129, 200, 205, 209,
    210, 233, 236, 237, 260, 262, 321,
    337
New York Welfare Department, 119,
    120
Nixon, E. D., 195
Nixon, Richard M., 26, 115, 248, 250
Nkosi, Lewis, 223
North Carolina
    fear of communism at the University
        of, 166
    the Joan Little case (*see* Little, Joan)
    Ku Klux Klan in, 197, 216n32,
        217n35
    racial violence in, 196–97, 216n35
Norton, Eleanor Holmes, 250–53, 254,
    255, 267

Obama, Barack
    American pluralism and, 341–42
    approach to race in the 2008
        campaign, 339–44
    The Audacity of Hope, 339–40, 349
    compared to Martin Luther King Jr.,
        351–52
    death threats against, 335
    "dog-whistle" politics and, 331,
        347–48
    economic justice and, 352–53
    "fist-bumping" and use of black
        vernacular style, 347–48
    inaugural address, 350–51

invocations of Abraham Lincoln,
    331–32, 340, 344–46, 347–49
invocations of Martin Luther King
    Jr., 329–30, 331, 332–33, 340,
    341, 348, 349, 351, 352
the Jeremiah Wright controversy,
    336, 342
the Lincoln Memorial and, 349
the "magic Negro" effect and, 339
"More Perfect Union" speech,
    342–44, 346
narratives of self-realization and,
    344
notions of "we the people," 340–41
postracialism and, 7, 331–32,
    332–44, 354–57
racism in America and, 333–37,
    354–57
redemption of the American dream
    and, 353–57
relationship with older black leaders,
    342
2008 voter demographics, 337,
    338–39
Obama, Michelle, 347
Obama: The Dream Fulfilled, 333
O'Dell, Jack, 178, 183
Off Our Backs, 201
Okihiro, Gary, 79
*Once upon a Time When We Were
    Colored* (Taulbert), 144–45
O'Neal Edward, 282
Opportunity, 45, 47, 51
Owens, Betty Jean, 195
Owens, Bill, 181

pacifists, 34n37
Palin, Sarah, 334, 335–36
Parks, Rosa, 125, 195, 199, 203
Parson, Albert "Buck," 185
Parting the Waters (Branch), 330
"Pata Pata" (song), 230

Patrick, Duval, 313
Patriot News, 332
Paul, Jerry, 191, 198, 200–201, 205, 206, 207, 210–11, 212, 213
Paul, Rand, 356
peace activists, 178–81
Peavy, Elias, 282–83
Pemberton, Bruce, 299n18
Pendleton, Clarence, 259–60
Penn, Mark, 346
Pepsi Cola, 86
Perkins, Gertrude, 195
Perry, Lincoln (Stepin Fetchit), 44, 45, 47, 49
Perry County (Alabama), 305, 313–14, 319
Perry County Civic Association (PCCA), 319, 321
Perversion for Profit (film), 172–73
"Pirate Jenny" (song), 231–32
Pittsburgh Courier, 47, 51, 52, 228–29
Political Affairs, 125, 128, 129
Poor People's Campaign, 352
Popular Front
    black freedom struggle in the New Deal era, 14–15
    Black Power movement and, 25
    chronology of, 15, 23
    lack of national charismatic leadership, 25
    in the long civil rights movement narrative, 17
    role of southern white activism in, 19
    southern conservative defeat of, 113–14
Population Registration Act (South Africa), 225
Porgy (film), 61
pornography and obscenity, postwar opposition to, 172–73
Posner, Alan, 332

postracialism, 7, 331–32, 332–44, 354–57
Potash, Irving, 114
Powell, Adam Clayton, Jr., 34n40
Powell, John, 249
presidential election of 1916, 287–92
presidential election of 2000, 277, 297
presidential election of 2008
    race and Barack Obama's campaign, 334, 335–44
    voter demographics, 337, 338–39
President's Committee on Civil Rights, 23–24, 36n51, 86
Presley, Julia, 142
Putnam, George, 172–73
Putnam, Michael, 316–17

quotas, 254, 256, 271n60

race relations
    impact of wartime migration on, 71–72, 73, 77
    in postwar America, 81, 85–89
    postwar commitment of the YWCA to interracial relations, 71, 81–84, 89–91
    See also multiracialism
Race Relations Institute, 77
race riots, 196
Racial and Civil Disorders in St. Augustine (report), 181–83
"racial capitalism," 15
racial violence
    black children's awareness of, 145–46
    lynchings, 89
    in Mississippi, 127–28
    murder of Emmett Till, 22, 128, 137–38
    in North Carolina, 196–97, 216n35
    race riots, 196
Randolph, A. Philip, 17, 18, 19, 25
Randolph, Alexis, 204

rape
    antirape activism, 192, 194–95,
        199–200
    the Joan Little case (*see* Little, Joan)
Rape Crisis Center, 201
rape crisis centers, 217nn43, 44
Ray, William and Geneva, 142
Reagan, Ronald
    EEOC resistance to, 6, 259, 260–67
    nominees to civil rights positions
        and, 259–60
    opposition to the renewal of the
        Voting Rights Act, 247, 255
    racism and, 255
    scaling back of civil rights policy, 6,
        247, 253–56, 311
Reagon, Bernice Johnson, 203
Republican Party
    "ballot integrity" program, 315
    black voters and disfranchisement
        controversies in St. Louis,
        286–95, 296
    racism and the 2008 presidential
        election, 334, 335–37
    Tea Party and the racist treatment of
        Barack Obama, 355, 356–57
    voting fraud investigations and, 316,
        318, 320, 321, 326n48
    residential segregation ordinances,
        287
    "reverse discrimination," 255
Reynolds, William Bradford, 254–56,
    259, 261, 262, 263
Richardson v. Ramirez, 278
Richmond (Virginia), 297
Rights of White People, 197
riots, 196
Roach, Max, 228–29, 237
Roane, Mabel, 60
Roberson, Rosa Ida Mae, 206
Roberts, John, 247
Roberts, Porter, 49

Roberts Temple Church of God in
    Christ, 137, 139
Robeson, Paul, 120
Robinson, Ann Gibson, 22
Robinson, Bill "Bojangles," 44
Robinson, Jackie, 86
Robinson, Jo Ann, 195
Robnett, Belinda, 92
Roe v. Wade, 199
Roosevelt, Franklin Delano, 19,
    39–40, 287
Rosenberg, Julius and Ethel, 114, 242n14
Rowan, Carl T., 265
Rubio, Marco, 357
Rudwick, Elliott, 15
Russell, Bill, 141, 144, 147
Russell, Bob, 228
Russell, Charlie, 141
Russell, Richard B., 169
Rustin, Bayard, 18, 19, 178, 179, 183,
    185
Rye, Tom, 299n18

Sambo character, 41, 44
Sanders, Hank, 310, 313, 317
San Diego Union Tribune, 347
Sandman, Theodore, 293
Schiffman, Frank, 54
Schmoll, John, 290
Schrecker, Ellen, 165
Schwellenbach, Lewis, 120
Scott, Tim, 357
Sears, Roebuck & Co., 249, 252, 266
Seay, Rev. Solomon, Sr., 195
sedition laws. *See* Smith Act
Self, Robert, 15
Sellers, Cleveland, 151–52
Selma (Mikell), 184
Selma-to-Montgomery march
    murder of Viola Liuzzo, 183–84
    smear campaigns linking political
        and sexual deviancy, 184–86

Selznick, David O., 56
Sessions, Jefferson, 312, 316, 318
sexual harassment, 252
sexuality, women jazz artists and, 233–36
sexual violence
    activism against, 192, 194–95
    the Joan Little case (*see* Little, Joan)
    in slavery, 192
Sharpton, Rev. Al, 321, 342
Shelley, Joseph, 167, 176, 178
Shelton, Robert, 233
Siler, James, 292
Simone, Nina, 224, 231–33, 237, 240
Sitkoff, Harvard, 11
sit-in protests
    in Florida in 1963, 167, 168
    at Howard University, 19–20
slavery, sexual exploitation of black women, 192
Smith, Frank, 317
Smith, J. Clay, 259, 260–61
Smith, William French, 247, 262, 263
Smith Act
    Esther Cooper Jackson on, 121
    indictment of communist leaders under, 112–13, 114
    the NCDNL on, 120
    Yates v. United States decision, 130
Smith v. Allwright, 20, 22
social movements, 21
Sojourners for Truth and Justice (STJ), 195, 224
Soros, George, 355
South Africa
    banning of *We Insist! Max Roach's Freedom Now Suite,* 229
    history of apartheid, 225
    "overlapping diaspora" relationship with the United States, 224–26, 240–41

Southern Christian Leadership Conference (SCLC)
    Birmingham march, 168
    campaign in St. Augustine, Florida, 175–78
    in the civil rights movement, 21, 22
    Florida Spring Project, 182
    the Joan Little case and, 203
    local politics in the Alabama Black Belt and, 305–6, 307–8, 310–11, 317
    Montgomery bus boycott and, 125
    survival after 1968, 26
    Williamstown, North Carolina, and, 216–17n35
Southern Conference Educational Fund, 12, 114, 183
Southern Conference for Human Welfare (SCHW), 12
"Southern Diaspora," 139
Southern Negro Youth Congress (SNYC), 3, 9, 12, 194
Southern Organizing Committee, 317
Southern Poverty Law Center (SPLC), 201, 335
Southern Regional Council, 317
Southern Student Organizing Committee, 178
"speak-outs," 192
Speight, Mamie, 312
Spellman, Karen Edmonds, 145–46, 147, 148, 149–50, 151
Springarn, Arthur, 54
Springsteen, Bruce, 353
St. Augustine (Florida)
    civil rights activities in 1963, 166–67
    Johns Committee report on civil rights activism in, 181–83
    nighttime marches, 176
    SCLC's campaign in, 175–78
St. Augustine Record, 175

St. Louis (Missouri)
  "colonization conspiracy," 288–89
  Great Migration and, 286
  residential segregation ordinance,
    287
  state control of city police, 302n65
St. Louis Argus, 288, 289, 290, 291,
  292
St. Louis Browns, 86
St. Louis Daily Globe Democrat, 292
St. Louis Republic, 288
St. Louis Woman controversy, 58–61,
  62
Stachel, Jack, 114
Stallings, George, 181
Stantis, Scott, 347
Star-Ledger, 333
Steele, Charles, 321
steel industry, 249
Steinberg, Sidney, 114
Step by Step with Interracial Groups
  (Height), 90–91
Steve Allen Show (television show),
  233
Stoner, J. B., 176–77
Stormy Weather (film), 53
Straight Ahead (album), 237
"Strange Fruit" (song), 227
Strickland, R. J., 167
Strider, Clarence, 138
Strudwick, Christine, 204
student activism, 164
Student Group for Equal Rights
  (SGER), 178
Student Nonviolent Coordinating
  Committee (SNCC)
  activism of black veterans and, 140
  in the civil rights movement, 21, 22
  collapse of, 26
  freedom politics in Alabama, 307,
    308, 310–11
  Timothy Jenkins and, 159–60n43

leadership in, 29n1
local politics in the Alabama Black
  Belt and, 305–7, 308, 310–11
radicalism and, 164
Southern Student Organizing
  Committee and, 178
Student Peace Union, 166
Students Act for Peace (SAP), 168,
  169, 180
Students for a Democratic Society
  (SDS), 160n43
Sugrue, Thomas, 25
Sullivan, James E., 293
Sullivan, John L., 294–95, 296
Sumter County (Alabama), 309
Suppression of Communist Act (South
  Africa), 237–38

Taft-Hartley Act, 18
Takechi, Dorothy, 77, 79, 93, 109n174
Tallahassee Democrat, 174
Taulbert, Clifton, 144–45
Taylor, Recy, 20, 194–95
Tea Party, 355, 356–57
"Tears for Johannesburg" (song), 229
Tennessee
  the Cornelius Curtis
    disfranchisement case, 278,
    279–85, 295, 296–97
  infamy judgments, 279–81, 299n12
Tennessee Court of Appeals, 278, 285
Tennessee Supreme Court, 278, 285
Thirteenth Amendment, 35–36n50
This Is My Husband (Cooper Jackson),
  120–22
Thomas, Clarence
  affirmative action and, 256, 257–58
  clashes with the Reagan
    administration, 6, 247, 261–66
  as head of the EEOC, 6, 247,
    256–58, 259, 261–66
Thomas, James, 310

Thompson, E. P., 26
Thompson, Robert, 114
Till, Emmett Louis
  Mamie Till Bradley and, 133n28
  legacy of, 22, 128, 146, 150–55,
    156n7
  murder of, 22, 128, 137–38
Till generation
  black migration and, 140
  defined, 156–57n8
  Joyce Ladner's coining of the term,
    138
  legacy of Emmett Till's murder, 146,
    150–55
Till-Mobley, Mamie, 141, 142, 154.
    See also Bradley, Mamie Till
Time magazine, 176, 332
Title V, 160n43
Title VII, 251
To Secure These Rights (report), 86
Toure, Sekou, 237
Townsend, Chauncey, 45
Trickey, Minnijean Brown, 143
True Selma Story, The, 184–86
Truman, Harry S., 18, 23, 36n51, 86
Trumka, Richard, 337–38
Tuck, Stephen, 28
Tucker, Mrs. Legrand, 85
Turner, Albert, Jr., 319, 320, 321, 322
Turner, Albert, Sr., 310, 313–14, 319
Turner, Evelyn, 313
Tuskegee Airmen, 20
Twentieth Century-Fox, 39, 40
21st Century Youth Leadership
    Movement, 317
Tyree, Connie, 317

Underwood, Bessie J., 324n28
United Auto Workers, 18
United Council of Church Women,
    87
United States Constitution, 340, 350

United States Supreme Court
  attacks on affirmative action, 255–56
  Brown v. Board of Education, 18,
    225 (*see also Brown v. Board of
    Education*)
  civil rights cases and, 86
  Guinn v. United States, 279
  overturn of the California Alien
    Land Law, 86–87
  Richardson v. Ramirez and
    disfranchisement, 278
  Roe v. Wade, 199
  Smith v. Allwright, 20, 22
  U.S. v. Dennis, 113, 114, 121
  Yates v. United States, 130
University of Florida, 168, 169
University of North Carolina at Chapel
    Hill, 166
University of Oklahoma, 89
University of South Florida, 164–65
university students, the Johns
    Committee investigations of,
    164–65, 178
Urban League, 21, 26
U.S. v. Dennis, 113, 114, 121
USA Today, 337

Valentine, Lewis J., 75
Veterans of Foreign Wars, 87
Vivian, C. T., 175
vote buying, 321
voter registration
  in the Alabama Black Belt, 305–6
  following the Voting Rights Act,
    216n25
  1964 NAACP drive in Florida, 169
voting fraud investigations, 311–22,
    326n48
Voting Rights Act of 1965, 216n25,
    247, 255

Wagner, Walter, 40

"Walk for Peace," 179–81
Wallace, George, 168
Wallace, Henry, 12
Walsh, Julius S., Jr., 292
Ward, Brian, 42, 235
War Relocation Committees, 75
War Resisters League, 178
Washington, Booker T., 41
Washington, Fredi, 47
Washington Daily News, 197
Washington Examiner, 348
Washington Post, 251, 254, 271n60, 354
Watkins, Nathan, 311–12, 318
Watson, Annie Clo, 82
Weill, Kurt, 231
We Insist! Max Roach's Freedom Now Suite (album), 228–29, 236
Weisman, Michael, 291
Wells, Ida B., 192
West, Cornel, 334, 342
Westbrooks, Richard E., 121
White, Deborah Gray, 56, 59
White, Walter
  belief in racial justice, 41
  criticized by black actors and actresses, 55–58
  on the effects of black film stereotyping, 49–50
  Hollywood Bureau proposal, 42–43, 54–58, 61–62
  Hollywood campaigns of the NAACP, 39, 40, 41, 42, 43, 52–53
  St. Louis Woman controversy, 58–61, 62
  support for integration of the YWCA, 85
White House Office of Management and Budget, 256
white supremacy
  Brown v. Board of Education in the dismantling of, 225
  in North Carolina, 197
  South African women's resistance to, 225
  in St. Augustine, Florida, 176–77
Wiley, John, 140
Wilkins, Helen J., 82, 83, 101n73, 109n174
Wilkins, Roger, 101n73, 255
Wilkins, Roy
  article in the YWCA's monthly magazine, 84
  on black actors opposing the Hollywood campaigns, 57
  Leadership Conference on Civil Rights and, 18
  opposition to black film stereotyping, 39, 48
  St. Louis Woman controversy and, 60
  on Walter White and the Hollywood campaigns, 43
  Helen Wilkins and, 101n73
  work with the NAACP in Hollywood, 63
Wilkinson, John A., 220n88
Williams, Aubrey, 183
Williams, Edmund, 283
Williams, Fannie Barrier, 192, 194
Williams, Fannie May, 312–13
Williams, Hosca, 308
Williams, Jessie, 204
Williams, Linda F., 236, 239–40
Williams, Paul W., 129
Williams, Robert, 170
Williamson, John, 114
Williamstown (North Carolina), 216–17n35
Willkie, Wendell, 39, 54
Wills, Garry, 346
"Wilmington Ten," 197, 216n33
Wilson, Woodrow, 287
Winchell, Walter, 62
Winston, Henry, 113, 114, 120, 125–27, 128

Winter, Carl, 114
wiretaps, 177
Woman's Press, 84
Women's Christian Temperance
    Union, 87
Women's International League for
    Peace and Freedom, 178–79
Women's League (African National
    Congress), 224
Women's League Defense Fund, 201
Women's Political Caucus, 22
Women's Political Council (WPC), 195
Woodridge, Anna Marie. *See* Lincoln,
    Abbey
Woods, Calvin, 333
workers' rights, 36n50
World War I "Great Migration," 139, 286
World War II
    impact of domestic migration on
        America's racial landscape,
        71–72, 73
    impact on the black freedom
        struggle, 17, 52
Wright, Jeremiah, 336, 342
Wright, Marjorie, 191
Wright, Michael, 9
Wright, Moses, 151
Wright, Richard, 146

Yates v. United States, 130
Young, Bill, 181
Young, Whitney M., 18
Young, William, 288, 289, 292
Young Men's Christian Association
    (YMCA), 88, 105n134
Young People's Socialist League, 168,
    169, 178
Young Women's Christian Association
    (YWCA)
    aid to Japanese Americans during
        forced resettlement, 72–77
    balancing multiracialism with the

    biracial civil rights struggle,
        93–95
    black women in, 76, 92
    branches resistant to integration, 90
    collaboration with other
        organizations, 77, 84
    first black National Board president,
        101n73
    focus on integration of black and
        white communities, 83–84
    fostering of a multiracial and
        ecumenical community, 91–92
    Dorothy Height on *interracial work,*
        90–91
    integration of, 84–85, 87–88
    internal study of interracial
        practices, 73
    Interracial Charter, 3, 82, 85, 87–88, 89
    *Interracial Practices in Community
        YWCAs* report, 81–82
    multiracialism and, 3, 77–81, 91–95
    multiracial membership figures,
        108n162
    1946 National Convention, 71, 81–82, 85
    postwar commitment to interracial
        relations, 71, 81–84, 89–91
    postwar race relations in southern
        branches, 80–81
    reintegration of Japanese Americans
        and, 77–80
    student involvement in race
        relations, 89
    Dorothy Takechi's career with, 93,
        109n174
    wartime migration of African
        Americans to the West Coast and, 77
    the YMCA and, 88
YWCA Magazine, 94

Zanuck, Darryl, 40
Zippert, John, 313, 317, 321
Zyglis, Adam, 333

CPSIA information can be obtained at www.ICGtesting.com
Printed in the USA
BVOW070739201011

274075BV00002B/2/P